SCIENTIFIC AMERICAN®
GUIDE TO SCIENCE
ON THE INTERNET

AN INTERNET
TRAVEL GUIDE™

AVAILABLE NOW

The Ultimate Dinosaur
Robert Silverberg, Editor

Are We Alone in the Cosmos?
The Search for Alien Contact in the New Millennium
Ben Bova and Byron Preiss, Editors

The New Dinosaurs
by William Stout

Eclipse
Voyage to Darkness and Light
by David H. Levy

COMING SOON

Scientific American's The Big Idea
David H. Levy, Editor

Share your thoughts about these and other ibooks titles
in the new ibooks virtual reading group at
www.ibooksinc.com

SCIENTIFIC AMERICAN GUIDE TO SCIENCE ON THE INTERNET

ED RENEHAN

ibooks
new york
www.ibooks.com

DISTRIBUTED BY SIMON & SCHUSTER, INC

An Original Publication of ibooks, inc.

Pocket Books, a division of Simon & Schuster, Inc.
1230 Avenue of the Americas, New York, NY 10020

ibooks, inc.
24 West 25th Street
New York, NY 10010

The ibooks World Wide Web Site Address is:
http://www.ibooksinc.com

You can visit the ibooks Web site for free
first chapters of all the ibooks titles:
http://www.ibooksinc.com

ISBN 0-7434-0722-9
First ibooks printing November 2000
10 9 8 7 6 5 4 3 2 1
POCKET and colophon are registered trademarks of Simon & Schuster, Inc.

Cover design by Tom Draper
Interior design by Debbie Silva

Printed in the U.S.A.

CONTENTS

INTRODUCTION:

What is the Internet?

Knowledge is of two kinds. We know a subject ourselves, or we know where we can find information upon it.

—Dr. Samuel Johnson

The Internet. It seems so fundamental to our lives. Looking back over the last few—in fact, very few—years, we wonder how we ever lived without its numerous, readily-available resources just as we wonder how we ever lived without desktop computers themselves, digital notebooks, and cellular phones.

Of course, most scientists have been on familiar terms with the Internet for quite some time. The fabled network of networks was, after all, first created by scientists themselves with scientists in mind. Up until a few years ago, the Internet was used almost exclusively by engineers, scientists, academics and students as a vehicle for sharing information and research. In 1985 the Internet boasted only 1,961 host computers and numbered its users in the tens of thousands. But as many scientists know only too well, the once-pristine electronic frontier of the Internet has now been overrun by new settlers. In fact, the Internet has doubled in size every ten months for the past ten years. Today the number of Internet users increases by a more than two million new logins each month.

Along with vast numbers of "lay" Internet users have come vast numbers of purveyors of all sorts of information: the new gold of the electronic frontier toward which so many settlers rush. Scientific information certainly continues to have its place in the newly settled territories of the Internet. And scientific resources continue to grow in number. However, scientific information on the Net no longer constitutes the majority share. Scientific information plays second fiddle to financial information, religious information, erotic information, political information, literary information, and so on.

On the "plus" side, the information resources of the Internet seem to increase at almost as fast a rate as do the number of Internet users. The steadily growing profusion of information options—including information options related to the sciences—is wonderful. It is also utterly confusing.

WHAT IN THE WORLD IS THE WORD WIDE WEB?

The most popular aspect of the Internet is, of course, the World Wide Web. The "Web"—as it is familiarly called—provides access to virtually all those computers (servers) on the Internet that offer hypermedia-based information and documentation.

Hypermedia is a technology that presents and relates information by using nonlinear, nonsequential links rather than linear sequences. (Less formally put, hypermedia and hypertext enable users to navigate both the World Wide Web and the documents on it with point-and-click ease. To navigate, one "clicks" on words, phrases, and icons in a document, which provide links that enable you to jump at will to a new location in the document, or even to a new document altogether.) In short, the Web is a uniquely intuitive and information-rich environment.

Additionally, the Web is hospitable to graphic images, photographs, audio, and even full-motion video. Thus the Web has a multimedia capability that is of great value to scientists and those interested in science. Astronomers can view full-color space images on-line. Oceanographers can access real-time "remote sensor" data from key oceanographic sites around the world 24 hours a day. Students of chaos theory on the East Coast can connect and watch fractal trees generate on a minicomputer in Los Angeles. And paleontologists can get audio and image clips of Stephen Jay Gould giving a series of lectures at Harvard.

An additional perk of Web technology is that the Web provides easy tools for inexpensive on-line publication. Combining global connectivity and individual empowerment, the Web enables anyone who has a computer and the proper Internet connection to become a multimedia publisher. With the right tools (most of them available as free downloads from sits highlighted in this book) and a little effort, you can easily translate scientific papers into electronic Web documents (also known as "pages" or "sites") that the entire world can access. The same goes for reports. calls for papers, conference proceedings, announcements, course catalogs, etc. For more on this see the section later in this chapter entitled "A Few Web Fundamentals/ General Web Resources."

WHERE DID THE WEB COME FROM?

Appropriately enough, the idea for the Web came from scientists—just as had the original idea for the Internet.

In 1989 Tim Berners-Lee, a physicist at the European Particle Physics Laboratory (CERN), proposed the concept of the Web as a system for transferring ideas and research among scientists in the high-energy-physics community.

Berners-Lee's original proposal defined a very simple implementation that used hypertext but did not include multimedia capabilities. Something very much like this was introduced on Steve Jobs's NeXT computer system in 1990. The NeXT implementation allowed users to create, edit, view, and transmit hypertext documents over the Internet. The system was demonstrated for CERN committees and attendees at the Hypertext '91 conference.

In 1992 CERN began publicizing the World Wide Web (WWW) project and encouraging the development of Web servers at laboratories and academic institutions around the world. At the same time, CERN promoted the development of WWW clients (browsers) for a range of computer systems including X Windows (Unix), the Apple Macintosh, and PC/Windows. (Today, the two most popular and useful of these browsers are Netscape Communicate and Micorosft Internet Explorer—both of which are available via free download on the Internet.)

THE RAISON D'ÊTRE FOR THIS BOOK

Today there are literally millions of documents on the Web Every subject known to humankind can be found here. But finding what you want amid this mountain of data can be more than time-consuming.

Even if you use one of the popular search-engines on the Web to isolate all Web sites containing information on a given topic such as comets (or thermodynamics, or lipids, or polychlorinated biphenyl's, etc.), you will still have to spend a fair amount of time browsing through the many documents called up by your search in order to see which ones provide the richest information base.

One comet page, for example, may contain nothing more than a collection of 200-year-old observations of Comet Halley with no accompanying links, while another page will provide a cornucopia of information and resources on all aspects of the study of comets from ancient times right up to the present day, with a long list of related links, including an appropriate description of (and a link to) the limited Comet Halley page for those who want it.

Which of these two documents is more useful? Which would you prefer to spent time on? The latter document is the one you will find discussed in this book.

In writing this book I have endeavored to provide a guide to the most useful and informationally rich resources for scientists on the Web. I have scoured the various Web information options in a range of scientific disciplines and cut out the shallow and trivial in favor of the deep and meaningful. Thus, this book comprises a directory to the most ambitious science pages on the web, not only rich in links that leverage to the utmost the possibilities of hypertext but also rich in layers of vital, current data as represented in text, graphics, and audio.

HOW CAN I CONNECT TO THE WEB?

Times was when only a privileged few could get on the Internet superhighway and drive. That's not so anymore. These days, there are more and more "on-ramps" for the highway, and tolls on the road are decreasing every day. Today you can speed around the Net and the Web or little more than the price of a subscription to the fruit-of-the-month club. Your connection options include permanent direct connections, dial-up connections to local hosts, and connection to the Web via a commercial on-line service.

* Permanent Direct Connections: Web Nirvana

Those of us affiliated with universities, research labs, and corporations—as well as those of us with direct connections often by our cable television suppliers—are usually able to connect to the Internet via the fastest route possible: a TCP/IP (Transmission Control Protocol/Internet Protocol) network. Whether you are at your home cable modem, a corporate office, a university, or a public library, you are likely to have access to a PC hooked to such a network connection.

Permanent direct connections are clearly the vest and quickest way to travel to and across the Internet, as they allow fast data throughput capable of dealing swiftly with memory-fat Web graphics. Such high-speed access is vital for many applications related to scientific research and communications (such as video conferencing), which require extremely fast transmissions of large amounts of data.

* Local Host Dial-Up Connections: The Next Best Thing

The next most attractive alternative is to use your computer's modem to dial-up to the network of an Internet service provider. These service providers are usually called local hosts. A local host computer runs with applications software that uses the TCP/IP protocols to communicate with other Internet. (Note that for web surfing a minimum modem speed of 28.8 bps [bits per second] is highly recommended.)

To communicate with the Web via your local host, you must use software that enables your computer to use the TCP/IP language to communicate over local telephone lines. Here you have two choices. The first is SLIP (Serial Line Internet Protocol) and the second and newer option is PPP (Point-to-Point Protocol). These low-cost alternatives provide full peer access to the Internet. The difference between the two is fundamental. SLIP does not provide error correction or data compression, but it still works well for home and small-business applications. PPP was specifically developed to rectify SLIP's error correcting weakness. PPP checks incoming data and asks the sending computer to retransmit when it detects an error in an IP packet. Thus, of the two protocols, I recommend PPP. It'll save you time and hassles.

There are hundreds of dial-up Internet providers across the country, many of them regional, and a number of them national. Among these are several that cost absolutely nothing, such as freeInternet. com (http://www.freeinternet.com).

Other popular options nationwide include Mindspring (http://www.mindspring.net), Earthlink (http://www.earthlink.net/), and MCI (http://www.mci.net). All of these outfits have proprietary SLIP or PPP software packages, complete with browsers, that they'll be happy to send to you and with which you can connect to their services.

* Connection via Commercial On-line Services

For the least-efficient, least-satisfying, though most thoroughly idiot-proof means of connecting to the Internet, check out major on-line services such as American On-line (http://www.aol.com), CompuServe (http://www.compuserve.com) and Prodigy (http://www.prodigy.com). Each offers easy-to-use proprietary software, but the easy software comes with trade-offs. Load times can often by very slow, depending on the volume of people on the network at any given time. Also, the proprietary browsers used by the services often leave something to be desired: images can come out looking pretty bad. However, depending on how much time you have and how important multimedia and other memory-intensive elements are to you, these on-line services can provide economical (and certainly simple) access to the Internet.

WHAT TOOLS ARE AVAILABLE TO HELP ME USE THE INTERNET?

* Browser Tools

As mentioned earlier, on-line services often provide their own browser software, as do many dial-up hosts. The best two items of browser software on the market however, are Netscape Communicator and Microsoft Internet Explorer. Most new PCs ship with one or both of these browsers preinstalled. But should you not have them, they are readily available as free downloads from the Internet.

To download Netscape Communicator go to
http://home.netscape.com/comprod/mirror/index.html
To download Microsoft Internet Explorer go to
http://www.microsoft.com/windows/ie/default.htm
* General Interent/Web Tutorials On-line

A number of Web pages provide excellent hypertext tutorial instructions on the ins and outs of the Internet and the Web. Here is a quick listing of a few of the best:

How to Search the World Wide Web
http://204.17.98.73/midlib/tutor.htm
Learn the Net
http://www.learnthenet.com/english/
World Wide Web Tutorial
http://www.educ.sfu.ca/tutorial/
Yahoo Internet How-To
http://howto.yahoo.com/

HTML EDITORS FOR CREATING YOUR OWN WEB DOCUMENTS AND PAGES

Many readers of this book will want not only to read what others have published don the Web, but also to do some Web publishing themselves.

The tool that you use to create hypertext documents for the World Wide Web is called HyperText Markup Language (HTML). If you want to create your own homepage, or render a document in a form readable on the Web, you need to get a good HTML editor and learn how to use it. This involves assigning document tags and working with basic text structures. You may also want to learn how to incorporate images into your HTML documents.

You'll be glad to hear that HTML is not all that hard to master. One of the best introductions to HTML is freely available on the Web itself:
Introduction to HTML
http://www.cwru.edu/help/introHTML/toc.html
Another very good alternative is:
HTMLelementary
http://labrocca.com/htmlementary/
Before you can learn to use an HTML editor, however, you have to have one available on your platform. Many excellent HTML editors are available on the Web for Macintosh, Windows and UNIX machines. Here are some addresses where you'll find them available for download:
ANT HTML (PC Windows & Macintosh versions)
http://telacommunications.com/ant/

Download a demo version of this great macro for effortlessly converting Microsoft Word documents into HTML.

COFFEECUP HTML EDITOR ++ (PC Windows)

http://www.coffeecup.com/

Download CoffeeCup HTML Editor ++ for a 30-day free trial. CoffeeCup HTML Editor++ is a full-featured HTML editor that includes Expresso FTP for uploading and downloading; an image gallery with quick-linking images; highlighted tags; style sheet help; automatic image sizing; a line reader; and tips. It comes with 30 background images, more than 175 animated GIFs, upwards of 140 Web icon graphics, 60 JavaScript scripts, a frame designer, and an HTML stripper. You can work on and test multiple pages at once. Other features include an internal browser for testing and surfing, an image-previewing utility, a sound gallery, on-line help, and a step-by-step Web design guide and references for the latest HTML 4.0 tags.

HOT DOG WEB EDITOR (PC Windows)

http://www.sausage.com/

Download a free 30-day trial version of any one of several fast, flexible, and friendly versions of the Hot Dog Web Editor for Windows.

HTML GRINDER (Macintosh)

http://www.matterform.com/grinder/

Download a free, fully functional demo copy of HTML Grinder, a robust HTML editor for the Mac. Decide you don't like it? Then just let the software expire and keep its highly useful "Find and Replace Tool" as a gift from the good folks at MatterForm Media. Note: Macintosh SE/30 or better, System 7, 8MB RAM (16MB RAM recommended). Compatible with MacOS 8.

INTERNET LIST KEEPER (PC Windows)

http://www.drweb.com/

Go to "Dr. Web's" home page to download a free coy of Internet List Keeper, a very simple, template-based HTML tool for creating Web pages.

Simple HTML Editor (S H E) version 2.9 (Macintosh)

http://www.lib.ncsu.edu/staff/morgan/simple.html

Simple HTML Editor (S H E) is just that, a simple editor for creating hypertext markup language (HTML) documents. It is in the form of a HyperCard stack, and therefore, it requires HyperCard or Hyper-Card Player, as well as a Macintosh. Take a free download of the software and try it on for size.

SITEAID HTML EDITOR (PC Windows)

http://www.siteaid.com

More than just your average HTML editor, SiteAid is a tool for managing your entire site. From creating HTML, Javascripts and Style Sheets, to uploading them to your Internet server, SiteAid has you covered. You are invited to download and test drive this shareware free of charge.

ULTRAEDIT HTML EDITOR (PC Windows)

http://www.ultraedit.com/

Download the full version of this great shareware HTML editor for Windows.

UNIX HTML EDITORS

http://www.xcelco.on.ca/~johnston/html5.html

Here is a wonderful megalist of dozens of powerful Unix-oriented HTML editors available for downloading through quick-click hyperlinks.

SEARCH ENGINES ON THE WEB

This book should be your first stop when searching for scientific resources on the Web. But should you need information or resources beyond what you find here, there are several very reliable and useful options for searching the Web. All of these resources are available 24 hours a day for the mere price of oxygen. In other words, they are free. And they all operate very simply. Just enter some keywords for a search, survey the results, and click on those hyperlinks you'd like to follow.

The Web search engines I most highly recommend are:

Altavista

http://www.altavista.com/

HotBot

http://www.hotbot.com

Lycos
http://www.lycos.com
WebCrawler
http://www.webcrawler.com
Yahoo
http://www.yahoo.com

I should say that I am particularly fond of WebCrawler and Yahoo.

WebCrawler was developed by Brian Pinkerton at the University of Washington. Given a set of parameters. WebCrawler creates indexes of documents it locates on the Web and then lets you search the indexes. WebCrawler presents results in a prioritized order. The first item listed is the one with the highest number of "hits" within the text of the page for the keywords you have specified. Links noted at the bottom of a set of WebCrawler results are thus less likely to be what you are looking for than items at the top.

Yahoo is an extensive database of Web sites—tens upon tens of thousands, in fact. Yahoo's various pages are organized in subject categories, and you have the option of searching within a given category or to search the entire database. Once again. as with WebCrawler, a prioritized list of hyperlinks appears as the result of your search. To follow the links, just click.

Because of subtle differences in the manner in which they search the Web, WebCrawler and Yahoo can, at times, produce remarkably dissimilar results for the same set of parameters. A site that one misses, however, the other is sure to catch. That's why I recommend using both WebCrawler and Yahoo in tandem to ferret out the Web information you need.

ON WITH THE SHOW

That being said, the book you hold in your hand is intended to save you a great deal of time in searching for scientific resources on the Internet. It is the result of many hours of roaming cyberspace—appraising, accepting and rejecting hundreds of various scientific sites based on their wealth of content, ease of navigation, and overall usefulness and accessibility. In other words, what you have here—to embrace both an old cliché and a mixed metaphor—is the cream of the crop. Enjoy.

—EJR

I

ANTHROPOLOGY

Anthromorphemics: Anthropology & Archeology Glossary
http://www.anth.ucsb.edu/glossary/index.html

Here is a comprehensive hypertext glossary created by John Kantner and Kevin Vaughn, both of the University of California, Santa Barbara. Dr. Kantner—http://monarch.gsu.edu/faculty/jkantner.htm—currently directs the Lobo Mesa Archaeological Project, which focuses on prehistoric Anasazi groups who inhabited northwestern New Mexico between A.D. 850 and 1200. The goal of this research is to identify the processes by which complex social and political regional institutions emerge from communities of comparatively simple horticulturists. Kantner's early research was on Spanish Colonial archaeology and the ethnohistory of the Southwest, but he has also conducted investigations in Costa Rica, the U.S. Plains, and the U.S. Rocky Mountains. Kevin Vaughn is a doctoral candidate in the anthropology program. Their extensive online glossary embraces hundreds of anthropological and archeological terms, from acculturation to varnes caste, from abrasive stone to XTENT modeling, and—in the world of physical anthropology—from absolute dating to zygotic mortality. You can scroll through alphabetical lists in each specialty, or search for a pecise term using a robust search engine that quickly takes you to the key term your interested in. Note that this fine Web resource is a Selection of the Scout Repot—http://scout.cs.wisc.edu/report/sr/current/index.html—a highly respected weekly report highlighting the best and most useful of sites on the Internet of interest to scholars, researchers, and educators.

Anthropology Tools for Cultural Resource Management
http://library.lib.binghamton.edu/subjects/anthro/crm.html

Anthropologists worldwide are required to adhere to the guidelines set down by many different national and international laws, councils, treaties and relating to historic preservation and cultural protection. This web site organizes and presents the very best web resouces designed to help anthropologists navigate these various legalistic and logistical hurdles. Here you'll find links to dozens of key web resouces, among them the home pages for The International Council on Monuments and Sites, the full text of UNESCO's "Convention concerning the Protection of the World Cultural and Natural Heritage," and the American Cultural Resouces Association. Here you also have links to a complete online directory of U.S. State Archaeologists & State Historic Preservation Offices nationwide, Brian Gill's splendid online directory of U.S. state archeological laws, and key Native American Indian Cemetery Removal and Reburial New Rules. Other interesting links take you to the Repatriation Offices of the Smithsonian Institution and the Peabody Museum of Archaeology and Ethnology (Harvard), contract archeological pofessionals across the United States, and key university archeological research labs around the world. The latter category includes the famous Arkansas Archeological Suvey, the Wake Forest University Archeological Laboratories, and Public Archeologial Facility at the State University of New York, Binghamton. By the way, it is the anthro department at SUNY Binghamton that we have to thank for this splendid web site.

Anthroplogists Fieldwork Handbook (online edition)
http://www.truman.edu/academics/ss/faculty/tamakoshil/index.html

This great online guide to anthropological fieldwork comes to us courtesy of Dr. Laura Zimmer-Tamakoshi, Associate Professor Of Anthropology, Truman State University. Covering all aspects of planning (proposals, pep, field site selection), field methods, and the writing of fieldnotes and final reports, Dr. Zimmer-Tamakoshi's Web pages are rich in beautiful photographs from her own trips as well as insightful essays on the the art, science and profession of anthropology. What is more, Dr. Zimmer-Tamakoshi makes a point of leveraging the Web's multimedia potential by including sound-enhanced visual clips from her own fieldwork among the Gende tribe of New Guinea. Dr. Zimmer-Tamakoshi also provides an in-depth glossary of anthropological terms, an extensive bibliography of key references, and a sensitive essay on what it is like to leave the field—not to mention a culture into which one has thoroughly immersed, aborginal friends to which one has become attached, and ancient ways of thinking one has come to appreciate and understand—and return home to the culture shock of what some call the civilized world. But as Zimmer-Tamakoshi points out, fieldwork never really ends. In finding a distant land and people to become intimate, the good anthropologist adopts (in part, at least) a new culture, develops a new family, and wins a second home, to which he or she can and should always plan to return.

Anthropology in the News (updated daily)
   http://www.tamu.edu/anthropology/news.html

Here it is. All the anthropology news that's fit to print. Call this The New York Times of anthro, the Chicago Tribune of all that is new in the study of human culture. Want the latest on doctors in Ghana working with traditional healers, Spokane native Americans threatening suicide unless their ancestral lands are left unspoiled, or the restoration of ancient 12th century Egyptian aqueduct? This is the type of thing you will find at this great web site, brought to you courtesy of the Anthropology Department at Texas A&M. Learn about paleontologists unveiling the most complete "Apeman" skull ever excavated, DNA studies on the "Kennewick Man," and the strange tale of the world's "oldest hat." In other words, from the vital to the absurd, it is all here in a page updated weekly without fail. In addition to core anthropology news, you also get specific reports from the frontlines of various specialties including Bioanthropology, Socio/Cultural Anthropology, Linguistics. There is, believe it or not, important and engaging news on the linguistics front. Did you know the native language of Labrador is headed for extinction, with only a few speakers left walking the world? Did you know that a baby's first words are usually

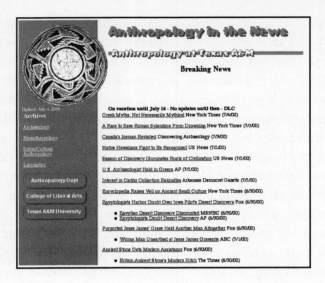

uttered in sign language, or that it isn't just Dr. Dolittle who can talk to the animals? Find out more at the Anthropology in the News web site.

Anthropology Review Database
http://wings.buffalo.edu/anthropology/ARD/

The Anthropology Review Database (ARD) is intended to improve the level of access of anthropologists to anthropological literature by making them more aware of what is being published and helping them to evaluate its relevance to their own interests. Unlike the more traditional print journals, ARD is not constrained by production deadlines and has few running costs. ARD can keep abreast of the production of new materials, and do so in a much more timely fashion than the traditional media. Envision an almost continous flow of information from publisher to reader, by way of this database. ARD has no volumes, issues, or page numbers, just the name and date of the review, and the site's URL to reference them. They also occasionally feature multiple reviews of more controversial items as well as links to reviews published elsewhere. ARD for is a brand new resource for anthropology and a first-rate example of the new species of online publication. Unlike traditional periodicals, ARD reviews are published individually, as soon as they clear the editorial process. Documents are housed in an online database where they can be accessed at any time. This is web publishing at its best—timely, easy-to-navigate, information rich, and focused on important material. At this writing, ARD houses no less than 1287 vital reviews. Editor in Chief and Webmaster is Hugh Jarvis of the Department of Anthropology, University at Buffalo.

Antiquity: an international journal of expert archaeology
http://intarch.ac.uk/antiquity/

This quarterly publication has been the main journal of international anthropological and archaeological debate and reporting for 74 years. Papers range in time focus from Palaeolithic to present and include reporting from all parts of the world on new methods and technologies, heritage issues and museums, theory and ethics, and management and landscapes. Recent articles published online as well as in the paper edition address such topics as the use of henbane (Hyoscyamus niger L.) as a hallucinogen at Neolithic 'ritual' sites . . . Cosmology, calendars and society in Neolithic Orkney . . . and the development of the International Ancient Egyptian Mummy Tissue Bank at the Manchester Museum. Other recent pieces address the introduction of the lapidary engraving wheel in Mesopotamia, the radicarbon evidence regarding the neolithization of Siberia and the Russian Far East, and the palaeoethnobotany of the Indus Civilization. Here you also have interesting investigations of the "oldest ever" brush hut plant remains from Ohalo II in the Jordan Valley, and cimex lectularius L., the common bed bug from Pharaonic Egypt. The web site includes an archive of the contents from recent back issues, a full index to the complete 74 years of the magazine's publication, and notes for would-be contributors along with editorial contact information and details on contributing editors. (By the way, the journal is edited by Caroline Malone assisted by Simon Stoddart, both of the University of Cambridge.)

Council for Museum Anthropology (CMA)
http://luna.cas.usf.edu/~curtis/cma.html

According to its charter, the Council for Museum Anthropology is "an all-volunteer membership organization that serves anthropologists and museum professionals dealing with anthropological collections and issues through the journal Museum Anthropology, a regular column in The Anthropology Newsletter, and occasional meetings, seminars, and special publications. Its mission is to foster the development of Anthropology in the context of museums and related institutions." This information-rich web site includes an in-depth index to the contents of the Council for Museum Anthropology's journal, Museum Anthropology. It also delivers regular reprints of the monthly column from The Anthropology Newsletter, listings of CMA's officers (complete with contact information), and the full text of the bylaws for the CMA. Here you will also find a highly useful collection of links to anthropology museums on the web (among them the Field Museum, the Arizona State Museum, the Peabody Essex Museum and Wake Forest University's Museum of Anthropology), along with links of interest to museum professionals of all stripes and classes (including the American Association of Museums and the Internation Council of Museums). Perhaps most importantly, the CMA also provides an extensive index of links to univeristy departments around the globe offering specific museum training for anthropology students, these including the anthro departments at Brown, Harvard, Penn State, Seton Hall and Tufts.

Cultural Survival: Helping Save Indigenous Cultures
http://www.cs.org/

Cultural Survival, founded in 1972, is a recognized leader anibg educational and cultural organizations speaking out for the rights, voice and vision of indigenous peoples. Cultural Survival believes that indigenous peoples should be able to determine their own futures on their own lands (and on their own terms). Through its website and publications, student conferences and educational outreach, Cultural Survival draws attention to the issues confronting

indigenous peoples, and promotes the cause of self-determination. Cultural Survival's projects emphasize the need to build partnerships with and between indigenous peoples and their program serves as a means of pro-indigenous advocacy. Here at the web site. Cultural Survival provides important and, above all, carefully analyzed information concerned with reconciling economic development and human rights in an era of globalizing capitalism. Related topics of interest include the prospects for multiculturalism in pluriethnic societies This web site includes online indexes to Cultural Survival's magazine, Cultural Survival Quarterly, along with reports on Cultural Surval events and projects, and in-depth articles on a range of topics, among them a fascinating piece on the Macuxi, Wapixana, Ingarikó and Taurepang of Raposa-Serra do Sol in which an anthropologist documents the struggle of indigenous people to have their ancestral land protected—rather than despoiled—by the Brazilian government. Tune in here for the news corporate media is not likely to mention, let alone highlight.

Current Anthropology: Journal from Univ. of Chicago Press, online edition
http://www.journals.uchicago.edu/CA/home.html

Current Anthropology is a transnational journal devoted to research on humankind, encompassing the full range of anthropological scholarship on human cultures and on the human and other primate species. Communicating across the subfields, the journal features papers in a wide variety of areas, including social, cultural, and physical anthropology as well as ethnology and ethnohistory, archaeology and prehistory, folklore, and linguistics. Articles for the online edition are available as Full Text, Postscript, and PDF files—take your choice. Editions of the journal available online begin with Volume 40, number 5 (in other words, every edition since December 1999. Although this presently makes for a fairly limited digital backlist, all future editions of the journal will be published and archived on the web, so the library will quickly grow in weight and usefulness. Recent articles include "The Social Behavior of Chimpanzees and Bonobos: Empirical Evidence and Shifting Assumptions," "Cheating at Musical Chairs: Territoriality and Sedentism in an Evolutionary Context," "The Distributional Approach: A New Way to Identify Marketplace Exchange in the Archaeological Record," and "Sex, Sound Symbolism, and Sociolinguistics." The site also includes listings and contact info for the editors and editorial board, details on how to submit articles for publication, and a handy searchable index items published in the journal.

Documents on Anthropological Multimedia
http://www.rsl.ox.ac.uk/isca/marcus.banks.02.html

What is the proper role for interactive multimedia technology in anthropological research, development and publication? The papers gathered at this web site endeavor to answer this question—a complex question, and one not easily answered. In the course of the one of the articles cited here, the author is wise to paraphrase Lévi-Strauss, who always said we should to avoid the trap of thinking (or letting others think) that new technology is merely bien à manger (i.e. that the consumption of new technology is inherently good and brings its own inherent rewards). As the writer suggests, technology best serves the purposes as anthropologists when they realise it is also bien à penser. One item particularly worth reading here is Marcus Banks's "Interactive multimedia and anthropology: a sceptical view." Banks—a Reader in Social & Cultural Anthropology and a Fellow of Wolfson College, Cambridge—has done more research and thinking on the role of multimedia in the teaching of anthropology than just about anyone else on the planet. His insights are invariably plentiful, hard-won, and pertinent. Banks argues, with justice, that interactive multimedia is bound, in the long run, to hurt more than help in the research and teaching of anthropology. As he says, all pure research is a linear, and thus bound to be corrupted (rather than enhanced) by invasive technology.

Journal of Field Archeology
http://jfa-www.bu.edu/

The Journal of Field Archaeology is an international, refereed quarterly serving the interests of not only archaeologists, but also anthropologists, historians, scientists, and others concerned with the recovery and interpretation of archaeological data. Its scope is worldwide and is not confined to any particular time period. The Journal publishes field reports whose results in terms of interpretive content or of techniques and methods employed seem clearly to be of more than regional interest . . . technical and methodological studies that relate to actual archaeological data, are also of general rather than only regional significance, and would be comprehensible to most readers . . . review articles such as updated regional or topical summaries designed to appeal to a fairly wide professional readership . . . occasional essays on the history of archaeology in major geographical areas, or with respect to research topics of general archaeological concern . . . and brief preliminary reports describing the results of recent fieldwork or other research. Visit this web site to search the journal archives and read journal articles online. Here you'll also find details on the members of the editorial board, and information on how to submit articles for publication. You can perform searches by keyword, author, or—nicely—by geographic region related to the topic addressed in any given article. All editions of the journal are archived back to the autumn of 1998.

Film Archive of Human Ethology of the Max-Planck-Society
http://erl.ornithol.mpg.de/~fshuman/EngHomep/eindex.html

Based on the pioneering work of Prof. Dr. Irenaeus Eibl-Eibesfeldt and Prof. Dr. Hans Hass begun in the 1960s, as many as 205 films on Human Ethology and Ethnology have been published based on the resources resources of the Film Archive of Human Ethology of the Max-Planck-Society in co-operation with the Institute for Scientific Film (Institut fuer den Wissenschaftlichen Film, IWF) in Goettingen, Germany and most recently with the Federal Austrian Institute for Scientific Film (Österreichisches Bundesinstitut fuer den Wissenschaftlichen Film, ÖWF) in Vienna, Austria. Most of the published films were included in the Encyclopaedia Cinematographica (EC) of the IWF, either because they met the rigid standards for scientific documentation or because they were judged to be of great importance for the scientific community. Each of these films documents a certain scene of primitive life in detail. The films are accompanied by publications in which the verbal interactions and songs are transcribed and all important side information is collated. Much of this data—incuding clips, supporting materials, and a complete catalogue of films houses in the archive—are to found at this web site. The films in question record unstaged and undisturbed social interactions of everyday life, rituals and other activities—and thus provide documentation that will prove continually valuable to anthropologists and ethnologists through the years.

Food Habits Anthropology
http://www.ilstu.edu/class/anth273-foodways/foodbib.html

From cannibalism to floating markets on the Mekong Delta in Vietnam, here you'll find a comprehensive bibliography listing hundreds of incisive and engaging studies of the foods of peoples around the world, and how they are impacted by and in turn impact culure. Topics include ecology and food systems, eating attitudes, fasting and body image, festivals and feasting, famine and starvation, malnutrition and disease, meat-eating vs. vegetarian diets, the nutritional anthropology of nonhuman primates, food rituals, and food taboos. Regions covered include Africa, Australia, the Caribbean, Central America, Mexico, East Asia, Europe, the Middle East, North America (both European and indigenous), Oceania, South America, South Asia, Southeast Asia, and West and Central Asia. Articles address subjects that range from the dialetics relating to the sacred cows of India to the typical American diet of 100 years ago, from scholarship on contemporary American "foodways" (as opposed to folkways) to "soul" and traditional Southern food practices, customs, and holidays. Here you'll also find references to such interesting articles as "Chinese Tables Manners: You Are How You Eat," "The Origins and Ancient History of Wine," "Food Classifications and the Diets of Young Children in Rural Egypt," and "The Folk Foods of the Rio Grande Valley and of Northern Mexico." As language, climate and history are to culture, so too is food—an engaging and appetizing area of study, to say the least.

Guide to Library Research in Cultural Anthropology
http://www.as.ua.edu/ant/libguida.htm

The literature on cultural anthropology is large, diffuse, confusing, and hard to get a handle on. This page is designed as a remedy to the situation. As a primary goal, it seeks to enhance and simplify the library research projects of anthropology students by suggesting a search strategy for locating materials relevant to cultural anthropology, and by listing a wide variety of anthropological reference materials. The page also introduces users to anthropological resources on the Internet by providing a jump station to Web sites that are particularly useful for anthropologists. The jump station is desgined with the novice in mind and is divided up into sections on Internet Basics, Internet Directories, Interesting Anthropology Sites, Regional Studies, and Maps. The jump station identifies and summarizes dozens of the most useful and in-depth anthropological Web resources available anywhere. Supplementing this, the detailed bibliographies provide complete information on Classic Introductory Texts, General Guides to Research in Cultural Anthropology, Handbooks and Manuals, Atlases, Biographical Sources, Guides to Anthropological Serials, Book Reviews in Anthropology, Anthropological Catalogs, Histories of Anthropology, Anthropological Directories, Guides to the Funding of Anthropological Research, Guides to Anthropological Ethics, and more. All this comes to us courtesy of webmaster Michael Dean Murphy, a professor of Anthropology at the University of Alabama, Tuscaloosa.

Huarochirí: A Peruvian Culture in Time
http://wiscinfo.doit.wisc.edu/chaysimire/

Here is an in-depth ethnographic and historical tour of Huarochirí, a fascinating Andean province near Lima, Peru. Among the highlights of this web page are significant extracts from the Huarochirí Quechua Manuscript, which alone among colonial documents explains a pre-Christian tradition in an Andean language. The web site also provides riveting memoirs of recent visits to modern highlanders who still, to this day and despite all obstacles, inhabit and interpret the beautiful and mythic landscape of the Andes. Huarochirí, though close to Lima, is an area of harsh economic conditions. Several non-governmental organizations collaborate with Huarochirí villagers to promote reforestation, improved crop storage, Mothers' Clubs, restoration of agricultural terraces, improved irrigation techniques, appropriate technology, improved diet, and biological pest control. Among these are the Instituto de Desarrollo y Medio Ambiente (IDMA), Diaconía, Perú-Francia, etc. Agronomists and other technical personnel travel the Province by truck and motorcycle attending village meetings and work bees. Two notable tendencies are the prioritization of "bio-development", meaning ecologically sustainable production with a minimum of chemical inputs, and micro-regional approaches bringing together the communties of each river catchment. Governmental agencies at national and Department level provide ad-hoc project aid to ventures such as reservoir improvement and school building. Visit this informative, lushly illustrated web site for more details.

Internet Archeology: an e-journal
http://intarch.york.ac.uk/

Covering key topics of anthropology as well as archeology, Internet Archaeology—a part of the Electronic Libraries Programme (http://www.ukoln.ac.uk/services/elib/)—is the first fully refereed electronic journal in its discipline. The editors have set themselves the task of publishing articles of a high academic standing which also try to utilize the potential of electronic publication. The journal currently has 22962 registered readers (registration is currently free as of this writing). The breadth of this biannual publication includes excavation reports (incorporating text, photographs, data, drawings, reconstruction diagrams, interpretations), analyses of large data sets along with the data itself, visualisations, programs used to analyse data, and applications of information technology to archeology. Articles in Internet Archaeology are chosen for their quality academic content and for their use of the electronic medium—there are no chronological or geographical restrictions, and papers in languages other than English are very welcome. Internet Archaeology is steered by a consortium made up from representatives from the British Academy, the Council for British Archaeology and the Universities of Durham, Glasgow, Oxford,

Southampton and York. The Journal is hosted on behalf of the consortium by the Department of Archaeology and Prehistory at the University of York, and the editor is Judith Winters of the same department at the University of York.

Kinship and Social Organization: An Interactive Tutorial
   http://www.umanitoba.ca/faculties/arts/anthropology/kintitle.html

Kinship is the most basic principle of organizing individuals into social groups, roles, and categories. Some form of organization based on parentage and marriage is present in every human society. In modern industrial communities family structures have been weakened by the dominance of the market economy and the provision of state organized social services. However, the nuclear family household is still the fundamental institution responsible for rearing children and organizing consumption. In nonindustrial contexts, kinship units normally have a much wider array of functions. They often serve as basic units of production, political representation and even as religious bodies for the worship of spiritual beings, who are themselves considered members of the kingroup. Brian Schwimmer of the University of Manitoba explores the implications of all this—and does so brilliantly—in his stunning, web-based, interactive tutorial on kinship and social organization. Beautifully illustrated with photographs of indigenous humans and their artifacts, this tutorial explores (among other things) systems of descent (unilineal descent and cognatic descent), kinship terminology, marriage systems (exogamy and incest, taboos, endogamy, cross cousin marriage, parallel cousin marriage), and residence rules. Schwimmer takes his ethnographic examples from a Turkish peasant village, the Yanomamo of the Amazon Forest, the Ancient Hebrews, the Akan of West Africa, and the Dani of New Guinea.

University of Kansas Museum of Anthropology
http://www.ukans.edu/~kuma/

You may not realize how long people have been living in Leavenworth County, Kansas. Come to the web page of the University of Kansas Museum of Anthropology to learn of a place located on a bluff overlooking the Missouri River where scientists have discovered evidence of human occupation going back 10,000 years. Most of the artifacts date to two periods: 4000-500 B.C. and A.D. 900-1400. A wide variety of different artifact types has been recovered, including axes, celts, spear and arrow points (also known as projectile points), knives, ceramic sherds (vessel fragments), grinding stones or manos, hammerstones for making stone tools, hematite or "ocher," and charred wood, nutshells, seeds, and corn. Study of how these artifacts were made, how they were used and worn, what they were made from and where they were found has allowed researchers to answer some basic questions about the site and the human activities that took place there. The Museum's web page includes extensive details on current research such as this, and also describes the Museum's rich collection of over 8,000 artifacts from various expeditions throughout North America (Western Greenland, Plains, Southwest, California, Northwest Coast, Mexico), South America (Amazonia, Gran Chaco, Andes), Oceania (Polynesia), Australia, New Guinia, and Africa (Sahara Sudan, East and South, Central, West).

Univereity of Kent Anthropology Resources/CASC Ethnographics Gallery
http://lucy.ukc.ac.uk/

This web site hosted by the University of Kent's Center for Social Anthropology and Computing (CASC) provides an extensive collection of resources and brilliantly crafted research studies. One highlight are the web pages belonging to Stephen Lyon—a Ph.D. student in Anthropology at the University of Kent—was, until September 1999, doing fieldwork in a village in Pakistan. His web pages include an archive of weekly updates and monthly reports about his research and

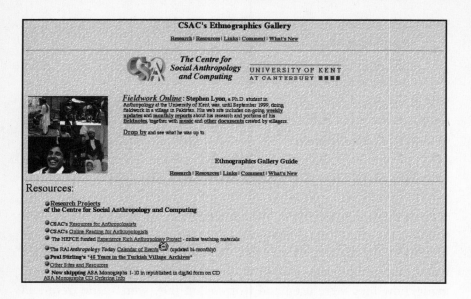

portions of his fieldnotes, together with music and other documents created by villagers. Other resources include CSAC's Resources for Anthropologists, CSAC's Online Reading for Anthropologists, the HEFCE-funded "Experience Rich Anthropology Project," the RAI Anthropology Today Calendar of Events (updated bi-monthly), and Paul Stirling's "45 Years in the Turkish Village Archives." Here you will also find interesting information on other CASC research projects including those that address sustainable semi-arid development, traditions of the Cook Islands, VIMS: The Virtual Institute of Mambila Studies, BLERBS: British Library Ethnographic Research on Bibliographic Services, texts of exploration, TAP: The Text Analysis Project, the Contrade System for exploring territory and identity, culture as distributed cognition, and the 1999 Eclipse Anthropology Project. The webmasters are Michael D. Fischer (an anthropologist who has worked mainly in the Punjab and Swat in Pakistan) and David Zeitlyn (Senior Lecturer in Social Anthropology, Department of Anthropology, University of Kent).

Margaret Mead 2001 Centennial Web Site
http://www.mead2001.org/

Come to this great web site for complete information on anthropologist Margaret Mead and her centennial. Mead (1901 to 1978) contributed vastly to the field of anthropology. Her 44 books (among them the classic Coming of Age in Somoa) and more than 1,000 articles have been translated into virtually all languages. Her data has been carefully catalogued and preserved. She was the first anthropologist to study child-rearing practices. Her work on learning theory and "Learning Through Imprinting," a method by which children learn, is currently being studied further. One of the founders of the "Culture and Personality School of Anthropology", she was the first to conduct psychologically-oriented field work. She was instrumental in forging interdisciplinary links between anthropology and other fields. Her writings and lectures covered a vast array of important topics, what she called "Unmapped Country". She wrote on subjects ranging from mental and spiritual health to ethics and overpopulation. A strong proponent of family, she believed that "Children are our vehicles for survival-for in them there is hope, and through them what has been, and what will be will not only be perpetrated, but also united." In addition to a full biography and bibliography, this site also includes links to online resources relating to Mead's research, a guide to print and film archives, and more.

National Anthropological Archives
http://www.nmnh.si.edu/naa/

Established in 1879 as the archives of the Bureau of American Ethnology, the National Anthropological Archives (NAA) is now a unit of the Department of Anthropology in the National Museum of Natural History. It preserves papers of anthropologists, records of anthropological organizations (including certain Smithsonian units) and other documents of use to anthropologists. The Archives' 7000 linear feet of field notes, photographs, correspondence, journals, sound recordings, and works of art are available for use through visits to the reading room and, as possible, through correspondence.

Many Native Americans use the collection to study their cultural past. Highlights include ethnological and linguistic documents concerning North American Indians collected by the Smithsonian Institution since the 1850's and by federal geological surveys during the 1870's. George Gibbs, John Wesley Powell, and Franz Boas are among the very many anthropologists who contributed to the collection. Archaeological documents include materials of Cyrus Thomas' survey of mounds east of the Rocky Mountains, periodic reports of the Work Projects Administration, and the records of the River Basin Surveys, as well as materials of individual archaeologists and a collection of so-called "grey" literature. There is also a large photograph collection of original glass film negatives and vintage prints, a relatively large collection of American Indian ledger book drawings, and other works of art, as well as a small but important collection of sound recordings, including material collected by John P. Harrington, James Henri Howard, and John Lyle Fischer.

National Museum of Natural History (Smithsonian) Dept. of Anthropology
http://www.nmnh.si.edu/anthro/

Anthropology at The National Museum of Natural History is all about what makes us human, our place in nature, our common concerns and our differences. National Museum of Natural History anthropologists explore these issues through laboratory and collections-based research at the Museum and at field sites throughout the world. The National Museum of Natural History anthropology staff build and maintain the Museum's world class collections which now include more than 600,000 objects documenting the diversity and accomplishments of humankind. Museum anthropologists also teach others about what they have learned through exhibits, school age educational programs, public programs and opportunities for advanced training. This thorough, thought-provoking web site also includes outside links to research projects conducted by the National Museum of Natural History and other institutions, among them the Field Museum's New Guinea Research Program, a a fascinating multidisciplinary endeavor bringing together expertise in archaeology, social

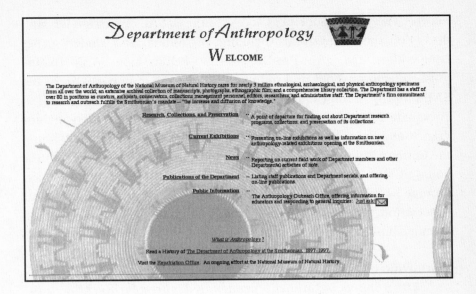

anthropology, human biology, museum studies, and data analysis to explore the history and human diversity of the southwest Pacific. Since 1987 the New Research Program (NGRP) has been using the world-famous ethnological collections at the Smithsonian and other institutions as a starting place "benchmark" for researching the social life, prehistory, and contemporary cultural change on the Sepik Coast of New Guinea.

Society for the Anthropology of Europe
http://www2.h-net.msu.edu/~sae/

The Society for the Anthropology of Europe (SAE) was first conceived in 1986 and its first elections were held in the Fall of 1987. The purposes of the organization, as announced in the organizing letter that went out in 1986, were to strengthen national and international networks between colleagues, to provide forums for discussion and debate, to encourage comparative research, to enhance the visibility and legitimacy of Europeanist anthropology (both within the discipline and among other Europeanist groups), to facilitate the dissemination of information about employment opportunities and grants, and to promote the professional integration of students specializing in

Europe. This web site includes access to the H-SAE discussion list, and details on special programs including the annual SAE student paper competition, the SAE Pre-Dissertation Fellowship, SAE's Distinguished lecturer series and roundtables, and the online edition of the SAE's journal Europea: The Journal of the Europeanists. You can also click here for various subgroups of SAE, including the Network for French and Francophone Cultures, The Hungarianist Research Group, the German Studies Network Bibliography, the East European Anthropology Group, and the Anthropology of Italy Network. (By the way: Strange as it may seem. SAE is a division American Anthropological Association, referenced above. Membership in one entitles you to membership in the other.)

Worldwide e-mail Directory of Anthropologists
*http://wings.buffalo.edu/academic/department/anthropology/
weda/*

The Worldwide Email Directory of Anthropologists (WEDA) is a searchable database of address and research information about anthropologists from around the world. This is a completely volunteer project, established to encourage and aid scholarly communication. Here, anthropology is taken in its widest sense, to include physical, earth, and social scientists, as well as their colleagues in the humanities. Students and scholars, applied anthropologists, professionals and avocationalists are all to be found here: at last count, 2,020 institutions and 4,919 individuals. There are four different ways to search: by using all or part of a person's name, by title of an institution or business, by geographic location, and by research specialty. Click on the appropriate button, and you can add your own e-mail address and profile details to the database. This site attracts more than 3,000 visitors a month and is rapidly becoming one of the most popular anthropology resources on the Internet. As a bonus, it also offers very useful links to other anthropology-related search tools on the Web. The Worldwide e-mail Directory of Anthropologists is available in English, French and Spanish versions, and is hosted by the State University of New York at Buffalo Department of Anthropology.

Anthropology E-mail Discussion Groups

ACRA-L
> American Cultural Resources Association—send message "subscribe acra-l your name" to listproc@listproc.nonprofit.net

ANSS-L
> Discussion Forum for Information Specialists in Anthropology, Sociology and Related Fields—send message "subscribe anss-l your name" to listserv@uci.edu

AnthEurasia-L
> Anthropology of the Former Soviet Bloc—send message "subscribe AnthEurasia-L your name" to majordomo@fas.harvard.edu

ANTHRO-L
> Anthropology in general—send message "subscribe anthro-l your name" to listserv@listserv.acsu.buffalo.edu; Home page & archives at http://www.anatomy.su.oz.au/danny/anthropology/anthro-l/index.html; mirror of archives at http://listserv.acsu.buffalo.edu/archives/anthro-l.html

ANTHRO-LIB
> Liberation anthropology—send message "subscribe anthro-lib your name" to listproc@lists.colorado.edu

ANTROPOL
> majordomo@iinet.net.au

AnthroWomen
> Women anthropologists networking with other anthropology professionals and students—send message "subscribe" to Majordomo@list.pitt.edu

ANTHTHEORY-L

Anthropology theory—send message "subscribe anththeory-l your name" to listserv@list.nih.gov

ARTIFACT

Material culture study/methods—send message "subscribe artifact your name" to listserv@umdd.umd.edu

ASAONET

Anthropology of Oceania—send message "sub asaonet your name" to listserv@listserv.uic.edu

CELTLING

Celtic linguistics—send request to celtling@mitvma.mit.edu

Ceramics-L

Prehistoric ceramics—send message "sub ceramics-l first-name last-name" to listserv@listserv.acsu.buffalo.edu

CONSDIST {moderated}

For professionals engaged in conservation of cultural materials—send request to consdist- request@lindy.stanford.edu

CRFA-L

Center for Research and Fieldwork in Anthropology, University of Texas at Arlington—send message "subscribe crfa-l" to listserv@utarlvm1.uta.edu

EASIANTH

East Asian anthropology—"subscribe easianth your name" to list-serv@vm.temple.edu

ETHMUS-L

Ethnomusicology—send message "subscribe ethmus-l your name" to listserv@umdd.umd.edu

ETHNET-L

Irish & British Ethnography—send message "subscribe ethnet-l your name" to listserv@ysub.ysu.edu

ETHNO

Ethnomethodology/conversation analysis—send message "subscribe ethno your name" to comserve@vm.ecs.rpi.edu

ETHNO-BIO

Ethnobiology (use of plants and animals by native peoples worldwide)—send message "subscribe ethno-bio" to major-domo@sfu.ca

FOLKLORE

Folklore—send message "subscribe folklore your name" to listserv@tamvm1.tamu.edu

H-SAE

Anthropology of Europe—send message "subscribe h-sae your name" to listserv@msu.edu

INTERCUL

Intercultural communication—send message "subscribe intercul your name" to comserve@vm.ecs.rpi.edu

MAPC

Materialist Anthropology and the Production of Culture Work-shop—send message "subscribe mapc your name" to listserv@vm.utcc.utoronto.ca

NAGPRA-L

Discussion of Native American Graves Protection and Repatria-tion Act—send message "subscribe nagpra-l" to majordomo@world.std.com

NAT-LANG

Native American indigenous languages—send message "subscribe nat-lang your-first- name your-last-name" to listserv@tamvm1.tamu.edu

NATFOOD-L

Native American Foods—send message "subscribe natfood-l your name" to listproc@listproc.wsu.edu

PAN-L

Physical Anthropology—send message "sub pan-l your name" to listserv@freya.cc.pdx.edu

SBANTH-L

Anthropology graduate students—send message "subscribe sbanth-l your name" to listserv@ucsbvm.ucsb.edu

WOMANTH-L

Women in anthropology—send message "subscribe coswa-l your name" to listserver@relay.doit.wisc.edu

XCULT-X

Intercultural communication—send message "subscribe xcult-x your name" to listserv@psuvm.psu.edu

Anthropology Usenet Discussion Groups

alt.native—Native American issues (superceded by
soc.culture.native)
rec.food.historic—ancient foods
sci.anthropology—anthropology
sci.anthropology.paleo—evolution of humans and other primates
soc.culture.native—Native American issues (supercedes alt.native)
sci.lang—linguistics
soc.misc—miscellaneous social issues

2

ARCHEOLOGY

American Antiquity: A Journal of the Society for American Archaeology

http://www.saa.org/Publications/AmAntiq/amantiq.html

American Antiquity is a principal journal of the Society for American Archaeology (SAA). This web page provides tables of contents—and complete article abstracts in both English and Spanish—for all issues beginning in 1995, as well as e-mail links for the journal's editorial staff. Topics of recent articles include the Solutrean Settlement of North America, Archaeology and Native North American Oral Traditions, The Recovery and First Analysis of an Early Holocene Human Skeleton from Kennewick (Washington), and Rural Communities in the Black Warrior Valley (Alabama). Additional articles address Women and Children at the Old Baton Rouge Penitentiary, Paleoindian Colonization of the Colonization of the Americas, Paleoindian Colonization of the Colonization of the Americas, Prehistorical Ceramics and People in Southeast Missouri, and Cannibalism, Warfare, and Drought in the Mesa Verde Region during the Twelfth Century A.D. For would-be contributors, the web site also includes the journal's style guide and information on the journal's editorial policy. For those interested in casting a wider net, this web site also offers links to the Journal of Latin American Antiquity and associated newsletters and bulletins of the SAA, among them the Newsletter of Archeology and Public Education and various other little publications, all of them available in online hypertext editions.

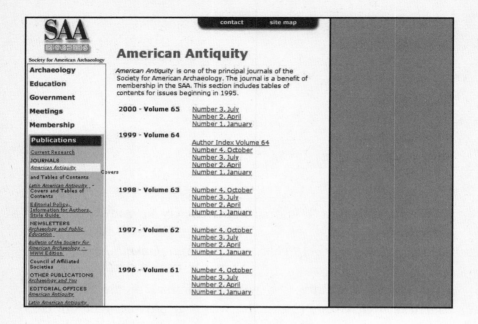

Anistoriton: History, Archaeology, ArtHistory
http://users.hol.gr/~dilos/anistor/cover.htm

Anistoriton is an electronic journal published only on the Internet. It is a free and independent magazine of History, Archaeology and ArtHistory edited by D. I. Loizos and an Editorial Committee. Anistoriton is the Greekword for "ignorant in history". The journal is an attempt to bridge the gap between professional historians and archaeologists and their specialized research, on the one hand, and the general public, the true history and archaeology lovers, on the other. Contributions of undergraduate and graduate students (papers, analysis etc) as well as other non-specialists are also welcome and encouraged. Anistoriton publishes essays on any topic related to History, Archaeology and ArtHistory of any era and any part of the world provided it is of interest to the general educated public and undergraduate students. Also, it includes student Viewpoints, Archaeology News and History News, Internet Meesages from the major electronic Mailing Lists related to History and Archaeology, Primary Sources, and the sections In Situ and An Object of Art. It also contains a special page with announcements of Conferences worldwide. Anistoriton

SCIENTIFIC AMERICAN GUIDE TO SCIENCE ON THE INTERNET

welcomes submissions of electronic manuscripts for any of its sections especially by trained Historians, Archaeologists and ArtHistorians who would like to reach a broader public. Other Scholars, Researchers, or Students are also invited to submit their manuscripts for the section entitled "Viewpoints."

ArchNet: The World Wide Web Virtual Library for Archaeology
http://archnet.uconn.edu/

ArchNet serves as the World Wide Web Virtual Library for Archaeology. This server provides access to archaeological resources available on the Internet. Information is categorized by geographic region and subject. Catalan, Dutch, French, German, Italian, and Spanish language versions of the home page are also available. The webmasters are Thomas Plunkett of the Graduate Center of the City University of New York and Jonathan Lizee of the University of Connecticut, and the resources are virtually (no pun intended) endless. Come here for hundreds of links on such topics as Archaeometry, Botanical Archeology, Cereamics, CRM and Government Agencies, Educational Materials, Ethnohitory/Ethnoarcheology, Faunal Archeology, Geo-Archeology, Historic Archeology, Lithics, Mapping and GIS, Method and Theory, and Archeological Software. Click on that latter category for free downloads of such great offerings as The Bonn Archaeological Statistics Package, a terrific DOS and Mac radiocarbon calibration program from the University of Washington, Macintosh mapping software for caves and rockshelters, a user-friendly geographical information system for Windows called Map Maker, and Point, a DOS-based projectile point classification program by Tara Prindle (UCONN). This highly useful program utilizes morphological data to classify projectile points from the northeastern United States. Whatever the specific subject of your quest, be sure to make ArchNet your first stop when browsing for archeology-related information on the web.

Archeological Institute of America
http://www.archaeological.org/

The Archaeological Institute of America (AIA) has been dedicated to the encouragement and support of archaeological research and publication and to the protection of the world's cultural heritage for more than a century. A nonprofit cultural and educational organization chartered by the US Congress, it is the oldest and largest archaeological organization in North America, with more than 11,000 members around the world. The Archaeological Institute of America/Institut Archéologique d'Amérique (AIA/IAA-Canada) was incorporated in Canada in 1994 as an independent affiliate of the Archaeological Institute of America (AIA-US). Members of the Institute have conducted fieldwork in Africa, Asia, Europe, and North and South America. The AIA has further promoted archaeological studies by founding research centers and schools in seven countries and maintains close relations with these institutions, including the American School of Classical Studies at Athens, the School of Classical Studies at the American Academy in Rome, and others. Come to this web page for information on AIA membership as well as AIA programs, including publications, lecture series, scholarships, internships, fellowships, and local affiliates. The web site also provides a complete directory to the archives of the AIA, from its founding in 1879 to the present day. In addition to the daily operations of the Institute, the records deal with Institute sponsored foreign schools, excavations, explorations, publications, lecture tours and Local Societies.

Archeological research in Northeastern Nigeria
http://www.informatik.uni-frankfurt.de/~sfb268/c7/c7.htm

Since 1991 the Africa section of the Prehistory Departement of the Johann-Wolfgang-Goethe-University at Frankfurt am Main, Germany, has engaged in research in Northeastern Nigeria, specifically Borno and Yobe States. Research has concentrated on three areas. First, excavations started around the present town of Gajiganna, NE of Maiduguri, the capital of Borno State. Here various Later Stone Age and Early Iron Age sites have been discovered. The second region consists of the vast clay plains (locally called firki), south of Lake Chad, where four extensive mound sites have been trenched. Research here concentrated on the Later Stone Age layers in those mounds but also on Iron Age and Medieval periods up to the onset of Colonial times. Additionally, considerable attention has been given to the social and political structures of the present societies, as various cultural influences both from the islamic empire of Borno as well as the local indigenious traditions merge in this area. The third area is the region around River Yobe. The most fascinating find so far is a fully preserved boat at the site of Dufuna, between Potiskum and Gashua on the Komadugu Gana. The radiocarbon dates for the boat are: 7264 ± 55 bp (KN-4683) and 7670 ± 110 bp (KI-3587) (uncalibrated). This makes it the oldest known boat in Africa and one of the oldest in the world.

Archeological Resource Guide for Europe
http://odur.let.rug.nl/arge/

Archeological Resource Guide for Europe (ARGE) comprises more than 1,500 categorized links served from 42 countries. Begun in early 1995 by Sara Champion and Martijn van Leusen as a service within the European Archaeological Heritage Web, Archeological Resource Guide for Europe presents an ordered collection of hypertext links pointing to current archaeological communication and information resources across Europe. Search the links by country, by subject, or by period. Archeological Resource Guide for Europe is different from other guides to archaeological resources on the Web because new links are actively sought out, visited, and evaluated before being posted in our new links section. Archeological Resource Guide for Europe always aims to present information in its original language, and is currently working on the implementation of multilingual access and searching. Search topics ranging from ancient land management to urban archeology, from environmental archeology to statues and stelae. Here you will also find links to extensive pages introducing the Valetta treaty (including links to the official text and an overview of available fact sheets), details on the history and excavations in the Roman city of Neuss (Germany), and the fascinating story of an amazing archaeozoological find: an extinct antelope (Myotragus Balearicus) found associated with mesolithic human occupation remains in two rock shelters on the island of Mallorca.

Archeology Magazine: The Official Publication of the Archeological Institute of America
   http://www.he.net/~archaeol/index.html

Founded in 1948, ARCHAEOLOGY Magazine covers all aspects of the human past. It is an official publication of the Archaeological Institute of America, the country's oldest and largest professional organization devoted to archaeology. Lavishly illustrated and written with clarity and wit, ARCHAEOLOGY conveys the excitement of worldwide exploration and discovery. Its engaging and entertaining stories written by leading experts bring the past into the 21st century. The full texts of newsbriefs and selected longer articles are available online; abstracts of other departments and features are also available. Help solve the puzzle of mysterious burial urns found in caves deep within the Amazon jungle. Discover fabulous geoglyphs, the remains of bunkers and pillboxes built to stymie a Nazi invasion of England, and the "extraordinary folly" of Asia's greatest brick monument. Take guided tours of Rome as it was at the time of the first-millennium, the Shenandoah Valley as it was in the mid 1800s, or Hamlet's castle. Join the world's top archeologists as they unearth the secrets of Roman life on the Danube, Armageddon, the physical evidence of the Battle of the Nile, Roman-era tombs southwest of Cairo, and the legendary square-rigger Bounty. Search articles by topic, title or author. Then enjoy full texts of selected items plus dazzling online illustrations.

Athena Review: Journal of Archaeology, History, and Exploration
   http://www.athenapub.com/

The Athena Review: Journal of Archeology, History, and Exploration features well-written, informative articles addressing current news items in archaeology, history, and exploration . . . profiling and explaining relevant field or research projects in archaeology and history . . . reviewing of key books, journals, videos, and CD-ROMS in

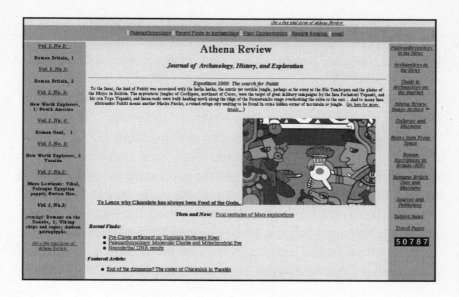

these areas. Recent areas of focus include Pre-Clovis settlement on Virginia's Nottoway River, Neanderthal DNA results, the search for the Incas' legendary land of Paititi, and Roman inscriptions in Britain. Here you can also get the scoop on Andean petroglyphs, evidence of the first people to populate the region in and around central Scotland, Palenque Egyptian papyri, and Roman Gaul. Also be sure to check the Athena Review's great image archive presenting splendid photographs of unique archeological sites in Britain, Bulgaria (Ancient Thrace), Cambodia, Egypt, France, Italy, Scandanavia and elsewhere. And don't miss the stunning collection of online maps, including Athena's maps of Buddhist Monasteries in Tibet, Caesar's crossings in Britain, Celtic tribes and Caesar's campaigns of the Gallic Wars (58-50 BC), Rome (Domus Aurea and the baths of Trajan), sites of tomb treasures in Bulgaria, site plan for Angkor (Cambodia), and Columbus's first voyage as shown on the a period map, the famous Map of Antilles (1492).

CBA guide to UK archaeology online
http://www.britarch.ac.uk/info/uklinks.html

Access hundreds of links associated with archeology of, for and about the United Kingdom. Categories include: Government offices,

Virtual tours and presentations (site specific), Government agencies and Royal Commissions, Virtual tours and presentations (regional/national), National organizations and professional bodies, Virtual tours and presentations (thematic), Local government curators, Online journals and magazines, Contracting units, trusts and consultancies, Specialist archaeological book services, University archaeology departments, Museums, Special interest groups, Projects and services, Other online directories, and Regional and local societies. This web site is an especially valuable source for local regional archeological societies throughout the length and breadth of the British Isles, many of them offering engaging reports of research on little-known yet fascinating British archeological sites—so called "little Stonehenges"—rife with mysterious roots. Local links include the Astons' Local History Group, Bangor Archaeological Society, Birmingham & Warwickshire Archaeological Society, Dradon Archaeological Group, Chester Archaeological Society, City of London Archaeological Society, Colchester Roman Society, Cumberland & Westmorland Antiquarian & Archaeological Society, Derbyshire Archaeological Society, Edinburgh Archaeological Field Society, Hastings Area Archaeological Research Group, Hendon & District Archaeological Society, and the Isle of Wight Industrial Archaeology Society. Additional local listings include the Kent Archaeological Society, Lanark & District Archaeological Society, Leicestershire Archaeological & Historical Society, London & Middlesex Archaeological Society, Manshead Archaeological Society of Dunstable, and the Northamptonshire Archaeological Society.

Classics and Mediterranean Archeaology
http://rome.classics.lsa.umich.edu/welcome.html

Come here for hundreds of links of interest to classicists and those interested in Mediterranean archeology. Search by category amid Texts, Projects, Journals, Bibliographies, Indexes of Links to Other Sites, Exhibits, Web Documents and Sources of Images, Field Reports and Site Specific Pages, Associations and Organizations, Departmental Descriptions, Course Material and Teaching Resources, Museums, Atlases and Geographic Information, and much more. Links include the University of Michigan's Papyrus digitalization project. With over 10,000 individual fragments on hand, the University of Michigan is home to one of the largest collections of papyri in the world. Through their webpage they hope to provide the public with access not only to our own papyrological collections but to many other papyrological resources as well. Currently you can search approximately 2,500 papyri images. Another fascinating link is to The Medieval Review. Since 1993, The Medieval Review (formerly the Bryn Mawr Medieval Review) has been publishing reviews of current work in all areas of Medieval Studies, a field it interprets as broadly as possible. The electronic medium allows for very rapid publication of reviews, and provides a computer searchable archive of past reviews, both of which are of great utility to scholars and students around the world. These are just two of the hundreds of splendid resources you can access via the Classics and Mediterranean Archeaology web site.

Current Archeology

http://www.archaeology.co.uk [Editor: Note updated URL from what was on original site map]

This is the home page of Current Archaeology, Britain's leading archaeological magazine. If you have an interest in anything to do with archaeology, this is the place to find out about digs, discoveries, and the latest news. As the editors inform us, Current Archeology was founded in response to a dream. "We dreamed of a magazine for the ordinary archaeological enthusiast. A magazine that would keep him (or her!) up to date with what is happening in the world of archaeology; that would describe the latest excavations, illustrating them in full colour and with lots of maps and plans, and would explain them all in language that the ordinary person could understand. With Current Archaeology, that dream has come true. Over the years,over 900 sites have been described, more than 1200 books reviewed, the Science Diary has described all the latest scientific advances, and the Diary has given the latest news of people and ideas." The web site is contrived to give an elegant foretaste of this splendid magazine. Beautifully designed and illustrated, it includes complete rundowns on the contents of recent issues, useful archeological newbytes, lists of current excavations seeking volunteers, a full hypertext directory of over 900 British archeological insitutions and clubs, and more.

Institute of Egyptian Art and Archaeology (University of Memphis)
http://www.memst.edu/egypt/main.html

The Institute of Egyptian Art & Archaeology, founded in 1984, is a component of the Department of Art of The University of Memphis, in Memphis, Tennessee (USA), and is a Tennessee Center of Excellence. It is dedicated to the study of the art and culture of ancient Egypt through teaching, research, exhibition, and community education. As part of its teaching and research, the Institute conducts an epigraphic survey in the Great Hypostyle Hall of Karnak Temple in Luxor, Egypt. The Institute's collection of antiquities resides in the Art Museum of The University of Memphis. Over 150 objects range in date from 3500 B.C.E. to 700 C.E. There are mummies, religious and funerary items, jewelry, and objects from everyday life. One uniqe item in the collection is nothing less than a 4000 year old loaf of bread. This loaf of bread placed with other objects under the foundation of Mentuhotep II's mortuary temple

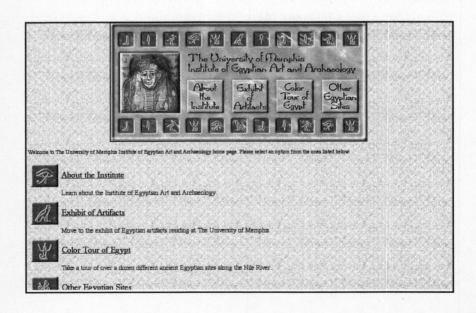

at Deir el Bahari in Western Thebes. The objects placed in foundation deposits for ancient Egyptian temples were intended to symbolically stabilize and protect the four corners and the boundary walls of the temple, because the temple itself was believed to be a microcosm of the universe. One reward gained from a stable universe was food in abundance. The loaf of bread symbolizes that value. View the bread, and other artifacts, in a stunningly rendered online exhibit.

The Glyph: The San Diego Society of the Archeological Institute of America
http://www.theglyph.com/

The San Diego Society is one of nearly 100 local chapters of the Archaeological Institute of America. The institute and its members are dedicated to the recovery, care, study and publication of archaeological material and the conservation and preservation of archaeological sites world wide. A major activity of the San Diego Society is its program of periodic lecture meetings featuring many of the world's leading archaeologists. These scholars present timely topics on their own excavations and research. Visitors are always welcome and most lecture programs are free and open to the public. Click on San Diego Society Lectures and Events icon for the current schedule. Their quarterly publication, THE GLYPH—available here in an abbreviated online edition—offers archaeological news, both local and worldwide. The information is timely, educational, and often fun. Recent articles include "Answering the Question of Slavery in Ancient Egypt," "The Archaeology of Canada's Arctic," "California's Lost Spanish Settlement at Bodega Bay," "Ramses II in Jordan," and "Redating the Sphinx: The Voice of Reason." The web page also gives you guidelines for would-be authors who would like to contribute to THE GLYPH, information on how to contact the editorial staff, and related links.

Institute of Nautical Archeology
http://nautarch.tamu.edu/INA/index.htm

The Institute of Nautical Archaeology was incorporated as the American Institute of Nautical Archaeology in 1972 in Philadelphia,

Pennsylvania, and founded as a nonprofit scientific/educational organization with the purpose of gathering knowledge of human past from the physical remains of maritime activities, and disseminating this knowledge through scholarly and popular publications, seminars, and lectures. Its funding has been from its Board of Directors, the National Geographic Society, the National Endowment for the Humanities, the Institute for Aegean Prehistory, the National Science Foundation and various other foundations and donors Additionally, it draws support from over 950 members, twenty Supporting Institutions (universities, museums, and archaeological organizations), and a modest endowment to pay staff salaries and other operating expenses. Headquarters and research facilities in College Station, Texas are graciously provided by Texas A&M University, but INA owns extensive equipment and facilities at its overseas center in Bodrum, Turkey. In addition to all of the camping and diving equipment required to mount a major excavation, the Institute owns a sixty-five-foot steel vessel, Virazon, with a double-lock recompression chamber, darkroom, and compressors. Come to this web page for more information on the Institute and for beautifully illustrated, hypertext tours of its various research projects.

Irish Archeology: The Swedish Archaeological Excavations at Carrowmore, Co. Sligo, Ireland [Note, this item has changed since site map]
   http://www.hgo.se/carrowmore

The Swedish Archaeological Excavations at Carrowmore (1977-1982) revealed a series of data that made possible alternative explanations to the appearance of the megalithic tradition in Ireland and Europe, as well as the underlying settlement-subsistence systems. The importance of the rich marine resources to the megalith-building population in the Knocknarea area was strongly emphasized. The investigation highlighted the complicated, and artificial, boundary between the Mesolithic and the Neolithic periods, suggesting a slow, local, successive transformation, rather than a migration of farmers. The archaeological results were strongly supported by the paleoecological studies in the area. The remarkable early dates from the three tombs that produced datable material, tombs nos 4, 7 and 27, placed Carrowmore among the earliest megalithic cemeteries in Europe, and thereby in the world, and stressed the necessity of a re-thinking of the Irish megalithic tradition. The results from the Carrowmore excavations have since gained strong support from excavations in other areas in Europe, notably Brittany in France, where a series of dates now show that the megalithic tradition in western France began already before 5000 B.C., and that the underlying economy was heavily oriented towards marine resources. Come to this fascinating web site for more details and engaging photographs of the "dig."

Irish Archeology Online
http://www.xs4all.nl/~tbreen/ireland.html

This comprehensive guide to Irish archaeology on the web is geared to meet the information needs of both for the interested layman and the professional archaeologist. The offerings include an E-mail directory for Irish archaeology supplying E-mail addresses of archaeologists involved in Irish research at home and abroad, Archaeological and historical journals in Ireland (some with lists of contents), and the Newsletter of the Irish section of the Paleopathology Association (on-line edition). Come here for information on Current research, specific regions and individual sites, Monuments, Artifacts, Industrial archaeology, Excavations and other projects, Universities, Government institutions, Museums, Local societies, People engaged in Irish archeology, Books and other publications, Photographs, and Conferences, summer schools, tours and other events. Be sure to check out the link named "A Brief Guide To Irish Archaeological Sites," which features illustrated details on Wedge Tombs, Ceremonial enclosures, Bronze Age Burials, Barrows, Cairns, Stone Circles, Fulachta Fiadh, Ringforts and Cashels, Souterrains, Medieval Moated Sites, and Mottes. Further exploration will yield beautiful photographs and descriptions of the Ahenny and Kilkieran High Crosses near Carrick-on-Suir, which date from the 8th Century. The North Cross at Ahenny is perhaps the most fascinating with its symbolism and detailed tracery (including old celtic patterns of intercalary and spirals), but the North Cross at Ahenny is also quite interesting and alluring.

Museum of Antiquities

http://museums.ncl.ac.uk/archive/

The Museum of Antiquities is the joint museum of the Society of Antiquaries of Newcastle upon Tyne and the University of Newcastle upon Tyne. It is the principal museum of archaeology in north east England. Come to the Museum's web pages to experience The Virtual Mithraeum: A temple to the Roman god Mithras. Click the button for Wallnet: the Hadrian's Wall Education Website. Click another button and go to Flints and Stones, an exhibition which takes you to the world of the Late Stone Age hunter gatherers. Next view and learn about popular "Objects of the Month." These include Carved and Inscribed Stones, Ceramics, Metalwork, Personal and Ornamental Objects, and Coins. Metal objects include a Bronze Axehead, a Capheaton Hanging Bowl, a Dodecahedron, a Helmet Cheek Piece, a Reaverhill Bronze Dagger, a South Shields Harness Mount, and a Bronze Age Shield. The carved and inscribed stones include Alnmouth Cross Shaft, the Head of Antenociticus, the Bremenium Dedication Slab, the Doddington Cist Cover, a Hadrianic Building Inscription, the Temple of Mithras, the Tombstone of Aurelius, the Tynemouth Cross Shaft, the Statue of Heracles, the Cup Marked Rock, the Tomb of Anicius, and more. The last highlight of this web page is "Armamentarium: The Book of Roman Arms and Armour."

National Archeological Database

http://www.cast.uark.edu/products/NADB/

National Archeological Database—a computerized communications network for the archeological and historic preservation community—is an internationally recognized source of information on public archeology. NADB ("Nad-Bee") was established to meet a congressional directive to improve access to information on archeological activities nationwide. NADB-Reports is an expanded bibliographic inventory of approximately 240,000 reports on archeological planning and investigation, mostly of limited circulation. This "gray literature" represents a large portion of the primary information available on archeological sites in the U.S. The last update occurred in November 1997 when some 110,000 reports were added to the database. NADB-Reports can be queried by state, county, worktype, cultural affiliation, keyword, material, year of publication, title, and author. NADB-NAGPRA provides the full text of the Native American Graves Protection and Repatriation Act, up-to-date information on regulations and guidance, and summaries of inventory and repatriation activities. Divided into five document categories, any one of the more than 200 records can be downloaded. Finally, NADB-MAPS (Multiple Attribute PresentationSystem) is a graphical application which contains a variety of maps (GIS) showing national distributions of cultural and environmental resources across the U.S. by state and county levels. Updated information and new data modules are added to NADB on a regular basis. The NADB network is maintained through a cooperative agreement between NPS and the Center for Advanced Spatial Technologies (CAST) at the University of Arkansas.

Review of Archeology
http://www.reviewofarchaeology.com/

Featuring reviews of current archeological literature, the twice-yearly Review of Archeology may be read with profit and enjoyment by anyone with strong interests in archaeology, palaeoanthropology, palaeontology, palaeobotany, geoarchaeology, and dating methods. The reviews may focus on a single publication or upon several. For the most part the subjects are research reports and syntheses of research issued in the form of books, monographs, and, even, short articles. ROA articles are generally lengthy, allowing the authors to consider broadly, and in depth, the matters brought up by the publication. For the reader the resulting articles are thus interesting, searching, informative, and intellectually challenging. (On occasion, the review article may be as long or longer than the publication itself. In addition to the normal literature reviews with their typically diverse coverage, from time to time the Review now brings out Special Issues devoted to one particular subject. Recent reviews have assayed such topics as: The Archaeology of the European Neanderthals: East and West, Agricultural Origins in North America Climate and Punctuated Cultural Change, Dating Monte Alegre in South

America, and the Demise of the "Gran Chichimeca." Other subjects have included: Dental Variation and Human History, the Ice-Age Amazon, the De Soto Entrada Into the Southern United States, and the Prehistory of British Columbia from 10,500 to 5,000 BC.

Scrolls From the Dead Sea: The Ancient Library of Qumran and Modern Scholarship
http://sunsite.unc.edu/expo/deadsea.scrolls.exhibit/intro.html

The Library of Congress's online exhibition "Scrolls From the Dead Sea: The Ancient Library of Qumran and Modern Scholarship" brings before the American people a selection from the scrolls which have been the subject of intense public interest. Over the years questions have be en raised about the scrolls' authenticity, about the people who hid them away, about the period in which they lived, about the secrets the scrolls reveal, and about the intentions of the scrolls' custodians in restricting access. The Library's exhibition describes the historical context of the scrolls and the Qumran community from whence they may have originated; it also relates the story of their discovery 2,000 years later. In addition, the exhibition encourages a better understanding of the challenge s and complexities connected with

Welcome to

SCROLLS FROM THE DEAD SEA

The Ancient Library of Qumran and Modern Scholarship

an Exhibit at the Library of Congress, Washington, DC

The exhibition Scrolls From the Dead Sea: The Ancient Library of Qumran and Modern Scholarship brings before the American people a selection from the scrolls which have been the subject of intense public interest. Over the years questions have be en raised about the scrolls' authenticity, about the people who hid them away, about the period in which they lived, about the secrets the scrolls reveal, and about the intentions of the scrolls' custodians in restricting access. The Library's exhibition describes the historical context of the scrolls and the Qumran community from whence they may have originated; it also relates the story of their discovery 2,000 years later. In addition, the exhibition encourages a better understanding of the challenge s and complexities connected with scroll research.

The exhibition is divided into five sections:

- Introduction -- The World of the Scrolls
- The Qumran Library
- The Qumran Community
- Today -- 2,000 Years Later
- Conclusion

The original exhibition included nearly 100 objects: scroll fragments, artifacts from the Qumran site, and books and illustrations from the Library of Congress' collections. The online exhibit includes images of 12 scroll fragments and 29 other objects lo aned by the Israel Antiquities Authority for this exhibition.

You may view the exhibit by selecting any of the above sections or you may choose to browse the entire exhibit by selecting

- Outline of Objects and Topics in Scrolls from the Dead Sea

scroll research. The exhibition is divided into five clickable sections: Introduction—The World of the Scrolls. The Qumran Library. The Qumran Community. Today—2,000 Years Later. Conclusion. The original exhibtion included nearly 100 objects: scroll fragments, artifacts from the Qumran site, and books and illustrations from the Library of Congress' collections. The online exhibit includes images of 12 scroll fragments and 29 other objects loaned by the Israel Antiquities Authority for the exhibition.

Society for American Archeology Bulletin
http://www.anth.ucsb.edu/SAABulletin/

The Northwest Research Obsidian Studies Laboratory announces the availability of an annual research grant for up to $1,000 worth of analytical services (X-ray fluorescence trace element analysis and/or obsidian hydration analysis) for any M.A. or Ph.D. student whose research is concerned with an Oregon archaeological site and/or obsidian source. The Federal Emergency Management Agency (FEMA) and the National Task Force on Emergency Response are recruiting conservation and preservation professionals for postdisaster assistance teams and mitigation research. And UCLA and the J. Paul Getty Trust are creating a master's degree in the conservation of archaeological and ethnographic materials that is unique in its focus among conservation training programs in the United States. The program will provide students with a cultural orientation to conservation, and a strong base in materials science, anthropology, and fieldwork. Where do you turn for news and notes of this stripe? Why, to the Bulletin of the Society for American Archeology, of course. Come here, to the online edition of the Bulletin, to learn about a host of opportunities, including those offered by Archaeology Abroad which—based at the Instite of Archaeology, University College, London—does a great job of publicizing more than 1,000 places for volunteers, professional staff, and specialists on a wide variety of projects of all periods in diverse locations worldwide.

The Newstead Research Project

http://www.brad.ac.uk/acad/archsci/field_proj/newstead/new-stead.html

The Newstead Research Project is investigating the region surrounding the Roman fort of Trimontium near Newstead, on the River Tweed in the Borders region of southern Scotland. Field research has concentrated both on the Roman military complex of Trimontium itself and on the Iron Age settlement sites in the surrounding region. Trimontium was one of the most important Roman centers of the northern frontier in Britain, and was occupied from the late first century AD through the second. It was extensively excavated in the early years of the twentieth century, producing an outstanding collection of Roman artefacts, from humble wooden tent pegs to highly decorated military parade helmets, all now in the National Museums of Scotland in Edinburgh. The surrounding region is among the most fertile areas for arable farming in modern Scotland. Its importance seems to have been similar in antiquity, with one of the two biggest of Scotland's hillforts, Eildon Hill North, lying very near Trimontium, and some 150 settlement sites known in the 25 x 25 km area of the Research Project's survey region. Come to this web page for interesting, extensively illustrated reports from the field documenting research conducted by the staff, students and interns associated with the Department of Archaeological Sciences, University of Bradford, UK.

USA TODAY archeology articles

http://www.usatoday.com:80/life/science/ancient/lsaindex.htm

All the archeological news that's fit to print. There's always late-breaking news from thousands and millions of years ago, and USA TODAY has it. Consider: Four recently discovered spears made 400,000 years ago are the oldest hunting weapons ever found and prove mankind's early ancestors were much more savvy than imagined. Consider: Scientists who drilled core samples from the ocean bed said recently they have found "smoking gun" evidence that a huge asteroid smashed into the Earth 65 millions years ago and probably killed off the dinosaurs. Consider: New evidence that humans lived in

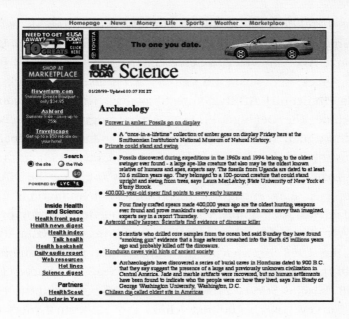

southern Chile 12,500 years ago, some 1,300 years earlier than previously believed possible, could radically revise theories about how humans migrated to North America. And consider: Archaeologists have discovered a series of burial caves in Honduras dated to 900 B.C. that they say suggest the presence of a large and previously unknown civilization in Central America. Jade and marble artifacts were recovered, but no human settlements have been found to indicate who the people were or how they lived. So says Jim Brady of George Washington University, Washington, D.C. From Clovis to Rome, from the arctic to the Ucatan, USA TODAY goes out of its way to bring you cutting-edge archeological news from the four corners of the earth. And they do so in a timely and informed manner.

Virtual Museum of Nautical Archeology
http://nautarch.tamu.edu/INA/vm.htm

Take wonderful virtual tours of the Institute of Nautical Archeology's many expeditions and projects over the past three decades, illustrated with more than 1000 splendid images! Follow INA research in the Mediterranean Sea, the Red Seas, North America, the Caribbean, and elsewhere. Projects include: a Bozburun Byzantine Shipwreck, a Tektas Shipwreck, a Cape Gelidonya Bronze Age Shipwreck, a Uluburun Bronze Age Shipwreck, a Serce Limani 11th Century AD Byzantine Shipwreck, a Yassiada 4th Century AD Roman Shipwreck, and a Yassiada 7th Century AD Byzantine Shipwreck. North American projects include The Denbigh Project: Archaeology of a Confederate Blockade Runner, and various projects in Lake Champlain, including the excavation of canal boats, War of 1812 shipwrecks, and the 19th century Lake Champlain Horse Ferry. In the Caribbean, the INA takes you along as they engage in archeological investigations at Port Royal, Jamaica. As a bonus, you also get inside information on various INA coastal surveys, including the Crimean Coastal Survey (1997), the 1998 Brownsville Reconnaissance survey around the mouth of the Rio Grande, the Georgia Black Sea Coast Survey (1999), the 1998 Palacios Survey in Matagorda Bay (Texas), and the Turkish Coastal Survey (1998). Additional links provide virtual tours of the INA's Conservation Research Laboratory (CRL) and Archaeological Preservation Research Laboratory (APRL).

Archeology E-mail Discussion Groups

ADS-ALL

Digital archiving of archaeological data—send message "join ads-all your name" to mailbase@mailbase.ac.uk; archives at http://www.mailbase.ac.uk/lists-a-e/ads-all/archive.html

AEGEANET

Pre-Classical Aegean World—send message "subscribe aegeanet" to majordomo@acpub.duke.edu

AIA-L {moderated}

Archaeology and Technology—send message "subscribe aia-l" to majordomo@brynmawr.edu

ANE

Ancient Near East—send message "subscribe ane" to majordomo@oi.uchicago.edu

ARCHAEOBOTANY

Archaeobotany—send message "subscribe archaeobotany your name" to listproc@eng-h.gov.uk

ARCH-ARCTIC

Arctic archaeology—send message "subscribe arch-arctic" to maiser@natmus.min.dk

ARCH-DE

German archaeology/Mailingliste zur deutschsprachigen Archae-ologie (primarily in German/Ueberwiegend deutsch)— send message "subscribe arch-de" to majordomo@charon.ufg.uni-freiburg.de

ARCH-L

Archaeology—send message "subscribe arch-l your name" to list-serv@tamvm1.tamu.edu

ARCH-METALS

Archaeology/history of metallurgy—send message "join arch-metals your name" to mailbase@mailbase.ac.uk

ARCH-STUDENT

Students of Archaeology—send message "subscribe arch-student your name" to listproc@listserv.ttu.edu

ARCH-THEORY

Archaeological theory in Europe—send message "join arch-theory your name" to mailbase@mailbase.ac.uk

ARCHCOMP-L

Archaeological computing—send message "sub ARCHCOMP-L your name" to listserv@listserv.acsu.buffalo.edu

ARHEOLOGIE-L

Romanian archaeology—send message "subscribe ARHEOLOGIE-L yyour name" to listproc@pcnet.pcnet.ro

ARQUEOANDINA {moderated}

For professionals interested in Andean archaeology—send message "subscribe arqueoandina" to listasrcp@rcp.net.pe

AUSARCH-L

Australian archaeology—Contact Peter Hiscock at Peter.Hiscock@anu.edu.au

AZTLAN

Precolumbian Mesoamerican studies—send message "subscribe aztlan your name" to listserv@ulkyvm.louisville.edu

Britarch

Discussion in British archaeology—send message "join britarch first-name last-name" to mailbase@mailbase.ac.uk

C14-L
Carbon fourteen dating issues—send message "subscribe c14-l your name" to listserv@listserv.arizona.edu

EAAN
East Asian Archaeology Network (early East Asian Archaeology and History)—send message "subscribe eaan" (without quotes; also without signature and subject line, if possible) to lstsrv@ccat.sas.upenn.edu

GAARCH-L
Georgia archaeology—send message "subscribe gaarch-l your name" to listserv@sun.cc.westga.edu

GISARCH
GIS and Archaeology—send message to mailbase@mailbase.ac.uk with the following two lines: subscribe gisarch your name stop

GREEKARCH
Archaeology of the ancient Greek world—send message "subscribe greekarch your e-mail address" to majordomo@rome.classics.lsa.umich. edu

HISTARCH
Historical Archaeology—send message "subscribe histarch your name" to listserv@asuvm.inre.asu.edu

IND-ARCH
Industrial Archaeology—send message "join ind-arch your name" to mailbase@mailbase.ac.uk

MEROITIC
Sudanese archaeology—send message "subscribe MEROITIC your name" to listproc@lists.cudenver.edu

Mil-Arch

Discussion of issues relevant to military archaeology—send message "SUB MIL-ARCH" to listproc@ukans.edu

Italian-archaeology

Information and discussion for archaeologists (prehistoric, classical or medieval) interested in Italy—send message "join italian-archaeology firstname lastname" to mailbase@mailbase.ac.uk

LITHICS-L

Analysis of archaeological lithics, natural and artificial—send message "sub lithics-l your name" to listserv@acsu.buffalo.edu

PACARC-L

Pacific Rim archaeology—send message "subscribe pacarc-l your name" to listserv@listproc.wsu.edu

PAPY

Papyrology and history/epigraphy/archaeology of Greco-Roman Egypt—send request to papy@igl.ku.dk

ROCK-ART

Petroglyphs, pictographs, etc.—send message "subscribe rock-art your name" to listserv@asuvm.inre.asu.edu

ROMARCH

Art and archaeology of ancient Italy and the Roman provinces—send message "subscribe romarch" to majordomo@rome.classics.lsa.umich. edu; archives at http://www .sys.uea.ac.uk/Research/ResGroups/JWMP/ostia/ROMARCH.html and http://www.vol.it/mirror/ROMARCH/ROMARCH.html

SAS-net

Society for Archaeological Sciences (primarily for members)— contact Jim Burton {jhburton@macc.wisc.edu}

SOPA

> Society for Professional Archeologists—send message "subscribe sopa your-name your-e-mail-address" to majodomo@mail.smu.edu

SPANBORD

> History and archaeology of the Spanish Borderlands—send message "subscribe spanboard your name" to listserv@asuvm.inre.asu.edu

Standpipe-L

> Discussion of Caribbean archaeology and ethnology—send message "subscribe standpipe-l first-name last-name" to listserv@lists.vcu.edu

SUB-ARCH

> Underwater archaeology—send message "subscribe sub-arch your name" to listserv@asuvm.inre.asu.edu

TXARCH-L

> Texas Archeological Society (TAS; restricted to current members of TAS)—refer to http://www.txarch.org/join.html

XYLHIST-L

> History and archaeology of timber-framed construction—send message "subscribe xylhist-l your name" to listserv@bloxwich.demon.co.uk

Archeology Usenet Discussion Groups

sci.archaeology—archaeology
sci.archaeology.moderated—same as above, but moderated
sci.archaeology.mesoamerican—Archaeology of Mesoamerica

3
ARTIFICIAL
INTELLIGENCE

American Association of Artificial Intelligence
http://www.aaai.org/

As its web site states, the American Association for Artificial Intelligence (AAAI) is a nonprofit scientific society devoted to advancing the scientific understanding of the mechanisms underlying thought and intelligent behavior and their embodiment in machines. AAAI also aims to increase public understanding of artificial intelligence, improve the teaching and training of AI practitioners, and provide guidance for research planners and funders concerning the importance and potential of current AI developments and future directions. Major AAAI activities include organizing and sponsoring conferences, symposia and workshops, publishing a quarterly magazine for all members, publishing a series of books, proceedings, and reports, and awarding grants and scholarships. Conferences on which you'll find information include the Annual National Conference on Artificial Intelligence and the Annual Innovative Applications of Artificial Intelligence Conference. Note that AAAI Members receive password access to controlled portions of AAAI's web, where they can find full-text versions of the latest AI Magazine, along with other members-only materials. The web site also provides information on various awards the AAAI bestows to selected members each year. These honors include election to Fellows status, the Allen Newell Award, the Innovative Applications of Artificial Intelligence Awards, the National Conference on Artificial Intelligence Best Paper Award, and the Robot Competition Awards.

Artificial Intelligence Resources from the Institute for Information Technology
http://ai.iit.nrc.ca/ai_point.html

Come here for hundreds of artificial intelligence Internet resources of various stripes and varieties. Click on the various links for archive sites for some of the AI news groups and mailing lists, searchable bibliographic databases of AI literature, descriptions of books and ordering information, and companies whose main business involves AI. Here you will also find CFPs (calls for papers) for most upcoming AI conferences, job postings for AI workers, Frequently Asked Questions about AI, information on various AI journals, and various AI research groups (organized geographically). Additional links deliver a list of AI News Groups and AI-related News Groups (with live links), pointers to lists of AI personal pages, pointers to publishers that carry some AI books or journals, national and international AI societies (a list maintained by SIGART), various AI related software products, a list of Canadian Companies involved in AI, a list of AI projects in Canada, an interactive guide to finding on-line Computer Science papers (including AI), and an excellent on-line dictionary of computing terminology. More than 246,000 visitors have made good use of this web site since it was launched in October of 1996. If you are interested in any aspect of AI, you will definitely want to add yourself to this number.

Association for Computing Machinery (ACM) Special Interest Group for Artificial Intelligence (SIGART)
http://sigart.acm.org/

SIGART is the ACM Special Interest Group on Artificial Intelligence. This web site serves as an excellent repository for AI related resources and information. Here you can read selections from intelligence Magazine, order AI related books from Amazon.com, or even submit announcements for your AI related events or resources. Among the editions of intelligence Magazine available online you'll find the legendary first issue, featuring COSPACE (a 3-D Web environment), a consideration of how to build Intelligent Dialog Systems, and an in-depth contemplation of the famous (some would say infamous) "Chinese Food Problem." Further articles look at the possibility for defining AI through co-citation analysis. And there is even a complete special issue on Ontologies. The Web page also includes links to proceedings of conferences sponsored by, or in cooperation with, SIGART, along with information on The SIGART Doctoral Consortium, which provides an opportunity for a selected group of Ph.D. students to discuss and explore their research interests in an interdisciplinary workshop together with a panel of established researchers. The web page further provides information on SIGART officers, Information on SIGART locals organization, and an on-line SIGART membership form. All together, this collection of web pages provides resources that will prove indispensable to any and all AI professionals (or would-be professionals).

Cal Tech Robotics Home Page
   http://robby.caltech.edu/

Here you have the the Web, gopher, and ftp server for the Robotics Group in the Department of Mechanical Engineering at Caltech. These pages provide complete details on the Group's ongoing research projects concerning Sensor Based Motion Planning, Robotic Locomotion, Grasp and Fixture Analysis/Planning, Applied Control Theory, Hyper-Redundant Robotics Systems, Medical Robotics, and Modular Robots. Papers available online address such topics as Sensor Based Planning and Nonsmooth Analysis, Sensor Based Planning, Part I: The Generalized Voronoi Graph, Sensor Based Planning, Part II: Incremental Construction of the Generalized Voronoi Graph, Sensor Based Planning for a Rod Robot, New Bounds on the Number of Frictionless Fingers Required to Immobilize Planar Objects, and The Stability of Heavy Objects with Multiple Contacts. Additional papers explain Stratified Motion Planning with Application to Robotic Finger Gaiting, Objective and Frame-Invariant Kinematic Metric Functions for Rigid Bodies, Kinematic Metric Functions, Feedback Algorithms for the Control of Robotic Locomotion, Nonholonomic Mechanics and Locomotion, The Mechanics of Undulatory Locomotion, The Control of Mechanical Systems with Symmetries and Nonholonomic Constraints, and Geometric Perspectives on the Mechanics and Control of Robotic Locomotion. Want more? Then take a test of articles discussing Construction and Modelling of a Carangiform Robotic Fish, Controllability with Unilateral Control Inputs, and Stabilization of Systems with Changing Dynamics.

Cambridge University Speech, Vision & Robotics Group
http://svr-www.eng.cam.ac.uk/

The Speech, Vision and Robotics (SVR) Group at Cambridge University, UK, was founded by the late Professor Frank Fallside in the early 1970's when the main interests were in speech processing and control applications. In the mid 1980's the group developed a strong interest in the theory and application of neural networks and this led to a widening of the group's research to include vision and robotics. Today the guiding principle of all research in the group is that a well-designed engineering system must be based on a sound mathematical model. In this regard, neural networks represent just one of a wide range of applicable techniques. Others include stochastic processes such as hidden Markov models, Bayesian inference, invariant transformations in 3D-geometry, Wiener and Kalman filtering,

---

UNIVERSITY OF CAMBRIDGE   **DEPARTMENT OF ENGINEERING**

Speech Vision and Robotics Group

Welcome to the home page of the Speech Vision and Robotics Group. There is an overview of the group available.

The SVR group is part of the Information Engineering Division. To see how we fit into the structure of research groups within the Department of Engineering, see the Research Groups home pages page.

Announcements

- The MPhil in Computer Speech and Language Processing; studentships available.

Research Topics

The work of this group is primarily concerned with

- Speech recognition, coding and synthesis: HMM and Neural Network techniques, the HTK toolkit, and applications of speech recognition.
- Computer vision: interpretation of visual motion, visual tracking, robot guidance, face detection and tracking, image segmentation and compression.
- Robotics: Cambridge University Robot Language (CURL), rehabilitation engineering, robot hand-eye co-ordination.
- Neural networks: statistical techniques in healthcare, models for speech analysis, and large vocabulary continuous speech recognition.
- Biomedical engineering: freehand 3D ultrasound, the Stradx system, quality assurance in maternity care, and transplant rejection risk management.

There is a list of current research projects available.

People

The SVR group is run by Professor Steve Young. It consists of academic staff, research fellows, research assistants and associates, and research students. There is also a list of recent members of the group.

Publications

The SVR group maintains an index of many of our publications, including links to abstracts and the documents themselves, and a search facility.

Research Seminars and Courses

---

classification and regression trees, and genetic algorithms. Come to this web page for complete information on the Group's research. Topics covered include: Neural networks, pattern recognition and machine learning . . . radial basis functions, and recurrent networks . . . signal processing, non-stationary time-series analysis, speech coding and compression . . . speech recognition using both neural networks and hidden Markov Models . . . image processing and object recognition (including 3-D reconstruction from 2-D images, image segmentation, and face recognition) . . . and aspects of robot assembly, including path planning, hand-eye coordination and quality inspection.

Carnegie–Mellon University (CMU) Artificial Intelligence Repository
http://www.cs.cmu.edu/Web/Groups/AI/html/repository.html

The CMU Artificial Intelligence Repository was established by Mark Kantrowitz in 1993 to collect files, programs and publications of interest to Artificial Intelligence researchers, educators, students, and practitioners. Come to this exhaustive web site for an extensive AI-related Software Collection . . . home pages dedicated to Lisp, Prolog and Scheme . . . useful AI-related FAQs . . . complete AI-related Newsgroup Archives . . . and the complete, HTML edition of the book "Common Lisp, the Language, 2nd Edition." The software links are particularly useful, and include free downloads of dozens of great shareware and freeware packages addressing Agent Architectures, Artificial Life and Complex Adaptive Systems, Simulated Annealing, Blackboard Architectures, Cellular Automata, Constraint Processing, Distributed AI, and Machine Discovery and Data-Mining. Here you'll also find software for Expert Systems and Production Systems, Fuzzy Logic, Game Playing, Genetic Algorithms and Genetic Programming, Knowledge Representation, Neural Networks and Systems , Connectionist Systems, Natural Language Processing (NLU, NLG, Parsing, Morphology, Machine Translation), Planning and Plan Recognition, Reasoning, Robotics, Speech Recognition and Synthesis, Virtual Reality, Computer Vision, and Testbeds, Simulators, and Micro-Worlds for Planning, Agents, and Robotics. There is perhaps no more extensive a collection of artificial intelligence resources and links anywhere on the Internet.

The Computation and Language E-Print Archive
http://arXiv.org/cmp-lg/

Computing research relies heavily on the rapid dissemination of results. As a result, the formal process of submitting papers to journals has been augmented by other, more rapid, dissemination methods. Originally these involved printed documents, such as technical reports and conference papers. Then researchers started taking advantage of the Internet, putting papers on ftp sites and later on various web sites. But these resources were fragmented. There was no single repository to which researchers from the whole field of computing could submit reports, no single place to search for research results, and no guarantee that information would be archived at the end of a research project. This changed in 1998 with the founding of The Computation and Language E-Print Archive, a fully automated electronic archive and distribution server for papers on computational linguistics, natural-language processing, speech processing, and related fields. No longer updated, the Archive nevertheless contains an enormous wealth of past work in all these fields, searchable by topic, subject and author. The Archive was the brain child of Stuart M. Shieber, the Gordon McKay Professor of Computer Science at Harvard. For information on more current, cutting-edge AI research, check out the E-Print Archive's legitimate heir, the online Computing Research Repository (CoRR), located at the URL http://www.acm.org/pubs/corr/

The European Association for Logic, Language and Information
http://www.folli.uva.nl/

FoLLI: The European Association for Logic, Language and Information was founded in 1991 to advance the practising of research and education on the interfaces between Logic, Linguistics, Computer Science and Cognitive Science and related disciplines in Europe. FoLLI was first conceived by Martin Stokhof, a prominent, Amsterdam-based semanticist. His idea was that the exciting but still sparsely inhabited interface between logic, linguistics and computer science needed some visible platform—and that creating this might be a European initiative, given the volume of relevant research activities going on in Europe. The resulting umbrella organization managed to gather several enterprises under its aegis, including the Amsterdam Colloquia in Formal Semantics, the London-based Interest Group in Pure and Applied Logic (IGPL), and most conspicuously, the European Summer Schools in Logic, Language and Information. Moreover, as Lenin once pointed out, a political party is a mob with a newspaper—and hence, FoLLI started an academic journal of its own, published with Kluwer. Gradually, other activities were added to this portfolio, such as a TEMPUS program for academic exchange with Central and Eastern Europe, a series of small Research Workshops, both sponsored by European community funds, a Newsletter, and recently at last, an operational Book Series. Visit the web site for far more details on FoLLI.

Freeware Expert Systems Shells
http://knight3.cit.ics.saitama-u.ac.jp/ai/expert.html

This terrific collection of free, downloadable expert system shells includes links for BABYLON: a development environment for expert systems, CLIPS: a C Language Integrated Production System, ES: a Public Domain Expert System, ESFM: a Prolog Expert System for Forestry Management, ESIE and Logic-Line: an Expert System Shell and AI Retrieval/Correlation Tool, Expert: An expert system written in ADA, FRulekit: a Frame-based RETE production system, the HUGIN Expert System (in demo versions for Solaris, Sun4, and Windows), LES: a Learning Expert System; MIKE: a Free and portable expert system teaching system, OPS5: a RETE-based expert system shell, PROTEST: a Prolog Expert System Building Tool, and G2: a real-time expert system shell. Several of these packages stand out. The HUGIN Explorer is a graphical expert system shell for construction and execution of model based expert systems in domains characterized by inherent uncertainty. MIKE (Micro Interpreter for Knowledge Engineering) is a full-featured software environment designed for teaching purposes at the UK's Open University. It includes forward and backward chaining rules with user-definable conflict resolution strategies, and a frame representation language with inheritance and 'demons' (code triggered by frame access or change), plus user-set-table inheritance strategies. Automatic 'how' explanations (proof histories) are provided for rule execution, as are user-specified 'why' explanations. Coarse-grained and fine-grained rule tracing facilities are provided, along with a novel 'rule graph' display which concisely shows the history of rule execution.

Harvard Robotics Lab
http://hrl.harvard.edu

Founded in 1983 by Professor Roger Brockett, the Harvard Robotics Laboratory is engaged in extensive, ongoing research concerning computational vision, neural networks, tactile sensing, motion control and

VLSI systems. Come to this web site for complete details on all these projects. In recent years hands-free, human-to-machine interfacing of speech signals has become increasingly popular and practical. Examples of this technology range from the speaker phone in an office or noisy car to devices designed to focus on a single conversation in a crowded room or auditorium. These phenomena are the focus of Professor Michael Brandstein's research into Robust Speech Acquisition. Then consider Dr. Brandstein's work on Hybrid Systems for Source Tracking. The goal of this project is to combine both acoustic and visual information to locate and track moving sources in a variety of environments. Applications for this work include videoconferencing units, automated television studios, and surveillance systems. At the same time, Professor Roger Brockett 's Pulse Computing Project is focuses on discovering methods for designing and analyzing analog devices that can accurately perform computational tasks. It seems that pure analog methods can not be made to be sufficiently robust and that one needs to develop methods of data representation that are better adapted to computation and communication. Recent work has concentrated on the role of pulse-like waveforms in the design of dynamical systems.

Iowa State University Artificial Intelligence Research Group
http://www.cs.iastate.edu/~honavar/aigroup.html

Founded in 1990 by Dr. Vasant Honavar, the Artificial Intelligence Research Laboratory is housed in the Department of Computer Science at Iowa State University and works on a range of basic and applied research problems in AI. In the area of AI and cognitive science, the lab gives extensive attention to Artificial Neural Networks; Autonomous Robots; Automata Induction; Computational Learning Theory; Computational Organizational Theory; Data Mining, Knowledge Discovery and Visualization; Decision Support Systems; Distributed Knowledge Networks; Intelligent Agents, Mobile Agents, and Multi-Agent Systems; Knowledge Representation and Inference; Machine Learning; Parallel and Distributed AI. In the aread of Biological Computation the lab focuses on Computational Neuroscience; and Evolutionary, Cellular, and Neural Computation). The lab also studies Bioinformatics and Computational Biology (Genetic Regulatory Networks; Protein Structure-Function Prediction; Computational Genomics; Metabolic Pathways; Distributed Knowledge Networks for Bioinformatics); Complex Adaptive Systems (Neural Computation, Cellular Computation, Evolutionary Computation); Network Information Systems (Distributed Knowledge Networks; Distributed Databases, Mediators, and Data Warehouses; Intelligent Agents, Mobile Agents,and Multi-Agent Systems); and Applied AI (Diagnosis; Bioinformatics; Complex Systems Monitoring and Control; Intrusion Detection). Visit the Lab's information-rich web pages for complete details on all the Lab's various past, present and forthcoming research.

Journal of Artificial Intelligence Research
http://www.cs.washington.edu/research/jair/home.html

The Journal of Artificial Intelligence Research covers all areas of artificial intelligence (AI), publishing refereed research articles, survey articles, and technical notes. Established in 1993 as one of the first electronic scientific journals, The Journal of Artificial Intelligence

Research is indexed by INSPEC, Science Citation Index, and Math-SciNet. JAIR reviews papers within approximately two months of submission and publishes accepted articles on the Internet immediately upon receiving the final versions. JAIR articles are published for free distribution on the Internet by the AI Access Foundation, and for purchase in bound volumes by Morgan Kaufmann Publishers. Search articles by topic, title or author. Download articles as brief abstracts, or in their complete form as zipped or unzipped PostScript files, or convenient PDF files. Recent articles addres such topics as "Reasoning on Interval and Point-based Disjunctive Metric Constraints in Temporal Contexts," "Exact Phase Transitions in Random Constraint Satisfaction Problems," and "Robust Agent Teams via Socially-Attentive Monitoring." Additional recent articles address "The Complexity of Reasoning with Cardinality Restrictions and Nominals in Expressive Description Logics," "Randomized Algorithms for the Loop Cutset Problem," and "Semantic Similarity in a Taxonomy: An Information-Based Measure and its Application to Problems of Ambiguity in Natural Language."

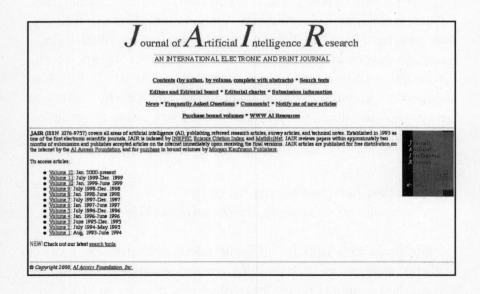

Knowledge Representation Meta-Site
http://www.cs.man.ac.uk/~franconi/kr.html

"Knowledge Representation" bills itself as a web site offering "A list of Knowledge Representation, Automated Reasoning, Computational Logics, and Advanced Database projects, people, conferences and specific resources." To this end, it gathers a large collection of links related to Artificial Intelligence bibliographies, conferences, FAQs, journals, associations, projects, courses, organizations, and publishers. Not stopping there, this web site also offer links related to ontology (projects, people, and conferences), mechanized deduction, formal methods, and more. The web site is maintained by Enrico Franconi, Senior Lecturer in the Department of Computer Science, University of Manchester, UK. Professor Franconi's research interests are in Description Logics, Knowledge Representation, Knowledge Representation and Databases, Ontology, Temporal Logics, Computational Logics, Artificial Intelligence, and Natural Language Semantics. Professor Franconi is also the principal investigator in the European ESPRIT Long Term Research project and a leading co-investigator with the British Engineering and Physical Sciences Research Council (EPSRC) project on flexible source integration in distributed knowledge-based query processing for bioinformatic information sources (TAMBIS-II). With all these different demands on his time, it is a wonder Professor Fanconi manages to keep the "Knowledge Representation" web site as tidy, as timely and as interesting as it is. Come here for all your information needs related to Knowledge Representation and its applications.

KQML: Knowledge Query and Manipulation Language
http://www.csee.umbc.edu/kqml/

KQML (Knowledge Query and Manipulation Language) is a language and protocol for exchanging information and knowledge. It is part of a larger effort, the ARPA Knowledge Sharing Effort which is aimed at developing techniques and methodology for building large-scale knowledge bases which are sharable and reusable. KQML is both

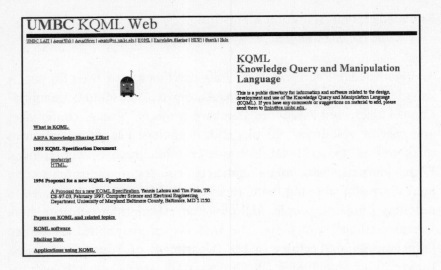

a message format and a message-handling protocol to support run-time knowledge sharing among agents. KQML can be used as a language for an application program to interact with an intelligent system or for two or more intelligent systems to share knowledge in support of cooperative problem solving. KQML focuses on an extensible set of performatives, which defines the permissible operations that agents may attempt on each other's knowledge and goal stores. The performatives comprise a substrate on which to develop higher-level models of inter-agent interaction such as contract nets and negotiation. In addition, KQML provides a basic architecture for knowledge sharing through a special class of agent called communication facilitators which coordinate the interactions of other agents. Come to this outstanding Web site to download the complete KQML compiler along with full source code, documentation, and extended instructions for deployment of the language in a range of environments.

University of London: Queen Mary and Westfield College
Distributed Artificial Intelligence Research Unit
http://www.elec.qmw.ac.uk/dai/

The DAI (College Distributed Artificial Intelligence Research) Unit, headed by Professor Nick Jennings, is part of the Intelligent Systems Group in the Department of Electronic Engineering at Queen Mary and Westfield College (part of the University of London). The Unit has developed and applied agent and multi-agent techniques to real world problems in a wide range of commercial and industrial domains. Applications which have been addressed include: telecommunications network management, business process management, electricity management, patient care, concurrent engineering, 3-D scientific data interpretation, digital libraries, electronic commerce, and process control. The Unit has also worked on formalising a number of key types of behaviour which can be observed in multi-agent systems. This work has used a variety of formal techniques to investigate social rationality, cooperative problem solving, negotiation, argumentation, social laws and coordination in multi-agent systems. The Web pages for the DAI Unit include a complete hypertext edition of the *The Journal of Autonomous Agents and Multi-Agent Systems*. Also, from the web page for the DAI Unit you can click once and go directly to AgentLink, Europe's ESPRIT-funded Network of Excellence for agent-based computing. AgentLink is a coordinating organisation for research and development activities in the area of agent-based computer systems funded by the European Commission.

The Maine Cooperative Distributed Problem-Solving Research Group
http://bronte.umcs.maine.edu/

The Maine Cooperative Distributed Problem Solving Research Group is part of the Maine Software Agents and AI Laboratory, which is part of the Department of Computer Science of the University of Maine. The Group's research focuses on developing ways of getting groups of autonomous and semi-autonmous systems to cooperatively accomplish tasks. They have ongoing research projects in self-organization/reorganization and task assignment (both part of the CoDA Project, which used to be called the MAUV Project), intelligent control of autonomous systems (the Orca project), deciding what to say during collaborative problem solving (part of the CoCo project), and developing a low-bandwidth conceptual language for CDPS systems (the COLA project). They collaborate with several other laboratories, including researchers at the Autonomous Undersea Systems Institute (AUSI), the Naval Postgraduate School (NPS), and the UM Spatial Engineering Department. Their primary domain is cooperative problem solving by groups of autonomous underwater vehicles (AUVs). Aside from an interesting and challenging domain in which to develop and test CDPS methods, AUVs in general and cooperative systems of AUVs in particular have immense potential for science and industry as well. The CDPS group involves both undergraduate and graduate students in AI research. There are usually five to ten students in the group, with equal numbers of men and women.

Multi-Agent Systems Laboratory
http://mas.cs.umass.edu/

The Multi-Agent Systems Laboratory, under the direction of Professor Victor Lesser, is concerned with the development and analysis of sophisticated AI problem-solving and control architectures for both single-agent and multiple-agent systems. The laboratory has pioneered work in the development of the blackboard architecture, approximate processing for use in control and real-time AI, and a wide variety of techniques for coordination of multiple agents. The MAS Laboratory is part of the Department of Computer Science at the University of Massachusetts at Amherst. Research into Multi-Agent Coordination includes studies of Generic Coordination Strategies for Agents (GPGP) . . . Task Analysis, Environment Modeling, and Simulation . . . Distributed Detection and Diagnosis Algorithms . . . Multi-Agent Simulation . . . Java Agent Frameworks . . . and Finite State Machine Coordination Frameworks. Research into Multi-Agent Negotiation includes focuses on Automated Contracting , Coalition Formation, Electronic Commerce, Cooperation Among Heterogeneous Agents, Negotiation among Knowledge-Based Scheduling Agents, and Negotiation among Computationally Bounded Self-interested Agents. And research into the Scheduling of Computational Tasks includes studies of Design-to-Criteria Scheduling, Design-to-time Real-time Scheduling, Integrating Decision Making with Real-time Scheduling, Control Issues in Parallel Knowledge-Based Systems, and Contingency Analysis in Design-to-Criteria Scheduling. visit the Lab's

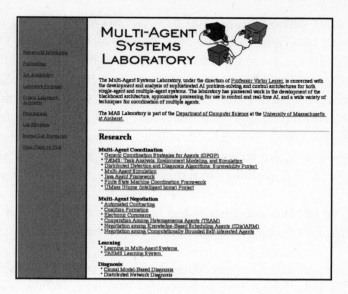

web page for complete information on all these projects, notes on faculty and staff, and updates regarding ongoing research.

University of Massachusetts Laboratory for Perceptual Robotics
http://www-robotics.cs.umass.edu/lpr.html

The Laboratory for Perceptual Robotics (LPR) is in the Computer Science Department at UMass. The Laboratory for Perceptual Robotics research areas include dexterous manipulation (reaching and grasping), mobile robot navigation, geometric reasoning, assembly planning, and the application of learning theory to robotics. Here you will also find a link to the UMass Interactive Intelligence Laboratory. The Interactive Intelligence Laboratory focuses on the origins of conceptual knowledge and on biologically-based dynamic motor control. The staff of the laboratory address central issues in cognitive science and artificial intelligence: the origins of conceptual systems, the role of native structure, computational and complexity issues, knowledge representation, and experimental methods. The goal of the research is to advance computational accounts for sensorimotor and cognitive development. Visit the web site for updates on research, a video gallery of projects, introductions to personnel, and a virtual tour of the various labs. While you are here, be sure to check out the UMass Torso. The UMass Torso consists of two two Whole Arm Manipulators (WAMs) from Barrett Technologies, two Barrett Hands, and a Bi-sight stereo head. The WAMs are 7 DOF manipulators, whose kinematics are roughly anthropomorphic. The individual joints are actuated through tendons and have a low gear ratio. These properties allow a natural compliance in interacting with the world, and allow for the simulation of additional dynamic properties (e.g. of muscle properties).

University of Michigan Distributed Intelligent Agents Group
http://ai.eecs.umich.edu/diag/homepage.html

This page describes the current research being conducted by DIAG, the Distributed Intelligent Agents Group, at the University of Michigan, Department of Electrical Engineering and Computer Science, Artificial Intelligence Laboratory. Specific project descriptions are available for: Multiagent Planning and Coordination as Distributed Search, Multiagent Planning and Coordination for Unmanned Ground Vehicles, Coordination through Plan Recognition, Organizational Self Design, Intelligent Agent Infrastructures for Supporting Collaboration, Recursive Agent Modeling, Procedural Reasoning, Distributed Constraint Satisfaction, and Strategic and Adaptive Reasoning in an Information Economy. There is a particular focus on Distributed Constraint Satisfaction. Many distributed problem solving (DPS) scenarios involve the construction, in a distributed fashion, of partial solutions that "fit together." That is, the distributed partial solutions are in some ways mutually constraining. Thus, a subset of DPS involves constraint satisfaction, and often a decentralized strategy for solving such constraint satisfaction problems (CSPs) makes sense. The lab's work in this area builds on the rich core of work in CSPs to study how CSPs can be efficiently solved in a distributed manner, covering such issues as how agents determine local variable bindings in parallel, when they propagate their information, and who should make changes when conflicts arise.

MIT Artificial Intelligence Laboratory
http://www.ai.mit.edu/

The MIT Artificial Intelligence Laboratory conducts research in many aspects of intelligence. The Lab's aims are two-fold: to understand human intelligence at all levels, including reasoning, perception, language, development, learning, and social levels, and to build useful artifacts based on intelligence. Since Marvin Minsky and John McCarthy formed the Lab in 1959 it has always been a place where significant new tools and applications have been developed. The great strength of the AI Lab has always been a willingness to put together large scale systems in ways that others have either not dared or for which they have not been able to marshal the required resources. Since the very early days the Lab has also been a place where robotics and computer vision have been great strengths. In all areas the Lab has had much success in the building of software and computer hardware systems. These traditions are all alive and well, and the last few years have seen significant applications emerge based on the Lab's robotics, vision, language, and circuit design technology. They have recently pioneered new methods for image guided surgery, wired the Whitehouse, made haptic interfaces a reality, produced new generations of micro displays, and changed the way NASA explores planets. Twenty active companies have spun off from the Lab in just the last few years. Visit the Lab's web page for more details.

Neurality: The Neural Networks Meta-Site
http://sun.icenet.it/icenet/neurality/home_uk.html

Come to this web page for complete information on current, multidisciplinary research projects concerning neural applications to industry, finance, and the virtual world of cyberspace. The team behind Neurality is is composed of Alberto Fanelli, Michele Fanelli and Luca La Ferla, respectively experts in computer science, structural engineering and economics. "Through this site," they write, "we aim to contribute to the spreading of neural network potentialities, offering you theoretical and practical examples of applications." Neural samples at the site include Damnet: a neural network for designing arch dams ... Leathernet: a neural network-based damage detector for natural leather processing ... and more. You can also download software for NeuroTetris and NeuralFractal, for building neural networks that recognise and plot fractals. The three webmasters of Neurality also give you an extensive, carefully selected collection of Neural Links from around the world. Whether you are interested in developing your own neural nets or incorporating preprogrammed, stand-alone neural applications into existing industrial or financial systems, Neurality: The Neural Networks Meta-Site delivers the expertise, software, and core-knowledge you need to get the job done quickly, efficiently, and without breaking the bank. Rely on Neurality as your one-stop neural network information resource.

Oxford University Robotics Research Group
http://www.robots.ox.ac.uk/

This is the home page for the Robotics Research Group in the Department of Engineering Science, University of Oxford. Come here for overviews of the Group's ongoing research into Robot Sensor Systems , Manufacturing, Mechatronics, Medical Image Analysis, Pattern Analysis, Visual Geometry, Visual Dynamics and Active Vision. The Sensor Systems group has evolved from the mobile robots group in Oxford, and typically works on applications related to the questions: "Where am I? What am I looking at?" Different smart sensors for range and position information have been developed during last few years and a lot of the Group's work now is to do with picking out suitable features from sensor data to classify various aspects of a scene. In this regard, they are working on Ultrasound, r.f. imaging (especially in soils), inertial sensors (gyros, accelerometers), and vision data. Characteristic of the work is the use and development of low cost real time algorithms based on a good understanding of the physics of the sensor. Most work is applied and done with industrial support and interest. There are close links to agricultural engineering through collaboration with Silsoe Research Institute. The Group concentrates on developing low cost real time algorithms, based on a good understanding of the sensors presently in use.

Stanford Dextrous Manipulation Lab

http://www-cdr.stanford.edu/Touch/touchpage.html

The Dextrous Manipulation Laboratory is affiliated with the Center for Design Research (CDR) which is part of the Design Division in the Mechanical Engineering Department at Stanford University.

The areas of research in the laboratory are: modeling and control of dextrous manipulation with robotic and teleoperated hands, tactile sensing and haptic exploration with robotic fingers, and haptics and force-feedback in telemanipulation and virtual environments. Come to the Lab's web page to get complete details on lab projects related to Tactile Sensing, Haptic Exploration, Haptic Environment Identification with Friction, Dexterous Telemanipulation, Haptics in Education, Biomimetic Robotics, and Object Proximity Sensing for a Robot Arm. The Haptic Environment Identification research is a joint project with Interval Corporation. Although friction is becoming increasingly important in manipulation, the current state of the art in terms of identifying, modeling and displaying frictional properties through a haptic interface is primitive. Thus the Lab is undertaking a series of experiments and analyses aimed at identifying the main frictional properties of small devices and displaying them through a haptic interface.

The Dexterous Telemanipulation research is a joint project with Virtual Technologies. Virtual Technologies are the makers of the Cyberglove, a device for measuring the position and configuration of the human hand. Dexterous telemanipulation enables a user to interact with a hostile environment from a safe location.

University of Surrey Mechatronic Systems & Robotics Research Group

http://robots.surrey.ac.uk/

The Mechatronic Systems and Robotics Research (MSRR) Group have been active in the field of robotics and automation since 1976. The group is led by Professor Graham Parker and consists of three academic and 2 full time researchers in addition to a number of research students and visiting overseas scholars. The group is historically best known for its work in industrial robot calibration and, more recently, for its engineering approach to the development of robotic stereo vision systems. Current research themes include the use of augmented reality (AR), haptic feedback, and telepresence for operations in remote or hazardous environments; advanced specialist vehicular technologies (including sensors for mobile vehicles, sewer robots and autonomous road sweepers) and machine vision for automated inspection and non-destructive testing (NDT). Additional areas of research include Image Processing for Non-destructive Testing, Sensors for Robotic Welding, Assessing Quailty Assurance in Mammography, Development of an open-architecture PUMA 560 robot controller, active vision for Robot Guidance, and Robot calibration. Along with research activities the scientists of the Group also teach courses to undergraduate (BEng and MEng), graduate MPhil/PhD, and modular MSc in Advanced Manufacturing Management Technology (AMMT) students.

The AI and Statistics Electronic Mailing List

Messages for distribution: ai-stats@watstat.uwaterloo.ca

Messages not for distribution: dfisher@vuse.vanderbilt.edu
(moderator, Doug Fisher)

To subscribe, send a message "subscribe ai-stats", or to unsubscribe, send a message "unsubscribe ai-stats", or to get help,
send a message "help ai-stats" to
Majordomo@watstat.uwaterloo.ca

AI Newsgroups

The following News Groups are directly related to AI:

comp.ai—general AI
comp.ai.alife—artificial life
comp.ai.edu—education
comp.ai.fuzzy—fuzzy logic
comp.ai.games—AI applied to games
comp.ai.genetic—genetic algorithms
comp.ai.jair.announce—Journal of AI Research, article announcements
comp.ai.jair.papers—Journal of AI Research, articles
comp.ai.nat-lang—natural language
comp.ai.neural-nets—neural networks
comp.ai.nlang-know-rep—natural language and knowledge
 representation
comp.ai.philosophy—Philosophy of AI
comp.ai.shells—expert system shells
comp.ai.vision—machine vision

4

ARTIFICIAL LIFE

Applets for Neural Networks and Artificial Life
http://www.aist.go.jp/NIBH/%7Eb0616/Lab/Links.html

Here is the Web's best directory of downloadable Java applets related to Competitive Learning, Backpropagation Learning, Neural Nets for Constraint Satisfaction and Optimization, Artificial Life, Simulated Annealing, Cellular Automaton, Bayesian Networks, and Turing Machines. Be sure to check out the software for Bayesian Self-Organizing Maps (BSOM). A self-organizing map is a statistical model in which learning is regarded as an estimation algorithm for its parameters. Hyperparameters are also estimated, and ultimately a probability densty function for data is estimated. Other interesting software applets include Biomorph, The Game of Life, Boids, Virtual Darwin World: Evolving Bugs, the Edge of Chaos Cellular Automata Generator, and a robust Binary Hopfield Neural Network Applet. A Hopfield network is an associative memory that works by calculating how much a node is in agreement with the nodes that it is connected to. The preferred states of agreement (that is, whether a node value should be like or unlike a certain neighbor) are determined by the patterns that are initially imposed upon the nodes. These states of agreement are inherently distributed over the nodes, so no single connection can be thought of as "storing" a pattern. This leads to to the rather nice properties of graceful degradation and categorization in an overloaded space.

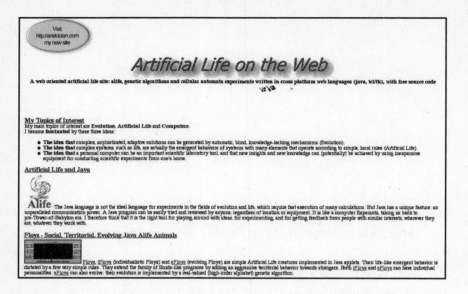

Artificial Life Games Homepage
http://www.alifegames.com/

Download and play free ALife games! This firm's first freely downloadable game is not a full fledged virtual world but a set of small arenas where you can meet artificial life entities who will search you out and attack you. The setting for this is a 3D-world rendered with Microsoft's Direct3D technology. The people at ALife Games have not tried to compete with the current crop of first-person shooters by creating a world that looks very much like the real world, but have focused on creating a game world where everything you see is significant and might have an influence on what you do next. Fighting in one arena typically lasts 10 to 20 minutes, and during this time your attention is fully engaged. Having played other shooter games does not prepare you for the monsters you'll find here, who don't look like much (being made up of 9 polygons each) but whose behavior is more lifelike than anything seen in other games. If you want to get good at fighting them, you will have to observe their behavior until you understand what makes them tick, and you can manipulate them. This is a unique challenge, and you can look forward to some engaging gaming. Have fun!

Artificial Life on the Web
http://arieldolan.com/

This web site contains the Floys Alife applets, the GA Playground genetic algorithm toolkit, and the online Alife Database of Alife-related sites on the net. The Alife experiments are written in Java or Tcl/Tk and the source code is free to download. Other sections include the Dolls 3D assemblage pictures, the Java Annotated Picture Browser, and various experiments in web design and XML. What, you ask, are Floys? Floys belong to the flocking Alife creatures variety, sharing with them the social tendency to stick together, and the life-like emergent behavior which is based on a few simple, local rules. They differ from most other Alife flocking (Boids-type) implementations by being territorial animals that defend their territory against intruders. They are implemented as Java applets. The more advanced applets allow changing traits and personality of individual Floys (iFloys & eFloys), and also breeding and evolving the population (eFloys). This web site also invites you to download GA Playground, a general purpose genetic algorithm toolkit where the user can define and run his or her own optimization problems. The toolkit is implemented in the Java language, and requires (when used as an application, in its full mode), a Java compiler and a very basic programming knowledge (just enough for coding a fitness function).

Artificial Life Online
http://alife.org/

Examing all aspects of Artificial Life development and research, this site includes great collections related to ALife news, events, and even a fascinating, ongoing ALife forum. Online resources include the papers "How to study to prepare for ALife" and "How to give an introductory ALife talk." Various Web links deliver mediations on current ALife Issues, an ALife Lexicon, a listing of essential ALife Books and Journals, guides to ALife Software, a virtual "room" for ALife Chat, an exhaustive ALife Link Database, and much more. The Web site's software library includes dozens of downloadable programs related to

Cellullar Automata, Evolutionary Dynamics, Genetic Algorithms, Multi-Agent Simulation Systems, Neural Networks, and Simulations. Of particular interest in the Genetic Algorithm category is GALib: a great set of C++ genetic algorithm objects. The library includes tools for using genetic algorithms to do optimization in any C++ program using any representation and genetic operators. The documentation includes an extensive overview of how to implement a genetic algorithm as well as examples illustrating customizations to the GAlib classes. This software is perfect for all implementations of genetic algorithms. It is also fast and reliable and behind the scenes there is a very good structured object oriented system.

Biota: The Digital Biology Project
http://www.biota.org/

The mission of Biota.org is to promote and assist in the engineering of complete, biologically-inspired, syntheticecosystems and organisms. This involves the creation and deployment of digital tools and environments for simulation, research, and learning about living systems both natural and artificial. These tools could range from simple genetic algorithms all the way up to full multi-user virtual environments. Biota.org will seek to nourish a community of interest and to bring the experience of interacting with digital biota to a large audience through the medium of the Internet. Cyberbiology is Artificial Life made visible through Cyberspace. The dissemination of interdisciplinary concepts is an important aspect of promoting the field of cyberbiology. To this end Biota.org welcomes members from all scientific disciplines including evolutionary science, microbiology, medicine, computer science, robotics, nanotechnology, paleontology, social science, and artificial intelligence. Biota also encourages artists, technologists, philosophers, and educators to join in and add their input to the developing body of experimental work. Biota.org holds conferences and workshops on its key themes to specifically encourage a multidisciplinary approach. These events aim to foster lively debate on methods for the creation of digital biota, as well as looking at the philosophical implications of such work, scenarios for the

incorporation of digital biota in virtual worlds, and the examination of the consequences of creating artificial lifeforms.

Boids: Flocks, Herds, Schools—A Distributed Behavioral Model
http://www.red3d.com/cwr/boids

In 1986, Craig Reynolds made a computer model of coordinated animal motion such as bird flocks and fish schools. It was based on three dimensional computational geometry of the sort normally used in computer animation or computer aided design. He called the software Boids. Each boid has direct access to the whole scene's geometric description, but reacts only to flockmates within a certain small radius of itself. The basic flocking model consists of three simple steering behaviors: Separation (steer to avoid crowding local flockmates), Alignment (steer towards the average heading of local flockmates), and Cohesion (steer to move toward the average position of local flockmates). In addition, the more elaborate behavioral model included predictive obstacle avoidance and goal seeking. Obstacle avoidance allowed the boids to fly through simulated environments while dodging static objects. For applications in computer animation, a low priority goal seeking behavior caused the flock to follow a scripted path. Boids is an example of an individual-based model, a class of simulation used to capture the global behavior of a large number of interacting autonomous agents. Individual-based models are being used in biology, ecology, economics and other fields of study. Come here for a free downlaod of the software, complete documentation, and various papers Reynolds has presented through the years.

COGS Evolutionary and Adaptive Systems CSRPs from the University of Sussex
http://www.cogs.susx.ac.uk/lab/adapt/easy_csrps.html

The School of Cognitive and Computing Sciences (COGS) at the University of Sussex produces, annually, an immense body of research in its areas of expertise. Here you have an immense collection of these research papers, all of them available as abstracts, and some available in their full text versions via anonymous ftp. All of these Cognitive Science Research Papers (CSRPs) comrprise technical reports relevant to evolutionary and adaptive systems research. CSRPs are produced within the COGS school. Topics include: A cybernetic perspective on the role of noise in the iterated prisoner's dilemma; Truth-from-trash learning and the mobot footballer; Attractor basins of discrete networks; Computation, dynamics and sensory-motor development; and Evolutionary robotics and the radical envelope of noise hypothesis. Additional topics include: The application of a distributed genetic algorithm to a generic scheduling system; Unsupervised constructive learning; A new crossover operator for rapid function optimisation using a genetic algorithm; and Cellular encoding for interactive evolutionary robotics. Enthusiasts will also want to check out articles addressing: A computational model of speciation in non-uniform environments without physical barriers; An empirical exploration of computations with a cellular-automata-based artificial life world; and Evolving electronic robot controllers that exploit hardware resources.

Complex Adaptive Systems and Artificial Life
http://lslwww.epfl.ch/~moshes/alife_links.html

What are Complex Adaptive Systems? Within science, complexity is a watchword for a new way of thinking about the collective behavior of many basic but interacting units, be they atoms, molecules, neurons, or bits within a computer. To be more precise, the definition is that complexity is the study of the behavior of macroscopic collections of such units that are endowed with the potential to evolve in time. Their interactions lead to coherent collective phenomena, so-called emergent properties that can be described only at higher levels than those of the individual units. In this sense, the whole is more than the sum of its components, i.e., the Complex Adaptive System. This web site includes links to key journals addressing issues related to Complex Adaptive Systems, including Adaptive Behavior, Advances in Complex Systems, Artificial Life, Artificial Life and Robotics, BioSystems, Complexity, Complexity International (e-journal), Complex Systems, Evolutionary Computation, Evolutionary Optimization, Evolution of Communication, Genetic Programming and Evolvable Machines, and more. Additional journals and magazines include InterJournal (e-journal), International Journal of Modern Physics, IEEE Transactions On Evolutionary Compu-

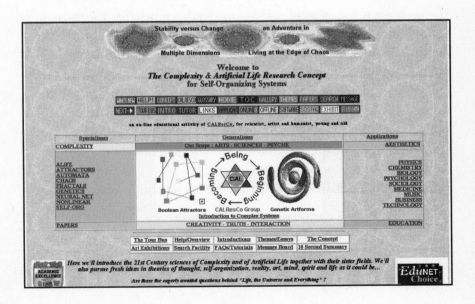

tation, Journal of Memetics—Evolutionary Models of Information, Transmission (e-journal), Journal of Physics, The Journal of Transfigural Mathematics, The Journal of NanoTechnology, NanoTechnology Magazine, Nature, New Scientist, Physica, Science and Scientific American.

The Complexity & Artificial Life Research Concept
http://www.calresco.org/

CALResCo is a non-profit organization dedicated to promoting the wider aspects of the Complex System sciences by education, synthesis and by the integration of the theories into the mainstream viewpoints of arts, philosophy and science. The Complexity Theory idea covers many separate scientific research fields, nominally designated by such titles as ALife, Cellular Automata, Fractals, Genetic Algorithms, Neural Networks and Nonlinear Systems. The ideas used in these fields are complementary to each other and are all ways of approaching the study of those difficult areas involving many connected variables—complex systems. This site will relate and contrast all these approaches, and highlight their applications to both new areas of research and to long standing problems within conventional science and the humanities. CALResCo provides a non-technical introduction for those who have not met any of these ideas before. The web page also provides more in-depth knowledge for those new to these fields and also offer a wider perspective for any visiting specialists. CALResCo's objectives are to create the best initial entry point to Complexity Theory on the web, to provide comprehensive introductions to all aspects of the subject, related to conventional ideas, to give easy access to diverse online tutorials on all of the complex system sciences, and to supply direct access to the best specialist resources available on the subject.

Downloadable Artificial Life Software for the PC & Unix Workstations
http://alife.santafe.edu/alife/software/

Check out great PC and Unix workstation software for ALife implementations. For Unix, you have JVN, the classic implementation of the John von Neumann Universal Constructor . . . Primoridal Soup: an artificial life system that spontaneously generates self-reproducing organisms from a sterile soup . . . Discrete Dynamics Lab (DDLab), a program for the study of discrete dynamical networks from Cellular Automata to Random Boolean Networks, including their attractor basins . . . Echo, an ecological simulation system . . . Polyworld, an artificial-world for evolutionary studies . . . Tierra, a system for studying ecological and evolutionary dynamics . . . and a great C++ Multi-agent simulator. For PCs you have the Biotopia Physical Evolutionary Darwinistic Artificial Life Eco System . . . collections of various Behavioral Evolution Simulations and Tutorials . . . and Rudy Rucker's fantastic suite of Alife and cellular automata programs for Windows machines (including CELLAB, BOPPERS, and CAPOW). Here you will also find Discrete Dynamics Lab (DDLab), a program for the study of discrete dynamical networks from Cellular Automata to Random Boolean Networks, including their attractor basins . . . a stunning Alife screen saver for Windows 95 and Windows NT . . . Cybercillin, which runs under DOS and simulates the growth of a colony of bacteria and the effects of an 'antibiotic . . . and the famous Iterated Prisoners Dilemma software by Philippe Mathieu.

Macintosh Artificial Life Software
http://www.ccnet.com/~bhill/elsewhere.html

Download, among other things, Simon Fraser's "MacTierra," an implementation on the Macintosh of Tom Ray's "Tierra." MacTierra creates an ecosystem of interacting and competing machine code programs living in an environment which emulates a massively parallel computer. The archive includes the very latest documentation in HTML format. You may also download Genebank, a small application that simply dumps MacTierra's Genebank file to a text file, giving you data on the genotypes that have arisen during a run. Additional offerings include LetterLearner, Robert Orenstein's letter-recognizing neural network. Once taught a few examples of different letters, it can recognize subsequent versions of those letters even though they are hand-drawn by the user. This HyperCard stack requires HyperCard or HyperCard Player in order to run. Also of interest: Tresvita, Alexander

Kasprzyk's three-dimensional LIFE program for Macintosh which allows the user to set rules under which cells live, die, and are reborn, create custom cell patterns, and much more. Enthusiasts will also want to have a try with Reggie McLeod's "Easy_Life-2.0," a Macintosh version of the most widely-known two-dimensional cellular automata, "LIFE." This program shows several forms of cyclical, recurring, and coherent moving forms that are possible under the simple set of LIFE rules.

Manna Mouse interactive artificial life simulation
http://www.caplet.com/MannaMouse.html

With Manna Mouse, you see the evolution of two separate populations of creatures. A creature's genotype encodes two values—an x coordinate and a y coordinate. The phenotype is expressed as a dot on the display area. For each population, the first generation is determined randomly. Without a fitness function to selectively steer reproduction, subsequent generations of creatures appear to be moving randomly through the 2-d space. The population size can be changed. When increased, the new creatures are placed in randomly-determined locations. The mutation rate defines the percentage of the evolving population that has a random bit flipped. These random mutations can increase the genetic diversity over what is seen with crossover alone. A Gray representation encodes the genotype in a way that results in adjacent positions differing only by one bit. Binary representations do not have this property. If a transformation happens to invoke the hardware's carry operation, adjacent positions will have very dissimilar genotypes. Come to this web site to download the Java software and documentation, along with friendly power-user tips on how to get the most out of the simulation software for PCs. Note: the Genetic Algorithms used in this software were invented by John Holland, author of the classic book *Hidden Order*.

Phil's Good Enough Complexity Dictionary
http://www.cs.buffalo.edu/%7Egoetz/dict.html

Allometry: relative growth of a part in relation to an entire organism; also: the measure and study of such growth. Allopatry : A pattern of species distribution such that the ranges of species in question do not overlap (sympatry) or adjoin (parapatry); when used in the context of evolution (e.g. "allopatric speciation") it means that a species evolved in isolation from its ancestral lineage. Alloparental: "Alloparental behavior" usually means the exhibition of behaviors that one expects from parents, but expressed by someone other than an individual's actual parents. Having the neighbors come baby-sit your kids involves alloparental behavior. Autotroph: 1: An organism which needs only carbon dioxide or carbonates as a source of carbon and a simple inorganic nitrogen compound for metabolic synthesis. 2: An organism which doesn't need a specified exogenous factor for normal metabolism. And so on . . . all the way to the Wilson-MacArthur equilibrium theory of island biogeography, zero-sum games, and Zipf's law. Although coming from various sources, all explanations of key words are stunningly complete, offering a full description of the root and meaning of the word in question. In sum, Phil's "Good Enough" dictionary is much better than that. It is excellent.

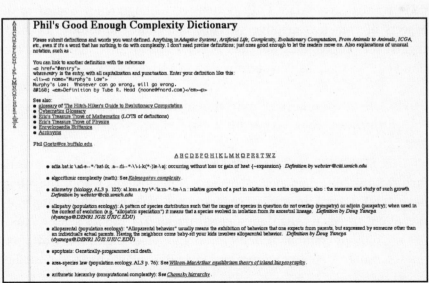

Artificial Life Links Collection
http://www.aridolan.com/ad/adb/AL.html

Here you will find a terrific list of virtually every resource available online with regard to ALife. Check out listings of scarce artificial life employment opportunities. Access an extensive directory of download invitations for some of the coolest ALife software to be had on the planet. Read Ph.D. papers on the range of ALife topics, along with detailed, comparative reviews of competing (and sometimes complimentary) ALife simulators. Discover the complex beauty of three-dimensional cellular automata, a fast pixel-level implementation of Conway's Game of Life, and scores of great web pages hosted by leading ALife research labs from around the country and around the world. Additional links provide c++ genetic algorithms for evolutionary computation, an artificial life model and simulator of controlled complexity using endogenous fitness, and a great set of pointers to even more resources related to complex adaptive systems. Check out software that postulates organisms as computer software loops that live in a shared memory space and self-reproduce. Visit The Genetic Algorithms Archive at the Navy Center for Applied Research in Artificial Intelligence. And consider an innovative cellular automation model of bi-directional traffic that might one day change the way we structure all ALife simulators. Additional links deliver exhaustive ALife FAQs, extensive bibliographies related to all aspects of complex adaptive systems, and robust directories of ALife conference proceedings. Consider making this great ALife links collection your first stop as you surf the web of complexity.

POPBUGS—A Simulation Environment for Track-driven Robots
http://www.cogs.susx.ac.uk/users/christ/popbugs/intro.html

The POPBUGS package (implemented in Poplog) lets you experiment with simple, simulated robots in a 2-dimensional world. The robots have "tank-tracks" instead of legs and are thus controlled simply by specifying speeds for the right and left tracks. The robot's sensory abilities are fully programmable but typically provide some variety of proximity sensing. All object parameters, including color, shape, pentrability and mass, can be manipulated independently. The simulation provided by theis freely downloadable software package is relatively realistic. Robots have inertia and proper tank-track dynamics. This means, for example, that locking one of the tracks causes the robot to pivot about the central point of that track rather than about the robot's centre. Sensors and motors can be arbitrarily noisy. At present, however, there is no way of introducing track-slippage; i.e., the tracks are assumed to have perfect grip. Various POPBUG videos include at the web site include one entitled "Centering." A bug with a single proximity sensor moves around a circular space. By changing direction each time there is a change in the sign of the sensed proximity changes, the bug effectively manages to keep moving towards the centre of the space.

Karl Sims Retrospective
http://www.biota.org/ksims/

Karl Sims studied computer graphics at the MIT Media Lab, and Life Sciences as an undergraduate at MIT. He currently leads GenArts, Inc. in Cambridge, Massachusetts, which creates special effects software for the motion picture industry. Of special interest here is Sims's 1994 video titled "Evolved Virtual Creatures." This video shows results from a research project involving simulated Darwinian evolutions of virtual block creatures. A population of several hundred creatures is created within a supercomputer, and each creature is tested for their ability to perform a given task, such the ability to swim in a simulated water environment. Those that are most successful survive, and their virtual genes containing coded instructions for their growth, are copied, combined, and mutated to make offspring for a new population. The new creatures are again tested, and some may be improvements on their parents. As this cycle of variation and selection continues, creatures with more and more successful behaviors can emerge. The creatures shown are results from many independent simulations in which they were selected for swimming, walking, jumping, following, and competing for control of a green cube. The web page also includes links to many other Sims creations, one more fascinating than the other.

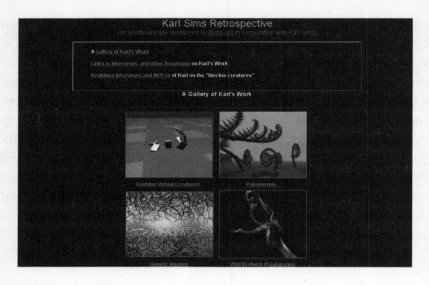

Virtual ALife Library
http://www.cs.brandeis.edu/~zippy/alife-library.html

This web page includes links to the home pages of such ALife innovators as Vince Darley, Patarick Tufts, Carl Sims, Jeffrey Ventralla, Luc Steels, Craig Reynolds, Dave Hiebeler, Brian Keeley, John Koza, and Maja Mataric. It also provides links to the full texts of many major articles by Mataric, including "Interaction and Intelligent Behavior," (MIT EECS PhD Thesis, May 1994, MIT AI Lab Tech Report AITR-1495, August 1994), "Learning to Behave Socially," "Kin Recognition, Similarity, and Group Behavior," and "Behavior-Based Systems: Key Properties and Implications." Articles from Craig Reynolds include "Evolution of Corridor Following Behavior in a Noisy World," and "Competition, Coevolution and the Game of Tag(ps)." And articles from Luc Steels include: "The Homo Cyber Sapiens, the Robot Homonidus Intelligens, and the artificial life approach to artificial intelligence," "When are robots intelligent autonomous agents?," "Intelligence—Dynamics and Representations," "A case study in behavior-oriented design," " Mathematical analysis of behavior systems," "Building Agents with Autonomous Behavior Systems," "Emergent functionality through on-line evolution," and "The artificial life roots of artificial intelligence." Also be sure to check Jeffrey Ventralla's. "Attractiveness vs. Efficiency: How Mate Preference Affects Locomotion in the Evolution of Swimming Organisms." Many of these papers are classics in their field, seminal utterances by leading researchers.

mailing list:

Artificial Life
    alife@cognet.ucla.edu
    The alife mailing list is for communications regarding artificial
    life, a formative interdisciplinary field involving computer science,
    the natural sciences, mathematics, medicine and others. Send mail
    to alife-request@cognet.ucla.edu to be added to the list.

newsgroup:

comp.ai.alife

5

ASTRONOMY

All-Sky Low Energy Gamma Ray Observatory (ALLEGRO)
http://www.astro.nwu.edu/astro/allegro/

ALLEGRO is a proposed MidEx class instrument providing all-sky monitoring of low-energy gamma-rays at unprecedented sensitivity. Unlike previous hard X-ray experiments, there is no time-averaging, data-selection, or triggering on-board: ALLEGRO transmits all events, time-tagged to 1/8th ms and with full energy information. This produces a database of uniformly high resolution in both energy and time, permitting non-triggered, unbiased detection of transient and pulsed events. ALLEGRO is the natural descendant of NASA's several High Energy Astrophysics Observatories. The first of these was launched aboard an Atlas Centaur rocket on 12 August 1977 and operated until 9 January 1979. During that time, it scanned the X-ray sky almost three times over 0.2 keV–10 MeV, provided nearly constant monitoring of X-ray sources near the ecliptic poles, as well as more detailed studies of a number of objects through pointed observations. The second of these was launched into an approximate 100-min low Earth orbit on 13 November 1978. Renamed the Einstein Observatory, it operated (with one significant interruption) until April 1981 and made over 5,000 targeted observations. Come to this web page for information on the latest of Nasa's observatory ventures, now focused on low-energy technology.

American Astronomical Society
http://www.aas.org/

Come to this web page for online editions of recent newsletters of the American Astronomical Society, as well as digital editions of *The Astronomical Journal* and *The Astrophysical Journal.* Affectionately known as Ap.J. and A.J., the journals are the most respected and important in astronomy. They have chronicled astronomy's journey from the turn-of-the-century debate over whether the Milky Way made up the entire cosmos to the present view that Earth's galaxy is one obscure smudge of stars and gas hurtling apart from billions of others in the wake of the Big Bang. Recent A.J. articles discuss THE X-RAY PROPERTIES OF $z > 4$ QUASARS, THE VELOCITY AND MASS DISTRIBUTION OF CLUSTERS OF GALAXIES FROM THE CNOC1 CLUSTER REDSHIFT SURVEY, THE 11 YEAR PERIOD IN OJ 287 REVISITED: IS IT A TRUE LONG-ENDURING PERIOD, and WEAK LENSINGINDUCED CORRELATIONS BETWEEN 1 Jy QSOs AND APM GALAXIES ON ANGULAR SCALES OF A DEGREE. Additional topics include MULTIWAVELENGTH OBSERVATIONS OF THE SECOND-LARGEST KNOWN FANAROFF-RILEY TYPE II RADIO GALAXY, NVSS 2146+82, A STRONG JET-CLOUD INTERACTION IN THE SEYFERT GALAXY IC 5063: VLBI OBSERVATIONS, and MAPPING THE EVOLU-TION OF HIGH-REDSHIFT DUSTY GALAXIES WITH SUBMILLIMETER OBSERVATIONS OF A RADIO-SELECTED SAMPLE. Download articles as abstracts, full hypertext, or in PDF or Postscript versions.

Amateur Telescope Making Home Page
http://www.atmpage.com/

The ATM Page is intended as a resource for both beginning and advanced Amateur Telescope Making. ATMs are, at once, optical engi-neers, machinists, woodworkers, electrical engineers, programmers, and a few other more obscure callings. Here you will find Reference and Design Info including links to books, vendors, opticsl design scope plans, and guides to mountings, drives, mirror-making and more (including observatory plans). Telescope plans offered online include those for a 12.5" Split Ring Newtonian (a great telescope for visual and CCD astrophotography use), The Zonto (a TeleVue Pronto clone made from a surplus Zeiss Tessar triplet), Construction notes and diagrams for a dual grating prominence telescope, Notes on the Construction of a Portable 8" Dobsonian Telescope by Ron Ravneberg, and design and construction notes for a Wright reflector. Meanwhile, the online collection of Mounting and Clock Drive plans, ideas and tips includes a Sidereal Clock (a simple clock program for Windows 95 that shows local, UTC, and sidereal time, plans for my Split Ring Mount, a Voltage Inverter (in other words, a dual axis drive corrector can run either 240V/50Hz or 120V/60Hz synchronous motors from a 12V battery), plans and instructions for an Equatorial Platform using cylindrical vice conical bearings, plans for an easy to build binocular mount (complete with measured drawings), and plans for a simple wedge to mount your ETX or Questar to a Celestron or Meade tripod.

Armagh Observatory
http://star.arm.ac.uk/

Irelands Armagh Observatory conducts ongoing research into Solar Physics, Planetary Systems, the Solar System, Solar-Terrestrial issues, Star Formation, Stellar Evolution, Stars and Massive Stars. Areas of scrutiny include Polar coronal holes: utilising data from the SOHO spacecraft to derive the properties of the corona and solar wind streams . . . The chromosphere and the transition to the corona: examining oscillations in extreme ultraviolet emission lines . . . The transition region: explosive events at a dynamic interface -contrasting the quiet sun and the active sun . . . and Solar Magnetohydrodynamics : wave phenomena and heating in the atmosphere. Also of interest to the researchers at Armagh: Light variations of massive stars (alpha Cyg variables), Cyclicities in the light variations of Luminous Blue Variables, the analysis of emission lines in the spectrum of P Cygni, and stellar evolution as it relates to Extreme helium stars (B- and A-type supergiants, rich in carbon and nitrogen but practically devoid of hydrogen), Hot subdwarfs (O and B-type stars lying just beneath the main-sequence, often helium-rich, and always less massive than the Sun), Hydrogen-deficient binaries (A-type supergiants in binary systems with orbital periods 1—12 months, comparatively young stars, with masses 1–3 times the Sun) R Coronae Borealis stars which fade unpredictably by factors of up to 1000. Visit the web site for complete details on Armagh's ongoing research.

Astronomer Magazine Online
http://www.demon.co.uk/astronomer/

The first issue of The Astronomer magazine appeared under the title of The Casual Astronomer in May 1964. The lead editorial of the charter issue summed up the editorial slant of the magazine—and the organization behind it—very well. "... Owning a telescope, by itself, makes no one an astronomer. Enthusiasm is the vital requisite; and enthusiasm is born, not made. Every month a hundred newcomers buy a telescope and equip themselves. Every month a hundred disillusioned amateurs gradually bring out their instruments less and less often as the first keenness dies down and they seek something else to occupy their leisure hours. ... The Casual Astronomer does not intend to operate in the manner usual to a society. There will be no regular meetings. It does not intend to lay down observational policies. does not intend to organise members into observing groups. The society feels that an observer does his best telescopic work when observing on his own account. It therefore exists simply to collect and publish observations from its members and print them as quickly as possible in a monthly bulletin." In addition to the online edition of the magazine, here you also have links to vital astronomical software and equipment, as well as tips, techniques and strategies from leading experts.

Astronomy Cafe
http://wwwtheastronomycafe.net

"Is there an asteroid that will hit the Earth in the near future?" "If you could survive a trip into a black hole, what would you see?" "What existed in space prior to the Big Bang?" "What is Time?" "Will travel at light speed ever be possible?" "Is there a center to the Universe?" These are just some of the hundreds of questions professional astronomer Sten Odenwald answers in The Astronomy Cafe. In fact,

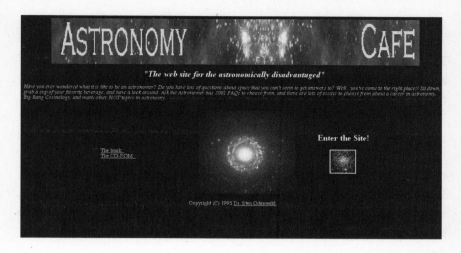

Odenwald answers no less than 365 of the most popular questions asked by real people about all things astronomical. Organized around topics such as "The Sun," "The Origin of the Universe," "The Solar System," "Telescopes and Star Gazing," "Special and General Relativity," and "Strange Sightings," The Astronomy Cafe lets you quickly findthe answers you need without having to wade through long, technical essays. And the answers are not text alone, but in fact a wonderful flow of related images and ideas about one particular topic combined with useful tables, on-line resources, and a glossary. Dip in at random or use it The Astronomy Cafe to find out everything you've ever wanted to know about astronomy and space, but were afraid to ask.

Astronomy Magazine Online
http://www.kalmbach.com/astro/astronomy.html

ASTRONOMY bills itself as the most popular English-language magazine in the universe for astronomy enthusiasts. Tune into the web page for "Astro News this Week," in which you'll find late-breaking reports from the frontiers of astronomical science. For instance, did you know Astronomers searching for planets outside the solar system have just crossed a critical threshold? They have found the first planets around sunlike stars that could be less massive than Saturn. Or do you know Scientists have recently released data from an Air Force satellite that mapped the entire plane of the Milky Way Galaxy at mid-infrared wavelengths? This survey, the highest resolution view yet at these wavelengths, yields detailed information about the structure of the galaxy and dramatically improves our knowledge of the space environment and its components. And do you realize that, using the power of adaptive optics to achieve incredibly high resolution, a team of astronomers has peered deep into the heart of an emerging star cluster? The international team, led by Wolfgang Brandner of the University of Hawaii's Institute for Astronomy, believes the results may yield new insights into the origin of field stars and the recently discovered population of free-floating brown dwarfs in the vicinity of the sun.

Astroweb: Astronomy & Astrophysics on the Internet
http://www.cv.nrao.edu/fits/www/astronomy.html

Astroweb comprises an extensive collection of pointers to astronomy-related information available on the Internet. The database is maintained by the AstroWeb Consortium, a collaboration involving no less than 9 individuals at 7 institutions. The links are extensive and include information on Telescopes (331 records), Astronomical survey projects (70 records), Telescope observing schedules (26 records), Metereological information (11 records), Data and Archive Centers (142 records), Astronomy Information Systems (38 records), Astronomy & astrophysics preprints & abstracts (57 records), Abstracts of Astronomical Publications (28 records), Full-texts of Astronomical Publications (90 records), Astronomical Bibliographical Services (29 records), Astronomy-related Libraries (47 records), Other library resources (13 records), Personal Web pages (793 records), Jobs (37 records), Conferences and Meetings (46 records), Newsgroups (at least somewhat astronomy-related) (32 records), Mailing Lists (at least somewhat astronomy-related) (16 records), Educational resources (258 records), Astronomy Departments (500 records), Astronomical Societies (169 records), Space Agencies (45 records), Astronomy software servers (132 records), and Document Preparation Tools (TeX,etc) (8 records). Also bear in mind: Radio Astronomy (113 records), Optical

Astronomy (178 records), High-Energy Astronomy (75 records), Space Astronomy (174 records), Solar Astronomy (78 records), the history of Astronomy (20 records), and more.

Comet Observation Home Page
http://encke.jpl.nasa.gov/

Here you have details on all the coolest, visible comets around, including the famous Hale-Bopp. This comet was discovered on July 23, 1995 UT (Universal Time = Greenwich, England time, which astronomers use as a common time for reporting observations) by Alan Hale, New Mexico, and Thomas Bopp, Arizona. This is the first discovery for both, although Alan Hale is one of the top visual comet observers in the world having seen about 200 comet apparitions. The orbit of this comet is of long period (~4200 years since the last appearance and because of gravitational tugs by the planets, particularly Jupiter, the next appearance will be in about 2380 years). It has been through the inner solar system before. That is, it is not a new comet from the Oort Cloud. Its orbit is a very long, stretched out ellipse and the comet is part of our solar system in orbit around our Sun. There have been reports that this comet is very large. Actually, the heart of the comet, the nucleus, is obscured by the dust and gas that forms the head of the comet. Nobody knows how large the nucleus is. We can't see it! The nuclei of comets range in size from a few miles (kilometers) or smaller to over 100 miles (~160 kilometers) in diameter.

Digital Sky Survey
http://archive.stsci.edu/dss/

The Catalogs and Surveys Branch of the Space Telescope Science Institute has been digitizing the photographic Sky Survey plates from the Palomar and UK Schmidt telescopes in order to support HST operations and provide a service to the astronomical community. These plates cover 6.5 x 6.5 degrees of the sky and have been digitized using a modified PDS microdensitometer with a pixel size of either 25 or 15 microns (1.7 or 1.0 arcsec respectively) and the resultant images are stored on optical discs. These images are 14000x14000 (0.4GB) or 23040x23040 pixels (1.1GB) in size and are difficult to access quickly. In order to provide convenient access to these data, the images have been compressed using a technique based on the H-transform to reduce the data volume. Although the technique is lossy, it is adaptive so that it preserves the signal very well. The Digitized Sky Surveys were produced at the Space Telescope Science Institute under U.S. Government grant NAG W-2166. The images of these surveys are based on photographic data obtained using the Oschin Schmidt Telescope on Palomar Mountain and the UK Schmidt Telescope. The Second Palomar Observatory Sky Survey (POSS-II) was made by the California Institute of Technology with funds from the National Science Foundation, the National Geographic Society, the Sloan Foundation, the Samuel Oschin Foundation, and the Eastman Kodak Corporation.

European Space Agency
http://www.esrin.esa.it/

Investments made through the European Space Agency by its Member States have yielded a number of scientific and technological achievements of the highest order in the fields of space science, Earth observation, telecommunications and space transportation. Examples are the exceptional series of original and exciting space science missions such as ISO (Infrared Space Observatory), the Cassini-Huygens mission to Titan and SOHO (Solar and Heliospheric Observatory). And Ariane 5 is the most modern high tech expendable launch vehicle in the world today. ESA is also a major partner in the largest cooperative endeavour in space, the International Space Station, which is already a reality. Other projects such as the XMM (X-ray Multi-Mirror) satellite or Envisat, one of the world's most sophisticated environmental satellites, are due for launch in 2000. All these investments have helped and will help to maintain the competitiveness of European industry and to improve the quality of life for the citizens of Europe. At a time of great change in the space business world-wide, one of the biggest challenges confronting Europe's space industry is the competition it faces from world markets. At present, ESA together with its Member States is defining a European space policy for the coming years that will enable Europe to pursue world class space science and technology development.

Galileo Project

http://www.jpl.nasa.gov/galileo/

The Galileo Project is a NASA unmanned mission to explore the planet Jupiter and its surrounding moons and magnetosphere. The spacecraft, which started its journey on October 18, 1989 with the launch of the Space Shuttle Atlantis, consisted of an atmospheric entry probe (Galileo Probe) designed to enter Jupiter's atmosphere, and an orbiter (Galileo Orbiter) designed to orbit the planet and observe Jupiter, its moons, and radiation belts. This homepage is devoted to background information and scientific results from the Galileo atmospheric entry probe portion of the mission. The Galileo Probe successfully descended into Jupiter's atmosphere on December 7, 1995 and directly measured the atmosphere of a Giant Planet for the first time. Results from this most difficult atmospheric entry in the solar system have permitted us to better understand many of the scientific mysteries of the largest planet in our solar system. The Galileo Probe no longer exists and is now part of Jupiter's atmosphere as expected. The Galileo Orbiter successfully entered orbitn well above the cloud tops

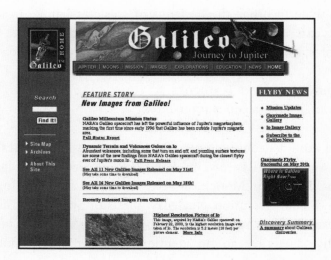

of Jupiter on December 7, 1995 and is currently observing the Jupiter system. Most recently, NASA's Galileo spacecraft has successfully flown past the largest moon in our solar system—Ganymede, which orbits around Jupiter. Visit the web page for complete details and beautiful illustrations in splendid, vivid color.

The Best of the Hubble Space Telescope
http://www.seds.org/hst/

Imagine seeing stars and planets as if they were just outside your living room window. From this window seat to the universe, you could see the birth and death of stars and galaxies as they appeared billions of years ago. The Hubble Space Telescope is your window seat to the universe. Hubble has provided us with front row seats to fragments of a comet slamming into Jupiter and stars being born in huge craggy towers of cold dark gas. Deployed April 25, 1990 from the space shuttle Discovery, Hubble is one of the largest and most complex satellites ever built. Hubble's deployment culminated more than 20 years of research by NASA and other scientists. The telescope is named for American astronomer Edwin P. Hubble, who first discovered that countless island cities of stars and galaxies dwell far beyond our Milky Way. With Hubble, astronomers are getting a clearer picture of the universe. The telescope's stunning photos are showing the world about the wonders of space. Many of the world's foremost astronomers are using Hubble to probe the horizons of space and time. Designed to last 15 years, Hubble is providing intriguing new clues to monster black holes, the birth of galaxies, and planetary systems around stars.

Astronomy Hypertext Textbooks
http://zebu.uoregon.edu/text.html

Here are great online textbooks introducing such topics as Cosmology and the Origin of Life, Solar System Geology, Properties of Galaxies, Planetary Motion, Inverse Square Law, The Interstellar Medium, Stellar Evolution, Nucleosynthesis in Stars, and The Evolution of Star Clusters. You also get introductions to key topics in physics, Alternative Energies, not to mention multimedia presentations on such topics as The Scientific Basis for the Man Nature Partnership, the Solid State Physics of CCD detectors, Cosmological Issues, and more. The web site also includes an intricate online lab discussing the digital spectra of the stars. The lab demonstrates one thing clearly: Since the light from galaxies represents the integrated contribution of its consitutient stars, we can learn about stellar populations in galaxies by modelling their light by summing up individual stellar spectra for different kinds of stars. Here, from the Ph. D. thesis of David Silva, you can experiment with and draw conclusions from the spectra of many different kinds of stars with wavelengths range from 3500 to 9000 angstroms. From main sequence stars to red and blue giants and extreme molecular bandheads, all the different types of stars are here for you to delight in and learn from.

The Infrared Space Observatory (ISO)
http://isowww.estec.esa.nl/

The European Space Agency's (ESA) Infrared Space Observatory (ISO) is an astronomical satellite that was operational between November 1995 and May 1998. It operated at wavelengths from 2.5 to 240 microns, in the infrared range of the electromagnetic spectrum. Because the atmosphere acts as an 'umbrella' for most infrared wavelengths—preventing them from reaching the ground—a space telescope is needed to detect this kind of radiation invisible to the human eye and to optical telescopes. The satellite essentially consists of: a large liquid-helium cryostat; a telescope with a 60-cm diameter primary mirror; four scientific instruments and the service module. The overall dimensions of ISO are Height: 5.3 m, Width: 3.6 m, Depth: 2.8 m, and launch mass was 2400 kg. Infrared radiation is primarily 'heat', or thermal radiation. Even objects that we think of as being very cold, such as an ice cube, emit infrared radiation. For this reason ISO, operating at wavelengths from 2.5 to 240 microns, could observe astronomical objects that remain hidden for optical telescopes, such as cool objects that are unable to emit in visible light. Opaque objects, those surrounded by clouds of dust, are another specialty of ISO because the longer IR wavelengths can penetrate the dust, allowing us to see deeper into such clouds.

Johnson Space Center Home Page
http://www.jsc.nasa.gov/

Let the staff of the Johnson Space Center answer all your questions about space and space travel. For example: Question—How do you know what time it is in space? Answer—All the clocks on the shuttle are set to Mission Elapsed Time (MET). The MET clock does not start running until the launch into space, and when it does start running, it starts right at midnight. So, 1 hour after lift off, it is 1:00 a.m. Astronauts have a 16-hour day and then a sleep period. Mission Control uses both MET for the shuttle and Central time for public event times, so that everyone knows when particular events will occur on a mission. Question: What does a launch feel like? Answer—It is a very exciting, noisy, shaking ride for the first two minutes. Then the solid rocket boosters drop off and it gets a lot smoother, but there still is a strong push on the back of the astronauts' seats from all the power in the three main engines. Those three main engines burn fuel at an incredible rate—approximately 1,000 gallons every second. The shuttle goes from zero miles per hour (mph) on the launch pad to over 17,000 mph in just over eight minutes. That means it goes 2,000 mph faster every minute.

Macho Project
http://wwwmacho.anu.edu.au/

The MACHO Project is a collaboration between scientists at the Mt. Stromlo & Siding Spring Observatories, the Center for Particle Astrophysics at the Santa Barbara, San Diego, & Berkeley campuses of the University of California, and the Lawrence Livermore National Laboratory. Their primary aim is to test the hypothesis that a significant fraction of the dark matter in the halo of the Milky Way is made up of objects like brown dwarfs or planets: these objects have come to be known as MACHOs, for MAssive Compact Halo Objects. The signature of these objects is the occasional amplification of the light from extragalactic stars by the gravitational lens effect. The amplification can be large, but events are extremely rare: it is necessary to monitor photometrically several million stars for a period of years in order to obtain a useful detection rate. For this purpose they have built a two channel system that employs eight 2048*2048 CCDs, mounted on the 50 inch telescope at Mt. Stromlo. The high data rate (several GBytes per night) is accommodated by custom electronics and on-line data reduction. The team has taken ~27,000 images with this system since June 1992. Analysis of a subset of these data has yielded databases containing light curves in two colors for 8 million stars in the LMC and 10 million in the bulge of the Milky Way.

Mars Exploration Program Web Site
http://mpfwww.jpl.nasa.gov/

As world history illustrates, humans are compelled to discover new frontiers. Our exploration of the space frontier has already begun. Robotic missions and new technology are the first steps toward expanding human presence in the solar system. Human missions to the Moon, Mars and beyond may become a reality in the 21st century, and NASA is leading the way. The world's attention is focused on the exploration of the solar system more strongly now

than ever before. The discovery of possible ancient life on Mars and the Pathfinder examinations are credited with much of that attention. The rationale for exploring and settling space mirrors the spirit that has compelled explorers through the ages. NASA's mission to explore continues as they build a foundation of technology, experience, and scientific knowledge. During the first decades of the 21st century, explorers from Earth could well set foot on Mars. For now, however, we rely on unmanned craft such as Mars Pathfinder, the Mars Global Surveyor, and other such missions. This web page delivers explicit, illustrated details on all such ongoing adventures as they progress.

Messier Gallery
http://encke.jpl.nasa.gov/TIE/M.html

This web gallery gathers images taken at different wavelengths by a variety of ground-based and space-borne observatories. The human eye is a remarkable organ, but provides a mere sliver of insight into the richness of information that all celestial phenomena routinely provide. If we wish to understand the cosmos and its spectacular objects, we must collect and study radiation throughout the entire electromagnetic spectrum. With multi-wavelength data in hand, we can gain a more complete picture of celestial objects, and learn much about how scientific research often requires the skills of a good detective!

The primary purpose of this Gallery is to introduce users to the wealth of data available at wavelengths beyond the familiar visible light we are accustomed to seeing. You will discover some important characteristics of astronomical phenomena, and learn about which types of radiation are best suited to studying certain objects. By comparing images of objects obtained at different wavelengths, you will be able to interpret interesting features, and discover why certain objects emit little or no radiation at some wavelengths. As you tour the Gallery, take time to examine the images, make comparisons, and think carefully about the information accompanying the images. You can either visit your favorite objects, or take the a guided tour through the gallery from start to finish.

Meteorite Central
http://www.jonesville.com/meteor/

Here is the universe's greatest collection of Meteorite links. Have a friend? Why don't you send him or her a quick Cosmic Postcard? Choose from several of the latest images from NASA and Hubble ... And it's all free! Thirsty? Try a sip of Monahans -or- Zag! Nasa scientists that have been conducting research on meteorites have discovered purple halite crystals that contain small amounts of water. Learn about Nomad, the meteorite-hunting robot that recently located its first meteorite during a test in the Elephant Moraine region of Antarctica. Or join the Meteorite Mailing List and hear about meteorite news when it happens! (Don't worry. List traffic is moderate—usually just 10-20 posts a day). Read about Bob Verish who, recently spotted two stones in his rock collection that looked suspicious. After sitting in a box for almost twenty years, these have now been classified by Alan Rubin of UCLA as Martian basalt (shergottite)! Get a tutorial on why U.S. and Canadian cosmo geologists have announced that the unusually pristine pieces of the Carcross carbonaceous chondrite may make it one of the most important meteorite finds in more than 30 years. Here at Meteorite Central you get all the meteor buzz from around the world on a timely basis.

Nasa Home Page
http://www.nasa.gov/

NASA is deeply committed to using the Internet to spread the unique knowledge that flows from its aeronautics and space research. This commitment grows from the Agency's unique, original congressional mandate to "provide for the widest practicable and appropriate dissemination of information concerning its activities and the results thereof." Throughout the past three-and-a-half decades, NASA has accomplished this basic assignment through printed press releases, radio programming, television shows, educational materials and, more recently, the fax machine. The futuristic capabilities of the Internet promise to expand this outreach exponentially. Tune into Nasa's web site where you can download the latest imagery from the Hubble Space Telescope, read about recent uses of NASA-developed technology by private industry, watch a short video of the first human landing on the Moon or view the latest microgravity science experiment underway aboard the international Space Station. All of this and more is waiting for you on this special offramp on our Nation's Information Superhighway. You can also access Nasa's Strategic Plan and see how NASA is preparing to take America's aerospace program into the next century. And you can access invaluable FAQs, reference collections, and photo gallerys—all right online!

National Radio Astronomy Observatory
http://www.nrao.edu/

One of the coolest projects of the National Radio Astronomy Observatory is the Orbiting Very Long Baseline Interferometry Earth Station. One of the links here takes you to the National Radio Astronomy Observatory's Orbiting VLBI tracking station in Green Bank, West Virginia—one of four NASA tracking stations dedicated to support of Very Long Baseline Interferometry satellites. Current and future satellites extend interferometry baselines beyond the diameter of the earth. The trackings stations transmit a maser referenced timing tone to the orbiting satellites. The satellites sample the astronomical signals and transmit the data on a Ku band downlink back to the stations. The tracking stations record the data on wideband magnetic tape and ship it to correlators for further processing. The Observatory and tracking station are located in a valley at elevation 2750' , and are shielded from radio interference by mountains to the east and west. Other major initiatives, on which you'll find complete information at this web site, include the NRAO Space Very Long Baseline Interferometry Project, the Atacama Large Millimeter Array (ALMA), the NRAO VLA D-Array NVSS Sky Survey, the NRAO VLA B-Array FIRST Sky Survey, and the VLA Upgrade.

Near Earth Asteroid Tracking
http://huey.jpl.nasa.gov/~spravdo/neat.html

The Earth, and all the other planets in the solar system, have been continuously pelted by asteroids and comets ever since their formation. Just look at the moon through a small telescope or a good pair of binoculars. The surface is covered by craters that were created by impacting asteroids and comets. Similar craters have been observed on the surface of the Earth. One of the most spectacular is a ~1/2-mile-wide crater near Flagstaff, Arizona. If it weren't for the effects of erosion, and the cover of the oceans, the surface of the Earth would look much like the Moon or Mars. It is now known that an asteroid impact caused at least one mass extinction of life on Earth—the one that wiped out the dinosaurs. The remnant of the resulting crater lies off the coast of the Yucatan Peninsula in Mexico, mostly buried by ocean sediments. The most dangerous asteroids, capable of a global disaster, are extremely rare. The threshold size is believed to be 1/2 to 1 km. These bodies impact the Earth only once every 1,000 centuries on average. Comets in this size range are thought to impact even less frequently, perhaps once every 5,000 centuries or so. When the big one heads this way, the folks at the Near Earth Asteroid Tracking Station will be the first to know.

The Nine Planets: A Multimedia Tour of the Solar System
http://www.dkrz.de/mirror/tnp/nineplanets.html

The Nine Planets is a collection of information about our Solar System intended for a general audience with little technical background. No special expertise or knowledge is needed; all technical and astronomical terms and proper names are defined in the glossary. The bulk of this material should be familiar to planetary scientists and astronomers but they may find a few interesting tidbits, too. This document consists of about 90 WWW "pages", one page for each major body in the Solar System. Each page has, a large picture of its object and usually several smaller thumbnail images (all linked to their full-size originals), and some scientific and historical facts about it. If the

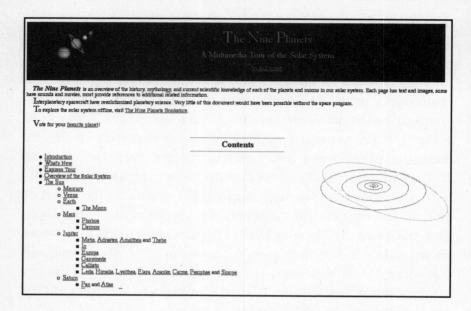

The Nine Planets

A Multimedia Tour of the Solar System

by Bill Arnett

The Nine Planets is an overview of the history, mythology, and current scientific knowledge of each of the planets and moons in our solar system. Each page has text and images, some have sounds and movies, most provide references to additional related information.

Interplanetary spacecraft have revolutionized planetary science. Very little of this document would have been possible without the space program.

To explore the solar system offline, visit The Nine Planets Bookstore.

Vote for your favorite planet!

Contents

- Introduction
- What's New
- Express Tour
- Overview of the Solar System
- The Sun
    - Mercury
    - Venus
    - Earth
        - The Moon
    - Mars
        - Phobos
        - Deimos
    - Jupiter
        - Metis, Adrastea, Amalthea and Thebe
        - Io
        - Europa
        - Ganymede
        - Callisto
        - Leda, Himalia, Lysithea, Elara, Ananke, Carme, Pasiphae and Sinope
    - Saturn
        - Pan and Atlas

object has satellites then its page has a table of data on them and links to their pages, links to more images and information about the object elsewhere on the Web, and a list of open issues for which we as yet have no answers. Many pages also include short sound clips and links to "movies" of a few objects. There are also a few miscellaneous pages on planetary science spacecraft.

Planetary Nebulae Observer's Home Page
http://www.blackskies.com/

This is a rather large, and seemingly always growing site about mainly one thing—the astronomical objects known as Planetary Nebulae, stars that have reached a stage of their solar life in which their primary fuel source (hydrogen) has been mostly depleted, and now will start converting the material that was created by the burning of hydrogen (mainly helium). As this site's webmaster writes: "I have attempted to make available on this site a mixture of wonderful images from amateurs, professional astronomers, and observatories both large and small. There are over 200 images on line, and with my CCD imaging setup, I am adding a few more as time and sky permits. They won't be great works of art like some of the images to be found here, but I do hope they will help in answering someone's question. I have combined two data bases into a single one with data on 1,143 planetaries. The data base is linked to the 600+ observing reports contributed by expert observers like Steve Gottlieb, Kent Wallace, Rich Jakiel, Yann Pothier and many others. There are many gaps of course, but thats part of the challenge—fill in that missing information."

Planetary Photojournal from Nasa
http://photojournal.jpl.nasa.gov/

This service, developed as a collaboration between NASA's Planetary Data System Imaging Node, the Solar System Visualization Project, and JPL's Media Relations Office, is designed to provide you with easy access to the publicly released images from various Solar System exploration programs. The system database is currently populated with approximately 2270 images; more are being added every day. You can search images by planet, by spacecraft/mission, by feature name, or by date. Recently added Galileo images include Ongoing Volcanic Eruption at Tvashtar Catena, Io . . . Snapshots of Chaac: Io's calderas up close . . . Stereo Image of Tvashtar Catena, Io . . . Stereo Image of Zal Patera and Neighboring Mountain, Io . . . and Colorized View of Zal Region, Io. Additional new pics include Shamshu Mons and Patera, Io . . . Lava Flows and Ridged Plains at Prometheus, Io . . . and Sulphur Dioxide on the Chaac Region of Io. Mars Global Surveyor Orbiter pics include A Typical Martian Scene: Boulders and Slopes in a Crater in Aeolis . . . and Defrosting Polar Dunes. Voyager photos include the Callisto basin, Ganymede, Io, Saturn's F ring, Saturn's shadow upon the rings, the Io Pele plume, Saturn's B rings, Titan, and much more.

The SETI Project
http://www.seti.org/

By the late-1970's, SETI programs had been established at NASA's Ames Research Center and at the Jet Propulsion Laboratory (JPL) in Pasadena, California. These groups arrived at a dual-mode strategy for a large-scale SETI project. Ames would examine 1,000 Sun-like stars in a Targeted Search, capable of detecting weak or sporadic signals. JPL would systematically sweep all directions in a Sky Survey. In 1988, after a decade of study and preliminary design, NASA Headquarters formally adopted this strategy, and funded the program. Four years later, on the 500th anniversary of Columbus' arrival in the New World, the observations began. Within a year, Congress terminated funding. With NASA no longer involved, both researchers and interested members of the public saw a diminished chance to answer, within their lifetimes, the profound question addressed by SETI. Consequently the SETI Institute is endeavoring to continue this large-scale program with private funding. Project Phoenix will concentrate efforts on that component of the NASA SETI project known as the Targeted Search. Its strategy is to carefully examine the regions around 1,000 nearby Sun-like stars. The world's largest antennas will be used, and these have already committed observing time for SETI. By pursuing the search now, Phoenix can take advantage of an historical window of opportunity. Within a decade, radio interference from terrestrial sources will grow significantly, compromising the ability to detect weak signals. Learn more at the SETI web page.

Sky & Telescope Magazine Online
http://www.skypub.com/

In the almost six decades of its existence, Sky & Telescope Magazine has seen a world of change in the way amateur astronomy is practiced in the United States and abroad. Just think of how it was in 1941: commercial telescopes and accessories were practically nonexistent. Now, you only need to thumb through Sky & Telescope to see the vast array of retail telescopes and equipment available all over the world. If you lived in a city of 100,000 people in 1941, odds are you would be the only amateur astronomer there and you'd have trouble finding anyone to share the hobby with; today, the Internet helps amateur astronomers to find fellow enthusiasts nearby and on the other side of the planet. Astronomical research has given us a model of how the universe works, while probes and telescopes in space, from Viking to Hubble, have contributed images of the cosmos that 1941 readers could only have dreamed of seeing. And Sky & Telescope has grown and changed along with the world of astronomy. Tune into Sky

& Telescopes's wonderful web site for complete details on the magazine, product reviews, late-breaking observational reporting, and all the latest astronomical news and information.

Spacezone
http://www.spacezone.com/

The neatest part of Spacezone is its great Space Hall of Fame. Here SpaceZone honors the men, women, missions and corporations who have made significant contributions towards the exploration of space and to the betterment of the human race by way of space exploration. The inaugural inductee is none other than Walt Cunningham. Cunningham is perhaps best known as America's second civilian astronaut. On October 11, 1968, he occupied the lunar module pilot seat for the eleven-day flight of Apollo 7—the first manned flight test of the third generation United States spacecraft. With Walter M. Schirra, Jr., and Donn F. Eisele, Cunningham participated in and executed maneuvers enabling the crew to perform exercises in transposition and docking and lunar orbit rendezvous with the S-IVB stage of their Saturn IB launch vehicle; completed eight successful test and maneuvering ignitions of the service module propulsion engine; measured the accuracy of performance of all spacecraft systems; and provided the first effective television transmission of onboard crew activities. The 263-hour, four-and-a-half million mile shakedown flight was successfully concluded on October 22, 1968, with splashdown occurring in the Atlantic—some eight miles from the carrier ESSEX (only 3/10 of a mile from the originally predicted aiming point).

Star Gazer Television Program Home Page
http://www.starhustler.com/

'STAR GAZER' is seen nationally on most PBS stations. Funding for Star Gazer provided by Orion Telescopes & Binoculars and the William J. and Tina Rosenberg Foundation, and the program is produced in cooperation with the staff of the Planetarium at the Miami Museum of Science. Scripts for all Star Gazer programs are to be found online, and include such episodes as "How To Use The Moon To

Find The Lion, The Virgin and The Scorpion," "How To Measure Distances In The Sky Using Just Your Fingers and The Big Dipper!", "Regulus and Denebola, The Heart and Tail of The King of The Beasts", and "The Closest Meeting of the Two Largest Planets In 20 Years!!" Additional episodes include "Day Star Day : A Celebration of The Summer Solstice and The Star We Call Our Sun", "The Great Mars/Jupiter/Saturn Sky Show Reaches Its Climax!", "Using The Big Dipper To Find Two Wonderful Stars", "How To Time Travel Through The Big Dipper", and "The Big Planetary Lineup Brou-Ha-Ha! You Won't Even Get Your Feet Wet!" As you can tell from some of the titles, the shows are not only educational, but also entertaining and just downright fun.

Stardust Project
   http://stardust.jpl.nasa.gov/

STARDUST is a comet sample return mission which will also be returning interstellar dust grains. These samples will be returned to Earth for analysis. A mass spectrometer derived from instruments flown on Giotto and Vega Halley missions will also be included on the payload to provide both complementary and corroborative data to the sample return results. For the comet Wild 2 encounter, the objective is to recover more than one thousand particles larger than 15 microns in diameter as well as volatile molecules on the same capture medium. The sample return objective for fresh interstellar grains is to collect over 100 particles in the 0.1 micron to 1 micron size range. They will be collected in a manner designed to preserve, at minimum, the elemental and isotopic composition for major elements in individual submicron particles. The first orbital loop is a 2-year VEGA path with a 171 m/s delta-V trajectory correction maneuver (TCM) near aphelion. This delta-V will set up the Earth swingby that will pump the orbit up to the 2.5-year loop, which the spacecraft will fly twice. At 160 days before encounter, a small delta-V of 66 m/s will set up the Wild 2 flyby. This will occur on 1 Jan 2004, at 1.86 AU and 97.5 days past Wild 2 perihelion passage.

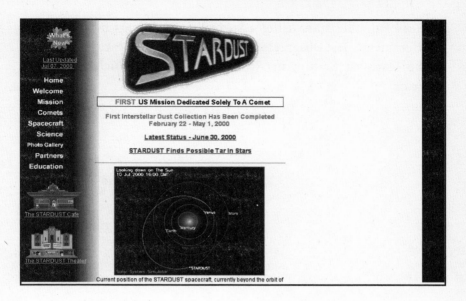

Current position of the STARDUST spacecraft, currently beyond the orbit of

United States Naval Observatory
http://www.usno.navy.mil/

The U.S. Naval Observatory performs an essential scientific role for the United States, the Navy, and the Department of Defense. Its mission includes determining the positions and motions of the Earth, Sun, Moon, planets, stars and other celestial objects, providing astronomical data; determining precise time; measuring the Earth's rotation; and maintaining the Master Clock for the United States. Observatory astronomers formulate the theories and conduct the relevant research necessary to improve these mission goals. This astronomical and timing data, essential for accurate navigation and the support of communications on Earth and in Space, is vital to the Navy and Department of Defense. It is also used extensively by other agencies of the government and the public at large. The largest telescope located on the Observatory grounds in Washington, D.C. is the historic 26-inch refractor, acquired in 1873, when it was the world's largest refracting telescope. Used in 1877 to discover the two moons of Mars, this telescope is now used chiefly for planetary satellite observations and for determining the orbital motions and masses of double stars using a special camera known as a speckle interferometer. The Observatory's largest optical telescope is located at the Flagstaff Station in Arizona. It is the 61-inch astrometric reflector.

Selected Astronomy Mailing Lists

HASTRO-L

> History of Astronomy Discussion Group
> To subscribe, send mail to: hastro-l-request@wvnvm.wvnet.edu

INTERNET AMATEUR ASTRONOMERS CATALOG / ARCHIVE (IAAC, netastrocatalog).

> A mailing list and Web archive dedicated to saving the deep-sky observations of amateur astronomers. Protocol for submitting observations is for one object or object group at a time, with observing instrument and object name both mentiond in the Subject:. To subscribe, send an email message with the text "subscribe netastrocatalog" in the body to the address: majordomo@latrade. com To access the Web archive: http://www.tiac.net/ users/lewkaren/netastrocatalog/maillist.html

METEOR OBSERVERS MAILING LIST (meteorobs)

> A mailing list with over 100 subscribers internationally, dedicated to all aspects of meteor observing and meteorics. To subscribe, send an email message with the text "subscribe meteorobs" in the body to the address: majordomo@latrade.com

6

BIOLOGY

American Association of Anatomists
http://www.faseb.org/anatomy/

This is the digital home for biomedical researchers in anatomy and anatomical science. Visit this site for information on the range of AAA programs, including the annual R.R. Bensley Lecture and Award. This is presented each year to someone who has made a distinguished contribution to the advancement of anatomy through discovery, ingenuity, and publications in the field of cell biology. The recipient gives a lecture at the AAA Annual Meeting and, at the AAA Annual Banquet, is presented with a certificate, a $500 honorarium, and travel reimbursement of up to $500. Another award of interest is the Charles Judson Herrick Award. Established in 1962, this award recognizes young investigators who have made important contributions to the field of comparative neuroanatomy and have demonstrated remarkable promise of future accomplishments. The area of comparative neurology is broadly defined for the purpose of the award; previous awardees are outstanding scientists who have made contributions to areas of neuroscience, including neurochemistry, development, neurocytology, neuroendocrinology, neurophysiology, and molecular neurobiology. Eligibility is restricted to individuals who have completed their doctorate degrees within the past 12 years. The web site also includes information on upcoming meetings of interest, various AAA publications, AAA membership, and available grants.

The American Society of Plant Physiologists
http://www.aspp.org/

The American Society of Plant Physiologists was founded in 1924 to promote the development of plant physiology, encourage and publish research in plant physiology, and to promote the interests and growth of plant science in general. Over the decades the society has evolved and expanded to provide a forum for molecular and cellular biology as well as serving the basic interests of plant science. ASPP's membership spans six continents and members work in such diverse areas as academia, government laboratories, industrial and commercial environments, as well as the student community. The society plays a key role in uniting the international plant science community. Come to this web site for complete information on the Soceity, as well as free e-text editions of the Society's Journal entitled Plant Physiology. Recent articles include "Ascorbate Biosynthesis in Mitochondria Is Linked to the Electron Transport Chain between Complexes III and IV," "Radiotracer and Computer Modeling Evidence that Phospho-Base Methylation Is the Main Route of Choline Synthesis in Tobacco," "Optical Coherence Microscopy: A Technology for Rapid, in Vivo, Non-Destructive Visualization of Plants and Plant Cells," and "Physiological Implications of the Kinetics of Maize Leaf Phosphoenolpyruvate Carboxylase." Articles are available as either abstracts or full text.

Baylor Biological Databases
http://mbcr.bcm.tmc.edu/MBCRdatabases.html

The Baylor Biological Databases include The Breast Cancer Gene Database, The Mammary Transgene Interactive Database, The Small RNA database, and The Tumor Gene Database. The latter is a database of genes associated with tumorigenesis and cellular transformation. This database includes oncogenes, proto-oncogenes, tumor supressor genes/anti-oncogenes, regulators and substrates of the above, regions believed to contain such genes such as tumor-associated chromosomal break points and viral integration sites, and other genes and chromosomal regions that seems relevant. The man behind the Tumor

Gene database is David Steffen, Ph.D., President of Houston's Biomedical Computing, Inc. The Small RNA databases focuses on Small RNAs broadly defined as the RNAs not directly involved in protein synthesis. These are grouped under three categories: 1) Capped small RNAs; 2) Noncapped small RNAs; and 3) Viral small RNAs. Sequences and references are included, and you can do wais searching with a keyword. The Mammary Transgene Interactive Database is an interactive database of literature on research designed to target transgene proteins to the mammary gland. Current emphasis is on biotechnology applications. Addition of tumor model and developmental model literature is planned. All of these databases are uniquely positioned to serve as essential tools for all serious biological researchers.

Bermuda Biological Station for Research (BBSR)
http://www.bbsr.edu/

One of the most interesting programs at this lab is their ongoing coral reef research into what they call the the "Marine Rainforest". Because coral reefs are threatened worldwide by both human activities and new diseases, research programs are essential to identify stresses and develop techniques for the better management of these ecosystems. BBSR is playing a major role in educating the next generation of marine science educators, with special emphasis on coral reefs, through the Munson Marine Sciences Graduate Fellowship Program. This program, initiated through a 1997 challenge grant from the Curtis and Edith Munson Foundation in Washington, D.C., provides funding for graduate to receive a rigorous blend of fieldwork, laboratory, and teaching experience at BBSR. A second grant received in 1997, from the San Francisco-based Richard and Rhoda Goldman Fund, supports creation of an Internet-based curriculum to accompany a coral reef camera on Bermuda's reefs. Also be sure to click the link to check the status of the lab's ongoing research into Studies of Bermuda's Air & Water Quality. Long-term projects have included the Bermuda Inshore Waters Investigation and the Marine and Atmospheric Program. Current research on Bermuda's environment range from studies of Bermuda's mangroves and seagrass communities to air quality studies to aquaculture.

Biological Searches Page
http://biomaster.uio.no/mdb/home.html#top

There is no better collection of biological links on the web than the one you'll find at the Biological Searches Page. Among the links are such goodies as Practical Biocomputing for the Bench Scientist, The Wonderfull Pedro's Research Tools page, Molecular Biology and BioInformations WWW sampler, Quick Utils for sequence analysis, Biological Sequence Search Palette, Protein Science Electronic Journal, Frontiers in the biosciences, Multiple Sequence Alignment, and more. You also get direct links to such Data Retrieval Systems as ATLAS MIPS/NBRF, SRS5, NCBI's Entrez browser, EMBL databases (gopher) , and Genbank databases (gopher). Need a sequence similarity search? Just point and click for Searches from the EBI, the Databases at the NCBI, Kabat's Database of Sequences of Immunological Interest, and IMGT—the Immuno Genetics Database (EBI). You can even get WWW based Sequence Analysis from BMC Gene Finder, Grail 1.3, and Pol3Scan (which recognizes the eukaryotic internal control regions A box and B box that are typical of tRNA genes and tDNA-derived elements), get Primer detection using Primer 2.2, and even engage in the Detection of CpG Islands in DNA sequences. Protein sequence & motif database searches are available via SWIS-SPROT, Blocks, NRL3D, OWL, PIR, ENZYME, Queries @ EBI , BLITZ, and other services.

Bio Online
http://www.bio.com

This site is most valuable as a linking intersection for various online biological/pharmaceutical journals. These include ACRE: UK Department of the Environment Advisory Committee on Releases to the Environment newsletters, AgBiotech Bulletins, AgBiotech News and Reviews (CABI), the Antiviral Agents Bulletin, the Australian National University: Biologic Applied Microbiology and Biotechnology BioTechniques (U.S. and Europe editions), the Bio/Technology/ Diversity News Bulletin, the Biotechnology and Development Monitor (University of Amsterdam), Biotechnology Letters (Science and Tech-

nology Letters), Biotechnology Techniques (Science and Technology Letters), BT Catalyst, published monthly by the North Carolina Biotechnology Center, Chromosoma, Current Genetics, The European Biotechnology Information Service, Genes and Development, The Genetic Engineer & Biotechnologist, Genetic Engineering News, The Genetical Society Newsletter, Genome Research, Human Molecular Genetics, Human Genome News, Iowa Biotech Educator, The Journal of Biological Chemistry, Mammalian Genome, Molecular Diversity, Molecular and General Genetics, Nature Biotechnology magazine, Network Science, Probe Newsletter from the USDA National Agricultural Library, Protein Science (a publication of the Protein Society published by Cambridge University Press), Science American Association for the Advancement of Science, The Scientist, Transgenic Research (Chapman & Hall), Transgenica: topics in clinical biotechnology, and The World Journal of Microbiology & Biotechnology (Rapid Communications of Oxford)

Biomolecular Engineering Research Center (BMERC)
http://bmerc-www.bu.edu/

The BioMolecular Engineering Research Center (BMERC) has two major research objectives: First, to develop statistical and other computational approaches which will detect syntactic and semantic patterns in DNA, RNA, and protein sequences. Second, to use statistical/computational approaches to identify structure, function, and regulation in these molecules. This identification has led to the formulation and testing of major hypotheses in the areas of molecular evolution, gene regulation, developmental genetics, and protein structure-function relationships. In meeting these objectives, the BMERC is continually developing new computer-assisted analytical approaches that address basic problems in molecular biology such as those noted above. The Center's support program provides DNA, RNA, and protein sequence databases and analysis tools on-line to a large local area community and to the larger research community via its anonymous FTP and gopher servers. The Center provides a distribution service of non-commercial software and support information for all developers, free of charge, to the scientific community as part of a larger dissemination program. In addition, the Center has provided support for a number of interdisciplinary meetings focused on the computational challenges arising in molecular biology. The Center's training program trains molecular biologists in statistics and computer methods, and educates engineers, biomathematicians and computer scientists in the contemporary computational problems in molecular biology.

Caenorhabditis elegans WWW Server
http://elegans.swmed.edu/

Caenorhabditis elegans is a small (about 1 mm long) soil nematode found in temperate regions. In the 1960's Sydney Brenner began using it to study the genetics of development and neurobiology. Since then the community of C elegans researchers has expanded to over a thousand. The Riddle Lab has written an introduction to C elegans for non-specialists, which you'll find here. And biologists unfamiliar with C elegans may find Mark Blaxter's "The Genetics of Caenorhabditis elegans, An Introduction" useful. Once again, this informative essay is just a click away via a link on the web site. Here you'll also find downloadable software of use to researchers, this including ACeDB, "A C elegans database", was written by Richard Durbin and Jean

Thierry-Mieg as part of the C elegans genome mapping and sequencing project. This hugely successful genome database program has replaced the paper versions of the genetic and physical maps in many (most?) C elegans labs. In addition, the ACeDB database engine has become the standard for other genomic mapping projects. Here you'll also find 4D microscopy software from the Fire Lab. This program is designed for acquiring and displaying images taken over time in a series of focal planes. In particular the program is useful in studying cell lineages and cell migrations during development. The program is for an DOS-based IBM compatible computer with an 80286 or more advanced processor.

European Molecular Biology Laboratory
http://www.embl-heidelberg.de/

The European Molecular Biology Laboratory (EMBL) was established in 1974 and is supported by sixteen countries including nearly all of Western Europe and Israel. EMBL consists of five facilities: the main Laboratory in Heidelberg (Germany), Outstations in Hamburg (Germany), Grenoble (France) and Hinxton (the U.K.), and an external Research Programme in Monterotondo (Italy). EMBL was founded with a four-fold mission: to conduct basic research in molecular biology, to provide essential services to scientists in its Member States, to provide high-level training to its staff, students, and visitors, and to develop new instrumentation for biological research. Over its 25-year history, the Laboratory has had a deep impact on European science in all of these areas. EMBL has achieved so much because it is a truly international, European institution, because it has achieved a critical mass of services and facilities which are driven by cutting-edge biological research, and because it regards education—at all levels—as a way of life. The Laboratory has a number of unique features. Its Outstations provide European biologists access to large instruments for the study of protein structures, some of the world's oldest and biggest databases of DNA and protein sequences, and a host of services operated by highly-trained biologists who are simultaneously involved in their own research.

Caenorhabditis elegans WWW Server

East Coast Worm Meeting **Worm Breeder's Gazette** **Midwest Worm Meeting**
Abstracts   **16(3)**   **Abstracts**

WormBase

Recent papers	Literature Search	Meetings
CGC	Labs	Researchers
EM Center	Announcements	Bionet.celegans
Software	(Thursday, July 6, 2000)	Nematodes
The Genome	Methods	Cells
Other Collections		

Caenorhabditis elegans is a small (about 1 mm long) soil nematode found in temperate regions. In the 1960's Sydney Brenner began using it to study the genetics of development and neurobiology. Since then the community of *C. elegans* researchers has expanded to over a thousand. The Riddle Lab has written an introduction to *C. elegans* for non-specialists. Biologists unfamiliar with *C. elegans* may find Mark Blaxter's The Genetics of Caenorhabditis elegans, An introduction useful.

Users in Europe may find access to the UK mirror of the *C. elegans* WWW Server more convenient.
What's New?   Please send us your comments!
(Tuesday, February 1, 2000)

Leon Avery (leon@eatworms.swmed.edu)
Last modified: Tue Jun 27 11:41:04 2000

ExPASy Molecular Biology Server
http://www.expasy.ch/

Come here for great downloadable tools and software. These include Proteomics tools for Identification and characterization, DNA -> Protein Similarity searches, Pattern and profile searches, Primary structure analysis, Secondary structure prediction, Tertiary structure studies, Transmembrane regions detection, and Transmembrane Alignment. Here you'll also find Melanie 3—Software for 2-D PAGE analysis, the SWISS-MODEL Automated knowledge-based protein modelling server, the Swiss-PdbViewer Macintosh/PC tool for structure display and analysis, and much more. With regard to databases, come here for SWISS-PROT and TrEMBL—Protein sequences, PROSITE—Protein families and domains, SWISS-2DPAGE—Two-dimensional polyacrylamide gel electrophoresis, SWISS-3DIMAGE—3D images of proteins and other biological macromolecules, SWISS-MODEL Repository—Automatically generated protein models, CD40Lbase—CD40 ligand defects, ENZYME—Enzyme nomenclature data, and SeqAnalRef—Sequence analysis bibliographic references. Also be sure to check the Swiss-Shop, a service that allows you to automatically obtain (by email) new sequence entries relevant to your field(s) of interest. New Protein Sequences, which are added to the SWISS-PROT database on a weekly basis, can be scanned following a user-defined query. The searches are performed on the current non-cumulative weekly additions only. This will allow researchers to be aware of new protein sequences, related to their interests, before the actual database release.

Federation of American Societies for Experimental Biology
http://www.faseb.org/

The mission of FASEB is to enhance the ability of biomedical and life scientists to improve, through their research, the health, well-being, and productivity of all people. FASEB is a coalition of independent Member Societies that serve the interests of biomedical and life scientists, particularly those related to public policy issues. FASEB facilitates coalition activities among Member Societies and disseminates information on biological research through scientific conferences and publications. FASEB also offers Member Societies headquarters facilities, and operational and logistic support. Founded in 1912 by three societies, FASEB has consistently provided educational meetings and publications to disseminate biological research results. The then six Member Societies met in 1989 to alter its focus and to reaffirm its mission. The Federation has since experienced significant growth, and is now composed of the following Member Societies: The American Physiological Society, The American Society for Biochemistry and Molecular Biology, The American Society for Pharmacology and Experimental Therapeutics, The American Society for Investigative Pathology, The American Society for Nutritional Sciences, The American Association of Immunologists, The American Society for Cell Biology, The Biophysical Society, The American Association of Anatomists, The Protein Society, American Society for Bone & Mineral Research, The American Society for Clinical Investigation, The Endocrine Society, and The American Society of Human Genetics.

Flybrain: An Online Atlas and Datbase of the Drosophilia Nervous System
http://www.flybrain.org/

The 'Basic Atlas' provides the user with a hypertext tour guide to the basic structural elements of the Drosophila nervous system. It links schematic representations, serial sections through the entire brain, and Golgi impregnations of individual cells. When appropriate, these are also linked to enhancer-trap images and to other gene expression data. It is hoped that the Basic Atlas will provide the novice with a usable overview of how the different parts of the nervous system are constructed and connected. It is intended that the Atlas links will provide a tour through the brain and its main structures, including JAVA applets and VRML manipulatable reconstructions. Teaching tools that can be used with the database are currently being developed by the University of Freiburg component of the database consortium. Schematic Representations: These provide diagrammatic views of the nervous system from a number of different perspectives. By clicking the cursor on a particular anatomical domain, the user will embark on a tour that links textual descriptions to images obtained by a range of different visualisation techniques. Flybrain 3D Project. This will include models, schematic models, and movies of confocal images of the brain or brain regions. Virtual dissections provide interactive guides to relationships amongst brain architectures.

Harvard Biological Laboratories
http://golgi.harvard.edu/

The Harvard Biological Laboratories compris a community of about 30 faculty, 80 graduate students and 180 postdoctoral fellows actively engaged in innovative research, discovery and training in modern biology. The research in the department covers a wide range of topics with special emphasis on: Biochemistry, Cell Biology, Genetics, Neurobiology, Development Genomics, Molecular Evolution, Gene Expression Immunology, and Structural Biology. They also, of course, offer instruction for undergaduates and graduates as well as numerous research opportunities for visiting scholars and summer students.

The Harvard program has a special interest in eukaryotic cell cycle progression. The activity of cyclin-dependent kinases (cdks) positively regulates cell growth and is believed to play an important role in the decision to initiate DNA replication and cell division. Although cyclin/cdk complexes are proposed to function by phosphorylating critical substrates required for transitions through the cycle, few substrates are known for these kinases. The retinoblastoma (pRB) tumor suppressor protein is perhaps the best candidate for a physiologic substrate of these kinases. pRB is thought to suppress growth at least in part by repressing the activity of the E2F transcription factor, which is believed to be important for the expression of key proteins needed for DNA replication. However, once phosphorylated by cyclin/cdks, prB can no longer bind E2F or inhibit its activity, thus reversing its role as a repressor.

Hawke's Nest: The Home of Zebrins
http://www.acs.ucalgary.ca/~rhawkes/

Spatially repeated patterns in developing organisms—from segmentation in the leech, through the patterned expression of homeodomain proteins in Drosophila, to somitic segregation in vertebrates—are a central problem in development. In the central nervous system, the mammalian cerebellum is an ideal tissue in which to explore pattern formation. A variety of molecules—ZEBRINS—are expressed in the cerebellum of the adult mouse brain in an elegant array of stripes, interposed by similar stripes of unlabeled cells. This pattern of stripes is, in turn, correlated closely with the pattern of axons bringing information into the cerebellum. This raises four broad sets of issues: i) what does neuroanatomy tell us about the modular organization of the adult cerebellum? ii) how do cerebellar modules reflect the receptive fields and serve cerebellar function (motor control)? (iii) how are the zebrin bands generated during development, and how is expression directed to the Purkinje cell? iv) how do the different ingrowing climbing fiber and mossy fiber axons recognize their appropriate targets? The information and resources at Hawke's Nest attempts to use cell and molecular biology techniques to approach these issues, including: raising monoclonal antibodies to zebrins and cloning the zebrin genes; using anatomical methods such as anterograde tracer transport, immunocytochemistry, and in situ hybridization; using surgical and pharmacological interventions in normal development; culture of cerebellar slices and dissociated neurons; electrophysiological mapping

Indiana University Bio Archive
http://iubio.bio.indiana.edu/

IUBio Archive is an archive of biology data and software. The archive includes items to browse, search and fetch public software, molecular data, biology news and documents. This archive, maintained at Indiana University Biology department since 1989, has moved recently from one computer to another. The archive maintains software for all computer systems important to biology. Public software categories served here include biology, chemistry, science, utilities, molecular biology sections including alignment, codon, autoseq, browsing, consensus, evolve, pattern, primer, restrict-enzymes, and rna-fold. Search services include GenBank nucleic databank (WAIS query of full release and weekly updates), Swiss-Prot and PIR protein databanks, Bionet news (full, searchable archive since Dec 1990), SRS (Sequence Retrieval System)—including Genbank, protein and others for both simple and sophisticated text/annotation queries of databanks, SRS-FastA—for sequence similarity searches against any user-defined subset of Genbank & protein data, including subsets for popular species Arabidopsis, Caenorhabditis, Drosophila, Oryza, Poaeceae, Rattus, Murinae, and Saccharomyces. fyi, in addition to web access, all IUBio Archive gopher services are now also available by e-mail, using GopherMail. For all IUBio services, including Genbank, Swiss-protein and other databank searches, Bionet news searches, and software archives, send a mail message to gopher@iubio.bio.indiana.edu

Lawrence Berkeley National Laboratory Human Genome Center
http://www-hgc.lbl.gov/GenomeHome.html

This site provides access to the human and Drosophila clones that have been sequenced at Lawrence Berkeley National Laboratory's

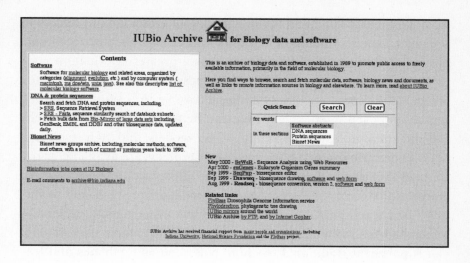

Human Genome Center and the Berkeley Drosophila Genome Project. Assembled regions that have not yet been submitted in that form to a public database are provided here as a service to the community. Users of the material provided here in advance of submission to public databases should not publish it or otherwise disseminate it without permission. Included here are Drosophila sequences, Human sequences and Mouse sequences. Online web tables list the overlapping clones in the tiling path in order from left to right across each chromosome arm. Data (hyperlinked as appropriate) include the GenBank accession number, the clone name(s), the cytological location (in situ if available, otherwise inferred (indicated by parentheses), the size of the clone or set of clones in the sequence accession (for low-coverage clones, the size is currently a number of sequence contigs; insert size estimates from CHEF gel electrophoresis coming soon), and known Drosophila genes, ESTs and sequenced P element insertions identified by sequence homology searches. There is no better resource for data such as this—and as timely as this—anywhere in the world.

Institute for Molecular Virology (Bock Labs, University of Wisconsin)
http://www.bocklabs.wisc.edu/Welcome.html

Visualizations of complex biological structures such as viruses are well-suited to distribution via the electronic medium of the World

Wide Web, complementing the peer-reviewed publication of figures in scientific papers. Animation and color can be employed to accentuate particular features of structure, and thus a greater information content can be imparted than would be possible with printed media. Structural information that is easily accessible in a standard, meaningful, and even interactive format can be an effective tool in teaching and research. Animations, interactive models, and high resolution color-coded images of viral particles and proteins are available, many of them exclusively, from this site. These virus visualizations enhance conventional virology instruction by offering unique resources to students and teachers. Animated or interactive visualizations of viruses allow students to interact in new ways with the course material and can supplement traditional teaching aids such as textbooks and lectures. With advances like the World Wide Web protocol and Kinemage, electronic publishing of virus structures have become decreasingly less platform-dependent and thus the are now accessible to a much wider audience. Check out two cutting edges at once: that of molecular biology, and that of multimedia web publishing for biological purposes.

Microbiology & Molecular Biology Reviews
http://mmbr.asm.org/

Microbiology and Molecular Biology Reviews, formerly Microbiological Reviews, continues to be recognized as the definitive, broad-based review journal in the expanding disciplines of microbiology, immunology, and molecular and cellular biology. Scope includes: Physiology and Enzymology, Molecular Biology, Genetics, Ecology, Host-Parasite Relationships Leading to Disease, and Cellular Biology. Recent articles—available as abstracts of in full text HTML of PDF— include Membrane Topology and Insertion of Membrane Proteins: Search for Topogenic Signals, Metabolic Engineering of Saccharomyces cerevisiae, Hepatitis B Virus Biology, Virioplankton: Viruses in Aquatic Ecosystems, Genetics of Mosquito Vector Competence, Higher Levels of Organization in the Interphase Nucleus of Cycling and Differentiated Cells, Microbial Relatives of the Seed Storage Proteins of Higher Plants: Conservation of Structure and Diversification of Function during Evolution of the Cupin Superfamily, Molecular Basis of Symbiotic Promiscuity, Aminoacyl-tRNA Synthetases (the Genetic Code and the Evolutionary Process), and more. Additional articles address lkaliphiles: Some Applications of Their Products for Biotechnology, Recombinational Repair of DNA Damage in Escherichia coli and Bacteriophage, Pathology and Epizootiology of Entomophaga maimaiga Infections in Forest Lepidoptera, Retroviral DNA Integration, Prions in Saccharomyces and Podospora spp.: Protein-Based Inheritance, and Adding the Third Dimension to Virus Life Cycles: Three-Dimensional Reconstruction of Icosahedral Viruses from Cryo-Electron Micrographs.

Molecular Biology Core Facilities/Dana-Farber Cancer Institute
http://mbcf.dfci.harvard.edu/

This in-depth web page itemizes all the services of the Institute labs and related facilities. These include Automated DNA Sequencing using ABI model 373/377 instrument and embracing the following tests: Single and double strand . . . Dye labeled dideoxyterminators . . . and Homologies, motifs, consensus sequence. The lab can also provide DNA Synthesis (for ABI model 3948) related to 40 nanomole purified (quantitated), 0.2 micromole, 1 micromole, S-oligos, Biotin, Aminolink, Dye labeled, RNA-oligos . . . Peptide Synthesis for Amino acid analysis, Analytical HPLC, Preparative HPLC . . . and Protein Sequencing for Protein digests and HPLC peptide mapping. There are also facilities for BIAcore AB protein ligand assays, Mass Spectrometry (Voyager DE-STR and Finnigan Lasermat) for In gel protein digests and analysis and Elucidation of post translational modifications. The web site also provides useful links to Cell and Molecular Biology Online (Pam Gannon's up-to-date Mol Bio site), The Association of Biomolecular Resource Facilities (If you work in a Molecular Biology Resource Facility, you'll want to know about this group), and The National Center for Biotechnology Information (sequence galore). Of course, Dana Farber is associated with the Harvard Medical School and is one of the leading oncological research and treatment institutions in the world.

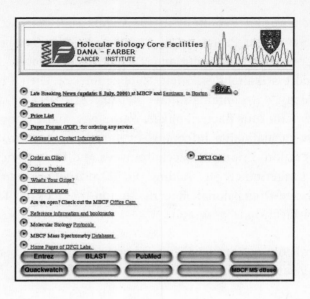

Pedro's BioMolecular Research Tools
http://www.public.iastate.edu/~pedro/research_tools.html

Here you have hundreds of great research links and tools including: 3D-ALI–Database relating Proteins Structures and Sequences at EMBL-Heidelberg . . . AA Analysis–Protein Identification in SwissProt and PIR using Amino Acid Composition at EMBL-Heidelberg . . . AA CompIdent–Protein Identification in SwissProt using Amino Acid Composition at ExPASy, Switzerland . . . AA CompSim–Compare the Amino Acid Composition of a SwissProt Entry with Other Entries at ExPASy, Switzerland . . . AA Sequence Analysis–Multiple Analysis of a Native or Modified Amino Acid Sequence at Rockefeller U. . . . AbCheck–Test an Antibody Sequence Against the Kabat Database at U. College-London, UK . . . ALIGN–Optimal Global Alignment of Two Sequences with No Short-cuts at EERIE-Nimes, France and Align at MIPS, Germany . . . AllAll–Check Relationships in a Set of Related Peptides at ETH-Zürich, Switzerland . . . AllAllDB–Search the All-Against-All Database of SwissProt at ETH-Zürich, Switzerland . . . AMAS–Analysis of Protein Multiple Sequence Alignments at U. Oxford, UK . . . ASC–Analytic Surface Calculation of PDB Protein Structures at EMBL-Heidelberg . . . ATLAS–Search DNA and Protein

Sequence Databases at MIPS, Germany...use the BCM Search Launcher at Baylor College of Medicine...and save time with BEAUTY—BLAST Enhanced Alignment Utility (see Documentation) at Baylor College of Medicine.

Society for the Study of Amphibians and Reptiles
http://www.ukans.edu/~ssar/

SSAR, a not-for-profit organization established to advance research, conservation, and education concerning amphibians and reptiles, was founded in 1958. It is the largest international herpetological society, and is recognized worldwide for having the most diverse program of publications, meetings, and other activities. Membership in the Society is open to anyone with an interest in herpetology. One benefit of membership is eligibility for the Society's popular Grants-in-Herpetology program. In addition to the GIH program, the Society's International Cooperation Committee recently has completed an extensive compilation of funding sources entitled International Grant Programs. The Society's Henri Seibert Awards are presented at each Annual Meeting to students presenting papers judged to be best in each of several categories. The Kennedy Award is

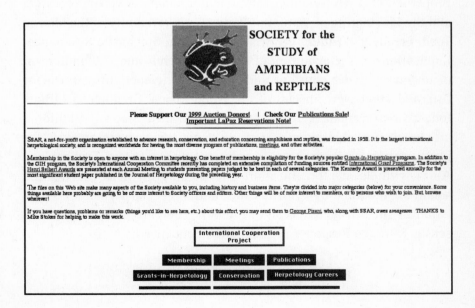

presented annually for the most significant student paper published in the Journal of Herpetology during the preceding year. The files on this Web site make many aspects of the Society available to you, including history and business items. They're divided into major categories (below) for your convenience. Some things available here probably are going to be of more interest to Society officers and editors. Other things will be of more interest to members, or to persons who wish to join. But, browse wherever!

World Wide Web Journal of Biology
   http://www.epress.com/w3jbio/

The World Wide Web Journal of Biology Features: Quality peer-reviewed research in diverse disciplines of the biological sciences. It also allows for Electronic mail and ftp submission of articles . . . Rapid consideration of manuscripts for fast publication . . . complete multimedia, hypertext presentations . . . Interactive forums via internet listserver for dynamic, ongoing dialog between authors and readers . . . No subscription fee for the on-line journal . . . postings and conference announcements, and more. Recent articles discuss The Effect of Infrasound Vibrations on Electrical Conductivity of Water and Optical Properties of DNA Aquatic Solution, Pulmonary Mechanoreceptors and the Modulation of Ventilator Pattern and Variability in the Marine Toad, Frequency Tuning on Red Noise Driven Stochastic Resonance: Implications to the evolution of sensory systems, and "A comparison of oogenesis under constant and fluctuating temperatures in Doctor fish, and Three New Species of the Wood Roach, Cryptocercus (Blattodea: Cryptocercidae), from the Eastern United States." Additional articles discuss: Morphometric study using wing image analysis for identification of Bactrocera dorsalis complex (Diptera Tephritidae), Apical cytoplasmic organization and polar growth in Rhizoctonia solani are modified by cytochalasins, and Molecular Dynamics Simulation Of The Estrogen Receptor Protein In Complex With A Non-Consensus Estrogen Response Element DNA Sequence In A 10.

biology mailing lists:

Biology andconservation of declining amphibians : SUBSCRIBE message to listproc@ucdavis.edu

Biology of fish and aquaria : SUBSCRIBE message to listserv@emuvm1.cc.emory.edu

American Society of Zoologists : SUBSCRIBE message to listserv@cmsa.berkeley.edu

Bat research : SUBSCRIBE message to listserv@unvma.unm.edu

Biological control regulations : SUBSCRIBE message to listserv@uafsysb.uark.edu

Research and information concerning bee biology : SUBSCRIBE message to listserv@uacsc2.albany.edu

Biomedical research/healthcare : SUBSCRIBE message to listserve@asuvm.inre.asu.edu

Bioacoustics : SUBSCRIBE message to listproc@cornell.edu

Biodiversity networks : SUBSCRIBE message to listserv@ftpt.br

Jobs for biologists : SUBSCRIBE message to majordomo@mtu.edu

Bionet newsgroups:

Archives for dozens of these groups can be found at the URL
http://www.bio.net/archives.html

7

Biosphere/Conservation /Ecology

Audubon Online
   http://www.audubon.org/

The mission of the National Audubon Society is to conserve and restore natural ecosystems, focusing on birds and other wildlife for the benefit of humanity and the earth's biological diversity. Founded in 1905, the National Audubon Society is named for John James Audubon (1785-1851), famed ornithologist, explorer, and wildlife artist. The National Audubon Society boasts 550,000 members, 508 chapters in the Americas, 100 Audubon Sanctuaries and nature centers nationwide, and 300 full time staff (including scientists, educators, sanctuary managers, regional and state directors, and a government affairs specialist). High Priority Campaigns and Key Legislative Programs include: Preserving wetlands, Lobbying to reauthorize the Endangered Species Act, Promoting a responsible U.S. population policy, Preserving America's endangered forests, Protecting and promoting growth of America's National Wildlife Refuges, Conserving marine wildlife through Living Oceans program, Restoration of water flows to enhance wildlife of the Platte River system, and protecting corridors for migratory birds through the Partners in Flight program. The organization's national headquarters "Audubon House," a century-old building in New York City, was renovated by a team of scientists, engineers and architects to be environmentally and fiscally responsible. Since its opening in December of 1991, it has served as a model of sustainable architecture and interior design for government agencies, institutions, and businesses.

Australian Environment
http://www.erin.gov.au/

The goals of the Australian Department of the Environment and Heritage is to develop, in the Australian national interest, a proper recognition of environmental, social and related economic values in government decision-making and activities; and to improve the quality of the decision-making process, program delivery and communication by ensuring that Government has available to it reliable information and advice and efficient delivery mechanisms. The Secretary of the Department of the Environment and Heritage is Mr Roger Beale. Mr Beale was formerly Associate Secretary of the Department of the Prime Minister and Cabinet with responsibility for the Economic, Industry Resources and Environment, and Corporate Services Divisions as well as the Cabinet Office. He was the Chair of the High Level Group of heads of departments responsible for implementing the Commonwealth Government's forest policy and was responsible for conducting major negotiations with State Governments and interest groups. From 1987 to 1993, Mr Beale was Associate Secretary for the Department of Transport and Communications. From 1984-1987, he was Commissioner of the Public Service Board. Visit this web site

for more information on other staff, and for details on various Department programs, including the Australian and World Heritage Group, the Biodiversity Group, the Environment Protection Group, and other divisions.

Biodiversity and Biological Collections Web Server
http://biodiversity.uno.edu/

This WWW server is devoted to information of interest to systematists and other biologists of the organismic kind. Within these pages you will find information about specimens in biological collections, taxonomic authority files, directories of biologists, reports by various standards bodies (IOPI, ASC, SA2000, etc), an archive of the Taxacom, MUSE-L and CICHLID-L listservs, access to on-line journals (including Flora On-line) and information about MUSE and Delta. Here you have hundreds of valuable links in the fields of Botany, Herpetology, Invertebrates, Entomology, Ichthyology, Mammalogy, Mycology, Microbiology and Ornithology. Here you'll also find relevant links under the headings: Announcements and Current News, Biological Societies, Biologist Directories and Publications, Data Models and Standards Reports, General Biodiversity, Geology & Earth Sciences, and Natural History Museums. Mammalogy links include: Whale Watching Web (WWW Virtual Lib.), Mammal species of the world, Faunmap (an electronic database for the late Quaternary distribution of mammal species in the US), The University of Texas at El Paso Centennial Museum, the Australian Mammal Society, the Northern Prairie Science Center (NBS), the Cornell University Mammal Collections, The Shrew Site, Images of mammals by Wernher Krutein, the American Society of Mammologists, the Unesco-IOC Register of Marine Organisms, and more.

Biodiversity Links
http://atlantic.evsc.virginia.edu/biodwrk98/links.html

Among the links you'll find here are those to Biodiversity Programs of the National Museum of Natural History (NMNH), the Biodiversity and Ecosystems NEtwork (BENE), the Canadian Biodiversity

Information Network, the Natural Heritage Network, the Convention on Biological Diversity, the U.S. Man and the Biosphere Program, Barry Lewis's article "Biodiversity: Why Should We Care;What Does it Mean?", and "Biodiversity and Conservation—a Hypertext Book" by Peter J. Bryant. The latter discusses the origin, nature and value of biological diversity, the threats to its continued existence, and approaches to preserving what is left. Chapters include: INTRODUCTION, Chapter 1: HISTORY OF LIFE, Chapter 2: THE AGE OF MAMMALS, Chapter 3: EXTINCTION AND DEPLETION FROM OVEREXPLOITATION, Chapter 4: WHALING AND FISHING, Chapter 5: OVEREXPLOITATION THREATENING LIVING SPECIES, Chapter 6: GLOBAL PATTERNS OF BIODIVERSITY, Chapter 7: VALUES OF BIODIVERSITY, Chapter 8: ENDANGERED SPECIES PROTECTION, Chapter 9: EXOTIC INTRODUCTIONS, Chapter 10: FORESTS AND DEFORESTATION, Chapter 11: ENDANGERED AQUATIC HABITATS, Chapter 12: ISLANDS, Chapter 13: PROTECTED AREAS, Chapter 14: HABITAT POLLUTION, Chapter 15: CAPTIVE BREEDING AND REINTRODUCTION, Chapter 16: HUMAN POPULATION GROWTH.

Boyce Thompson Institute for Plant Research Environmental Biology
http://birch.cit.cornell.edu/

The Boyce Thompson Institute for Plant Research Environmental Biology sponsors and conducts research in the areas of Biotechnology, Forest Biology, Insect Biology, Environmental Physiology, Genetics, Molecular Biodiversity, and Bio-pharming with Plants. The latter is of particular interest. "Bio-pharming" is an exciting new area of research that uses living organisms (or tissues and cells derived from them) to produce valuable organic molecules such as protein pharmaceuticals. Boyce Thompson has developed systems to create genetically engineered plants to produce these proteins, with special focus on vaccine antigens. Antigens are unique proteins that typically form the outer surfaces of bacteria or viruses. When these pathogens invade animals, the antigens are recognized by the immune system. Genetic engineering has provided new tools for the creation of vaccines; small segments of DNA are isolated from the pathogen and used to genetically engineer recipients to produce the antigen "subunit" (which is incapable of causing disease). Because subunit vaccines contain only specific proteins from the pathogen, they are much safer than live or killed whole-cell vaccines, which may actually cause disease. Boyce Thompson has shown that several different candidate vaccine proteins can be faithfully produced in plants. Feeding the plant tissue to mice can stimulate immune reactions; this tissue essentially constitutes an "edible vaccine." Boyce Thompson hopes to develop methods to increase production of foreign protein in plant cells and to engineer protein antigens that will enhance their potential as human and animal vaccines.

Chesapeake Bay Foundation
http://www.savethebay.cbf.org/

The Chesapeake Bay Foundation is a catalyst for bold and creative solutions to Bay problems. Staff members set the agenda, serve as watchdogs, and speak out on behalf of the Chesapeake Bay to business, government, and the public. CBF's Resource Protection Program has three focuses. First, they protect the Bay's natural resources from pollution and other harmful activities by fighting for strong and effective laws and regulations. They work cooperatively with government, business, and citizens in partnerships. When necessary, they use legal means to force compliance with existing laws. They restore the Bay's essential habitats and filtering mechanisms, such as forests, wetlands, underwater grasses, and oysters, through a variety of hands-on projects. And they involve citizens in CBF's environmental efforts by recruiting, training, and incorporating them as effective partners and leaders. Working with key partners, CBF restores habitat, educates others, and holds those who pollute accountable for their actions. The Chesapeake Bay Foundation's environmental education program introduces people to the wonders of the watershed and works to heighten sensitivity, increase knowledge, and empower citizens to take positive action toward the Bay's restoration. CBF's classroom curricula are supplementary middle school curricula designed to raise awareness of Bay issues and resources. Through activities that model subject integration, problem solving skills, and real life community action projects, students are empowered to take positive action towards restoring the Bay.

Earthwatch Institute
http://earthwatch.org/

Earthwatch Institute operates on a very simple but radical notion: that if you fully involve the general public in the process of science, you not only give them understanding, you give the world a future. The mission of the Earthwatch Institute is to promote sustainable conservation of our natural resources and cultural heritage by creating partnerships between scientists, educators and the general public. They accomplish this through three primary objectives. First, Research—Supporting the field work of research scientists worldwide collecting the base line data essential for sustainable management decisions Second, Education—Educating and inspiring the next generation of leaders in education, business and the general public both at home and overseas. Last, Conservation—Solving problems by active and ground-breaking collaborations with conservation and preservation partners. Unlike other environmental organizations, Earthwatch Institute puts people in the field where they can assist scientists in their field work. They are part of the action, they learn new skills, and develop a deeper understanding of their role in building a sustainable future. Earthwatch believes that teaching and promoting scientific literacy is the best way to systematically approach and solve the many complex environmental and social issues facing society today. Earthwatch Institute acts as a unique catalyst and a liaison between the scientific community, conservation and environmental organizations, policy makers, business, and the general public.

Earth Share
http://www.environment.org

Earth Share, a federation of America's leading non-profit environmental and conservation organizations, works to promote environmental education and charitable giving through workplace giving campaigns. Earth Share is an opportunity, a system, and an answer for environmentally conscious employees and workplaces to support dozens of environmental groups at once through a charitable giving drive. Earth Share's members work hard every day to safeguard your health and the environment. Its members are combating global warming and protecting ancient forests. They're guarding groundwater from toxic contaminants and saving endangered species. These efforts, and so many more, are supported by Earth Share's mission. Earth Share's goal is to continue expanding opportunities for working people to have an easy and effective way to help the environment, and in doing so, help ensure the preservation of our natural heritage. There are many things you can do to help protect and preserve the environment—from introducing an Earth Share charitable giving campaign at your workplace, to making small changes in your daily habits that will have a positive impact on the natural world. However you choose to contribute, your support makes a difference. Visit this web site to find out how you can get involved today!

Friends of the Earth
http://foe.org/

Friends of the Earth is a national environmental organization dedicated to preserving the health and diversity of the planet for future generations. As the largest international environmental network in the world with affiliates in 63 countries, Friends of the Earth empowers citizens to have an influential voice in decisions affecting their environment. Check out their three program areas: Focusing on the crucial economics of protecting our environment, Championing development that benefits people and the environment around the world, and Empowering citizens around the country to address environmental problems affecting them. One very cool aspect of the Friends of the Earth web site is their online publication, Atmosphere, available here in PDF format. Over ten years ago, Friends of the Earth began publishing Atmosphere as a service to its members and allies. Atmosphere focuses primarily on actions taken to preserve the earth's protective ozone layer and secondarily to highlight the work that FoE is doing to reduce global warming. Atmosphere will be published three times a year, to coincide with the major meetings of the parties

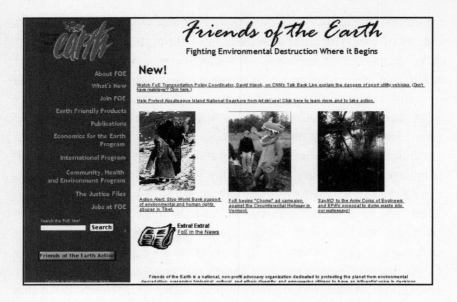

to the Montreal Protocol on Ozone Depleting Substances. The site also features a wealth of information on various FOE programs, policies and, of course, how to become a member.

Gaia Forest Conservation Archives & Portal
http://forests.org/

This site is dedicated to ending deforestation, preserving old-growth forests, conserving all forests, and commencing the age of forest restoration. The mission of Forests.org is to contribute to the conservation of rainforests, forests, biodiversity, indigenous cultures and the climate through targeted informational networking. The site lets you conduct full text searches of thousands of the Best Rainforest, Forest, Biodiversity, Temperate Forest and Climate Change sites on the Internet, and/or search the site's own extensive Archives of non-permanent Internet forest conservation news & information. Trees are sick and dying everywhere in the US. It seems clear that the dying trees are one more sign of danger, one more warning that something is terribly wrong. Why are the trees dying? The reasons are many and varied. In New England, New York, North Carolina, Tennessee, Georgia, Ohio, Indiana and Kentucky, it's a combination of acid rain and clear-cuts; in California it's killer smog; in Arizona and New Mexico and elsewhere, it's excessive ultraviolet light filtering through the earth's damaged ozone shield; other places, it's pesticides, or toxic heavy metals released by burning coal and oil; in Alaska and Florida it's rising temperatures and rising sea levels from global warming; in Colorado, Oregon and Washington state it's destructive forestry practices that leave forests weakened, unable to withstand extremes of weather or attacks by insects or fungi. Come to this web site for the facts.

Great Lakes Program at University at Buffalo
http://wings.buffalo.edu/glp/

The mission of the Great Lakes Program is to develop, evaluate, and synthesize scientific and technical knowledge on the Great Lakes ecosystem in support of public education and policy formation. In carrying out this mission, the Great Lakes Program attempts to involve UB faculty from a wide range of fields in multidisciplinary research and graduate education on the Great Lakes. Among the fields the Program has involved in Great Lakes research are: engineering, health sciences, natural sciences, social sciences, planning, and law. The Great Lakes Program has thirty-five faculty affiliates representing six faculties or decanal units. The short term goals of the Great Lakes Program are: 1. Enhance the recognition of the Great Lakes Program as a major multidiciplinary research and education program within the University of Buffalo community. 2. Involve more faculty from biological and chemical sciences and from economics/management in Great Lakes research. 3. Establish a major multidisciplinary research program in watershed management from Great Lakes watersheds. Managing water resources at the watershed scale is a major national trend that includes biological, ecological, hydrologic, chemical, engineering, socio-economic, law and policy, education, and planning/management research components. 4. Continue to develop collaborative research and education/outreach programs with other academic institutions, federal, state, and local government organizations, and private sector companies that have an interest in Great Lakes issues.

Greenpeace International
http://greenpeace.org/

Greenpeace is a global environmental campaigning organisation. They organise public campaigns for the protection of oceans and ancient forests, for the phasing-out of fossil fuels and the promotion of renewable energies in order to stop climate change, for the elimination of toxic chemicals, against the release of genetically modified organisms into nature and for nuclear disarmament and an end to nuclear contamination. The Greenpeace organisation consists of Greenpeace International (Stichting Greenpeace Council) in Amsterdam and Greenpeace offices around the world. Greenpeace currently has a presence in 40 countries. Greenpeace national or regional offices are licensed to use the name Greenpeace. Each office is governed by a board which appoints a representative (called a trustee). Trustees meet once a year to agree on the long-term strategy of the organisation, to make necessary changes to governance structure, to set a ceiling on spending for Greenpeace International's budget and to elect the International Board. Greenpeace International monitors the organisational development of Greenpeace offices. The International Board approves the annual budget of Greenpeace International and its audited accounts. It also appoints and supervises the International Executive Director who, together with senior managers, and consulting widely with national office staff, leads the organisation.

Hudson River Sloop Clearwater
http://www.clearwater.org

The story of the Hudson River Sloop Clearwater, Inc. is a history of people who have given of themselves as members, as supporters and as volunteers—people who have dreams for a better world and an unwavering belief that, as individuals, we can make a difference in bringing about a cleaner, safer world for ourselves and future generations. Clearwater conducts environmental education, advocacy programs and celebrations to protect the Hudson River, its tributaries and related bodies of water, and to create awareness of the estuary's

complex relationship with the coastal zone. A magnificent natural design blending the freshwater streams of the Adirondacks with the salt tides of the Atlantic, the Hudson's estuaries rank second only to rainforests in biological productivity. The centerpiece of Clearwater's public education program is the 106-foot wooden sailing sloop Clearwater, designed after the Dutch sailing sloops of the 18th and 19th centuries. In 1966, Pete Seeger had the idea that by learning to care for one boat and one river, the public could come to care for all our threatened waterways. He inspired a group of dedicated people who made the dream a reality. Serving as a movable classroom, laboratory and stage, the sloop Clearwater is now in her twenty-sixth sailing season. Across the country and abroad, more than a dozen programs have been successfully modeled after the programs pioneered by Clearwater.

Imaging Systems Laboratory, Department of Landscape Architecture, University of Illinois at Urbana-Champaign
http://imlab9.landarch.uiuc.edu/

Since 1986 the Imaging Systems Lab has conducted environmental perception research using computer-based technologies. The focus has been in the visualization and evaluation of large-scale environmental changes—the management of forest pests and fire, and harvesting practices. Projects include: SmartForest: An interactive forest visualizer (free download available), the East St Louis Action Research Project (aCooperative assistance and development program for East St. Louis, Illinois), EGRETS (East St. Louis Geographic Information Retrieval System (explore links and download data), SmartCity (Integrated support system for city planning (VRML interface to land-use data), Grand Canyon (a study of the effects of water flow regimes on recreation quality and satisfaction), Routt National Forest (a study of the effects of a severe forest blowdown followed by a spruce beetle outbreak), anbd more. Collaborations include Computing for the Arts (an Interdisciplinary program in Fine and Applied Arts), Environmental Rehearsal Studio (An interdisciplinary teaching and research initiative of the College of Fine & Applied Arts), and Human Dimensions of Environmental Systems (an interdisciplinary program of study with special emphasis on the socio-psychological aspects of natural resource use.) Journey to this web site for thrilling, scintilating online explorations of the human environment as represented by digital media. You'll be glad you did.

Lamont-Doherty Earth Observatory
http://www.ldeo.columbia.edu/

The Lamont-Doherty Earth Observatory in Palisades, N.Y., is a research division of Columbia University dedicated to understanding how planet Earth works. Scientific inquiry at the Observatory ranges from the origin and history of the planet to the processes taking place in and on it. More than 500 scientific, technical and support personnel, including 100 scientists and 100 graduate students, are involved in research that is often interdisciplinary and includes seismology, marine geology and geophysics, terrestrial geology, petrology, geochemistry, climate studies, atmospheric science, oceanography and paleontology. The Observatory, established in 1949 by Columbia geology professor Maurice Ewing, is located on a 125-acre estate donated to the University by the Thomas W. Lamont family. Lamont scientists devised prototypical seismic instruments for monitoring earthquakes and nuclear weapons tests and for exploring the Earth's deep interior and set up the first global seismic network. Lamont scientists also led a systematic global reconnaissance of the ocean floors, developing many of the first modern instruments to study the seafloor. Lamont is linked to Columbia's Department of Earth and Environmental Sciences, whose graduate students pursue research at the Observatory. Columbia professors are active researchers at Lamont and Observatory scientists play vital roles in advising students, directing student research, and enhancing the intellectual firepower of the outstanding education and research program. Lamont scientists also collaborate with two affiliated institutions, the American Museum of Natural History and the NASA Goddard Institute for Space Studies.

Long-Term Ecological Research Program
   http://lternet.edu/

The Long Term Ecological Research (LTER) Network promotes synthesis and comparative research across sites and ecosystems and among other related national and international research programs. This is entirely a collaborative effort involving more than 1100 scientists and students investigating ecological processes operating at long time scales and over broad spatial scales. The Network now consists of 24 sites representing diverse ecosystems and research emphases. A network office coordinates communication, network publications, and planning activities. The whole effort was started by the National Science Foundation in 1980 to support research on long-term ecological phenomena in the United States. Be sure to check out the online newsletter, loaded with news focusing on on the history and future of cross-site and synthetic research conducted by LTER scientists. From the beginning of the LTER program, cooperation among scientists has been one of the most important attributes of the network. The LTER concept itself encourages interdisciplinary within sites and fosters the development of research teams with common scientific goals. The stability of these research teams over time provides a unique opportunity to build understanding in the study ecosystems through a combination of long-term monitoring and experiments and short-term mechanistic studies.

National Estuary Program of the EPA
http://www.epa.gov/nep/nep.html

The National Estuary Program was established in 1987 by amendments to the Clean Water Act to identify, restore, and protect nationally significant estuaries of the United States. Unlike traditional regulatory approaches to environmental protection, the NEP targets a broad range of issues and engages local communities in the process. The program focuses not just on improving water quality in an estuary, but on maintaining the integrity of the whole system—its chemical, physical, and biological properties, as well as its economic, recreational, and aesthetic values. The National Estuary Program is designed to encourage local communities to take responsibility for managing their own estuaries. Each NEP is made up of representatives from federal, state and local government agencies responsible for managing the estuary's resources, as well as members of the community—citizens, business leaders, educators, and researchers. These stakeholders work together to identify problems in the estuary, develop specific actions to address those problems, and create and implement a formal management plan to restore and protect the estuary. Twenty-eight estuary programs are currently working to safeguard the health of some of our Nation's most important coastal waters. Visit the web site for more details.

National Gap Analysis Program
http://www.gap.uidaho.edu/gap/

Gap analysis is a scientific method for identifying the degree to which native animal species and natural communities are represented in our present-day mix of conservation lands. The mission of the Gap Analysis Program (GAP) is to provide regional assessments of the conservation status of native vertebrate species and natural land cover types and to facilitate the application of this information to land management activities. This is accomplished through the following five objectives: 1: map the land cover of the United States. 2: map predicted distributions of vertebrate species for the U.S. 3: document the representation of vertebrate species and land cover types in areas managed for the long-term maintenance of biodiversity, 4: provide this information to the public and those entities charged with land use research, policy, planning, and management. 5: build institutional cooperation in the application of this information to state and regional management activities. GAP is conducted as state-level projects and is coordinated by the USGS Biological Resources Division (BRD). It is a cooperative effort among regional, state, and federal agencies, and private groups as well as the BRD functions of inventory, monitoring, research, and information transfer. This web site delivers complete details on the GAP program as presently conducted.

Natural Resources Defense Council
http://www.nrdc.org/

The Natural Resources Defense Council's purpose is to safeguard the Earth: its people, its plants and animals and the natural systems on which all life depends. They work to restore the integrity of the elements that sustain life—air, land and water—and to defend endangered natural places. They seek to establish sustainability and good stewardship of the Earth as central ethical imperatives of human society. NRDC affirms the integral place of human beings in the environment. They strive to protect nature in ways that advance the long-term welfare of present and future generations. They work to foster the fundamental right of all people to have a voice in decisions that affect their environment. They seek to break down the pattern of disproportionate environmental burdens borne by people of color and others who face social or economic inequities. Ultimately, NRDC strives to help create a new way of life for humankind, one that can be sustained indefinitely without fouling or depleting the resources that support all life on Earth. Visit this web site for late breaking details on the NRDC's various missions, including their effort to outlaw Dursban. The most widely used insecticide in the country, Dursban is also among the pesticides most hazardous to human health, according to scientific studies and the findings of the U.S. Environmental Protection Agency.

National Wildlife Federation
http://www.nwf.org/

The National Wildlife Federation is the nation's largest member-supported conservation group, uniting individuals, organizations, businesses and government to protect wildlife, wild places, and the environment. For sixty years the National Wildlife Federation has been made up of sensible people saving the real places they know and love. Yes, during this time NWF has become one of the most respected forces for environmental protection in the political arena. Yes, NWF's staff has come to include committed educators, talented litigators, knowledgeable lobbyists, and renowned scientists. But the essence of NWF is and always has been the millions of Americans who join and support NWF with their precious time and hard-earned money. Working with NWF's state affiliates, regional offices, and like-minded organizations, NWF's cadre of committed volunteer activists are what distinguishes NWF among the expanding number of narrowly focused environmental organizations. They are, in many instances, active participants in the natural world, be it through hunting, fishing, gardening, hiking, boating or bird watching. From this participation comes a deep, intuitive knowledge that cannot be gleaned from books: they

know the value and fragility of functioning ecosystems; they know that we are not whole as humans without wild places and wildlife; they know that sustainable communities require a healthy environment as well as a healthy economy.

Oak Ridge National Laboratory Environmental Sciences Division
http://www.esd.ornl.gov/

One of the neatest things on this web site is something called the Fractal Landscape Realizer. What is the Fractal Realizer? The Fractal Realizer generates synthetic landscape maps to users' specifications. The alternative landscape realizations are not identical to the actual maps after which they are patterned, but are similar statistically (i.e., the areas and fractal character of each category are replicated). How does the Fractal Realizer Work? A fractal, or self-affine, pattern generator is used to provide a spatial probability surface for each category in the synthetic map. The Realizer arbitrates contentions among categories such that the fractal patterns of all categories are preserved in the resulting synthetic landscape. Also check out the lab's handy contaminant chemical adsorption models, coupled to simple one-dimensional hydraulic transport models, which you can download for use on your PC. All models were written with Visual Basic 6.0 and are compatible with Windows95/98 and WindowsNT platforms. You can change all significant input parameters for contaminant adsorption chemistry, transport configurations, and see their effects in graphical output. You do not need any other software other than the Windows operating system! Default values forall parameters are provided if you are unsure where or how to begin.

Riverkeeper
http://www.riverkeeper.org/

Riverkeepers do just what their name suggests. They take care of the river so that there are always plenty of fish and the water is clean and safe for everyone who lives around it. The idea comes from England. In the 1960s, Robert H. Boyle brought this idea to America when he wrote a book about the Hudson River. In his book, he said that the

Hudson could use a Riverkeeper. Then he made the Hudson River-keeper a reality. In 1983, the Hudson River Fishermen's Association, (a group Boyle founded), hired John Cronin, a former commercial fisherman and congressional aide, to patrol the Hudson full time. But Cronin does not work alone. He relies on a network of local fishermen, environmental experts and the legal system to stop corporations even as large as Exxon from polluting the Hudson. The fishermen help keep John informed of any suspicious activity on the river, and using the Clean Water Act, which Congress gave the public the right to enforce, Riverkeeper is able to collect evidence and file lawsuits against polluters. This hands-on, "blue-collar environmentalism" is key to the Riverkeeper philosophy. In 1984, attorney Robert F. Kennedy Jr. joined Riverkeeper. Kennedy is Riverkeeper's chief prosecuting attorney, and along with Karl Coplan, he co-directs the Pace Environmental Litigation Clinic where ten students and two professors do nothing but prosecute Hudson River polluters.

Save The Bay (Narragansett Bay)
http://www.savebay.org/

The mission of Save The Bay is to ensure that the environmental quality of Narragansett Bay and its watershed is restored and protected from the harmful effects of human activity. Save The Bay seeks carefully planned use of the Bay and its watershed to allow the natural system to function normally and healthfully, both now and for the future. In defense of Narragansett Bay and its watershed, Save The Bay's actions include: Watching over the activities and programs of government and the citizenry that degrade the environmental quality of the Bay, basin, and watershed. Leading the community by initiating programs and activities that increase the environmental awareness and knowledge of the public. Initiating action that will directly clean up the Bay. Save The Bay believes that education is a vital part of its mission to protect and restore Narragansett Bay. "Explore The Bay" programs connect people to Narragansett Bay andits watershed by emphasizing the significant relationship between this resource and our lives. Using Narragansett Bay's shores, salt ponds and marshes to teach about the natural world, Save The Bay's experiential education programs provide students with the valuable insight into the natural, cultural, aesthetic, and economic importance of Narragansett Bay. Since 1987, Save The Bay has worked with thousands of area school-children and members of the general public through "face to fin" educational programs.

Save The Bay (San Francisco Bay)
http://www.savesfbay.org/

Save The Bay (Save San Francisco Bay Association) seeks to preserve, restore and protect the San Francisco Bay and Sacramento/San Joaquin Delta Estuary as a healthy and biologically diverse ecosystem essential to the well-being of the human and natural communities it sustains. They have stopped thousands of acres of unnecessary fill in the Bay, and they're still fighting against unwise construction that threatens Bay habitat. Save The Bay is forcing pulluters to clean up toxic chemicals in the Bay, so people can fish, windsurf, sail and swim safely. They are making the Bay bigger, by targeting 100,000 acres of Bay and Delta for reclamation. Those areas were long ago diked and drained for farming or salt production. They work with landowners, businesses, citizens and government agencies to restore these "Baylands" to wetlands that provide vital food and habitat for endangered species, and precious open space for future generations. They fight for more fresh water from rivers and streams that feed the Bay to make it healthier. Save The Bay helped stop the Peripheral Canal and win increased water flows for endangered salmon in the Bay-Delta. They are promoting conservation programs to meet Califorinia's water needs without new dams and reservoirs that damage the Bay and its residents.

Sierra Club
http://sierraclub.org/

The advice to "climb the mountains and get their good tidings" has been followed by Sierra Club members since the organization's start, and the pursuit of this goal has played a key role in shaping the Club's history. Years before the founding of the Sierra Club, many of its future leaders and supporters were traveling the mountains of California and sharing with others the wonders they found there. John Muir was chief among these early wilderness explorers and visionaries. A immigrant who had been raised on a Wisconsin farm and educated at the University of Wisconsin, Muir had arrived in California in 1868 planning to stay only a few months before setting off to study Amazon botany. Virtually pennyless, he hired on as a shepherd's assistant, a job that took him to Yosemite Valley—and ultimately changed his life. "I have run wild," he later wrote of the effects of Yosemite's rugged grandeur. "As long as I live," he wrote, "I'll hear waterfalls and birds and winds sing. I'll interpret the rocks, learn the language of flood, storm, and the avalanche. I'll acquaint myself with the glaciers and wild gardens, and get as near the heart of the world as I can." Visit the web site for more info about the Sierra Club, yesterday and today.

Silviculture Laboratory at the University of Washington
http://silvae.cfr.washington.edu/

Come here for cool software. Check out, for starters, the Landscape Management System. The Landscape Management System (LMS) is an evolving application designed to assist in landscape level analysis and planning of forest ecosystems by automating the tasks of stand projection, graphical and tabular summarization, stand visualization, and landscape visualization. LMS is implemented as a Microsoft Windows (TM) application that coordinates the activities of other programs (projection models, visualization tools, etc.) that makeup the overall system. LMS is comprised of many separate programs that make projections, produce graphical or tabular displays, store inventory information, and connect these diverse programs into a cohesive system. Then consider Probabilistic classification of forest structures by hierarchical modelling of the remote sensing process. Satellite sensors observe upwelling radiant flux from the Earth's surface. Classification of forest structures from these measurements is a statistical inference problem. A hierarchical model has been developed by linking several sub-models which represent the image acquisition process and the spatial interaction of the classes. The model for blur assumes the underlying, unobserved image is degraded according to the system point spread function. The model for topographic effects assumes the unblurred pixel values are determined by the corresponding bidirectional reflectance distribution function (BRDF) and the mean spectral reflectance of each class. A discrete Markov random field (MRF) model provides information about the spatial contiguity of the classes.

Sustainable Agriculture World Wide Web Directory
http://www.floridaplants.com/sustainable.htm

Come here for hundreds of great links related to Sustainable Agriculture. Here you'll find Abstracts, Agencies, Animals, and Bibliographies. Here you'll also find info on Crops, Databases, Sustainable Farms, Forests, Grants, Permaculture, Soil and Water. Animal links include: The Department of Tropical Animal Health (part of the University of Edinburgh's Centre for Tropical Veterinary Medicine, CVTM), the Veterinary Field Station of the Royal (Dick) School of Veterinary Studies at Easter Bush (Midlothian), info on the Development of Sustainable Livestock Production in Developing Regions, and more. Additional links give you info on Livestock Behaviour and the Design of Facilities and Humane Slaughter, Livestock Research for Rural Development, The international journal for research into sustainable developing world agriculture (published by Fundación CIPAV, Cali, Colombia), details on Sustainable Ranching, and studies concerning the Use of Genetic Resources for Sustainable Livestock Development. Additional links identify cutting edge methods, tools and strategies for the sustainable development of a range of organic crops in large quantities, the mainteneance of sustainable woodlots, and the continuing refinement of approaches to preserving land and water while at the same time maximizing crop yield.

The Wilderness Society
http://www.wilderness.org/

Founded in 1935, the Wilderness Society works to protect America's wilderness and to develop a nation-wide network of wild lands through public education, scientific analysis and advocacy. Their goal is to ensure that future generations will enjoy the clean air and water, wildlife, beauty and opportunities for recreation and renewal that pristine forests, rivers, deserts and mountains provide. The Wilderness Society is headquartered in Washington, D.C., and has eight regional offices across the country, in Anchorage, Seattle, San Francisco, Boise, Bozeman, Denver, Atlanta and Boston. The Wilderness Society was instrumental in achieving the Wilderness Act, signed into law by President Lyndon B. Johnson in the rose garden of the White House on September 3, 1964. It enabled Congress to set aside selected areas in the national forests, national parks, national wildlife refuges, and other federal lands as units to be kept permanently unchanged by humans; no roads, no structures, no vehicles, no significant impacts of any kind. The 1964 Wilderness Act designated some nine million acres as wilderness. Since then, The Society has helped pass more bills, contributing a total of 104 million acres to the National Wilderness Preservation System.

World Conservation Monitoring Centre
http://www.wcmc.org.uk/

Established by IUCN—The World Conservation Union, the World Wide Fund for Nature (WWF) and the United Nations Environment Programme (UNEP), WCMC is an independent organisation and has become the planet's principal source of global biodiversity information. As an international conservation charity, WCMC provides objective, scientifically rigorous and focused information on global biodiversity. The mission of WCMC is to provide information services on conservation and sustainable use of species and ecosystems, and support others in the development of their own information systems. To support environmental protection, we need first to support others by supplying policy makers, planners and industry worldwide with accurate information on global biodiversity. The three principal services offered by WCMC are: 1. Information Services and Training: facilitating access to information on biological diversity; and helping others to gather, manage, interpret and use information. 2. Biodiversity Monitoring and Assessment Service: assessing the status, value and management of biological diversity. 3. Knowledge Management Services: includes secure storage, sharing and management of data on behalf of other agencies and networks. Come here for extensive links, great tools, superior information, and a healthy dose of hope for humanity and humanity's planet.

ecology mailing lists

EarthNet News mailing list
   sign up at the url http://www.envirocitizen.org/subscribe.html

For a complete directory of dozens more environmental/ecology
   mailing lists, go to the url http://www.themesh.com/ecoml.html

Usenet Environment Newsgroups

alt.earth.system.science

alt.org.sierra-club (Sierra Club)

alt.save.the.earth (General discussions on the environment)

ca.environment (California Only)

ca.environment.earthquakes (California Only)

clari.tw.environment (ClariNet-Commercial Service)

fidonet.environ (Fidonet-Worldwide)

francom.environnement (France)

sci.bio.ecology (General discussions on ecology)

sci.environment (General discussions on environment)

sci.geo.earthquakes

scot.environment(Scotland)

talk.environment (General discussions on environment)

tw.environment (Taiwan)

uiuc.misc.environment (University of Illinois)

uk.environment (United Kingdom)

za.environment (South Africa)

8

CHAOS AND FRACTALS

Applied Chaos Laboratory at Georgia Tech
  http://www.physics.gatech.edu/chaos/main.html

The mission of the Applied Chaos Lab is to deliver on the promise that engineering/physics is a "true" interdisciplinary science. They seek to expand, through creativity and hard work, the understanding of biological and adaptive systems. Such systems, which range from the behavior of coupled nonlinear electronic oscillators to the complex dynamics of the human brain, form the majority of the world around us and present the scientist with enormous challenges and unimaginable opportunities for the advancement of understanding of the natural world. The excitement of discovery and the promise of pushing the limits of science are the daily stimulants that the Applied Chaos Lab is designed to provide. Of special interest is Stimulated Pattern Formation and Synchronization Through Disorder. The normal thinking is that the synchronization an array of nonlinear oscillators—for example Josephson junctions or semiconductor lasers—is most easily achieved if all elements of such an array are identical. Recent work has shown that spatial disorder introduced into coupled oscillators can provide a nucleation for pattern formation and synchronization. It is the lab's intention to exploit upon this intriguing, counterintuitive result, to both understand the role disorder plays in spatial and temporal synchronization of nonlinear systems but to also develop detectors based upon both this principle and of spatio-temporal stochastic resonance.

The Beauty of Chaos

http://i30www.ira.uka.de/%7Eukrueger/fractals/

All images at this web site are pieces with a magnification factor of up to 10e13 cut out of the edge of the mandelbrot set. This set is named after the mathematician Benoit B. Mandelbrot, who discovered their fractal and self replicating structure and therefore founded the modern fractal geometry. It is mathematically described as the connected set of points c within the complex plane. The pictures are generated by computing the iterations for each point within a chosen rectangular area and resolution. The whole mandelbrot set looks like a man made of spheres or apples—therefore it is often called the apple man. This apple man may be found in many of the pictures due to the property of self replication. The points which are not belonging to the mandelbrot set are colored corresponding to the iteration depth at which the exclusion was discovered. The mandelbrot set itself is shown as a black area while areas of other colors are showing the edge of the set. In some cases the color black was also used at the edge for a better optical effect. Visit this web site to explore more than 500 fantastic fractal images.

Carlson's Fractal Gallery
http://sprott.physics.wisc.edu/carlson.htm

Some of these images were created using Clifford Pickover's quartic variation of Ushikis's "Phoenix" Julia set equations: $Z = Z*Z-.5Z + C$, $X = Z*Z-.5Y + C$, $Y = Z$, $Z = X$ (see "The World of Chaos" by Clifford A. Pickover, "Computers in Physics" Sep/Oct 1990). Others were created using a variety of equations, most involving transcendental functions. The colormap for these images consisted of two color ranges, each range varying in intensity linearly from light to dark. Which range was used for a particular pixel depended on whether the number of iterations at bailout was odd or even. The angle formed by a line joining the last two points in the orbit and the real axis was computed. The absolute value of this angle was converted to a colormap index in the proper color range, and the pixel was plotted using that color. Still others were created using a variation of another method developed by Clifford Pickover in which pixels are plotted in certain colors if the absolute value of either the real or imaginary component of Z falls below a specified value. In Carlson's variation of this method, this absolute value was converted to an index into one of two color ranges in the colormap, depending on whether the number of iterations was odd or even.

The Chaos Game
http://math.bu.edu/DYSYS/chaos-game/node1.html

The chaos game starts off as follows. First pick three points at the vertices of a triangle (any triangle works—-right, equilateral, isosceles, whatever). Color one of the vertices red, the second blue, and the third green. Next, take a die and color two of the faces red, two blue, and two green. Now start with any point in the triangle. This point is the seed for the game. (Actually, the seed can be anywhere in the plane, even miles away from the triangle.) Then roll the die. Depending on what color comes up, move the seed half the distance to the appropriately colored vertex. That is, if red comes up, move the point half the distance to the red vertex. Now erase the original point and begin again, using the result of the previous roll as the seed for the next.

That is, roll the die again and move the new point half the distance to the appropriately colored vertex, and then erase the starting point. From here, the complexity of the game grows, as does the complexity of the directions, all of which you'll find in beautiful illustrated detail at this web site.

Chaos at the University of Maryland, College Park
http://www-chaos.umd.edu/

The idea that many simple nonlinear deterministic systems can behave in an apparently unpredictable and chaotic manner was first noticed by the great French mathematician Henri Poincaré. Other early pioneering work in the field of chaotic dynamics were found in the mathematical literature by such luminaries as Birkhoff, Cartwright, Littlewood, Levinson, Smale, and Kolmogorov and his students, among others. In spite of this, the importance of chaos was not fully appreciated until the widespread availability of digital computers for numerical simulations and the demonstration of chaos in various physical systems. This realization has broad implications for many fields of science, and it is only within the past decade or so that the field has undergone explosive growth. It is found that the ideas of chaos have been very fruitful in such diverse disciplines as biology, economics, chemistry, engineering, fluid mechanics, physics, just to name a few. Since the mid-1970s, the Chaos Group at Maryland has done extensive research in various areas of chaotic dynamics ranging from the theory of dimensions, fractal basin boundaries, chaotic scattering, controlling chaos, etc. Visit this web page for complete details on the onbgoing chaos work at Maryland.

Chaos Matrix
http://www.chaosmatrix.com/

"At the time that Chaos Matrix was conceived," writes webmaster Fenwick Rysen, the only website I could find that was devoted to chaos magick was Tzimon's TOOLS of Chaos, and to be honest there wasn't a great deal there at the time. Most of the useful material about chaos magick was scattered around a half-dozen nearly impossible to access FTP servers located in remote parts of the internet. The alt.magick.chaos newsgroup had just been created and was a wonderful resource (it had a high signal-to-noise ratio in its early days), but dejanews and similar services had yet to be created to archive it. So in my own travels I greedily copied anything related to chaos magick that I found on the web onto my own local hard drive—this was mostly plain vanilla ascii files from FTP, threads from a.m.c., and a few posts to some chaos e-lists. I realized very early on that there weren't that many magick sites out there (at the time in 1995), let alone ones devoted specifically to chaos, so after I had learned HTML, it just made sense to put it all online in one place." And we are glad he did.

The Chaos Hypertextbook
http://www.hypertextbook.com/chaos/

In the 1980s, strange new mathematical concepts burst forth from academic isolation to seize the attention of the public. Chaos. A fantastic notion. The study of the uncontainable, the unpredictable, the bizarre. Fractals. Curves and surfaces unlike anything ever seen in mathematics before. Surely, these topics are beyond the comprehension of all but the smartest, most educated, and most specialized

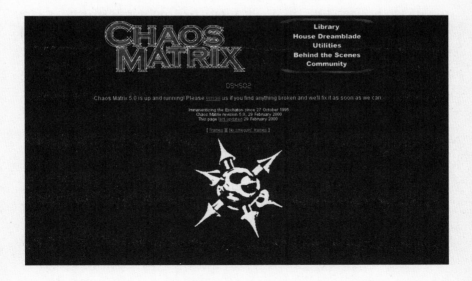

geniuses. Wrong! Chaos, fractals, and the related topic of dimension are really not that difficult. One can devote an academic lifetime to them, of course, but the basic introduction presented in this book is no more difficult to understand than the straight line and the parabola. This great hypertext book explains chaos and fractals in plain vanilla language for non-mathematicians and non-scientists. As the author reminds us: "I wrote this book for anyone with an interest in chaos, fractals, non-linear dynamics, or mathematics in general. It's a moderately heavy piece of work, requiring a bit of mathematical knowledge, but it is definitely not aimed at mathematicians. My background is in physics and I use mathematics extensively in problem solving. Like many educated people, I also enjoy math as a diversion. This is the audience I am writing for."

Chaos Systems in Art, Mathematics and Philosophy
http://www.esotericart.com/fringe/art/chaos.htm

Computers allows us to visualize reality in new ways. We can use them to map the known world, or simulate synthetic worlds looking for correlations and hidden synergies. Many technical studies are enhanced by computer graphics. The study of fractals, or fractional dimensions is one of these. With the right frame of mind, these studies can aid in light travel. They show the hidden order in chaos, and the inherent structure in replication. Self-defining structures are recursive by definition, and can give us a glimpse into mathematical eternity. Fractals are incredibly beautiful, and have an amazing range of application. Fractals were born out of a crisis in mathematics over the importance of continuous non-differentiable functions. The scientific imagination has been slow to accept the importance of these functions because they are very difficult to visualize. Scientists generally reject what they can't imagine and comprehend. Computers have made the visualization much easier. Now fractals are considered fashionable. Texts about them are available in all major bookstores. The web has dozens of sites with fabulous fractal images to see. One of the best tools for creating fractals is a shareware program called FractInt from Stone Soup, which you can download from this site.

Fractal Art Parade

http://www.cootey.com/fractals/index.html

Come here for great "fractal of the month" images, and an archive of same going back to 1994. In particular, check out the artist's Complex Newtons. These are are fascinating equations, that pose a particular challenge: It is tough to choose a palette for these images because of the bichromatic way the palette is mapped across the image. What would usually be a beautiful color spread for a Mandel-type equation would clash horribly on the Complex Newton. Thus they call for painstaking effort inediting the palette. Check out the various great images entitled Hidden Tsunami, Crustacean Doily, Noisy Nebula, Pollen, Halloween Slash, The Spook, Dark Cathedral, Ghoulish Torment, Bronchial Rainbow, Without Form and Void, Centered, Bioluminescent Spiral, Mandelbrot's Nightmare, Earth Star, Doily into Beyond, Iris into Infinity, Inside the Conch, Hot and Cold Spiral, Golden Eye, The Great Dance, Into the Dance, Further Into the Dance, The Dance Partner, The Edge of Night, Purple Kodomo, The Flower Spokes, Ghost Rigging, Night and Day, Flowers in the Dark, Red Stars, Tendrils of Sky, Reaching, Gateway, Ram, Galaxy Born, Soul in the Lattice, Colours in the Night, Atomic Fractal, A Night's Busy Work, and Onset of Fall.

Fractal Clouds

http://climate.gsfc.nasa.gov/~cahalan/FractalClouds/Fractal-Clouds.html

Come here for great images, advice and expertise regarding the fractal modelling of clouds. In particular, check out the information on iterative bounded cascade models in which the probability of horizontal transfer of liquid water approaches zero at small spatial scales. The simplest such model transfers a fraction $f*c^n$ at the nth cascade step, where the parameter f is typically about 1/2 and c about 4/5. The wavenumber spectrum decreases as a power $1-\ln_2(c^2)$, so that when $c = 2^{(-1/3)}$ (near 4/5), then the power = 5/3, close to that observed for California marine stratocumulus. Singular cascade models, by contrast, have nonzero transfers even when the spatial scale approaches zero, and as a result generally produce more slowly decreasing wave-number spectra than observed. Also of interest are fractal studies of Effective Cloud Liquid Water (W_eff) and Effective Cloud Thickness. The value of cloud liquid or optical thickness which allows a plane-parallel computation to obtain the correct cloud albedo when the cloud is inhomogeneous. Bounded cascades have an effective liquid water content (or effective thickness) approximately equal to the mean liquid (or thickness) times exp(-s^2/2) where s is the standard deviation of the natural logarithm of the distribution of liquid water (or optical thickness) in the cloud. Observed values of s vary geo-graphically, seasonally, and diurnally.

Fractal FAQ

http://www.faqs.org/faqs/fractal-faq/

This FAQ is posted monthly to sci.fractals, a Usenet newsgroup about fractals; mathematics and software. This document is aimed at being a reference about fractals, including answers to commonly asked questions, archive listings of fractal software, images, and papers that can be accessed via the Internet using FTP, gopher, or World-Wide-Web (WWW), and a bibliography for further readings. The FAQ does not give a textbook approach to learning about fractals, but a summary of information from which you can learn more about and explore fractals. Care for a sample qustion and answer? OK: What is topological dimension? Answer: A Topological dimension is the "normal" idea of dimension; a point has topological dimension 0, a line has topological dimension 1, a surface has topological dimension 2, etc. For a rigorous definition: A set has topological dimension 0 if every point has arbitrarily small neighborhoods whose boundaries do not intersect the set. A set S has topological dimension k if each point in S has arbitrarily small neighborhoods whose boundaries meet S in a set of dimension k-1, and k is the least nonnegative integer for which this holds.

Fractal Image Encoding

http://inls.ucsd.edu/y/Fractals/

Here is a great collection of links, including very cool download-able software. Consider, in particular, FracCompress, written by Jude Sylvestre. This is a Win-32 application based on a Visual C++ class named CFracComp. This class is based on Yuval Fisher's encoder and decoder C code. The class was written as part of an Honors Thesis in computer science at Hobart and Williams Colleges. It has been tested on Windows NT 3.5, Windows 95 Pre-release and Windows 3.1 with win32s extensions. This class can be considered as an Alpha version. Much of the code is being improved and modified in order to provide support for multiple graphic format, and increasing speed. The class library is able to save images in RAW format. Images can also be saved to the clipboard, but input files must be in RAW image format. The class library is provided AS-IS and as Freeware. A very useful program to use with this application is Paint Pro v3.0. It is able to read and write RAW image files quickly and easily. You can also download another cool item,a fractal coder featuring Entropy based split decision function, Variance based split decision function, Adap-tive splitting thresholds, Output quadtree partition in pgm format, Iterative decoding, Piramidal decoding, and more.

Fractal Video Art Gallery

http://snt.student.utwente.nl/~schol/gallery/

In additional to splendid fractal videos, this web page also con-tains a very useful bio of Benoit B. Mandelbrot, father of fractal sci-ence. Few scientists can claim to have started revolutions or generated new paradigms. IBM Fellow Emeritus Benoit Mandelbrot of the T.J. Watson Research Center is one of them. Mandelbrot, a mathematician at IBM, is an expert in processes with unusual statistical properties, such as those in which a random variable's average or its variance is infinite. His early work in the 1950's and 1960's suggested that the variations in stock market prices, the probabilities of words in Eng-lish, and the fluctuations in turbulent fluids, might be modeled by such strange processes. Later he came to study the geometric features of these processes and realized that one unifying aspect was their self-similarity. In the mid-1970s he coined the word "fractal" as a label for the underlying objects, since they had fractional dimensions. Fractals are shapes or behaviors that have similar properties at all levels of magnification or across all times. Just as the sphere is a concept that unites raindrops, basketballs, and Mars, so fractals are a concept that unites clouds, coastlines, plants, and chaotic attractors.

Fractal Microscope
http://www.ncsa.uiuc.edu/Edu/Fractal/Fractal_Home.html

The Fractal Microscope is a tool for exploring the Mandelbrot set and other fractals. The fractals you will be exploring are mathematical sets with extremely intricate and beautiful structure (so beautiful, in fact, that people using it have refused to believe that it had anything to do with mathematics!). What makes this a microscope? The microscopes we encounter in a laboratory are tools for getting a closer look at something we want to know more about. We put a specimen on a slide and look at it. Often we will see something that we want to look at more closely, so we use a higher powered lens to zoom in on that detail. The Fractal Microscope starts out with what you might call a pre-loaded slide that has a "specimen" on it known as the Mandlebrot set. As we look at this set we can see that, especially around the edges of the black area, there seems to be some detailed structure. What would that look like if we zoomed in on it? That is the kind of question that the Fractal Microscope is designed to answer. Think of this as a remote control microscope with an extremely powerful set of lenses that allow fantastic magnifications. You are the scientist controlling the microscope, and your job is to find out all you can about the structure of the mathematical "specimen".

Fractal Movie Archive
http://graffiti.u-bordeaux.fr/MAPBX/roussel/fractals/anim.html

Enjoy more than 200 fantastic fractal animations! Contributors include such great fractal artists and researchers as Kevin Adams (4 animations), Ian Badcoe (21 animations), Dave Bargna (1 animation), John Beale (1 animation), Booker C. Bense (1 animation), Eric Bigas (14 animations), Bruce Dawson (1 animation), Eric Deren (1 animation), Scott Draves (4 animations), Geoff Dutton (2 animations), Gerald A. Edgar (3 animations), Jim Grimes (1 animation), Nicolas Guerin (10 animations), Mike Henderson (2 animations), Frank M. Kappe (1 animation), Robert Kimmel (2 animations), Ara A. Kotchian (1 animation), Dave Kurtz (1 animation), Francois Le Coat (1 animation), Cyrille Le Cor (10 animations), Marvin Lipford (42 animations), Pascal Massimino (2 animations), Paul Melson (5 animations), Denis Pack (3 animations), Jason Pratt (6 animations), Eric Ostar Schol (7 animations), David Shortt (1 animation), Jason Stajich (1 animation), Marc Stengel (5 animations), Chris Ullrich (4 animations), Steve Vallis (1 animation), Ray Waldin (3 animations), Paul Way (14 animations). The animations include Julia sets, plasma, Mandelbrot sets, Mandelbrot waves, Newton fractals of the 2nd and third order, flybys through the Mandelbrot set, Ray-traced and fragtree images, fractals wrapped around and transitting on spheres, and much more.

Fractulus

http://www.fractalus.com/

"Once upon a time,," write the webmasters of Fractulus, "a fractal artist put up a web site. It's a story with a thousand variations. Web sites go up and down every day all over the world, and nobody cares. Personal web sites cause about as much stir on the net as a sneeze into your morning coffee—enough to make the person next to you say 'Yuck', but totally unnoticed across the street. Such is life." The goal of the proprietors of Fractulus is to show you the very best in fractal art. There are many reasons this site is still on the net, after nearly three years. "Mainly it's because we just love what we do," they write. "It's fun, relaxing, and an outlet for creativity. We hope you like what you see, and that you will come back again—we are always adding new material." Special care has been taken in the construction of this web site to have it work correctly (or at least reasonably so) in all major browsers, at all display sizes, and in all color depths. We do recommend, though, that your display be set to at least 800x600 in thou-

sands (not 256) colors. There are also a few pages which are specifically designed to exploit new browser features (DHTML, Java, etc.)
and these will not work correctly with older browsers.

Gallery of Interactive Geometry
http://www.geom.umn.edu/apps/gallery.html

Come here to download such cool software as WebPisces. Pisces is
a Platform for Implicit Surfaces and Curves and the Exploration of
Singularities. The goal of Pisces is to provide tools for researchers and
educators who want to compute the set of points that satisfy some
equation. Pisces is potentially useful to mathematicians and scientists
in a variety of fields, including algebraic geometry, astrophysics,
computer-aided geometric design, and dynamical systems. By using
interactive features of the World-Wide Web, it is possible to run Pisces
remotely at the Geometry Center and to have the results of the computation shipped across the Web to any graphics terminal. Although
Pisces can compute implicitly-defined curves in arbitrary dimension
and can also compute some implicitly-defined surfaces, this demonstration is restricted to the case of planar curves (that is, zero sets of
two-variable functions) in order to simplify the user-interface to
Pisces. Furthermore, Pisces contains five different algorithms that can
compute planar level sets, and the user can fully control the way that
each algorithm works. In this demonstration, However, you are only
allowed to choose from one of two algorithms, and you are not
allowed to alter the parameters for that algorithm.

Mandelbrot Exhibition of the Virtual Museum of Computing
*http://archive.comlab.ox.ac.uk/other/museums/computing/man-
delbrot.html*

What a terrific collection of links and resources. For historical
background, see short biographies of Benoit Mandelbrot (largely
responsible for the present interest in Fractal Geometry) and Gaston
Julia (of Julia set fame) in the MacTutor History of Mathematics
archive. Read an introduction to Julia and Mandelbrot Sets. Access
many beautiful Mandelbrot pictures and other fractal pictures and

Gallery of Interactive Geometry:

In order to enjoy this exhibit, you will need a Web browser that understands graphical Fill-Out Forms. See our list of browsers for more information.

Looking for math teaching resources? Check out COMAP!

WebPisces

This web-based interface to the Pisces program allows you to compute implicitly defined curves in the plane. You can choose from several pre-defined functions, and can modify their parameters and domains.

Build a Rainbow

How are rainbows formed? Why do they only occur when the sun is behind the observer? If the sun is low on the horizon, at what angle in the sky should we expect to see a rainbow? This laboratory, developed as part of the University of Minnesota Calculus Initiative, helps to answer these and other questions by examining a mathematical model of light passing through a water droplet.

QuasiTiler

Generate the famous Penrose tilings, or design your own nonperiodic tilings of the plane. In the process, you can select and visualize plane cross-sections of a lattice in anywhere from 3 up to 13 dimensions!

Kali
Kali-Jot *(with free-hand drawing, for X Mosaic only)*

Kali is an interactive editor for symmetric patterns of the plane, as seen in some of the woodcuts of M.C. Escher. It's also a fun way to learn about the 17 crystallographic symmetry groups of the plane.

animations are available from France. Try the powerful Mandelbrot and Julia Set Explorer, an interactive and colourful utility using a form with plenty of options and an "active map" image. Explore the Mandelbrot set interactively using an "active map" image. Use the Mandelbrot Exploreration web page from Greece, with its powerful selectable zoom in/out and drawing area. (This is extremely good if you have a reasonably fast Internet connection, otherwise forget about it.) LISTEN to the sound of Mandelbrot sets! View Mandelbrot movies from Department of Mathematics, University of Zagreb, Croatia. And get much more including Web references for Julia and Mandelbrot sets, on-line image generators, images and movies, courses and other information, software, fractal Frequently Asked Questions and a bibliography. Also check out Susan Stepney's wonderful online book entitled "Complexity and Self-Organisation: Chaos and Fractals."

Mandelbrot Explorer
http://surf.to/JMEnterprises

Learn how fractals work, and have fun exploring the most famous fractal of them all—the Mandelbrot Set. Download a free copy of Mandelbrot Explorer, which lets you interactively explore the Mandelbrot set. Mandelbrot Explorer offers a variety of powerful features, including: color cycling; user-definable fractal equations and palettes; support for up to 24-bit color fractals; the ability to save and restore interesting locations; a powerful zoom command; and the ability to turn any area of an image into your current Windows wallpaper. Software features: ntuitive user interface: Fast! User-definable fractal equations. User-definable palette (up to 24-bit colour). Colour cycling. Save and Restore interesting locations. Easily set (with 1 button!) cool areas as your Windows wallpaper. Zoom in over 1,000,000,000,000,000 times! Animated (ie. fun!) zoom in and zoom out. Comprehensive on-line help, including description of the Mandelbrot Set and its calculation. Runs on Windows 95, 98, NT and 2000. Note: This page makes extensive use of the Portable Network Graphics (PNG) format because it's the most appropriate for screen grabs. JPEGs are around if your browser can't cope. No matter how you cut it, however, Mandelbrot Explorer is not only a great learning tool, but also a great digital toy.

Mandelbrot and Julia Set Explorer & Generator
http://aleph0.clarku.edu/~djoyce/julia/explorer.html

These two explorers are the brainchildren of David E. Joyce, Associate Professor of Mathematics and Computer Science, Clark University, Worcester, MA. Plug in your parameters and create your own vibrant fractal images with a minimum of fuss, muss or bother. To begin with, you only see one image, the Mandelbrot set as a subset of the complex plane. The form is initially set so that if you click on that image, you'll get a second image on the form, namely, the Julia set determined by the particular point in the complex plane that you clicked at. If you continue to click on the Mandelbrot set, the Julia set image will be replaced by other Julia sets. You can pretty easily get a pretty good idea how the Julia sets are related to the Mandelbrot set. There are various ways you can view the Mandelbrot set. Typically, and by default, the μ plane is chosen. Then the iterating function is $f(z) = z2-\mu$. The set of quadratic functions can be parameterized in different ways. Another common parameter is lambda, and the iterating function is $f(z) = lambda\ z(1-z)$. The relation between lambda and μ is that μ = lambda2/4−lambda/2. Geometrically, converting from μ to lambda doubles the plane around the singularity of the cardioid which converts the cardioid into a pair of circles, and all the other circles remain circles.

Mandelbrot Set Java Based Explorer
http://www.mindspring.com/~chroma/mandelbrot.html

This is a little applet that lets you explore the Mandelbrot set. The Mandelbrot set is a type of infinitely complex mathematical object known as a fractal. No matter how much you zoom in, there is still more to see. There are many strange and beautiful sights to see when you explore the Mandelbrot set, ranging from the sublime to the psychedelic. In this applet, you can set the area you want to zoom in on by holding down the mouse button and dragging on the picture. You can also set the coordinates that you want to look at in the four text boxes. Press "Zoom In" when you are satisfied with the bounds you want to see. For instance, try changing "Xmax" to 1.1 and then click on "Zoom In." The program runs much faster if your computer has a floating point math processor such as that found in the Intel Pentium. You might try setting the size to "Small" until you find an interesting area and then have a look at the "Big" version. Also note that this applet seems to stop all other processing in Netscape, but looks OK with Sun's appletviewer. The Solaris version of Netscape won't run this applet at all, at least as of version 2.0b6.

Clifford A. Pickover Home Page
http://pickover.com/

The Los Angeles Times recently proclaimed, "Pickover has published nearly a book a year in which he stretches the limits of computers, art and thought." Pickover received first prize in the Institute of Physics' "Beauty of Physics Photographic Competition". His computer graphics have been featured on the cover of many popular magazines, and his research has recently received considerable attention by the press—including CNN's "Science and Technology Week", The Discovery Channel, Science News, The Washington Post, Wired,

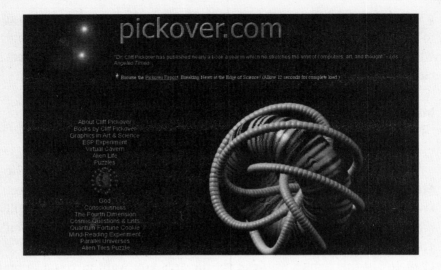

and The Christian Science Monitor—and also in international exhibitions and museums. OMNI magazine recently described him as "Van Leeuwenhoek's twentieth century equivalent". Scientific American several times featured his graphic work, calling it "strange and beautiful, stunningly realistic". Wired magazine wrote, "Bucky Fuller thought big, Arthur C. Clarke thinks big, but Cliff Pickover outdoes them both." Among his many patents, Pickover has received U.S. Patent 5,095,302 for a 3-D computer mouse, 5,564,004 for strange computer icons, and 5,682,486 for black-hole transporter interfaces to computers. Visit pickover.com for complete details on the life, work and thought of this inquisitive genius who so often spends his days riding the crest of the cutting edge in fractal science and chaos theory.

Spanky Fractal Database
http://spanky.triumf.ca/

As the webmaster writes: "This is a collection of fractals and fractal related material for free distribution on the net. Most of the software was gathered from various ftp sites on the internet and it is generally freeware or shareware. Please abide by the guidelines set down in the individual packages. I would also like to make a disclaimer here. This page points to an enormous amount of information and no single person has the time to thoroughly check it all. I have tested software when I had the resources, and read through papers when I had the time, but other than certifying that it is related to fractals I can't assume any other responsibility. Thanks to everyone who has contacted me, pointing out new and interesting fractal material. I try to respond to everyone but sometimes things just get too hectic or I get too disorganized. I also appreciate all your comments and criticisms, but please understand that it is impossible for me to impliment everything or reply to all." The collection of images is sizable, impressive, and brilliantly beautiful. As a bonus, you get the option for several splendid software downloads allowing access to great code for creating your own fractal images.

Three-D Strange Attractors and Similar Objects

http://ccrma-www.stanford.edu/~stilti/images/chaotic_attractors/nav.html

The objects seen in these pictures are calculated by iterating some function (next_point = fn(current_point)) many times (easily in the millions of iterations, often many more). The locus of all points hit by this iteration is the attractor of the function. The shape of the attractor is dependant on the parameters of the function, and sometimes on the initial point (although the functions used have attractors which are not dependant on the inital point). The pictures named fsh*.jpg were computed using a slight variant of the formula given in *Computers, Pattern, Chaos, and Beauty* by Clifford Pickover. This method can also render Quaternion Julia Sets by virtue of the Inverse Iteration Method, which computes a Julia set by iteratively calculating the inverse of the Julia set formula (forward: $z = z*z + c$, inverse: $z = +/- sqrt(z-c)$). Note that two inverses exist. In operation, one inverse is chosen randomly each iteration. The points in this iteration jump around on the boundary of the Julia set, forming a surface.

Unfortunately, certain points on the boundary are visited quite rarely, so will fill in very slowly. As luck would have it, these areas are some of the more interesting features of the sets, so Julia sets computed with this method are often incomplete.

Waterloo Fractal Compression Project
http://links.uwaterloo.ca/

The Waterloo Fractal Compression Project is part of a general research programme dedicated to the study of fractal analysis and Iterated Function Systems/Fractal Transforms from both theoretical as well as practical perspectives. The research has been funded primarily from grants from the Natural Sciences and Engineering Research Council of Canada (NSERC). It is also part of a international collaborative project involving the University of Waterloo, Ecole Polytechnique de l'Universite de Montreal, the University of Verona and INRIA Rocquencourt, France. One of the primary goals of this collaboration is to develop a new generation of image and signal compression methods which incorporate "fractal based" methods. The Waterloo research programme developed primarily from the collaboration between B. Forte and E.R. Vrscay of the Department of Applied Mathematics. (Since 1989, Prof. Forte has held a chair at the University of Verona in Italy.

Waterloo Fractal Compression Project

Table of Contents

1. Introduction

The Waterloo Fractal Compression Project is part of a general research programme dedicated to the study of fractal analysis and Iterated Function Systems/Fractal Transforms from both theoretical as well as practical perspectives. The research has been funded primarily from grants from the Natural Sciences and Engineering Research Council of Canada (NSERC). It is also part of a international collaborative project involving the University of Waterloo, Ecole Polytechnique de l'Universite de Montreal, the University of Verona and INRIA Rocquencourt, France. One of the primary goals of this collaboration is to develop a new generation of image and signal compression methods which incorporate "fractal based" methods. Some further details are given in Section 5 below.

The Waterloo research programme developed primarily from the collaboration between B. Forte and E.R. Vrscay of the Department of Applied Mathematics. (Since 1989, Prof. Forte has held a chair at the University of Verona in Italy. He currently holds an Adjunct Professorship to the AM Department and the collaboration with Prof. Vrscay continues.) The focus of this research has been the mathematical theory of Iterated Function Systems (IFS), in particular, the so-called "Inverse Problem of Approximation Using IFS".

Iterated Systems, Inc., the company founded by Michael Barnsley, formerly of Georgia Institute of Technology, has shown that fractal compression methods are viable competitors in the areas of image processing and communications. However, here is still much work to be done regarding the theoretical basis for such fractal transform methods as well as, of course, the practical/computational aspects. In fact, we have found that advances in the mathematical theory of IFS/fractal transforms have led to newer and more powerful practical algorithms for

He currently holds an Adjunct Professorship to the AM Department and the collaboration with Prof. Vrscay continues.) The focus of this research has been the mathematical theory of Iterated Function Systems (IFS), in particular, the so-called "Inverse Problem of Approximation Using IFS".

Mailing Lists:

N-LINEAR

    Chaos, Complexity, & Related Theories as they relate to Social Science

    Send "subscribe" message to: listserv@tamvm1.tamu.edu

Newsgroups:

alt.magick.chaos
alt.chaos
alt.sci.fractals

9

CHEMISTRY

Analytical Chemistry Databases and Publications
http://www.nist.gov/srd/analy.htm

The NIST(NATIONAL INSTITUTE OF STANDARDS & TECHNOL-OGY)/EPA/NIH Mass Spectral Library database is the product of a multiyear, comprehensive evaluation and expansion of the world's most widely used mass spectral reference library. The online NIST Chemistry WebBook contains IR spectra for over 7500 compounds, mass spectra for over 10,000 compounds, and UV/VIS spectra for over 400 compounds. Here you have Mass Spectra, Infrared Data, Surface Data, Diffraction Data, and UV/VIS information. The databases are updated and expanded on a regular basis. These PC databases have sophisticated software that enables searches taking only seconds. The National Institute of Standards and Technology is an agency of the U.S. Department of Commerce's Technology Administration. Established in 1901, NIST strengthens the U.S. economy and improves the quality of life by working with industry to develop and apply technology, measurements, and standards. It carries out this mission through a portfolio of four major programs: Measurements and Standards Laboratories, Advanced Technology Program, Manufacturing Extension Partnership, and Baldrige National Quality Award. NIST has an annual budget of about $800 million, employs about 3,330 people, and primarily in two locations Gaithersburg, Md., and Boulder, Colo.

Biological Mass Spectrometry Software
http://base-peak.wiley.com/msi/mssw.html

Download great software that includes: Isotope Pattern Calculator v1.6.6 for Macintosh (113k Download)—a shareware program that calculates isotopic ratio patterns for molecular fragments, Java Protein Analysis Tools (JPAT)—Java and JavaScript utilities for Mass Spectometry and peptide mapping, JCAMP-DX Interactive Mass Spectrum Viewer for Windows—a freeware program for interactive viewing of mass spectra, MASP for Windows—a freeware program predicting fragmentation-free mass spectra of libraries prepared by combinatorial synthesis, MMCalc v2.0 for Macintosh (54k Download)—a simple freeware program for the calculation of molecular and formula weights and elemental compositions, MoleCalc2.0 for Macintosh (161K download)—a Demo version of a molecular weight calculator program, Molecular Weight Calculator—a Freeware molecular weight and percent composition calculator for Windows 95, 3.x, and DOS, MSEQ Magnetic Sector Calculator (96K download)—a small Macintosh program that solves the equation: $m/q = r2*B2/E$, MolMass—a java applet that calculates all possible molecule masses on the basis the isotopes of the constituent atoms, and much, much more of value an interest to professional and amateur chemists alike.

The Boron-Mediated Aldol Reaction
http://www.ch.cam.ac.uk/MMRG/aldol1.html

These pages describe some of the results in modelling Z-enolborinates and provide the reader with the opportunity to manipulate the structures. In order to do this, you must have a program linked to Mosaic that is capable of reading pdb files. If you are using a unix workstation, Xmol and Rasmol are both suitable. If you are using a Macintosh, choose Preferences ... from the Option menu, click on Helper Applications ... and use the new menu to link files with a pdb extension to a program than can display them, such as Kinemage or CSC Chem3D Viewer. This web site is a joint effort by Dr Ian Paterson and Dr Jonathan Goodman at the University of Cambridge, and by Professor Cesare Gennari and Professor Anna Bernardi at the University of Milan. The research interests of all four scientists ranges across the total synthesis of various biologicallyactive natural products and structural analogues to the discovery and development of new synthetic methods, with particular interest in asymmetric reactions. Their focus is always on investigating organic structures and reactions using both organic synthesis and computational chemistry. Synthetic results lead to improved calculations, which then inspire new experiments.

Center for Chemical Education/Terrific Science Kits
http://www.terrificscience.org/

We all benefit from better science education. Today's students are tomorrow's leaders, voters, and employees. Miami University's Center for Chemical Education (CCE) brings chemistry and the companion sciences to life for teachers and students at all levels. Through programs begun in the mid-1980s, CCE fosters quality hands-on, minds-on chemical education that encourages teachers and students to work together to solve scientific challenges, think critically, and use their powers of observation. The Center for Chemical Education, through its ever-expanding nationwide network of educators and private-sector partners, has already reached about 12,500 teachers who teach more than 1 million students each year. CCE offers a variety of summer and academic-year workshop-style courses and noncredit academies for K-12 and college educators. While each workshop has a unique focus, all reflect current pedagogical approaches in science education, cutting-edge academic and industrial research topics, and classroom applications for teachers and students. Some courses are offered in a short course format, which provides opportunities for educators to enrich their science teaching in a limited amount of time. All courses offer graduate credit. Noncredit academies allow CCE graduates and other teachers to attend special one-day sessions presented by leading science educators from around the United States.

ChemCenter

http://www.ChemCenter.org/

The ACS is a self-governed individual membership organization that consists of 161,000 members—60% from industry, at all degree levels. This provides ample opportunity for peer interaction, regardless of your professional or scientific interests. There are 34 ACS divisions, representing a wide range of disciplines for chemists, chemical engineers and technicians. The ACS seeks to: Promote the public's perceptions and understanding of chemistry and the chemical sciences through public outreach programs and public awareness campaigns; Involve the Society's 161,000 members in improving the public's perception of chemistry; Assist the federal government with advice on scientific and technological issues involving the chemical sciences; Enrich professionals in academia and private industry through development programs, peer interactions & continuing educational courses; Host national, regional and local section meetings for the exchanging of ideas, information and chemical research discoveries; Provide career development assistance and employment

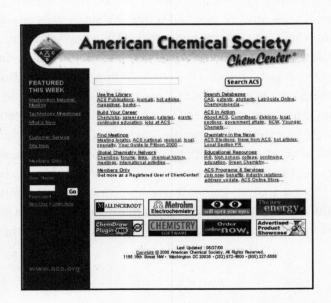

opportunities for students & professionals in academia & private industry; Foster communication and understanding between members, the chemical industry, the government and the community to enhance the quality of scientific research, support economic progress, and insure public health & safety. Investing in volunteer efforts in any organization can provide an alternate management or professional training track which might not be available through the full-time employer. In addition, involvement in the ACS will provide professional and peer relationships that can broaden your technical and interpersonal skills, thus challenging you and enriching your life.

Chemfinder

http://chemfinder.camsoft.com/

It's one thing to pop over to Lycos and do a search for all references to Aluminum Hydroxide. It's another thing to actually find them—especially if the information you want is at a site in Australia under the listing Aluminium Hydroxide. Or if there is simply a passing mention of the compound with CAS RN 21645-51-2. Or a compound with the molecular formula $Al(OH)3$. By working from a single master list of chemical compounds, the ChemFinder WebServer avoids these problems, and lets you find the information you want, faster. In generating this database, the webmasters have also taken pains to identify and correct the obvious errors (like 'mehtyl', as well as invalid CAS RNs) that account for 3-5% of of all chemical information on the WWW. "Very likely," write the webmasters, "we have introduced some new and exciting mistakes of our own, but we are confident that the overall quality of the ChemFinder WebServer data far surpasses the bulk of the information that it indexes. Because the ChemFinder Web-Server is a chemical database, it can also provide information that a general-purpose WWW index cannot, including physical property data and 2D chemical structures. This information is somewhat sparse at the moment, but is very good for the several thousand most-common compounds. The Webmasters are constantly working on getting more data, and they expect the ChemFinder WebServer only to keep improving."

Chemical Abstracts Service
http://info.cas.org/

Chemical Abstracts principal databases, Chemical Abstracts (CA), and REGISTRY now include about 15 million document records and more than 24 million substance records respectively. CAS also produces databases of chemical reactions, commercially available chemicals, listed regulated chemicals, and compounds claimed in patents. CAS is a division of the American Chemical Society. CAS is the producer of the largest and most comprehensive databases of chemical information. CAS Registry Numbers (often referred to as CAS RNs or CAS Numbers) are unique identifiers for chemical substances. A Registry Number itself has no inherent chemical significance but provides an unambiguous way to identify a chemical substance or molecular structure when there are many possible systematic, generic, proprietary, or trivial names. CAS Registry Numbers are used in many other public and private databases as well as chemical inventory listings and of course are included in all CAS produced databases. CAS offers print, CD-ROM, online, desktop, and web based access to databases covering science, engineering, technology, patents, business information, and much more. These products are designed to accommodate a wide range of information needs, whether you are an infrequent searcher who only needs a few quick answers, or a professional searcher who requires a more powerful and comprehensive set of search tools.

Crossroads Chemical Backgrounders
http://www.crossroads.nsc.org/chemicals.cfm

Here is a great safety reference for everyone working with chemicals. It includes details of every chemical for which documented evidence on reactive hazards has been found. Nearly 5000 chemicals are covered, and there are just as many entries for hazards involving two or more compounds. The profiles describe how to work safely with these chemicals, what to do in case of spills or exposure to them, and how to prevent exposure. Additional links click to such resources as Cornell University's Planning, Design and Construction MSDS database, which provides a compilation of approximately 325,000 MSDSs in a searchable format. The MSDS database is derived from U.S. Government Department of Defense MSDS database, The Vermont SIRI database, MSDSs from Cornell University Environmental Health and Safety, and other Cornell departments. Click once more and connect to: The EXtension TOXicology NETwork (EXTOXNET) is a searchable online toxicology database that provides pesticide information profiles, toxicology information briefs, toxicology issues of concern, fact sheets and newsletters. This site is a cooperative effort of University of California-Davis, Oregon State University, Michigan State University, and Cornell University.

Chemical Patents Plus
http://casweb.cas.org/chempatplus/

U.S. patents are issued every Tuesday. Full text for those patents is typically available from Chemical Patents Plus by Thursday morning, and page images become available incrementally by the end of the day. Chemical Patents Plus offers the full text for all classes of patents issued by the U.S. Patent and Trademark Office from 1975 to the present, including partial coverage from 1971-1974. Complete patent page images are available for patents issued from 1 January 1995. Chemical Patents Plus includes CAS Registry Numbers and complete subject indexing for all chemical patents covered in Chemical Abstracts, based on either the U.S. patent or an earlier issued foreign equivalent patent document of the same patent family. When available, you can request the 2-D and 3-D structure views for the CAS Registry Numbers for specific substances that are identified in the patent claims. Chemical Patents Plus offers easy, thorough, free searching for all U.S. patents by patent number, basic text, CAS Registry Number, CAS chemical indexing, inventor or assignee name, or in any of a variety of other specific patent data fields or combinations. Chemical Patents Plus complements the CAS Document Detective Service by delivering U.S. patents in a variety of text and image formats, as complete patent documents and as individual patent sections and patent pages.

Chemistry & Environmental Dictionary

http://EnvironmentalChemistry.com/yogi/chemistry/dictionary/

This dictionary contains definitions for most chemistry environmental and other technical terms used on this site as well as many other chemistry and environmental terms. The definitions are simple and to-the-point. Examples: "Kelvin (absolute temperature): the temperature scale used in chemistry, physics and some engineering calculations. Zero degrees Kelvin (–273 centigrade) is the temperature at which all thermal motion ceases. To convert from Kelvin into centigrade subtract 273 from the Kelvin temperature." "Atomic Mass Unit (AMU): a mass unit that is exactly 1/12th the mass of a carbon 12 (C12) atom (approximately 1.67E –24g)." "Molar Mass: is a unit that enables scientists to calculate the weight of any chemical substance, be it an element or a compound. Molar mass is the sum of all of the atomic masses in a formula." "Proton: a particle of matter with a positive electrical charge and a mass of 1 amu or 1.67E –24g. Although a proton has a mass 1837 times greater than an electron, it is nearly identical in mass to a neutron. Protons are constituents of the nuclei of all elements and an elements atomic number is dependent upon how many protons an element has."

Chemistry Central

http://users.senet.com.au/~rowanb/chem/

This great directory delivers: Basic Atomic Information, Information on the Periodic Table of Elements, Information on Chemical Bonding (metallic, ionic, covalent), Information on Organic Chemistry, and more. Outstanding chemistry links include: Yahoo's Science: Chemistry category, Yahoo's Chemistry Software category, Galaxy's Internet Chemistry Resource page, UMD's Chemistry Resources, Internet Chem Pointers, The Analytical Chemistry Springboard, A large list of Chem Teaching Resources, Jump to the Education Index Chemistry area, Links for Chemists—a free searchable chemistry index containing over five thousand chemistry resources in more than fifty categories, Database of Chemistry URLs, Rolf Claessen's Chemistry Index, SciSeek—a science and nature Internet Directory, Chemistry (and

Physics & Electronics) Software. You also get general chemistry pages related to the Usenet sci.chem newsgroup, UFL's Chem home page, and the Department of Chemistry at UCLA home page. Point and click for several great online periodic tables: WWW version of the Periodic Table of Elements, Web Periodic Table with fact sheets for all elements and includes some Bohr models, Gopher version of the Periodic table, Chemical Societies Network Periodic Table, and more. Also check out: The Chemist's Art Gallery, Pages devoted to Crystal Chemistry (text is in Italian), The Useful Chemistry Publishing website (home for the publishers of the great 'Save Time and Money through Chemistry' book), Some spectroscopic tools, the Wicked Science Bookstore, and Chemistry Jobs online.

CHEMystery

http://library.thinkquest.org/3659/

CHEMystery: An Interactive Guide to Chemistry, was created solely for the 1996 ThinkQuest Internet Contest. The production of this site was conducted at students' homes and the testing and research was conducted at the Process Modeling Laboratory of the State University of New York at Stony Brook. All material has been either created by the team itself or borrowed with written consent from other sources including World Wide Web sites. As the webmasters write: "We have created CHEMystery, a virtual chemistry textbook, to provide an interactive guide for high school chemistry students. In addition, CHEMystery allows you to further expand your chemistry knowledge by letting you interact with other Internet resources on the World Wide Web." From atoms and molecules to states of matter, chemical reactons, atomis structure, bonding, energy, thermodynamics, organic chemistry and nuclear reactions, CHEMystery covers virtually every aspect of chemistry. Don't bother approaching this site with the Netscape browser, as something about the programming of these pages causes them to crash Netscape. Knock on this door only with Microsoft Internet Explorer. This all comes to you courtesy of ThinkQuest—www.thinkquest.org—a unique and innovative Internet portal specializing in education-related content.

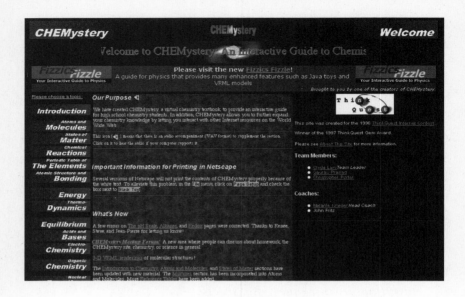

ChemWeb

http://chemweb.com/

The Internet has increasingly become the first port of call for locating chemical information. Users are accustomed to having free access to information on the internet but are often frustrated by the lack of quality of many web sites. This is usually caused by lack of investment and long-term effort in maintaining web sites. This is where ChemWeb comes in. ChemWeb is the World Wide Club for the Chemical Community, and as such has aimed from the start to provide a valuable and ongoing information source for chemistry research and communication. ChemWeb is one of the first Web services to be powered by Silicon Graphics Inc.'s Origin 2000 server, which supports all ChemWeb databases and information management technologies. The Origin 2000 server was chosen for its exceptional speed and responsiveness and because it is the most appropriate platform to run the MDL ISIS software and Chemscape. The live ChemWeb system operates on a network of Pentium machines, linked to the Silicon Graphics Origin 2000 processor via an Ethernet link operating at 100 Mbits/sec. Text searching is performed by the purpose-written search software, BiblioteK. BiblioteK was originally written for BioMedNet, but has been further developed for ChemWeb. It uses multi-level, tree-structured indexing to ensure fast searching, and it enables users to display increasingly detailed levels of information.

Global Intructional Chemistry
http://www.ch.ic.ac.uk/GIC/

This rich web page includes links to a set of practice problems in Pericyclic Mechanisms, prepared by Henry Rzepa for the for a second year course at the Department of Chemistry, Imperial College ... a consideration of the use of two-dimensional NMR and other spectroscopic data to interpret the three dimensional structures of molecules in solution ... and a wonderful Structural Classification of Proteins database. (Nearly all proteins have structural similarities with other proteins and, in some of these cases, share a common evolutionary origin. The SCOP database, created by manual inspection and abetted by a battery of automated methods, aims to provide a detailed and comprehensive description of the structural and evolutionary relationships between all proteins whose structure is known. As such, it provides a broad survey of all known protein folds, detailed information about the close relatives of any particular protein, and a framework for future research and classification.) Additional links address the Principles of Protein Structure, MOPAC modelling, statistics for chemistry, the CAUT computational chemistry project, stereochemistry, Asymmetric Synthesis, Valence Shell Electron Pair Repulsion Theory, Mechanisms of Organometallic Transformations, and much, much more addressing all aspects of chemistry instruction around the world.

Hazardous Chemical Database
http://ull.chemistry.uakron.edu/erd/

This database will allow the user to retreive information for any of 2662 hazardous chemicals or 'generic' entries based on a keyword search. Potential keywords include names, formula and registry numbers (CAS, DOT, RTECS and EPA). This data base and the information it contains were independently compiled by the author—Dr. James K.

Hardy or The University of Akron Chemistry Department, from a large number of sources, and the data included as well as the manner in which it is presented have been independently chosen by the author to provide what is deemed to be an academic publication. Among the published references available, particular mention should be made of 2000 Emergency Response Guidebook ERG2000, 2000; Hazardous Chemicals Data NFPA 49, PC-49-94, 1994; and The Merck Index, 11th edition, 1989. Dr. Hardy gives you a number of different search options.Take your pick.

Description Search: Simply describe the information that you want. For example, "Lead nitrate." Question Search: Ask a question that you want answered. For example, " What are the explosive limit for benzene?" Keyword Search: List important keywords relevant to your search topic. For example, "What are the explosive limit for benzene?" Boolean Keyword Search: Refine a keyword search using boolean operators.

Links for Chemists
http://www.liv.ac.uk/Chemistry/Links/links.html

Sponsored by The Royal Society of Chemistry and Advanced Chemistry Development Inc., this web site features more than 7500 Chemistry resources on the WWW. The links include connection for a free download of ACD/ChemSketch 4.0 Freeware software. This fantastic Windows software constitutes an absolutely splendid all-purpose chemical drawing and graphics package. Use templates or free-hand. Click and draw molecules, ions, stereobonds, text, polygons, arrows, etc. Automatic calculation of MW, and formula. See estimates of density, refractive index, molar volume, etc.—all with just a few clicks of your mouse. The latest version of the software includes new tools for drawing radicals and ion-radicals quickly and easily, supports Long File Names, and delivers instant on-line access to ACD/Labs prediction modules. Download and install ACD/I-Lab Add-on for ChemSketch, draw your molecule in ChemSketch 4.0, click on I-Lab button and your input molecule will be immediately sent to the Interactive Lab for any number of predictions: NMR spectra, log P and pKa, IUPAC name generation, and so on. ACD/ChemSketch 4.0 Freeware package now includes ACD/3D Viewer that allows you to convert two-dimensional structures from ACD/ChemSketch into their three-dimensional counterparts and view, measure and "handle" them in virtual 3D.

Making Matter
http://www.ill.fr/dif/3D-crystals/

There are only about 100 kinds of atoms in all the Universe, and whether these atoms form trees or tyres, ashes or animals, water or the air we breath, depends on how they are put together. The same atoms are used again and again. Structure determines not only the appearance of materials, but also their properties.

When an electrical insulator can become a superconductor, a pencil a diamond, a common cold a deadly virus, we begin to understand how important it is to understand the structure of materials. Every year we are making rapid progress in developing new tools to understand structure; X-rays and accelerators, electron microscopes and nuclear reactors are among many physical and chemical techniques. One of the most important tools is of course the computer, both for calculating structures and visualising them.

Combining computers with communication means that the secrets of structure, and the beauty of structure, can be revealed to everyone. "First," writes the author of these web pages, "we will try to understand why atoms naturally arrange themselves to form a structure. Then we will look at some common structures, and ask why diamonds are forever, but salt is of the earth—all of which will help us understand the different kinds of bonding between atoms."

Molecular Monte Carlo Home Page
http://www.cooper.edu/engineering/chemechem/monte.html

Molecular Monte Carlo: What Is It? Although Monte Carlo methods are used in a dizzingly diverse number of ways, in the context of molecular computations there are five types most commonly encountered: "classical" Monte Carlo, or CMC (samples are drawn from a probability distribution, often the classical Boltzmann distribution, to obtain thermodynamic properties, minimum-energy structures and/or rate coefficients, or perhaps just to sample conformers as part of a global conformer search algorithm); "quantum" Monte Carlo, or QMC (random walks are used to compute quantum-mechanical energies and wavefunctions, often to solve electronic structure problems, using Schroedinger's equation as a formal starting point); "path-integral" quantum Monte Carlo, or PMC (quantum statistical mechanical integrals are computed to obtain thermodynamic properties, or even rate coefficients, using Feynman's path integral as a formal starting point); "volumetric" Monte Carlo, or VMC (random and quasirandom number generators are used to generate molecular volumes and sample molecular phase-space surfaces); "simulation" Monte Carlo, or SMC (stochastic algorithms are used to generate initial conditions for quasiclassical trajectory simulations, or to actually simulate processes using scaling arguments to establish time scales or by introducing stochastic effects into molecular dynamics. "Kinetic Monte Carlo" is an example of an SMC method. So is "thermalization" of a molecular dynamics trajectory.) Visit this informative web page for more details.

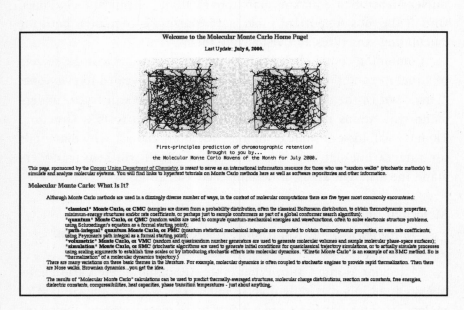

Welcome to the Molecular Monte Carlo Home Page!

Last Update: **July 6, 2000.**

First-principles prediction of chromatographic retention!
Brought to you by...
the Molecular Monte Carlo Mavens of the Month for July 2000.

This page, sponsored by the Cooper Union Department of Chemistry, is meant to serve as an international information resource for those who use "random walks" (stochastic methods) to simulate and analyze molecular systems. You will find links to hypertext tutorials on Monte Carlo methods here as well as software repositories and other information.

Molecular Monte Carlo: What Is It?

Although Monte Carlo methods are used in a dizzingly diverse number of ways, in the context of molecular computations there are five types most commonly encountered:

"classical" Monte Carlo, or CMC (samples are drawn from a probability distribution, often the classical Boltzmann distribution, to obtain thermodynamic properties, minimum-energy structures and/or rate coefficients, or perhaps just to sample conformers as part of a global conformer search algorithm);
"quantum" Monte Carlo, or QMC (random walks are used to compute quantum-mechanical energies and wavefunctions, often to solve electronic structure problems, using Schroedinger's equation as a formal starting point);
"path-integral" quantum Monte Carlo, or PMC (quantum statistical mechanical integrals are computed to obtain thermodynamic properties, or even rate coefficients, using Feynman's path integral as a formal starting point);
"volumetric" Monte Carlo, or VMC (random and quasirandom number generators are used to generate molecular volumes and sample molecular phase-space surfaces);
"simulation" Monte Carlo, or SMC (stochastic algorithms are used to generate initial conditions for quasiclassical trajectory simulations, or to actually simulate processes using scaling arguments to establish time scales or by introducing stochastic effects into molecular dynamics. "Kinetic Monte Carlo" is an example of an SMC method. So is "thermalization" of a molecular dynamics trajectory.)
There are many variations on these basic themes in the literature. For example, molecular dynamics is often coupled to stochastic engines to provide rapid thermalization. Then there are Nose walks, Brownian dynamics...you get the idea.

The results of "Molecular Monte Carlo" calculations can be used to predict thermally-averaged structures, molecular charge distributions, reaction rate constants, free energies, dielectric constants, compressibilities, heat capacities, phase transition temperatures - just about anything.

Chemsoc: The Chemistry Societies Network
http://www.chemsoc.org/

Chemsoc is a brand new site for chemists and the home of the international chemistry societies' electronic network. The site provides interesting features and useful services for the chemistry community. The information you find has been made available by various national chemistry societies for dissemination on a single site. Currently around 30 such societies are providing varying levels of information on chemsoc. There are several cool sections. First off, consider chembytes infozone, which is chemsoc's library providing daily science news, chemical industry news, product news, access to major chemistry information providers, information about new publications, a comprehensive guide to funding, and the chemsoc "art gallery". Then you have chembytes ezine–chemsoc's online magazine, with features on current "hot topics" in chemical science. Chemsoc also features the most comprehensive database of chemistry conferences and events available. Find out about meetings and conferences in your field of interest and link through to details on the organiser's Web site. You can search the conference database, or submit a new conference to the events list. Here you will as well find listings of the latest vacancies in industry and academia, plus advice on career-related topics such as effective job hunting, writing the perfect CV, improving your interview technique, etc.

Theory of Atoms in Molecules
http://www.chemistry.mcmaster.ca/faculty/bader/aim/

The molecular structure hypothesis–that a molecule is a collection of atoms linked by a network of bonds–was forged in the crucible of nineteenth century experimental chemistry. It has continued to serve as the principal means of ordering and classifying the observations of chemistry. The difficulty with this hypothesis was that it was not related directly to quantum mechanics, the physics which governs the motions of the nuclei and electrons that make up the atoms and the bonds. Indeed there was, and with some there still is, a prevailing opinion that these fundamental concepts, while unquestionably useful, were beyond theoretical definition. We have in chemistry an understanding based on a classification scheme that is both powerful and at the same time, because of its empirical nature, limited. Richard Feynman and Julian Schwinger have given us a reformulation of physics that enables one to pose and answer the questions "what is an atom in a molecule and how does one predict its properties?" Visit this great online tutorial to learn all you need to know about the theory of atoms in molecules as understood through the centuries.

ScienceBase

http://www.sciencebase.com/

SCIENCEbase.com is the place to be for reactive science communication on the web, and it's free.

SCIENCEbase.com is owned and managed by David Bradley Science Writer. Bradley is Contributing Editor and WebWorks columnist for the publication Analytical Chemistry. SCIENCEbase.com is aimed at everyone who has an interest in chemistry and related sciences. SCIENCEbase.com includes links to Bradley's Elemental Discoveries—a small but well-done e-zine whose purpose is to round up the latest happenings in chemistry (with some coverage of other areas). This is

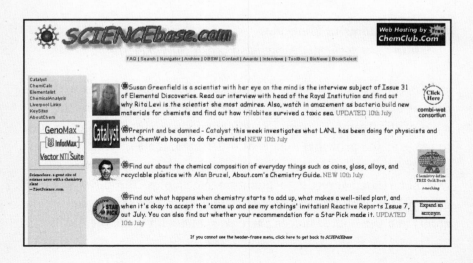

characterized by clear, concise writing backed up by an extensive knowledge of the field. In this day of overwhelming quantities of news on every subject, SCIENCEbase.com and Elemental Discoveries combine to form a definitely good resource, particularly for chemists. Also click on the link for Bradley's Reactive Reports. Learn about exciting developments in chemistry and related fields by checking out this Web-based chemistry magazine. Read about the molecule behind a Biblical plague, a marine bacteria that can bubble-wrap iron, and a compound found in a Native American herbal remedy that may hold the key to overcoming antibiotic resistance. The articles are accessible to a lay audience.

Chemistry Mailing Lists:

A splendid directory of chemistry related mailing lists can be found at the URL http://antoine.frostburg.edu/ chem/senese/101/mail/resources.shtml

Chemistry Newsgroups:

sci.chem

sci.engr.chem

sci.chem.organomet

sci.materials

sci.techniques.mag-resonance

sci.techniques.mass-spec

sci.techniques.microscopy

sci.techniques.xtallography

——————————o10

FUN STUFF

Bizarre Stuff You Can Make in Your Kitchen
http://freeweb.pdq.net/headstrong/

This site is an ever growing warehouse of the kinds of projects some of the more demented of us tried as young people, collecting in one place many of the classic, simple science projects that have become part of the collective lore of amateur science. It is a sort of warped semi-scientific cookbook of tricks, gimmicks, and pointless experimentation, concoctions, and devices, using, for the most part, things found around the house. These are the classics. Strange goo, radios made from rusty razor blades, crystal gardens . . . amateur mad

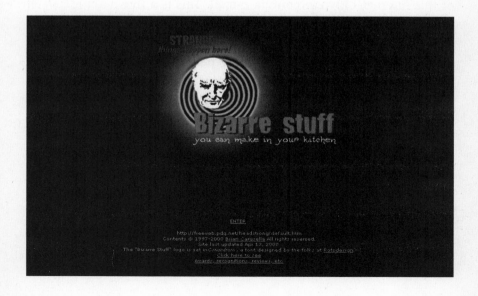

scientist stuff. If you happen to learn something in the process, consider yourself a better person for it. The projects are listed by a general alphabetical index, as well as by a general category listing. For the most part, the projects on this site are fairly safe. Use the info here to build a miniature airship. Out of matches? Start that fire the old fashioned Boy Scout way with a wooden bow and drill. Or build your own hypsomter and use it to calculate the height of nearby trees and water towers.

Dr. Fun
http://metalab.unc.edu/Dave/drfun.html

Each Doctor Fun cartoon is a 640x480 pixel, 24-bit color, JPEG image. The cartoons range in size from 80 to 150K. All of the previous Doctor Fun cartoons are archived and available for viewing. In addition to the cartoons themselves, there are a number of Doctor Fun logos available for viewing. Doctor Fun is the creation of David Farley, who works and plays at MetaLab, at the University of North Carolina in Chapel Hill. The various cartoons often have a scientific/ techie twist confronting head on the ironies of modern research and modern living as they collide with the realities of imperfect human nature. If you would like, you may arrange to receive a daily edition of this Internet-only cartoon via e-mail. This is a free mailing list set up by Nicholas Barnard for the enjoyment of all. Every day a nifty little program sends out a copy of the cartoon to all the subscribers via email as a MIME attachment with the help of eGroups. Visit the web site to view the archived cartoons and/or sign up for the mailing list. This is all absolutely free, and absolutely fun.

Hot Air: The Annals of Improbable Research
http://www.improb.com/

The Annals of Improbable Research (AIR) is the humor magazine of science, medicine, and technology.

AIR is known for hilariously genuine science, deadpan satire—and the annual Ig Nobel Prizes. The AIRheads are hard at work day and night, producing three streams of AIRy material: 1.AIR—the magnifi-

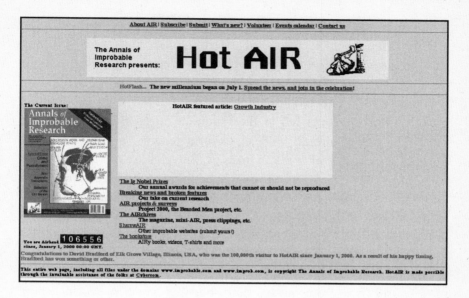

cent print magazine (with lots of nifty pictures!) that comes out six times a year. 2.mini-AIR—the (free!) monthly email newsletter, composed of tiny, timely tidbits. And 3.Hot AIR—the website. "About a third of what we publish is genuine research," write the editors," about a third is concocted, and about a third of our readers cannot tell the difference. (In the print magazine we always indicate which items come from the supposedly serious research journals—and we even give you the info to go look those things up and see for yourself.) Many people have been reading mini-AIR for years, and assume that the print magazine can't possibly exist. It does exist. Many scientists, doctors, and engineers tell us that AIR is the only journal they subscribe to that their family and friends also read. And many teachers tell us that they love to use AIR articles in the classroom, as a sneaky way to get kids curious about science."

International Human Powered Vehicle Association
http://ihpva.org/

The Human Powered Vehicle Association (HPVA) is a non-profit, all-volunteer organization, dedicated to promoting improvement, innovation and creativity in the design and development of human-powered transportation. "If one of your goals is to help develop and/or promote new forms of energy-conserving, non-polluting transportation—or if you are interested in keeping up with the latest developments, we invite you to join our organization," writes the webmaster. "The Cheetah broke the world speed record in 1992, 68.73 mph. 10 world records fell at the Colorado Speed Bike challenge in 1993. The Raven aircraft will set 4 world records in 1996/97. What humans are capable of really amazes us. Bicycles are not a 'hobby' for some of us. We are part of our own subculture. A Bike Culture. It's an addiction, it's a lifestyle. We're seeing some promising developments in the merger of human power and electric power. So this site is no longer purely about human power. It has expanded to accomodate appropriate transportation. This site is dedicated to visionaries and dreamers. Some dream of human-powered flight. Others have a vision of a world free from noisy, petro-burning cars. A world where humans can be maybe just a little more in tune with the Earth. This site is dedicated to people making our visions come true . . ."

Mad Science Home Page (First International Virtual Conference on Mad Science)
http://www.boxt.com/MadScience/

Mad science is a much maligned domain of human knowledge and its practitioners have for too long been relegated to B-movies and remote ancestral estates. The First International Virtual Conference on Mad Science (IVCMS) provides an international forum for the presentation, discussion and extension of research into these darkly powerful pseudosciences and dangerous technologies which fall beyond the scope of conventional science and good taste. The purpose of the conference is to promote a general understanding of mad topics within the broader scientific community, to encourage new researchers to dabble with things best left alone, to attract commercial sponsors to the potential benefits of mad science in the business world, and to replace the old drooling maniac stereotype of the mad scientist with a new drooling maniac image which is more appropriate to the modern era. The conference is hosted on the Web to avoid the overheads of unpredictable atmospheric conditions and revolting peasants. Topics of interest include, but are not limited to: Creating life to satisfy ego-centric motives. Unleashing entities beyond human control and comprehension. Tampering with the life-sustaining forces of the Universe. Exceeding the limitations of the human body via grotesque metamorphoses.

Museum of Questionable Medical Devices
http://www.mtn.org/quack/

Bob McCoy, proprietor of this museum, is a veritable encyclopedia of the world's most inane and useless information about how to cure and/or comprehend what may ail or puzzle you. Dubbed "The Quackery Hall of Fame" by the Copley Wire Service, the museum is the world's largest display of what the human mind has devised to cure itself without the benefit of either scientific method or common sense. It comprises the major collections on loan from The American Medical Association, The U.S. Food and Drug Administration, The St. Louis Science Center, The Bakken Library, The National Council for Reliable Health Information and is supported by the The Phrenology Company of Golden Valley, Minnesota. Check it out: soap that sudses off pounds. And if the soap doesn't work for you, how about a pair of

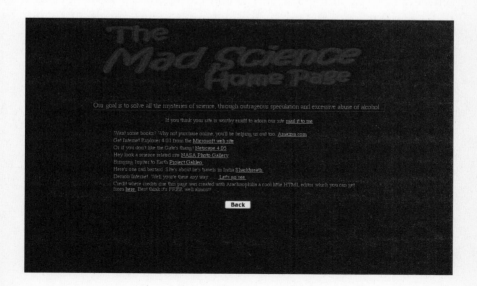

weight reduction glasses ? Stand in front of lights flashing prismatic colors that "guarantee" health and well being. Expose yourself to the "magic" of radio waves ... yes, quackery is alive and well, and painstakingly documented here in one of the weirder side alleys of cyberspace.

NeoScience Institute
http://www.necrobones.com/neosci/

According to the proprietors: "The NeoScience Institute was founded in the 1940's by our current director, and a small group of underground rogue scientists who broke away from the dawning nuclear age to start a new scientific foundation. Armed with the knowledge of their previous scientific careers, they based the initial organization on a few significant discoveries. Without the ethical constraints of society applying to them, they managed to make discoveries and advances that would not otherwise be possible, and now the Institute has grown to the point that it now spans the globe with over one million employees world-wide. Relativistic transport tubes allow for efficient pooling of resources from around the world, which facilitates rapid progress. The Institute's goal is to achieve world domination by the year 2099. Through the hard work and involuntary self-sacrifice of countless scientists and professionals, we believe this to be a valid goal. Before such domination ocurrs, we will in the meantime continue to bring you products and services, but only when it's convenient to do so and as long as it doesn't interfere with our experiments and research. We are, after all, primarily a scientific organization, not a mail-order service, got it?"

Tesla Web Links
http://www.amasci.com/tesla/tesla.html

A new millenium is time for reflection as well as anticipation. It's a good time to reflect on the important technologies of the 20th century that won't accompany us to the twenty-first. The phonograph is already gone from our lives, replaced by CDs. Movie watching today is more frequently by television than at the theater, and both movies

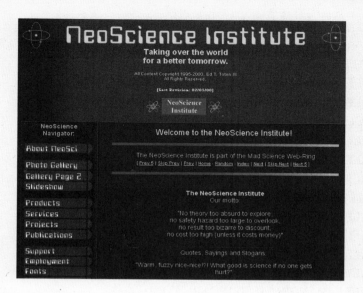

and television are going digital. (The Phantom Menace recently saw limited release in a purely digital format). Even the incandescent light bulb is steadily being replaced with fluorescent, HID lamps (High-Intensity Discharge—the arc lamp lives!) and other, more efficient lighting technologies. In short, many of Thomas Edison's most famous inventions—carbon microphone, phonograph, electric light, movie projector—are already obsolete or soon will be not far into the 21st century. On the other hand, fundamental electric technologies, such as 3-phase power distribution, the AC motor, wireless transmission, etc. will be with us far into the future. You may be surprised to learn that all of the latter inventions were strongly influenced by one man, a man many people today have never heard of: Nikola Tesla. Temperamental genius and megalomaniacal huckster, his invention of polyphase electric power alone earned him worldwide fame and fortune. At his zenith he was an intimate of poets and scientists, industrialists and financiers. Yet Tesla died destitute, having squandered both his fortune and scientific reputation.

Fun Stuff/Weird Science Newsgroups:

ALT.SCI.PHYSICS.NEW-THEORIES
ALT.SCI.NATURAL.PHENOMENA.UNUSUAL
ALT.SCI.TIME-TRAVEL
SCI.SKEPTIC
ALT.SKEPTIC.MAG
ALT.SKEPTIC.SOCIETY
ALT.PARANET.SKEPTIC
BIT.LISTSERV.SKEPTIC
ALT.PARANORMAL
ALT.PARANORMAL.MODERATED
ALT.PARANORMAL.CHANNELING
ALT.PARANORMAL.CROP-CIRCLES
ALT.PARANORMAL.REINCARNATION
ALT.PARANORMAL.SPELLS.HEXES
ALT.PARANET.PARANORMAL
ALT.PARANET.PSI
ALT.PARANET.METAPHYSICS
ALT.PARANET.UFO

II

GENERAL SCIENCE
RESOURCES AND SCIENCE
MUSEUMS

American Museum of Natural History
http://www.amnh.org/

View dozens of great exhibitions online, including the famous exhibit documenting Shackleton's famous antarctic expedition. The Exhibition at the American Museum of Natural History documented one of the greatest tales of survival in expedition history: Sir Ernest Shackleton's 1914 voyage to the Antarctic. Just one day's sail from the continent, the ship Endurance became trapped in sea ice. Frozen fast for ten months, the ship was crushed and destroyed by ice pressure, and the crew was forced to abandon ship. After camping on the ice for five months, Shackleton made two open boat journeys, one of which—a treacherous 800-mile ocean crossing to South Georgia Island—is now considered one of the greatest boat journeys in history. Trekking across the mountains of South Georgia, Shackleton reached the island's remote whaling station, organized a rescue team, and saved all of the men he had left behind. Also check out: Fighting Dinosaurs: New Discoveries from Mongolia. This exhibit features more than 30 of the best preserved and scientifically important dinosaur and other ancient animal fossils ever discovered in Mongolia's famed Gobi Desert. Never before seen in North America and designated a national treasure of Mongolia, the two Fighting Dinosaurs are a fierce Velociraptor that was apparently buried alive while attacking a plant-eating, shield-headed Protoceratops.

Access Excellence: Science Updates, Factoids and Interviews
http://www.accessexcellence.com/WN/

This web site divides into five major sections: Science Update—Regular reports on new and interesting developments from all areas of biology gleaned from a variety of sources including journals, conferences and the Internet. Here you will find: Newsmaker Interviews—Interviews with prominent researchers which delve into issues and controversies in science in an attempt to find the story behind the story; Factoids!—Amazing facts, such as "Major league baseball teams buy 182 pounds of special baseball rubbing mud each year from a farmer in Millsboro, Delaware;" Media Watch—Science programming on television, radio and the Internet; and The Editor's Desk—featuring news about the "man behind the curtain" . . . and links to science and web technology sites on the web. Webmaster Sean Henahan writes: "I was brought on board when AE was in the planning stages and asked to create the news area now known as What's News. Prior to joining AE I spent more than ten years as a professional journalist and science writer. After studying classical languages (Latin & Greek) at the UC Santa Cruz and later, Trinity College,University of Dublin, Ireland, I became a foreign correspondentfor the Medical Tribune, America's leading medical newspaper. I've since been a writer and editor for many medical newspapers, journals and popular magazines."

American Museum of Science and Energy
http://www.amse.org/

The museum opened in 1949 in an old wartime cafeteria. It was originally named the American Museum of Atomic Energy. Its guided tours took visitors through the peaceful uses of atomic energy. The present facility, opened in 1975, continues to provide the general public with energy information. The name of the museum was changed to the American Museum of Science and Energy in 1978. The American Museum of Science and Energy serves as an educational and communications forum to transfer information about the past and present programs of the Department of Energy to the American public of all ages. Created in January 1997, the AMSE Foundation

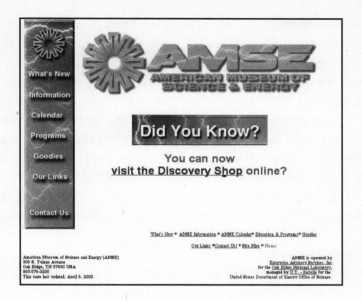

was created to provide a means for the communities surrounding AMSE to solicit and administer non governmental funding for AMSE programs and projects. The AMSE Foundation also organizes and sponsors the AMSE Tribute to Tennessee Technology, an award program recognizing the best in emerging and marketed technologies. Here you will find information on all aspects of the science of atomic energy. It should be stated, however, that the presentation is uniquely uncritical of atomic energy and tends to downplay the risks associated with the nuclear generation of electric power.

Bad Science
http://www.ems.psu.edu/~fraser/BadScience.html

This page is maintained by Alistair B. Fraser in an attempt to sensitize teachers and students to examples of the bad science often taught in schools, universities, and offered in popular articles and even textbooks. Bad Science abounds and comes in many guises. This page sets out to attack only one brand: well understood phenomena which are persistently presented incorrectly by teachers and writers, presumably because they either do not know any better or because they don't really care enough to get it correct. As Fraser writes: "For the purposes of this page, bad science does not mean pseudo-science. I realize that the boundary is permeable, but there is a useful distinction. The practitioners of (what scientists refer to as) pseudo-science generally know and even understand established scientific thought; they just reject it (for reasons which may have little to do with science itself). Treatments of pseudo-science and the paranormal are well treated elsewhere. Similarly, this page does not address contemporary controversies, about which the experts are still in active debate. Rather, it concerns itself with ideas and facts which are well established and well understood, but which persist in being presented incorrectly. As such, this page is about teaching rather than research."

The British Museum
http://www.thebritishmuseum.ac.uk/

The British Museum was founded in 1753 to promote universal understanding through the arts, natural history and science in a public museum. Since its foundation, the British Museum has been guided by three important principles: that the collections are held in perpetuity in their entirety; that they are widely available to all who seek to enjoy and learn from them and that they are curated by full-time specialists. In looking towards 2005, the 250th anniversary of its foundingthe British Museum will preserve these distinctive commitments to access, scholarship and care of the collections, whilst redefining them for the new millennium. The British Museum's international standing and its key role in the display of the world's and nation's heritage make it one of the most-visited public buildings in London, contributing to its cultural and economic life. As a social enterprise the British Museum has exceptional reach. It creates a context in which cultures can be seen, experienced and studied in depth or compared and contrasted across time and space to inspire and delight over five million visitors a year. Through its public, curatorial, exhibition and education programmes the Museum engages with the public to advance understanding of the collections and cultures they represent.

California Academy of Sciences
http://www.calacademy.org/

There is a place in San Francisco where you can take a deep sea dive without getting wet and explore the stars in the middle of the day; track wild African animals, explore Wild California, ride an earthquake and travel back 3 billion years in time! It's all under one roof at the California Academy of Sciences in San Francisco's Golden Gate Park. Each year one and a half million visitors enjoy the many exhibits at the Academy, a natural history museum, aquarium and planetarium rolled into one. Of specil interest is the natural history museum. From plate tectonics and earthquakes to animals native to California and Africa; from ancient seas and dinosaurs to scientifically humorous Far Side cartoons and a hands-on discovery room, the extensive Natural History Museum has something to stimulate your curiosity and imagination. Gems and minerals, asteroids, life- size elephant seals and seabirds, anthropological artifacts, and more, await you in engaging and informative displays. Also, educational and entertaining sky shows are presented daily in northern California's largest indoor universe, the Academy's Morrison Planetarium. Visitors experience a realistic simulation of the night sky as observed from any place on Earth, as well as numerous celestial events and cosmic phenomena.

Chicago Academy of Science
http://www.chias.org/

Founded in 1857, the Chicago Academy of Sciences established Chicago's first museum and only museum to specialize in the ecology and natural history of the Midwest from the Great Lakes to the prairies. Today, the Academy is a vital cultural and educational institution dedicated to promoting scientific literacy for all citizens. On October 23, 1999, the Academy opened the state-of-the-art Peggy Notebaert Nature Museum in Chicago's Lincoln Park, on the corner of Fullerton Parkway and Cannon Drive. The new Nature Museum serves as the cornerstone for all of the Academy's innovative scientific learning and environmental programs. The Academy advances scientific understanding by bringing outreach education programs, such as CAoS Club and Science on the GO!, to Illinois public schools, hosting science workshops for teachers and offering lectures, field trips, weekend workshops and other special programs for children and adults. The Academy's International Center for the Advancement of Scientific Literacy (ICASL) is the leading research organization in the world studying and measuring the impact of science and technology on public awareness. The Academy works in concert with a number of local and national organizations to support initiatives to inform citizens about science and the environment.

Earth and Sky Radio Series
http://www.earthsky.com/

This is an award winning daily science radio series heard by millions of listeners on over 950 commercial and public stations and their translators throughout the United States. It can also in be heard Canada, the South Pacific and on a variety of international networks, including Armed Forces Radio, World Radio Network and Voice of America. Each day, Deborah Byrd and Joel Block discuss popular science subjects that affect our everyday lives. Programs in the series explore the surface of Earth from the tallest mountains to the deepest trenches on the ocean floor. They explain dynamic processes such as the movement of tectonic plates. Some biology is presented; a recent program introduced the idea of life near hot-water vents on the ocean floor. Other shows focus on chemical processes in Earth's air and oceans. The series also takes people on imaginary journeys into space, with programs exploring the planets and sun, the possible birth of new solar systems, the evolution of stars and galaxies, and exotic objects such as quasars and pulsars. Listener questions are solicited on air and used at a rate of about one or two per week. Recent questions include, "How wide is lightning?" and "What does the sun look like from the planet Pluto?"

Exploratorium
http://www.exploratorium.edu/

The Exploratorium is a museum of science, art, and human perception located in San Francisco, California. Online since 1993, the Exploratorium was one of the first science museums to build a site on the World Wide Web. Included in the site are more than 10,000 Web pages and hundreds of sound and video files, exploring hundreds of different topics. They currently serve seven million visitors a year on the site—nearly seven times the number of visitors who show up in person at the museum in San Francisco. That makes this one of the most visited museum Web sites in the world. The Exploratorium's Web site is an extension of the experiences on the museum's floor. The webmasters have created "real" things for people to explore and interact with, not "virtual exhibits." The medium of the Internet makes it possible for the museum to reach homes and schools all over the world. This has changed the way formal and informal learning takes place, both in the classroom and in the home. The Exploratorium online, and the resources it provides, are available 24 hours a day, worldwide, to anyone with an Internet connection.

The Franklin Institute of Science Museum
http://sln.fi.edu/tfi/welcome.html

On January 1, 1934, The Franklin Institute Science Museum opened to the public. The Museum's hands-on approach to science and technology, combined with the Fels Planetarium, made the Institute a popular spot. As the end of the twentieth century drew near, major changes were beginning at the Institute. In May of 1990, The Mandell Center, Tuttleman Omniverse Theater (now known as the Tuttleman IMAX Theater), and Musser Theater opened, adding dramatically to the size and appeal of The Franklin Institute. The new exhibits, exciting Omnimax films, and interactive presentations continued the Institute's long tradition of making science and technology fun. The mission of The Franklin Institute Science Museum is to stimulate interest in science, to promote public understanding of science, and to strengthen science education. The Institute maintains an exemplary, innovative museum of science with engaging, educational exhibits and programs; supports a diverse set of partnerships with all levels of the formal educational system; interprets the social and historical impact of science and technology; recognizes outstanding achievement; and provides a forum for discussion of important scientific issues. The Franklin Institute also serves to perpetuate the legacy of Benjamin Franklin.

Goudreau Museum of Mathematics in Art & Science
http://www.mathmuseum.org/

The Math Museum features programs specially designed for you and your family. Some programs can be enjoyed by parents, youngsters, and educators together, while others are geared to either adult or child levels. Many programs involve a hands-on project that the participants can take home. The program topics include Videospheres, Tangrams, Origami, Math in Navigation, Math in Architecture, Egg Decorating, Calendars, Paper Airplanes, Music and Math . . . and more! The Math Museum has a large library of math resources to assist you on student projects, reports, and teacher curriculum development. Originally begun with founder Goudreau's own books, the

Library has grown through donations from educators, scientists, and engineers. Appointments can be made to use these books on the premises, both by individuals and by entire school classes. The Math Museum sponsors special, math-related events such as navigational cruises on the sloop Clearwater; a lecture by George Escher about his famous father, M.C. Escher; a lecture by Simon Singh, author of Fermat's Enigma; an annual Pi Day competition, and annual awards dinner to honor individuals for outstanding math achievements. The Museum is located in New Hyde Park, New York.

Institute and Museum of the History of Science (Florence)
http://galileo.imss.firenze.it/index.html

In addition to being one of the leading science museums in the world, the Institute is also the home for the new International Laboratory in the History of Science brings together junior and senior scholars for seven to ten days each year to confront a focused and novel research topic through hands-on contact with instruments, techniques, as well as the study of texts. Approximately a dozen postdoctoral fellows meet with five or six senior scholars, experts in the topic to be dealt with in the particular year, for an intensive seminar under the sponsorship of one of the five participating institutions. The goals of the International Laboratory in the History of Science are: (1) to expand the preparation of younger scholars in the history of science and related fields by exposure to sources and methods not ordinarily included in graduate training; (2) to introduce techniques and perspectives from other disciplines (e.g. archaeology, cognitive science, art history) as they intersect with problems in the history of science; (3) to promote interactions of junior and senior scholars around a focused topic across national boundaries; and (4) to stimulate research on new areas in the history of science by concentrating scholarly attention on them by means of the seminars.

Israel Museum of Science

http://www.netvision.net.il/~sci_muse/

Established in 1984, the unique Israel National Museum of Science—Daniel & Matilde Recanati Center is situated in the historic landmark Technion—Israel Institute of Technology Building, in mid-town Haifa. It features over 250 hands-on displays and exhibits—almost all manufactured in-house-demonstrate a broad range of scientific principles. Over 200,000 visitors (of whom 100,000 are students) take part in Museum activities annually, through participation in the vast range of programs offered by Museum exhibits and by the plethora of innovative educational activities for youngsters of all ages which its Science Education Center provides. The Center has developed innovative science curricula and designed and produced a host of teaching aids and laboratory experiments. It has trained student guides, refined teaching methods and techniques, and developed expertise in the design and construction of mobile scientific exhibits. The Museum's interactive exhibits and the specialized training of its highly professionalized staff, allow children, youth and adults, to experience diverse aspects of science and technology and to grasp their underlying principles, while at the same time enhancing their curiosity, deepening their knowledge and enabling them to have just plain fun.

Lawrence Hall of Science, UC, Berkeley
http://www.lhs.berkeley.edu/

If you've ever wondered what it feels like to be a scientist, come visit the Lawrence Hall of Science. You'll not only find out what scientists do- you'll actually do it yourself! Here visitors of all ages have fun exploring science by doing science. LHS features interactive exhibits on topics ranging from dinosaurs to space travel, what's below the earth to what's above it, how your brain works, and why it works that way, and many more intriguing topics. Free science videos are shown daily, program schedule permitting, in the auditorium. Weekend programs include special events, interactive planetarium shows, a biology laboratory filled with gentle animals, and evening stargazing. They also offer family workshops, a family Computer Lab, hands-on classes and camps, a gift and book store, and snack shop. The outdoor plaza and lawn feature spectacular views of the San Francisco Bay area and an array of unique climbing/learning structures. Be sure to check out the exhibit entitled Within the Human Brain. Activate your brain and find out what happens! Explore the changes your brain goes through when you try out activities such as magnetic mazes, constructing stories, and matching sounds. Use computers to journey into the inner space of your brain, and examine MRI images.

Miami Museum of Science
http://www.miamisci.org/

The Museum promotes science literacy and serves as a catalyst for continued science exploration by providing science education in a stimulating, enjoyable, non-threatening environment. The Museum plays a leadership role in informing and exciting South Florida's residents and visitors about all areas of science including, but not limited to, the physical and natural sciences, astronomy, technology, and the area's unique ecology. The Museum continues to assess the scientific and technological needs and interests of its broadly based community and service these needs through focused, on site and outreach initiatives. The Museum acts as a community resource on issues of science, health, technology, and the environment through timely dissemination of information and provision of learning opportunities for the public and other organizations, agencies, and institutions. Through the years, the Museum has enjoyed the full support of the Metropolitan Dade County Commission, Department of Parks and Recreation and School Board, the City of Miami and the State of Florida. Though the history of the institution can be charted by the growth of its facility, this story is ultimately one of people. For almost 50 years, the Miami Museum of Science and Space Transit Planetarium has been nurtured by a legion of tireless volunteers and generous contributors. Their abundance of vision and dedication has rarely been equaled by any other civic group in the city's history.

Museum of the History of Science at Oxford
http://www.mhs.ox.ac.uk/

The Museum of the History of Science houses an unrivalled collection of historic scientific instruments in the world's oldest surviving purpose-built museum building, the Old Ashmolean on Broad Street, Oxford. By virtue of the collection and the building, the Museum occupies a special position, both in the study of the history of science and in the development of western culture and collecting. The present collection of the Museum preserves the material relics of past science. As a department of the University of Oxford, the Museum has a role both in making these relics available for study by historians who are willing to look beyond the traditional confines of books and manuscripts as well as presenting them to the visiting public. The objects represented—of which there are approximately 10,000—cover almost all aspects of the history of science, from antiquity to the early twentieth century. Particular strengths include the collections of astrolabes, sundials, quadrants, early mathematical instruments generally (including those used for surveying, drawing, calculating, astronomy and navigation) and optical instruments (including microscopes, telescopes and cameras), together with apparatus associated with chemistry, natural philosophy and medicine. In addition, the Museum possesses a unique reference library for the study of the history of scientific instruments that includes manuscripts, incunabula, prints, printed ephemera and early photographic material.

Museum of Science (Boston)
http://www.mos.org/

In 1830, six men interested in natural history established the Boston Society of Natural History, an organization through which they could pursue their common scientific interests. Devoted to collecting and studying natural history specimens, the society displayed its collections in numerous temporary facilities until 1864, when it opened the New England Museum of Natural History at the corner of Berkeley and Boylston Streets in Boston's Back Bay. That Museum is now known world-wide as the Museum of Science. The Museum has remained on the cutting edge of science education by developing innovative and interactive exhibits and programs that both entertain and educate. Two of the Museum's more recent additions, the Hall Wing housing the Roger L. Nichols Gallery for temporary exhibits, and the Mugar Omni Theater, exemplify the Museum of Science's commitment to making science fun and accessible to all. The Mugar Omni Theater, opened in 1987, utilizes state-of-the-art film technology to project larger-than-life images onto a five-story high, domed screen, creating a "you are there" experience for viewers. More than 1.6 million people visit the Museum and its more than 400 interactive exhibits each year.

National Air and Space Museum (Smithsonian)
http://www.nasm.si.edu/

The Smithsonian Institution's National Air and Space Museum (NASM) maintains the largest collection of historic air and spacecraft in the world. It is also a vital center for research into the history, science, and technology of aviation and space flight. Located on the National Mall in Washington, D.C., the Museum has hundreds of artifacts on display including the original Wright 1903 Flyer, the "Spirit of St. Louis," Apollo 11 command module, and a Lunar rock sample that visitors can touch. The museum continues to develop new exhibits to examine the impact of air and space technology on science and society. In addition to the artifacts on display in the Museum downtown, hundreds more artifacts are currently housed at the Museum's Paul E. Garber Preservation, Restoration, and Storage Facility in Suitland, MD. Guided tours of selected artifacts on display and the restoration shop are available upon request. The Dulles Center, a new Museum extension under development near Dulles Airport in Virginia, will become the Museum's primary artifact restoration facility. Many aircraft and spacecraft never seen before in a museum setting will be displayed at the Dulles Center, scheduled to open in 2003.

National Atomic Museum
http://www.atomicmuseum.com/

The mission of the National Atomic Museum is to serve as America's museum resource for nuclear history and science. The Museum presents exhibits and quality educational programs that convey the diversity of individuals and events that shape the historical and technical context of the nuclear age. The National Atomic Museum is located on Kirtland Air Force Base in Albuquerque, New Mexico, approximately six miles from the airport. While owned by the United States Department of Energy (DOE), Albuquerque's, National Atomic Museum is operated by Sandia National Laboratories. Sandia is a multiprogram laboratory operated by the Sandia Corporation, a subsidiary of the Lockheed Martin Corporation and a prime contractor to the DOE. The Museum features a special exhibit on nuclear medicine. Nuclear medicine is the medical specialty that uses internally administered radioactive materials, called radioisotopes, to help diagnose and treat a wide variety of diseases. The National Atomic Museum has created this exhibit in the hope that it will inform and educate the public about the many aspects of the medical use of radioisotopes. The Atomic Energy Act, passed by Congress on August 1, 1946, created the Atomic Energy Commission. This act enabled the peaceful production of medical isotopes in an Oak Ridge reactor. The modern era of nuclear medicine had begun.

National Museum of Natural History (Smithsonian)
http://www.mnh.si.edu/

The Natural History Web is an internet resource compiled and maintained by the staff of the National Museum of Natural History. Here you will find documents and data about Museum research and the national collections, which comprise more than 120 million scientific specimens and cultural artifacts from around the world. You will also find information about programs and projects at the Museum or produced in cooperation with other organizations, supporting the Museum's mission of understanding the natural world and our place in it. Be sure to click the link for the Museum's educational programs. The Office of Education plans, coordinates, and conducts a variety of Museum activities for students, teachers, families, and the general public. The majority of these programs are free and open to all on a first-come, first-served basis. Students benefit from group tours of permanent and temporary exhibits, and the Museum has recently expanded its outreach to minority science students and their teachers. Families enjoy special weekend activities such as the annual Family Science Day and festivities offered in conjunction with temporary exhibits. Adults take part in daily highlights tours and a weekly film-and-lecture series. The latter features illustrated talks by staff and visiting scientists and occasional weekend film festivals.

The National Museum of Science and Industry (London)
http://www.nmsi.ac.uk/

The UK's National Museum of Science & Industry (NMSI) comprises the Science Museum, London, the National Museum of Photography, Film & Television, Bradford, and the National Railway Museum, York. The NMSI holds the world's largest and most significant collection illustrating the history and contemporary practice of science, technology, medicine and industry. It is governed by a Board of Trustees, appointed by the Prime Minister, and funded by Grant-in-Aid from the Department of Culture, Media and Sport. The origins of the Science Museum lie in the nineteenth-century movement to improve scientific and technical education. Prince Albert was a leading figure in this movement, and he was primarily responsible for the Great Exhibition of 1851 to promote the achievements of science and technology. The profits of the hugely successful Exhibition were used to purchase land in South Kensington to establish institutions devoted to the promotion and improvement of industrial technology. At the same time, the Government set up a Science & Art Department which established the South Kensington Museum in 1857, from which the Science Museum and Victoria & Albert Museum have developed.

National Science Teacher Association
http://www.nsta.org/

The National Science Teachers Association (NSTA), founded in 1944 and headquartered in Arlington, Virginia, is the largest organization in the world committed to promoting excellence and innovation in science teaching and learning for all. NSTA's current membership of more than 53,000 includes science teachers, science supervisors, administrators, scientists, business and industry representatives, and others involved in science education. To address subjects of critical interest to science educators, the Association publishes five journals, a newspaper, many books, and many other publications. NSTA conducts national and regional conventions that attract more than 30,000 attendees annually. NSTA provides many programs and services for science educators, including awards, professional development workshops, and educational tours. NSTA offers professional certification for science teachers in eight teaching level and discipline area categories. In addition, NSTA has a World Wide Web site with links to state, national, and international science education organizations, an on-line catalog of publications, and two "discussion rooms" to foster interaction and ongoing conversations about science education. NSTA's newest and largest initiative to date, "Building a Presence for Science," seeks to improve science education and align science teaching to the National Science Education Standards nationwide. The Exxon Education Foundation has funded the initial effort to bring the program to ten states and the District of Columbia.

New York Hall of Science
http://www.nyhallsci.org/

Programs include: EW! Molecule of Life—Always wondered what they mean when they talk about DNA testing? Now you can manipulate colored blocks to develop a better understanding of DNA base pairing, and isolate and take home your own DNA. Another cool presentation is The Five Senses. Learn how the five senses work together to percieve what is going on around us. Students visit discovery stations to conduct experiments, make observations and draw conclusions about the different senses. Also check Crazy for Crystals. Sharpen your observation skills while learning to classify minerals. Sort through the properties that make up our surrounding landscapes. Take home your own crystal growing kit. Then also consider It's a Small, Small World. This exhibit lets you see the very small through magnifying lenses and microscopes. Learn to look for tiny details. You may also be interested in Mystery in the Museum. Locate clues needed to solve a science mystery. In the process, learn basic research and problem-solving skills. Or embark upon Science Detective. Solve a crime using clues, fingerprints, paper chromatography, and coded messages. Analyze your own fingerprints. Make your own alphabet wheel to compose and decode secret messages.

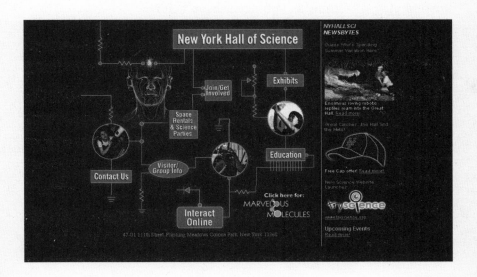

Ontario Science Center
   http://www.osc.on.ca/

As the webmaster writes: "Our science and technology programs for school groups are fun, engaging, interactive and educational—and they are carefully correlated to The Ontario Curriculum for Kindergarten to OAC! Selected for their educational value, curriculum links and cinematic excellence, the OMNIMAX films provide teachers and students with the opportunity to relate science and technology to each other and to the realworld." To enhance and expand on a visit to the exhibit halls, they recommend a school visit to the Ontario Science Centre include both a school program and an OMNIMAX film. "The Ontario Science Centre is proud to beyour partner in science and technology education," writes the webmaster. Be sure to check out the TIMESCAPE exhibit. Travel through tunnels of geological time into a huge archaeological dig site. The Science Centre's Procter & Gamble Great Hall is being rediscovered after the sands of centuries have buried it from view. TIMESCAPE features more than 20 interactive experiences, as well as special demonstrations, that will help you explore the past, present and future of the mysterious phenomenon we call time. What is time? How do we perceive time? How do we measure time? How is time an integral part of who we are? Visit this unique exhibition celebrating the Millennium—and touch, feel, measure and play with time, as you never have before.

Oregon Museum of Science and Industry
   http://www.omsi.edu/

OMSI began as an idea in the minds of a few Portland civic leaders who wanted to create a museum that didn't have "do not touch" signs on every exhibit. They believed interest in science is best cultivated in an active, engaging environment away from school books and blackboards, and that open-ended exploration of science would pique the interest of people of all ages. The Planetarium is especially cool. Since its opening in 1968, both OMSI's Kendall Planetarium and Murdock Sky Theater have served hundreds of thousands of visitors.

Over the years, it has evolved from a facility for teaching only the basic astronomy to modern, multi-purpose theater. Shows presented in the planetarium are dynamic and motivational, while providing visitors with the current knowledge about the universe we live in. OMSI's Murdock Planetarium takes a technological leap forward with a new Digistar II star projector. The new Digistar II projector displays a field of nearly 10,000 stars, and features three-dimensional space travel. The system's advanced technology showcases the true multimedia capabilities of the 200-seat, 52 foot domed Murdock Planetarium, the Pacific Northwest's largest public planetarium.

Scientific American Magazine
http://scientificamerican.com/

Let's let Scientific American's online editor speak for himself: "It's as interesting now as it was back in 1845. Things haven't changed that much—we're keeping Scientific American as vibrant as it always was, with the introduction of this new online edition. Here, on the World Wide Web, we are creating a new publication that pushes Scientific American into the frontiers of publishing in an electronic medium. Just as Scientific American has tracked key changes in technology for the past 150 years, we are now participating in the radical transformation driven by computer technology. We invite you to take a look. Each month, we will bring you the best of the current issue—augmented to take advantage of the unique capabilities of the WWW. You will find many of your favorite magazine features here, as well as at least two major articles in their entirety, with links that let you connect directly to the researchers and their work. You will want to keep coming back often. Scientific American on the WWW will be more than a showcase for the current issue. This site will include a number of features updated weekly and available only to readers of the Scientific American Online edition."

Society for Amateur Scientists
http://earth.thesphere.com/SAS/

The Society for Amateur Scientists (SAS) is a nonprofit research and educational organization dedicated to helping people enrich their lives by following their passion to take part in scientific adventures of all of all kinds. SAS is a unique collaboration between world-class professionals and "amateur" scientists. SAS is totally dedicated to helping everyday people find the limits of their own genius by developing their scientific skills and removing the roadblocks that today make it nearly impossible for people without Ph.D. degrees to do research. Members include people with no technical training whatsoever all the way to people with Ph.D.s in one field who want to explore fields outside their training. Their aim is to get everyone involved in stimulating projects on the front lines of science regardless of age, ethnicity or background. Their goal is to become the premiere support organization for amateur scientists. They define "amateur" to mean anyone who wants to do science simply for the love of it. Note: SAS is a conservative scientific organization dedicated primarily to advancing well-established experimental fields. SAS does not conduct research into paranormal phenomena. Also, they do not provide support for amateur theories of cosmology, creation, the unified field, or similar topics.

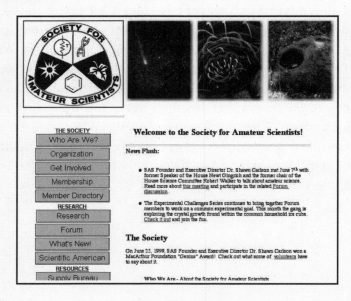

12

Geology

American Geological Institute
http://www.agiweb.org/

The American Geological Institute is a nonprofit federation of 35 geoscientific and professional associations that represent more than 100,000 geologists, geophysicists, and other earth scientists. Founded in 1948, AGI provides information services to geoscientists, serves as a voice of shared interests in the profession, plays a major role in strengthening geoscience education, and strives to increase public awareness of the vital role the geosciences play in mankind's use of resources and interaction with the environment. Member societies include: American Association of Petroleum Geologists (AAPG), American Association of Stratigraphic Palynologists (AASP), American Geophysical Union (AGU), American Institute of Hydrology (AIH), American Institute of Professional Geologists (AIPG), Association for Women Geoscientists (AWG), Association of American State Geologists (AASG), Association of Earth Science Editors (AESE), Association of Engineering Geologists (AEG), The Clay Minerals Society (CMS), Council on Undergraduate Research-Geology Division (CUR), Friends of Mineralogy, GeoInstitute of ASCE, Geological Society of America (GSA), Geoscience Information Society (GIS), International Association of Hydrogeologists/U.S. National Chapter (IAH), Mineralogical Society of America (MSA), National Association of Black Geologists and Geophysicists (NABGG), National Association of Geoscience Teachers (NAGT), National Association of State Boards of Geology (ASBOG), National Earth Science Teachers Association (NESTA), National Speleological Society (NSS), North American Commission on Stratigraphic Nomenclature, Paleobotany Section of the Botanical Society of America, and Paleontological Research Institution (PRI).

American Geophysical Union
http://www.agu.org/

American Geophysical Union is an international scientific society with more than 35,000 members in over 115 countries. For over 75 years, AGU researchers, teachers, and science administrators have dedicated themselves to advancing the understanding of Earth and its environment in space and making the results available to the public. Question: What do average Americans think about global warming, earthquake dangers, the availability of safe drinking water and other issues of geophysical sciences? And how do they view the scientists who study these and related phenomena? In 1997, AGU's Public Information Committee commissioned an independent study by Public Agenda to seek some preliminary answers. John Immerwahr of Public Agenda and Villanova University conducted the research and reported the results at 1999 Spring Meeting. The full text of his report is available here in HTML, PDF, and WordPerfect formats. Here you can also view the archived webcast of AGU President-elect Marcia McNutt's presentation at The White House as part of the Ninth Millennium Evening, hosted by President and Mrs. Clinton. Want more? How about information on great AGU books, such as Ellen Wohl's *Mountain Rivers*? What are the physical processes operating in mountain rivers and how do we know them? Mountain Rivers answers these questions and more. Here is the only comprehensive synthesis of current knowledge about mountain rivers available.

Bishop Museum's Geology Page (Hawaii)
http://www.bishop.hawaii.org/bishop/geology/geology.html

Because of it's volcanic and tectonic setting, Hawaii is an ideal place for geologists to study hot-spot volcanism, mid-ocean ridges, mantle-plume processes, and other geological and volcanological events. The Bishop Museum the Geology group has the facilities for petrographic analysis and sample preparation, as well as the capabilities for chemical analysis of geological specimens. Recent projects include an oceanographic research expedition to the southeast Indian Ocean to study the formation of the Indian Ocean Basin as India, Australia, and Antarctica separated starting 150 million years ago. The 53-day research cruise in February-April, 1996, collected seafloor rock samples from 98 sites along 1600 km of the Southeast Indian Ridge a ifting that occurs along the licollected multi-narrow beam swath sonar data used to construct bathymetric maps of the region. Other programs have include a geochemical study to investigate the structure of the Hawaiian hotspot by studying lavas erupted at Kilauea over much of it's history. "We will look at three very deep cores (1500-2000 meters long) that represent 100,000-200,000 years of eruptions at Kilauea. This will tell us how the compositions of lavas changed over most of Kilauea's life and from this we will learn about the hot spot's size and structure deep in the Earth's mantle."

California Earthquake Maps
http://quake.usgs.gov/recenteqs/

The earthquakes displayed on these maps and associated web pages have been detected and located by the combined seismographic

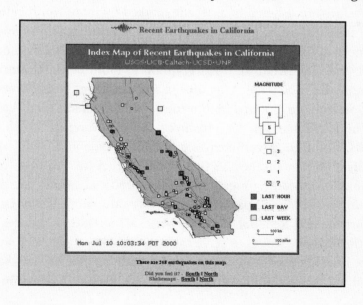

networks of the U.S. Geological Survey, Menlo Park and USGS, Pasadena, CA; the Seismological Laboratory, University of California, Berkeley; the Seismological Laboratory, California Institute of Technology; and the Seismological Laboratory, University of Nevada, Reno. Seismic signals are telemetered in real-time by radio and land lines from over 600 remote seismic stations in the region to one or more of the four centers. Real-time computer systems at each center continuously monitor the Earth for the occurrence of earthquakes. When an earthquake occurs, seismic waves are created, which propagate away from the focus or hypocenter. The fastest waves, the P-wave, travels outward at a speed of about 3 to 5 miles/second. As the P-wave passes each seismic station, its arrival time is detected and noted by the real-time computers. The computers use the list of arrival times to determine the location of the earthquake. The location is typically available within a minute or less after the occurrence of the earthquake. Once the location of the earthquake is known, a signal is sent to the computer that updates these web pages.

Cascades Volcano Observatory
http://vulcan.wr.usgs.gov/

The 1980 cataclysmic eruption of Mount St. Helens in southwestern Washington ushered in a decade marked by more worldwide volcanic disasters and crises than any other in recorded history. Volcanoes killed more people (over 28,500) in the 1980's than during the 78 years following the 1902 eruption of Mont Pelee (Martinique). Not surprisingly, volcanic phenomena and attendant hazards received attention from government authorities, the news media, and the general public. As part of this enhanced global awareness of volcanic hazards, the U.S. government significantly expanded the Volcano Hazards Program of the U.S.Geological Survey in response to the eruptions or volcanic unrest during the 1980's at Mount St. Helens (Washington), Mauna Loa and Kilauea (Hawaii), Long Valley Caldera (California), and Redoubt Volcano (Alaska)The USGS Cascades Volcano Observatory strives to serve the national interest by helping people to live knowledgeably and safely with volcanoes and related natural hazards including earthquakes, landslides, and debris flows in the western United States and elsewhere in the world. CVO assesses hazards before they occur by identifying and studying past hazardous events. They provide warnings during volcanic crises by intensively monitoring restless volcanoes and interpreting results in the context of current hazards assessments. They also investigate and report on hazardous events after they occur to improve assessment and prediction skills, and to help develop new concepts of how volcanoes work.

Cornell Geoscience Information Server
http://atlas.geo.cornell.edu/index.html

These web pages have been developed to disseminate data, knowledge, and information to researchers, educators, students, and the public. Most of the pages include terms, definitions, and information that are technical in nature and may not be informative for general public. However, some of the maps and tools could be of general interest to all interested parties. One interesting Cornell research project involves documenting active faults and constraining the rates of recent deformation along the northern Dead Sea fault system (DSFS) in western Syria and Lebanon. These results will provide critical information for future earthquake hazard assessments in the region. From a tectonic point of view, the region encompassing western Syria and Lebanon offers critical information on the transfer of strain between two relatively simple fault segments to the north and south. "Our research incorporates studies at both local and regional scales," they write. "Specific goals include constraining the long-term rates of fault slip and possible fault segmentation, as well as the timing and possible magnitudes of past events. Working with local scientists, detailed field investigations are being conducted involving the mapping of geomorphic and structural features along DSFS. Paleoseismic studies will extend the earthquake record further back in time and build upon a nearly 2,000 year record of historical seismicity."

Geological Society of America
http://www.geosociety.org/

The Geological Society of America is a nonprofit organization dedicated to the advancement of the geosciences. James Hall, James D. Dana, and Alexander Winchell founded GSA in New York in 1888. As a descendent of the American Association for the Advancement of Science, GSA is the first enduring society for the geosciences in America. Headquarters offices have been in Boulder, Colorado, since 1968. The management of the Society's affairs is under the control of its elected officers (Executive Committee and Council). GSA is an expanding global membership society with nearly 16,000 members in more than 85 countries. Twenty percent of its members are students. The Society's primary activities are organizing scientific meetings and conferences and publishing scientific literature. Other activities include disbursing research grants, operating an employment matching and interview service, honoring outstanding scientific contributors with medals and awards, assisting teachers in geoscience education, and fostering public awareness of geoscience issues. An individual may join GSA as a Member, Student Member, Student Associate or Teacher Member. Established GSA members may be nominated and elected to Fellow status. GSA offers reduced membership dues to all Students, Teacher Members, Senior Members and Senior Fellows. All members receive special benefits such as the monthly newsletter, GSA Today, and reduced rates on GSA publications and meetings. All members except Student Associates have full voting rights.

Geological Survey of Finland
http://www.gsf.fi/

The Geological Survey of Finland (GTK) is a modern research center that provides consultancy services and basic geological information essential for assessment of raw materials, nature conservation, environmental studies, construction, land use planning and for new applications, such as medical geology. Providing society with relevant and comprehensive geoscientific information and related data services is also an essential part of GTK's operational activities. The Geo-

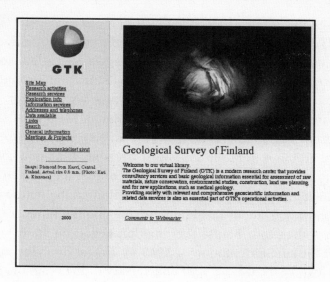

logical Survey of Finland, which was established in 1885, is a government funded agency responsible to the Ministry of Trade and Industry. It has a central administration based in Espoo and regional offices in Kuopio and Rovaniemi. The GTK is one of the leading geological organizations in Europe with a permanent staff of 700, including nearly 300 geologists, geophysicists and geochemists. It has an annual budget of USD 50 million. The GTK acquires, assesses and makes available geological information in promoting the balanced, long-term use of natural resources, particularly for exploration and mining companies and the construction industry, as well as for land use, environmental protection and public health authorities. The GTK offers its services to customers both in Finland and world wide. With its extensive data bases and wide range of experitise in the geosciences, the GTK is particularly well equipped for conducting multidisciplinary studies.

Hawaii Volcano Observatory
http://hvo.wr.usgs.gov/

Much of the present research on Hawaiian volcanoes is directed toward understanding how they work. Through interdisciplinary study of their geologic histories and structure, the geochemistry of their gases and erupted lavas, their historical eruptions, and their seismicity, HVO scientists and colleagues try to answer questions about the physical and chemical dynamics of magma formation, accumulation, ascent, storage, intrusion, eruption, structural evolution, and volcanic hazards. Be sure to visit the web pages here that are devoted to the June 1, 1000 50th anniversary of Mauna Loa's most spectacular eruption! The 1950 eruption was the largest and most spectacular historical eruption from the southwest rift zone of Mauna Loa. It was especially noteworthy, for lava was erupted from a nearly continuous 20-km-long fissure along the middle portion of the rift. One of the significant things about this eruption was that the flows reached the sea in less than four hours. The eruption began on June 1, 1950. It followed the summit eruption of 1949 by almost one year, consistent with the two years. On the 50th anniversary of the eruption, this article summarizes the high (and low) points of the eruption.

International Union of Geographical Sciences
http://www.iugs.org/

The International Union of Geological Sciences (IUGS) is one of the largest and most active non-governmental scientific organizations in the world. Founded in 1961, IUGS is a member of the International Council of Scientific Unions. IUGS promotes and encourages the study of geological problems, especially those of world-wide significance, and supports and facilitates international and interdisciplinary cooperation in the earth sciences. At present IUGS gives special consideration to: initiatives related to the identification and assessment of energy and mineral resources; global change; geologic hazards; and environmental geology. IUGS Commissions, Committees, and Boards are concerned with a wide range of geologic research of direct interest to governments, industry, and academic groups within the earth sciences. IUGS believes that it is of mutual benefit to establish close links with other organizations engaged in geoscience activities, and especially those organizations whose work relates to some of the major activities of IUGS. IUGS fosters dialogue and communication among the various specialists in earth sciences around the world. It achieves this by organizing international projects and meetings, sponsoring symposia and scientific field trips, and producing publications. Topics addressed span the gamut from fundamental research to its economic and industrial applications, from scientific, environmental and social issues to educational and developmental problems.

The Kelso Landslide
http://www.nwgeoscience.com/kelso/

There are forces acting on everything. Gravity and friction effect us in the simplest of tasks. Slopes are just as susceptible to the forces of gravity and friction as anything. Forces present on slope systems are dependent upon many different factors that combine and interact. The "type of material in the movement, topography, climate, vegetation, water amounts, and time" are all major factors governing slope systems . The main relationship in a slope system is between the driving forces and the resisting forces. Driving forces work to move materials such as rocks and soils down the slope. The resisting forces work to keep downslope motion from occurring. The main driving force on a slope is the weight of the material either in the slope system of built on top of it. These things can include the soil itself, rocks plants, and

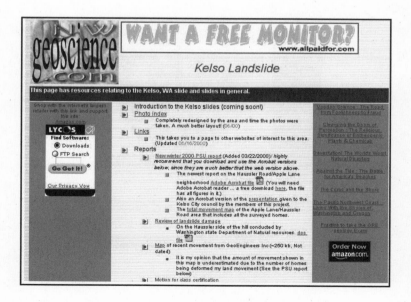

buildings. The main resisting force is the "strength of the slope materials acting along potentail slip planes." Slope stability can be expressed in terms of the Safety Factor. The safety factor is the ratio of the resisting forces to the driving forces. If the safety factor is greater than one the slope is stable, but if the safety factor is less than one, a mass movement may be imminent. Learn more at this informative web page.

Ocean Drilling Program
http://www-odp.tamu.edu/

The Ocean Drilling Program (ODP) is an international partnership of scientists and research institutions organized to explore the evolution and structure of Earth. ODP provides researchers around the world access to a vast repository of geological and environmental information recorded far below the ocean surface in seafloor sediments and rocks. By studying ODP data we gain a better understanding of Earth's past, present, and future. The ODP/TAMU web page provides relevant information to the news media, television/movie producers, scientific community, industry and educators regarding ODP science and engineering innovations. Presentation material is available such as videos, 35mm color slide sets, black and white pho-

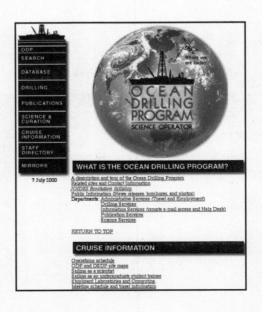

tos, written background material, and more for anyone working on projects related to scientific ocean drilling. The site includes information on the recently renamed research drilling ship JOIDES Resolution, which began operations in January 1985 as the Sedco/BP 471. The vessel is named for the HMS Resolution, commanded by Captain James Cook over 200 years ago, which explored the Pacific Ocean, its islands, and the Antartic region. Like its namesake, the purpose of the current Resolution is to sail for scientific exploration. But this time, those discoveries lie deep beneath the oceans.

Plate Tectonics
http://www.platetectonics.com/

This web site includes The Tectonic Globe—a unique globe that accurately describes all of the Earth's crustal tectonic features. Handcrafted to depict mid-ocean ridges, subduction zones, and island chains, this beautiful globe is unlike anything you will find anywhere else. You can also view the breathtaking panorama of world ocean floors. Browse and click around for selected close-ups of and commentary about Earth's tectonic features... and explore the wide ranging effects of plate tectonics on global climate, the origin of life an Earth, and the course of biological evolution. As the webamaster writes: "The story of plate tectonics is a fascinating story of continents drifting majestically from place to place breaking apart, colliding, and grinding against each other; of terrestrial mountain ranges rising up like rumples in rugs being pushed together; of oceans opening and closing and undersea mountain chains girdling the planet like seams on a baseball; of violent earthquakes and fiery volcanoes. Plate Tectonics describes the intricate design of a complex, living planet in a state of dynamic flux." Come to this comprehensive web site for exhaustive plate tectonic information of the very best kind.

San Andreas Fault
http://pubs.usgs.gov/gip/earthq3/

The presence of the San Andreas fault was brought dramatically to world attention on April 18, 1906, when sudden displacement along the fault produced the great San Francisco earthquake and fire. This earthquake, however, was but one of many that have resulted from episodic displacement along the fault throughout its life of about 15-20 million years. Scientists have learned that the Earth's crust is fractured into a series of "plates" that have been moving very slowly over the Earth's surface for millions of years. Two of these moving plates meet in western California; the boundary between them is the San Andreas fault. The Pacific Plate (on the west) moves northwestward relative to the North American Plate (on the east), causing earthquakes along the fault. The San Andreas is the "master" fault of an intricate fault network that cuts through rocks of the California coastal region. The entire San Andreas fault system is more than 800 miles long and extends to depths of at least 10 miles within the Earth. In detail, the fault is a complex zone of crushed and broken rock from a few hundred feet to a mile wide. Many smaller faults branch from and join the San Andreas fault zone. Almost any road cut in the zone shows a myriad of small fractures, fault gouge (pulverized rock), and a few solid pieces of rock. Visit the web site for more information.

Volcanic Home Page (Japan)
http://www.aist.go.jp/GSJ/~jdehn/v-home.htm

What, exactly, are volcanoes? Formally: apertures in the crust of a planet or natural satellite through which gases, LAVA, and solid fragments are discharged. The term is also applied to the conical mountain (cone) built up around the vent by ejected matter. Volcanoes are described as active, dormant, or extinct. On earth about 500 are known to be active. Belts of volcanoes are found along the crest of the mid-ocean ridge system under the ocean and at converging crustal plate boundaries (see the Plate Tectonics web page, above). There are also isolated volcanoes not associated with crustal movements, which may form from rising magma regions called hot spots. Eruptions range from the quiet type (Hawaiian) to the violently explosive (e.g., PELéE and KRAKATOA). In 1971 the Mariner 9 Space Probe revealed that the planet Mars also has volcanoes, including the largest in the solar system, Olympus Mons. Voyager 1 photographed (1979) at least eight active volcanoes on Io, a satellite of Jupiter, and Magellan provided (1991) evidence of widespread volcanism on Venus. Visit this great, profusely-illustrated web site for even more details on volcanoes and their related geology.

Volcano Hazards Program (USGS)
http://volcanoes.usgs.gov/

Many kinds of volcanic activity can endanger the lives of people and property both close to and far away from a volcano. Most of the activity involves the explosive ejection or flowage of rock fragments and molten rock in various combinations of hot or cold, wet or dry, and fast or slow. Some hazards are more severe than others depending on the size and extent of the event taking place and whether people or property are in the way. And although most volcano hazards are triggered directly by an eruption, some occur when a volcano is quiet. Volcano monitoring methods are designed to detect and measure changes in the state of a volcano caused by magma movement beneath the volcano. Rising magma typically will (1) trigger swarms of earthquakes and other types of seismic events; (2) cause swelling or subsidence of a volcano's summit or flanks; and (3) lead to the release of volcanic gases from the ground and vents. By monitoring these phenomena, scientists are sometimes able to anticipate an eruption days to weeks ahead of time and to detect remotely the occurrence of certain volcanic events like explosive eruptions and lahars. Visit the USGS Volcanic Hazards web page for more information.

mailing lists:

Find details on all of the following mailing lists at the url http://craton.geol.brocku.ca/guest/jurgen/list.htm

Geo-tectonics (the Discussion List of the Tectonic Studies Group)

Canadian Tectonics Group Discussion List

Yuruyuru (Mailing List of the young Japanese Structural Geologists) [Info (in Jap.) | recent Mails]

Geo-metamorphism (the Discussion List of the Metamorphic Studies Group)

Geo-Physics (the Discussion List of the Royal Astronomical Society and the Geological Society)

AI-GEOSTATS Mailing List (Communication about Spatial Data Analysis: GIS, Geostatistics, Geoinformatics, Spatial Statistics, Sampling Strategies . . .)

Geoscience Information Mailing Lists (by Wuchang Wei, Scripps Institution of Oceanography)

Software-Mine Mailing List (Disscussion Group on Exploration and Mining Software-related Issues)

MINGEOL -Software Mailing List (Information about Mining, Geology and other Earth Science Software.)

Newsgroups:

bionet.biology.deepsea
   Deep-sea marine biology, oceanography, and geology. (Moderated)

sci.geo.fluids
   Discussion of geophysical fluid dynamics.

sci.geo.geology
   Discussion of solid earth sciences.

13

HISTORY AND HEROES OF SCIENCE & INVENTION

Atomic Archive: History and Consequences of the Atomic Bomb
http://www.atomicarchive.com/

"At Los Alamos during World War II there was no moral issue with respect to working on the atomic bomb. Everyone was agreed on the necessity of stopping Hitler and the Japanese from destroying the free world. It was not an academic question , our friends and relatives were being killed and we, ourselves, were desperately afraid." So wrote Joseph O. Hirschfelder, chemist associated with the Manhattan Project. This site explores the complex history surrounding the invention of the atomic bomb—a crucial turning point for all mankind. AJ Software & Multimedia presents this site as an online companion to its CD-ROM, Atomic Archive. Follow a timeline that takes you down the path of our nuclear past, from the 1920s to the present. Read biographies of A-bomb father Robert Oppenheimer and other key scientists of the nuclear age. See the Trinity Test through Enrico Fermi's eye as you read his first hand account of that history making event. Examine maps of the damage to Hiroshima and Nagasaki, and summaries of arms-control treaties. You'll also find a gallery of exclusive photographs and animations of nuclear physics.

Benjamin Banneker
http://library.thinkquest.org/3337/banneker.html

Benjamin Banneker was a scientist, scholar, astronomer, and mathematical wizard. He was born a free man in the State of Maryland in 1731. Banneker was known and respected throughout America and Europe for his mathematics skills. He built the first wood en striking clock in America which kept accurate time for 53 years. President Jefferson chose Banneker to assist in developing plans for laying out the streets of Washington, DC. When L'Enfant, the architect for the project, left the project, Banneker d rew the plans for the city from memory. Banneker also published a "Farmer's Almanac" from 1892-1797. The Almanac won Banneker fame as far away as England and France. He used his reputation to promote social change: namely, to eliminate racism and war. He sent a copy of his first Almanac to Thomas Jefferson, with a letter protesting that the man who declared that "all men are created equal" owned slaves. Jefferson responded with enthusiastic words, but no political reform. Similarly, Banneker's attempts "to inspire a veneration for human life and an horror for war" fell mainly on deaf ears.

But Banneker's reputation was never in doubt. He spent his last years as an internationally known polymath: farmer, engineer, surveyor, city planner, astronomer, mathematician, inventor, author, and social critic. He died on October 25, 1806.

Alexander Graham Bell Institute
http://bell.uccb.ns.ca/

The Alexander Graham Bell Institute (The Bell Institute) of the University College of Cape Breton was incorporated on September 13, 1977. It is directed by a Board of Trustees representing the Bell family, University College of Cape Breton and members of the community. Over the years, the Bell institute has achieved several notable milestones including consolidating photographs, personal notes, and technical work of Alexander Graham Bell, completing a comprehensive index of these holdings, and conducting scholarly study of these materials. The Bell Institute is dedicated to the memory of Dr. Alexander Graham Bell and his work. Continued study of Dr. Bell's work ("Mining for nuggets") and development of new applied research projects are motivated by a desire to continue his high standard of principle, his practicle spirit and his social conscience. The Alexander Graham Bell family collection brings together a wide range of documents accumulated by Dr. Bell and his family during their time in

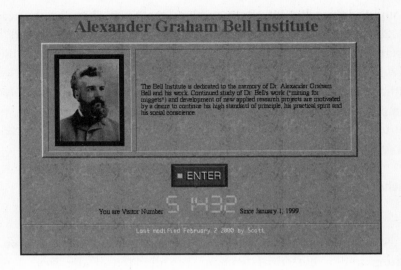

Baddeck, Nova Scotia. The Alexander Graham Bell institute has developed a comprehensive index of these materials. This index, with online access to several components of the Bell collection, can be accessed using the World Wide Web.

Niels Bohr Archive

http://www.asap.unimelb.edu.au/hstm/data/430.htm

Ernest Rutherford's model of the atom, developed at the turn of the century, pictured negatively charged electrons moving in circular orbits about a positively charged nucleus. Contradictory to electrodynamic theory the electrons did not emit electromagnetic radiation. Niels Bohr provided the explanation by incorporating Max Planck's quantum theory into Rutherford's atomic model. He envisioned specific discrete energy levels (i.e., shells) for the electrons within which they could move yet not emit radiation. Only if the electrons dropped to a lower energy level, or were raised to a higher level, would they emit or absorb electromagnetic radiation. That the energy of the emitted or absorbed radiation must equal the difference between the original and final energy levels of the electrons explained why atoms only absorb certain wavelengths of radiation. To Albert Einstein, Bohr's achievements were "the highest form of musicality in the sphere of thought". In recognition, Bohr received the Nobel Prize in physics in 1922. Later, Louis de Broglie and Erwin Schr"dinger described the electron as a standing wave rather than a particle, which "explained" how Bohr's electrons could move about within a defined energy level without emitting radiation. This led Bohr to his famous principle of complementarity, whereby the electron could be interpreted in two mutually exclusive yet equally valid ways: by either the particle or wave models.

Rachel Carson

http://www.dep.state.pa.us/dep/PA_Env-Her/rachel.htm

She was belittled as an antihumanitarian crank, a priestess of nature, and a hysterical woman. The director of the New Jersey Department of Agriculture believed she inspired a "vociferous, misinformed group of nature-balancing, organic gardening, bird-loving, unreasonable citizenry." An official of the Federal Pest Control Review Board, ridiculing her concern about genetic mutations caused by the use of pesticides, remarked, "I thought she was a spinster. What's she so worried about genetics for?"

Undaunted, Rachel Carson endured such attacks with a dignity, strength of conviction, and moral courage alien to her opponents. Just what had this native Pennsylvanian done to provoke these venomous and vengeful reactions? She wrote Silent Spring, a book destined to irrevocably change the course of world history. Rachel Carson never claimed to be anything more than a scientist and an author. A trained marine biologist, she devoted her life to exploring, understanding, and sharing—in exquisitely lyrical prose—the wonders of ocean life. Her decision to write Silent Spring, a book warning of the hazards of pesticide misuse and abuse, was not easy. Her earlier books had revealed the beauty, the diversity, and the incredible vitality of nature. With Silent Spring, however, Carson confronted the senseless destruction of nature by a society blinded by technological progress.

George Washington Carver

http://www.lib.iastate.edu/spcl/gwc/home.html

From inauspicious and dramatic beginnings, George Washington Carver became one of the nation's greatest educators and agricultural researchers. At the Tuskegee Institute, he gained an international reputation in research, teaching and outreach. Carver taught his students that nature is the greatest teacher and that by understanding the forces in nature, one can understand the dynamics of agriculture. He instilled in them the attitude of gentleness and taught that education should be "made common"—used for betterment of the people in the community. Carver's work resulted in the creation of 325 products from peanuts, more than 100 products from sweet potatoes and hundreds more from a dozen other plants native to the South. These products contributed to rural economic improvement by offering alternative crops to cotton that were beneficial for the farmers and for the land. During this time, Carver also carried the Iowa State extension concept to the South and created "movable schools," bringing practical agricultural knowledge to farmers, thereby promoting health, sound nutrition and self-sufficiency. Carver died in 1943. He received many honors in his lifetime and after, including a 1938 feature film, Life of George Washington Carver; the George Washington Carver Museum, dedicated at Tuskegee Institute in 1941; and the Roosevelt Medal for Outstanding Contribution to Southern Agriculture in 1942.

Nicholas Copernicus Museum at Frombork

http://www.frombork.art.pl/

While he was in Italy, Copernicus visited Rome, and it seems to have been for friends there that in about 1513 he wrote a short account of what has since become known as the Copernican theory, namely that the Sun (not the Earth) is at rest in the centre of the Universe. A full account of the theory was apparently slow to take a satisfactory shape, and was not published until the very end of Copernicus's life, under the title On the revolutions of the heavenly spheres (De revolutionibus orbium coelestium, Nuremberg, 1543).

Copernicus is said to have received a copy of the printed book for the first time on his deathbed. (He died of a cerebral haemorrhage.) Copernicus's heliostatic cosmology involved giving several distinct motions to the Earth. It was consequently considered implausible by the vast majority of his contemporaries, and by most astronomers and natural philosophers of succeeding generations before the middle of the seventeenth century. Its notable defenders included Johannes Kepler (1571–1630) and Galileo Galilei (1564–1642). Strong theoretical underpinning for the Copernican theory was provided by Newton's theory of universal gravitation (1687). Visit this fascinating web page for many more details on one of science's great geniuses.

Marie Curie

http://www.nobelprizes.com/nobel/physics/1903c.html

Marie Curie is the most famous woman of physics. She has been recognized for her work with Nobel Prize awards in both physics (1903) and chemistry (1911). She got a late start with her education obtaining her license in physics in 1893 and the corresponding degree in mathematics in 1894. In 1903, she finally received her doctorate. Choosing raioactivity as a thesis topic, Madame Curie examined a number of substances and found that thorium and its compounds behaved the same way as uranium. While examining pitchblende, a uranium ore, she discovered radium and polonium. In 1910 she succeeded in isolating pure radium metal. Marie Curie was also instrumental in setting up the Curie laboratory in Paris. She died in 1934 of leukemia, thought to have been brought on by her extensive exposure to the high levels of radiation involved in her studies. Her most quotable quote? "Nothing in life is to be feared. It is only to be understood." In addition to the url listed above, you can also find great information on Marie Curie, her work, her life and her times at the web page for Oxford's Marie Curie Research Group: http://www. mcri.ac.uk/default.html

Charles Darwin: Three Works
http://www.infidels.org/library/historical/charles_darwin/

Darwin was born on 12 February, 1809 in Shrewsbury, England. At age sixteen, Darwin left Shrewsbury to study medicine at Edinburgh University. Repelled by the sight of surgery performed without anesthesia, he eventually went to Cambridge Univeristy to prepare to become a clergyman in the Church of England. After receiving his degree, Darwin accepted an invitation to serve as an unpaid naturalist on the H.M.S. Beagle, which departed on a five-year scientific expedition to the Pacific coast of South America. Darwin's research resulting from this voyage formed the basis of his famous book, On the Origin of Species by Means of Natural Selection. Published in 1859, the work aroused a storm of controversy. Here Darwin outlined his theory of evolution, challenging the contemporary beliefs about the creation of life on earth. Darwin continued to write and publish his works on biology throughout his life. He lived with his wife and children at their home in the village of Downe, fifteen miles from London. Thought now to have suffered from panic disorder, as well as from Chagas' disease contracted during his travels in South America, Darwin was plagued with fatigue and intestinal sickness for the rest of his life. He died on 19 April, 1882, and lies buried in Westminster Abbey. This web site gives you digital editions of Darwin's books.

Dialogue Concerning Two New Sciences by Galileo
http://www.phys.virginia.edu/classes/109N/tns.htm

Galileo Galilei's father, Vincenzo Galilei (c.1520–1591), who described himself as a nobleman of Florence, was a professional musician. He carried out experiments on strings to support his musical theories. Astronomer and mathematician Galileo was born in Pisa, Italy. He entered Pisa University as a medical student in 1581, and became professor of mathematics at Padua (1592–1610), where he improved the refracting telescope (1610), and was the first to use it for astronomy. His bold advocacy of the Copernican theory brought severe ecclesiastical censure. He was forced to retract before the Inquisition, and was sentenced to indefinite imprisonment—though the sentence was commuted by the pope, at the request of the Duke of Tuscany. Under house arrest in Florence, he continued his research, though by 1637 he had become totally blind. Among his other discoveries were the law of uniformly accelerated motion towards the Earth, the parabolic path of projectiles, and the law that all bodies have weight. The validity of his scientific work was finally recognized by the Roman Catholic Church in 1993. This web site gives you a digital edition of one of Gelileo's greatest books.

Thomas Edison Papers at Rutgers
http://edison.rutgers.edu/

The extensive collection of papers preserved in the archive at the Edison National Historic Site—approximately 5 million pages in all—is the product of Thomas Alva Edison's sixty-year career as inventor, manufacturer, and businessman. Until now, the sheer size and organizational complexity of the archive have deterred researchers from delving extensively into its wealth of documentary resources. With the publication of the selective microfilm and book editions, these historically significant papers are for the first time readily available to scholars and other researchers. Edison and his associates used ledger volumes, pocket notebooks, and unbound scraps of paper on an irreg-

ular basis throughout the inventor's career. In 1877, however, Edison instituted a more regular practice for note keeping that, with some refinements, continued throughout his life. At first Edison used 9" _ 11" softcover tablets, whose sheets tore away from the top edge. Only a few of these notebooks were retained in their original condition. The majority were taken apart and, together with material on other loose pieces of paper, were organized according to the specific invention to which they related. Visit this informative web site for more details.

Albert Einstein
http://www.humboldt1.com/~gralsto/einstein/einstein.html

About 1912, Einstein began a new phase of his gravitational research, with the help of his mathematician friend Marcel Grossmann, by phrasing his work in terms of the tensor calculus of Tullio Levi-Civita and Gregorio Ricci-Curbastro. The tensor calculus greatly facilitated calculations in four-dimensional space-time, a notion that Einstein had obtained from Hermann Minkowski's 1907 mathematical elaboration of Einstein's own special theory of relativity. Einstein called his new work the general theory of relativity. After a number of false starts, he published the definitive form of the general theory in late 1915. In it the gravitational field equations were covariant; that is, similar to Maxwell's equations, the field equations took the same form in all equivalent frames of reference. To their advantage from the beginning, the covariant field equations gave the observed perihelion motion of the planet Mercury. In its original form, Einstein's general relativity has been verified numerous times in the past 60 years, especially during solar-eclipse expeditions when Einstein's light-deflection prediction could be tested. These insightful web pages reveal not only Einstein the scientist, but also the Eeinstein the man, the humanitarian, and the philosopher.

The Faces of Science: African Americans in the Sciences
http://www.princeton.edu/~mcbrown/display/faces.html

As the webmaster writes: "Profiled here are African American men and women who have contributed to the advancement of science and engineering. The accomplishments of the past and present can serve as pathfinders to present and future engineers and scientists. African American chemists, biologists, inventors, engineers, and mathematicians have contributed in both large and small ways that can be overlooked when chronicling the history of science. By describing the scientific history of selected African American men and women we can see how the efforts of individuals have advanced human understanding in the world around us." Consider, for example, astrophysicist George R. Carruthers. Born in 1939, George Carruthers received his B.S. Physics from University of Illinois in 1961, M.S. Physics in 1962, and his Ph.D. in aeronautical and astronomical engineering in 1964. Dr. Carruthers held the position of Rocket Astronomy Research Physicist from 1964 to 1982. He was Head of the Ultraviolet Measurements Branch of the Naval Research Laboratory. An inventor as well as physicist, George Carruthers was instrumental in the design of lunar surface ultraviolet cameras. Dr. Carruthers research focused on research in experimental investigations of atomic nitrogen recombination.

Enrico Fermi

http://www.fnal.gov/pub/fermi_biography.html

While studying the creation of artificially radioactive isotopes in the 1930s, Enrico Fermi became the first physicist to split the atom. His later research pioneered nuclear power generation. Born in Rome, Italy, Fermi graduated from the University of Pisa in 1922, became a lecturer at the University of Florence for two years and then a professor of theoretical physics at Rome. In 1934 he perfected his theory of beta ray emission in radioactivity, and went on to study the creation of artificially radioactive isotopes through neutron bombardment. His bombardment of uranium with slow neutrons caused reactions which were found later to be atomic fission. With Researcher Leo Szilard, he began work, first at Columbia then at the University of Chicago , on construction of an atomic pile which would make possible the controlled release of nuclear energy. This was accomplished in 1942. Transferred for a time to the Los Alamos nuclear laboratory , Fermi returned to Chicago in 1945 as a professor at the Institute for Nuclear Studies and in the same year became a United States citizen. He was awarded the Nobel Prize for physics in 1938 for his developments in harnessing nuclear power. Fermi is considered one of the most important architects of the nuclear age.

Richard Feynman
http://web.mit.edu/awhoward/www/feynman.html

As the webmaster writes: "Richard Feynman was an extraordinary man. Here was a man who could play every role: teacher, friend, father, musician, and even physicist. Feynman was born in a small town near New York City in 1918 and lived there until he went away to college at the Massachusetts Institute of Technology . After four years he went to Princeton University , then Los Alamos , Cornell , and finally Caltech . He was married three times during this peroid. Feynman passed away in February of 1988 from cancer. Feynman experienced many adventures during his life, and only a few of those are represented here. By making this page I hope to introduce you to Feynman with the hope that you will want to learn more about him in the future." Here you'll find plenty of Feynman wisdom. Example: "The questions of the students are often the source of new research. They often ask profound questions that I've thought about at times and then given up on, so to speak, for a while. It wouldn't do me any harm to think about them again and see if I can go any further now."

Galileo Museum in Florence
http://galileo.imss.firenze.it/museo/b/egalilg.html

The contributions made by Galileo to mechanics remain fundamental, despite the fact that this field of research met with less interest from the Medici Grand Dukes than Galileo's astronomical discoveries, perhaps because it was less spectacular. Galileo's investigations concerned the natural descent of bodies along planes of various inclinations, the formulation of the law which established the relationship between space traversed and time interval in free-fall, the isochronism of the oscillations of pendulums of equal lengths and, of particular importance, the motion of projectiles. At the end of the eighteenth century, from the necessity of displaying some of the mechanical principles discovered and demonstrated by Galileo, the Florentine Museum of Physics and Natural History had experimental devices constructed, such as the model of the inclined plane, the brachistochrone descent and the machine for raising water. The observations of the sky which Galileo carried out with his telescope led to the discovery of the satellites of Jupiter and to Galileo's increased adherence the Copernican System. The phenomena which were revealed little by little due to the increased possibility of larger lenses were described and illustrated by Galileo in Siereus Nuncius. The periods and frequencies of appearances of the satellites of Jupiter were studied by Galileo in order to develop a method for determing longitudes at sea. Visit the web page for more information.

Johann Carl Friedrich Gauss

http://www.phy.uct.ac.za/courses/phy104w/gauss.htm

Gauss published his second book, Theoria motus corporum coelestium in sectionibus conicis Solem ambientium, in 1809, a major two volume treatise on the motion of celestial bodies. In the first volume he discussed differential equations, conic sections and elliptic orbits, while in the second volume, the main part of the work, he showed how to estimate and then to refine the estimation of a planet's orbit. Gauss's contributions to theoretical astronomy stopped after 1817, although he went on making observations until the age of 70. Much of Gauss's time was spent on a new observatory, completed in 1816, but he still found the time to work on other subjects. His publications during this time include Disquisitiones generales circa seriem infinitam, a rigorous treatment of series and an introduction of the hypergeometric function, Methodus nova integralium valores per approximationem inveniendi, a practical essay on approximate integration, Bestimmung der Genauigkeit der Beobachtungen, a discussion of statistical estimators, and Theoria attractionis corporum sphaeroidicorum ellipticorum homogeneorum methodus nova tractata. The latter work was inspired by geodesic problems and was principally concerned with potential theory. In fact, Gauss found himself more and more interested in geodesy in the 1820's. Visit the Gauss web page for more info.

Jane Goodall

http://www.janegoodall.org/

The idea that we have much in common with chimps, including more than 98 percent of our genetic code, is now widely accepted. But chimp life was still a mystery in 1957, when, on a trip she had saved for years to make, a 23-year old Jane Goodall arrived in Kenya to visit a high school friend. Once there, in an effort to realize her dream of studying wild animals, she contacted Louis Leakey, a prominent anthropologist working at a Kenyan museum who would later become famous for his discoveries of early human remains at the Olduvai Gorge. She soon won a job assisting Leakey with his studies, doing everything from documenting monkey behavior to hunting for fossils. Leakey eventually encouraged Goodall to study chimpanzees, animals that he believed could provide us a window into our own beginnings. Many scientists were skeptical, even scandalized, by Leakey's suggestion that a young woman who had never gone to college could succeed as a lone field researcher in the chimpanzees' rugged mountain home. Nevertheless, in 1960, Goodall began her research at Gombe Stream National Park in the East African nation of Tanzania. Visit this web page for the rest of the story.

Edmond Halley

http://es.rice.edu/ES/humsoc/Galileo/Catalog/Files/halley.html

Halley was a major astronomer. He began observing seriously already as an undergraduate and published a paper on theoretical astronomy in the Philosophical Transactions at that time. He is known today primarily for A Synopsis of the Astronomy of Comets, 1705, but he made other important contributions: the catalogue of the southern skies (Catalogus stellarum australium, 1678), the method of measuring the astronomical unit via transits of Venus, the establishment of stellar motion and the secular acceleration of the moon. He published important editions of Apollonius and of other ancient geometricians as well as papers in pure mathematics. He is considered the founder of geophysics, especially for his paper on trade winds and his work on tides. He was one of the pioneers in social statistics by calculating annuities from the mortality tables of Breslau (1693). He was constantly concerned with the magnetism of the earth, and developed a general theory about this. He also experimented at determining the law of magnetic poles. He was concerned as well with weather, and published on the relation of barometric pressure to the weather.

Shirley Ann Jackson

http://www.princeton.edu/~mcbrown/display/jackson.html

Shirley Ann Jackson was born in Washington, D.C. in 1946. She received her B.S. from Massachusetts Institute of Technology in 1968 and her Ph.D. (Physics) in 1973. Shirley Jackson became the first African American female to receive a doctorate in Theoretical Solid State physics from MIT. Dr. Jackson became a Research Associate in Theoretical Physics at the Fermi National Accelerator Laboratory from 1973-1974 and served as a Visiting Science Associate at the European Organization for Nuclear Research (1974-1975). In 1975-76, Dr. Jackson returned to Fermi National Accelerator Laboratory as a Research Associate in Theoretical Physics. She spent 1976-77 at the Stanford Linear Accelerator Center and Aspen Center for Physics. Dr. Jackson then served on the Technical Staff of Bell Telephone Laboratories in theoretical physics from 1976 until 1978. In 1978 Shirley Jackson began working with the Technical Staff of the Scattering and Low Energy Physics Research Laboratory of Bell Telephone Laboratories. From 1976 to 1991 Dr. Jackson was appointed as Professor of Physics at Rutgers University in Piscataway, N.J. From 1991 to 1995, Dr. Jackson serving concurrently with her professorship at Rutgers as a consultant in semiconductor theory to AT&T Bell Laboratories in Murray Hill, N.J. Dr. Jackson was appointed as Commissioner of the Nuclear Regulatory Commission and assumed the Chairmanship on May 2, 1995.

Samuel Pierpont Langley

http://eosweb.larc.nasa.gov/education/Langley.html

As this web page informs us, Langley—one of the most prominent American scientists of a century ago—"started his scientific career as an astronomer in Ohio, where he became interested in measuring how much energy the sun was radiating. He built instruments, called calorimeters, to make these measurements. He built others, called bolometers, designed to make similar measurements on stars. Interestingly, the bolometers Langley built are very similar to the detectors scientists at NASA's Langley Research Center use to measure the Earth's radiation budget. Langley also became interested in heavier-than-air flight. He convinced the United States Navy to sponsor airplane building and testing, using his design. He competed with the Wright Brothers to build the first manned airplane that could fly under its own power. Unfortunately, Langley lost this contest. In the middle of his life, Langley moved to Washington, D.C. to become the third Secretary of the Smithsonian Institution. The brick building on the south side of the Mall in Washington (where the Washington Monument stands) was where Langley had his office nearly one hundred years ago. He published a book, called The New Astronomy, that still has many interesting perspectives on solar energy, sunspots, and our relationship with the environment."

Barbara McClintock

http://www.almaz.com/nobel/medicine/1983a.html

Barbara McClintock was born in 1902 just before Mendel's work on genetics was rediscovered. She studied as an undergraduate in the College of Agriculture at Cornell University and when on at Cornell to study both cytology and genetics as a graduate. McClintock received her doctorate in 1927. McClintock's first major contribution was made as a graduate student. She learned to identify each of the 10 maize chromosomes. McClintock was exclusively or partially responsible for many of the contributions made to cytology and genetics by the talented Cornell maize genetics group, including the cytological proof of genetic crossing over. On fellowships, she spent time as an instructor at Cornell, the California Institute of Technology and the University of Missouri. As an assistant professor at the University of Missouri, McClintock began to study chromosomes that had been broken by X radiation. Later, she devised a method for using these chromosomes to generate new mutations. She continued her work at Carnegie Institution and in 1944, she was elected to the National Academy of sciences and in 1945, to the presidency of the Genetics Society of America. In 1983, she received an unshared Nobel Prize for her discovery of transposable elements thirty-five years earlier. She died in 1992.

Sir Issac Newton

http://www.cannylink.com/historyissacnewton.htm

This noted English scientist and mathematician was born into a poor farming family. Luckily for humanity, Newton was not a good farmer, and was sent to Cambridge to study to become a preacher. At Cambridge, Newton studied mathematics, being especially strongly influenced by Euclid, although he was also influenced by Baconian and Cartesian philosophies. Newton was forced to leave Cambridge when it was closed because of the plague, and it was during this period that he made some of his most significant discoveries. With the reticence he was to show later in life, Newton did not, however, publish his results. Newton invented a scientific method which was truly universal in its scope. Newton presented his methodology as a set of four rules for scientific reasoning. These rules were stated in the Principia and proposed that (1) we are to admit no more causes of natural things such as are both true and sufficient to explain their appearances, (2) the same natural effects must be assigned to the same causes, (3) qualities of bodies are to be esteemed as universal, and (4) propositions deduced from observation of phenomena should be viewed as accurate until other phenomena contradict them. Visit the Issac Newton web site for more information.

J. Robert Oppenheimer

http://www.pbs.org/wgbh/aso/databank/entries/baoppe.html

Robert Oppenheimer was born April 22, 1904, in New York City. After graduating from high school he went to Harvard. He started as a chemistry major, but decided to switch to physics. He excelled in Latin, Greek, physics, and chemistry. After graduating in 1925 Oppenheimer sailed to England to study under Max Born for his decorate. Upon arriving back in the U.S., Oppenheimer became the head lecturer at the California Institute of Technology and the University of California at Berkley. In 1939 Oppenheimer married Katherine Harrison. They had two children. In 1942 Oppenheimer was asked to head a project to find a way to harness nuclear energy. This project took place in Los Alamos, New Mexico, and became known as the Manhattan Project. Oppenheimer was instrumental in the building of the atomic bomb which started in 1943 and ended in 1945. On July 16, 1945, the first atomic bomb was dropped at the test site in Alamogordo, New Mexico. On August 9, 1945, the first atomic bomb was dropped on Nagasaki, Japan. A second bomb was dropped three days later on Hiroshima, Japan. In 1954 Oppenheimer's clearance was revoked due to prewar involvement with communists. In 1963 Oppenheimer received the Enrico Fermi award, the highest award a physicist is able to receive. On April 22, 1967 Robert Oppenheimer died in Princeton, New Jersey.

James Clerk Maxwell

http://eosweb.larc.nasa.gov/education/Maxwell.htm

James Clerk Maxwell, who was born in Edinburgh, is generally regarded as one of the greatest physicists the world has ever seen. Einstein placed on record his view that the Scot's work resulted in the most profound change in the conception of reality in physics since the time of Newton. Maxwell's researches united electricity and magnetism into the concept of the electro-magnetic field. He died relatively young, and indeed some of the theories he advanced in physics were only conclusively proved long after his death. For example, he did not live to see proved in the laboratory his theory that when a charged particle is accelerated, the radiation produced has the same velocity as that of light: it is a unification that remains one of the greatest landmarks in the whole of science. It paved the way for Einstein's special theory of relativity. Maxwell's ideas also ushered in the other major innovation of twentieth-century physics, the quantum theory. Maxwell (1831–1879) graduated from the University of Edinburgh and went on to Cambridge. Maxwell was not accorded the honors, during his lifetime, that his many contributions and present rank in science would seem to have warranted. In part this was because contemporary scientists did not generally accept his theory of electromagnetism.

Louis Pasteur

http://www.ottawa.ambafrance.org/HYPERLAB/PEOPLE_pasteur.html

Over the course of 50 years-the second half of the 19th Century-Louis Pasteur's discoveries revolutionized chemistry, agriculture, industry, medicine, surgery and hygiene. These discoveries greatly improved the human condition. The diversity of his research, the brilliance of his intuitions, the rigor of his experimentations and the importance of the results he obtained dramatically advanced both science and its techniques. Each discovery in the body of Pasteur's work represents a link in an uninterrupted chain, beginning with molecular asymmetry and ending with his rabies prophylaxis, by way of his research in fermentation, silkworm, wine and beer diseases, asepsis and vaccines. In 1847 at the age of 26, Pasteur did his first work on molecular asymmetry, bringing together the principles of crystallography, chemistry and optics. He formulated a fundamental law: asymmetry differentiates the organic world from the mineral world. In other words, asymmetric molecules are always the product of life forces. His work became the basis of a new science-stereochemistry. Later, Emperor Napoleon III asked Pasteur to investigate the diseases afflicting wine which were causing considerable economic losses to the wine industry. Pasteur went to a vineyard in Arbois in 1864 to study this problem. He demonstrated that wine diseases are caused by microorganisms that can be killed by heating the wine to 55 C for several minutes. Applied to beer and milk, this process, called "pasteurization," soon came into use throughout the world.

Max Planck

http://www.windows.umich.edu/people/modern_era/planck.html

Planck's work on the quantum theory, as it came to be known, was published in the Annalen der Physik. His work is summarized in two books Thermodynamik (Thermodynamics) (1897) and Theorie der W"rmestrahlung (Theory of heat radiat ion) (1906). He was elected to Foreign Membership of the Royal Society in 1926, being awarded the Society's Copley Medal in 1928. Planck faced a troubled and tragic period in his life during the period of the Nazi government in Germany, when he felt it his duty to remain in his country but was openly opposed to some of the Government's policies, particularly as regards the persecuti on of the Jews. He was revered by his colleagues not only for the importance of his discoveries but for his great personal qualities. He was also a gifted pianist and is said to have at one time considered music as a career. Planck was twice married. Upon his appointment, in 1885, to Associate Professor in his native town Kiel he married a friend of his childhood, Marie Merck, who died in 1909. He remarried her cousin Marga von H"sslin. Three of his children died young, leaving him with two sons. He suffered a personal tragedy when one of them was executed for his part in an unsuccessful attempt to assassinate Hitler in 1944.

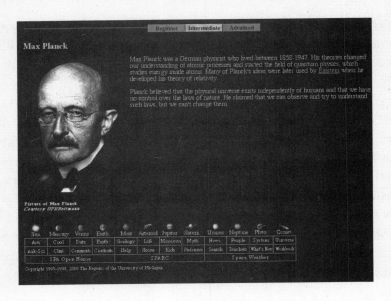

Ernest Rutherford
http://www.pbs.org/wgbh/aso/databank/entries/bpruth.html

Born in New Zealand in 1871, Rutherford studied under J. J. Thomson at the Cavendish Laboratory in England. His work constituted a notable landmark in the history of atomic research as he developed Bacquerel's discovery of Radioactivity into an exact and documented proof that the atoms of the heavier elements, which had been thought to be immutable, actually disintegrate (decay) into various forms of radiation. Rutherford was the first to establish the theory of the nuclear atom and to carry out a transmutation reaction (1919) (formation of hydrogen and and oxygen isotope by bombardment of nitrogen with alpha particles). Uranium emanations were shown to consist of three types of rays, alpha (helium nuclei) of low penetrating power, beta (electrons), and gamma, of exceedingly short wavelength and great energy. Ernest Rutherford also discovered the half-life of radioactive elements and applied this to studies of age determination of rocks by measuring the decay period of radium to lead-206. Rutherford recieved the Nobel Prize for Chemistry in 1908, was knighted in 1914, and made a peer in 1931. Visit this excellent web page for many more details on Rutherford's life, times, and science.

Leo Szilard Online

http://www.dannen.com/szilard.html

In the field of nuclear physics, Szilard's role as an inventor is well recognized, according to V.L. Telegdi of the University of California, San Diego, and CERN. The concept of a sustained nuclear chain reaction is credited to him, and a joint patent with Enrico Fermi covers all the essential features of the carbon-uranium reactor. "His proposals concerning accelerators, covered in applications for patents which never seem to have been issued, have not yet been publicized," says Telegedi. Szilard is also credited with inventing the cyclotron, the linear accelerator and the concept of phase stability, as well as drafting Albert Einstein's 1939 letter to President Franklin Roosevelt, which led to the Manhattan Project. Far from being limited to atomic physics, Szilard's interests ranged from statistical physics through information theory to biological evolution, from life phenomena through hot atoms to nuclear strategy and deterrance. In addition to being a creative physicist and biologist, Szilard's concern about how scientific discoveries might affect humanity led him to seek political solutions to enlarge the benefits and limit the damage caused by his work.

Alan Turing

http://www.turing.org.uk/

Many of the people who designed the early computers were both geniuses and eccentrics of the first order, and the English mathematician Alan Turing was first among equals.

In 1937, while a graduate student, Turing wrote his groundbreaking paper "On Computable Numbers with an Application to the Entscheidungsproblem." One of the premises of Turing's paper was that some classes of mathematical problems do not lend themselves to algorithmic representations and are not amenable to solution by automatic computers. Since Turing did not have access to a real computer (not unreasonably as they didn't exist at the time), he invented his own as an abstract "paper exercise." This theoretical model, which became known as a Turing Machine, was both simple and elegant, and subsequently inspired many "thought experiments."

A few years later Turing was destined to be a key player in the design and creation of Colossus, which was one of the world's earliest working programmable electronic digital computers. Turing was on the staff of the National Physical Laboratory at Teddington, London, working on ACE (Automatic Computing Engine); subsequently at the University of Manchester working on MADAM (Manchester Automatic DigitAlMachine).

14

KIDSTUFF

About Rainbows

http://www.unidata.ucar.edu/staff/blynds/rnbw.html

Ad Descartes wrote: "Considering that this bow appears not only in the sky, but also in the air near us,

whenever there are drops of water illuminated by the sun, as we can see in certain fountains, I readily decided that it arose only from the way in which the rays of light act on these drops and pass from them to our eyes. Further, knowing that the drops are round, as has been formerly proved, and seeing that whether they are larger or smaller, the appearance of the bow is not changed in any way, I had the idea of making a very large one, so that I could examine it better." Consider the path of a ray of monochromatic light through a single spherical raindrop. Imagine how light is refracted as it enters the raindrop, then how it is reflected by the internal, curved, mirror-like surface of the raindrop, and finally how it is refracted as it emerges from the drop. If we then apply the results for a single raindrop to a whole collection of raindrops in the sky, we can visualize the shape of the bow. Tune into this web site for more fun facts and folklore about rainbows.

All About Sharks

http://www.EnchantedLearning.com/subjects/sharks/index.html

Sharks are amazing fish that have been around since long before the dinosaurs existed. They live in waters all over the world, in every ocean, and even in some rivers and lakes. Unlike other fish, sharks have no bones; their skeleton is made of cartilage, which is a tough, fibrous substance, not nearly as hard as bone. Sharks have a variety of body shapes. Most sharks have streamlined, torpedo-shaped bodies that glide easily through the water. Some bottom-dwelling sharks (e.g. the angelshark) have flattened bodies that allow them to hide in the sand of the ocean bed. Some sharks have an elongated body shape (e.g., cookiecutter sharks and wobbegongs). Sawsharks have elongated snouts, thresher sharks have a tremendously elongated upper tail fin which they use to stun prey, and hammerheads have extraordinarily wide heads. The goblin shark has a large, pointed protuberance on its head; its purpose is unknown. There are many different species of sharks that range in size from the size of a person's hand to bigger than a bus. Fully-grown sharks range in size from 7 inches (18 cm) long (the Spined Pygmy shark), up to 50 feet (15 m) long (the Whale shark). Most sharks are intermediate in size, and are about the same size as people, 5-7 feet (1.5-2.1 m) long. Half of the 368 shark species are under 39 inches (1 m) long. Visit this web site for more fascinating deteails.

Ask Dr. Science!
http://www.ducksbreath.com/

As the webmaster writes: "Ask Dr. Science Web Site, the home of America's foremost authoritarian on the world around us. Or at least the world around him. "There is a thin line between ignorance and arrogance," he says, "and only I have managed to erase that line." Dr. Science is heard daily on radio stations throughout America and the world. We'll send you his Daily Question for free by e-mail. You can also see the 3D version of Dr. Science at the DotComix web site or pick up a few points on your IQ by shopping at the Doctor Science S-Mart. How does Dr. Science know the secrets of the universe? He has a Masters Degree . . . in Science!" Who is Dr. Science? For a man who weighs over 300 pounds, who is well past the prime of his life, who has neither bathed nor dabbled in social intercourse for over a decade, Dr. Science is surprisingly normal. Despite his girth and the aroma that follows him around his secret laboratory, the Fortress of Arrogance, Dr. Science presents an attractive and wholesome picture of the typical scientist at work. One unnatural subject currently under study by Dr. Science is those pesky UFO's frequently spotted by Kansas farmers and recreational chemical enthusiasts. If you thought Fox Mulder was an expert, wait until you hear what Dr. Science has to say about flying saucers.

Beakman's World Television Program
   http://www.beakman.com/

In 1993 a show was introduced in syndication ... a show that starred a guy with Frankenstein's Wife's hairdo, an old, fat guy in a giant rat suit, and an eager beaver young girl fielding questions. That show was called ... Beakman's World. Producers of the show ran about one season before CBS picked it up and ran with it for another three or four years. The show of fun, facts, and flatulence delighted viewers of ALL ages, even while on the Kid's Saturday Morning lineup. This page is chock full of information the much loved show Beakman's World. Beakman was taken off the air when CBS decided to cancel the show, but it is back five days a week on various stations across the country! For those of you new to the World of the Beakmeister, this was a fabulous show (BOKU EMMYS!!!) for sound design (An average of 1500 different sound cues per show), phenomenal directing and editing, and incredibly fresh performances. Fast and furiously paced, this show teaches why the energy of the universe is structured the way it is in one moment, and has you rolling on the ground the next.

Bear Den
   http://www.nature-net.com/bears/

Did you know: Koala bears from Australia are not real bears. They belong to a group of animals called marsupials. Marsupials have a pouch where they carry their young. Kangaroos are also marsupials. For a long time, scientists believed that giant panda bears from China were more like raccoons than bears. Today, we know that giant pandas are really bears. Only brown bears, polar bears and American black bears live in the United States and Canada. In Canada, only the province of Prince Edward Island has no American black bears. In the United States, 32 states have American black bears living in the forests. Brown bears, which live along the sea coast in Alaska and a land called Kamchatka in Russia, grow the largest. They feed on salmon, a type of fish. Some of these bears live on Kodiak Island near Alaska. They are called Kodiak bears. Much like dogs, the fur of a bear falls out and grows back each year. This is called molting. Some American black bears are white in color. These bears are called Kermode bears. They live on islands off the coast of British Columbia, Canada. They are not albino bears. They have brown eyes and a black nose like other bears. Visit this web page for other wonderful facts and fancies about bears of all kinds.

Children's Butterfly Site
http://www.mesc.nbs.gov/butterfly/Butterfly.html

This great web site includes: A coloring page that shows the life cycle of the Monarch butterfly; Some answers to frequently asked questions about butterflies and moths; Some references to butterfly and moth books and videos suitable for young people, including Butterfly Gardens, Activities with Butterflies, and Teacher Resources; Some hot-links to other World Wide Web sites that will provide additional information about these fascinating insects; and a wonderful

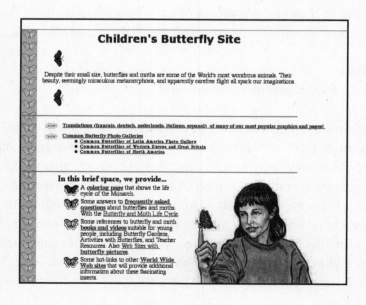

Gallery of full-color Butterfly photographs. Question: How many kinds of butterflies and moths are there? Answer: Butterflies and moths are found on all continents except Antarctica, and scientists estimate that there are approximately 12-15,000 species of butterflies and 150-250,000 species of moths. There are still thousands of moth and butterfly species that have not been found or described by scientists. In the United States and Canada, more than 750 species of butterflies and 11,000 species of moths have been recorded. Many species of moths and a few kinds of butterflies are still being discovered. There is much to be learned. The site gives you answers to dozens of other common questions about butterflys and their cousins, the moths.

Cool Kids Fishing
   http://www.ncfisheries.net/kids/index.html

WHY DO WE HAVE FISHING REGULATIONS? There are good reasons for fishing laws. All are intended to conserve and improve fish populations. Fisheries biologists study bodies of water to check on fish numbers and the health of fish populations. If there is a problem with a fish stock, regulations are created to help keep the fish population healthy. Marine Patrol officers check to make sure that fishing regulations are being obeyed. There are several types of fishing regulations. Limits on the number of fish that can be caught are meant to keep anglers from taking too many fish at one time. Size limits are meant to protect fish of spawning size before they are caught. Fishing seasons protect fish during spawning and limit the catch on heavily fished waters. Fishing laws are meant to protect fish and make sure there is fishing to be shared by everyone. If you fish, it's important that you know the rules and regulations. Ignorance of the law is no excuse. Fishing is a wonderful privilege; obeying fishing regulations is the responsibility that goes with it. Visit this web site for all sorts of information on how to have fun fishing while at the same time staying within the rules that are meant to protect wildlife.

Dan's Wild Weather Page
http://www.whnt19.com/kidwx/

Here are answers to scores of common weather question. For example, what is relative humidity? The relative humidity tells how much water the air is holding compared to how much it could hold at a certain temperature. If our blob of air has a relative humidity of 50% then that means it is holding half of the amount of water a blob of air 80 degrees could hold. The relative humidity can change if the moisture changes or if the temperature changes. And what is the dew point? The dew point is the temperature at which the air will be holding all the moisture it can if cooled. Or . . . another way of putting it. The dew point is the temperature at which the relative humidity reaches 100%. CONFUSED? Lets talk about our blob of 80 degree air. It has water vapor in it, and remember that warm air can hold more water than cold air. If we start cooling our blob of 80 degree air . . . it will eventually reach a temperature at which it can no longer hold the water vapor in it. Lets say that in this case our blob of air forms a cloud when we cool it to 50 degrees. Then 50 degrees in the dew point of our blob of air! Note that the dewpoint does not depend on the temperature like Relative Humidity!

Dr. Internet's Science Resources for Kids
http://www.ipl.org/youth/DrInternet/

Did you ever wonder why sometimes your hard boiled egg yolks have that icky gray ring around them? Well the this site will show you why! If you are itching to do some chemistry in the kitchen, this site is for you! Why does an ice cube float in water and not sink? This site will teach you about the structure of water, as well as show you how to do experiments in your classroom. Also: What will happen when an empty plastic bottle filled with warm air is placed in cold water? What happens? The bottle collapses! But why did the bottle collapse? By placing the bottle in the hot water the air inside became warm. The warm air expanded and took up more room in the bottle. When Morgan put the cap on it sealed a specific amount of air in the bottle. Then when the bottle was placed in the cold water the air cooled. Cool air doesn't take up as much room as warm air. The bottle then collapsed. Dr. Internet has tons of cool experiments and explanations for you at his web site. Check it out.

Explorers Club (from the EPA)
http://www.epa.gov/kids/

Here is the Explorers' Club—the US Environmental Protection AGency's website for kids ages 5 through 12. Get ready to explore your environment and learn about the neat things you can do to protect it. there are games, pictues and stories and other fun things. You can use most of the activities without special software. When specal plub-ins are needed. There will be instructions to help you download the software. You can find information on this great web page a couple of different ways—by clicking on a picture of an environmental subject or by clicking on one of the rooms in the clubhouse. Or, if you prefer, you can use a text-based page. Check out: Recycle City: a game in which an interactive storybook and other puzzles will teach you hundreds of ways a whole town can reduce, reuse, and recycle. Explore an 11-page Happy Earth Day Activity Book full of tips for making the Earth a better place. Have fun with the What's Wrong with this Picture? game. Can you find all the ways that we pollute the water around us? Click on the picture to learn about some of the most common things to avoid.

Fun Science Gallery
http://www.funsci.com/

Here you will find instructions showing you how to build scientific equipment from relatively cheap materials. This site is a must for the amateur scientist. Projects include instructions for making telescopes, microscopes, batteries, sidereal indicators, and several other instruments. Moreover, you will find programs on the lexical analysis of texts and the determination of the readability of texts. For example, you can build a simple light microscope. One of the first microscopes, invented by Anton van Leeuwenhoek, used a simple spherical glass lens as its objective. This might sound way too primitive to produce a useful image, but that's not the case. This article, part of a larger site devoted to "fun science," not only explains how such a microscope works—it also gives you and your students instructions on how to build one! The Fun Science Gallery os loaded with great laboratory activities such as performing scientific experiments or building instruments. Practical experiments are advantageous in that they call upon many of our faculties, not just those connected to language. They also have the important advantage of motivating children to engage in science.

Good Green Fun: The Rainforest for Kids
http://www.efn.org/~dharmika/oldindex.htm

A talented singer/songwriter brings you great Rain Forest related songs and activities. Teachers, parents, and children enjoy using Good Green Fun! to learn about forest ecology. For each song, you can cover habitats and systems, cycles, adaptations, and issues and interactions. The concepts listed in the chart below give a framework to work in, but they are not fixed. If a song inpires curiosity about a particular topic, go in that direction. If you already know of useful activities that convey a concept, use those; if not, there are many lesson plans and activites to work with, on and off of the internet. You can work with any learning

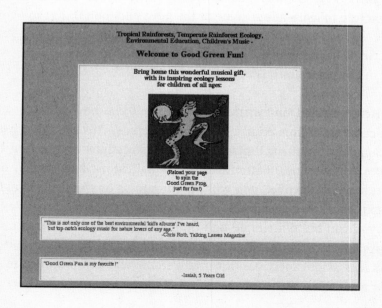

activities that teach about ecology, especially when the song-stories in Good Green Fun! enhance the concepts being studied. Games, puzzles, facts, quizzes, and and other fun learning activities are also fun and useful. You can also help by sharing with us any great game or activity that you know about that pertains to the ecology concepts listed. Don't miss the beautiful songs and useful activities you'll find at this web site.

Helping Your Child Learn Science (Online Book)
http://www.ed.gov/pubs/parents/Science/index.html

This online book provides examples of a few simple activities we can do with our children. It is an introduction to the wealth of material in many other books available in libraries and bookstores. It might also inspire us to make up our own experiments to see why and how things turn out the way they do. Science is not something mysterious. Being "scientific" involves being curious, observing, asking how things happen, and learning how to find the answers. Curiosity is natural to children, but they need help understanding how to make sense of what they see. Parents help their children learn—by reading to and with them, by helping them learn to count and calculate, by helping them begin to write, and in many other ways. Most parents, though, say they do not—or cannot—help their children with science. But we don't need degrees in chemistry or physics to help our children. All we need is a willingness to observe and learn with them, and, above all, to make an effort and take the time to nurture their natural curiosity.

Hurricane: Storm Science for Kids
http://www.miamisci.org/hurricane/

A hurricane is a powerful storm that measures several hundred miles in diameter. Hurricanes have two main parts. The first is the eye of the hurricane, which is a calm area in the center of the storm. Usually, the eye of a hurricane measures about 20 miles in diameter, and has very few clouds. The second part is the wall of clouds that surrounds the calm eye. This is where the hurricane's strongest winds and heaviest rain occur. Hurricanes are born over warm, tropical oceans. Hurricanes are fueled by water vapor that is pushed up from the warm ocean surface, so they can last longer and sometimes move much further over water than over land. The combination of heat and moisture, along with the right wind conditions, can create a new hurricane. The colors in hurricane radar images indicate the amount of rain falling in a given area. Each raindrop reflects the energy from the radar. Therefore, the more raindrops in a certain area, the brighter the color in the radar image of that area. The brighter the color on the radar image, the more moisture in the air. The bright red color around the eye indicates the area of heaviest rainfall. The green colored area has a moderate amount of rain, while the blue areas represent the least amount of rain. Visit the web site for lots more great hurricane information!

Magnet Man

http://www.execpc.com/~rhoadley/magindex.htm

The study of the magnetism found in the planets and the sun of our solar system has been a very exciting field during the last 100 years. Of course, trying to understand the magnetism within our own planet earth has been going on for a very long time, and only recently (within the 1990s) has a reasonable model been made which closely mimics how the magnetic field is created and how it changes over time. There are also models of the expected strength and direction of the magnetic field seen on the surface of the earth at various locations. But there is more to the Earth's magnetic field than what we can measure at various locations on its surface. There is also the effect the earth's magnetic field has on the solar wind coming from the sun. The solar wind is what the stream of particles created by the sun is called. It travels as fast as 1.7 million miles per hour (800 km/sec) and goes out in all directions from the sun! When special eruptions occur on the sun, we can measure the effects on Earth about 52 hours later. Several scientists have been studying the shape of the magnetic field of the earth out in the space around our planet, and have been able to obtain a good understanding of its shape and how it varies over time.

The Microbe Zoo

http://commtechlab.msu.edu/sites/dlc-me/zoo/

What is Microbial Ecology? Well, it is many things. Microbial ecology is the study microbes in their environment. Microbes are found in water, in soil and in the atmosphere. Microbial ecology is the study of the role of microbes which appear to be necessary for the functioning of life on Earth. Microbial ecologists seek to understand how microbes affect the environment on a global scale. Microbes probably contribute to global change, nutrient cycling, and ozone depletion. Microbial ecology is the study of microbial interactions with plants and with animals and with other microbes. Microbial ecology is an applied science. Knowledge of microbial ecology contributes to environmental protection, agriculture, mining, food production, and chemical and pharmaceuticals production. And Microbial ecology is a rapidly developing scientific discipline. The reasons for this include the realization that microbes are essential for a healthy environment; they are important in helping us understand the mechanics of evolution; and they are important in biotechnology. And What is a microbe? A microbe is any living organism that spends its life at a size too tiny to be seen with the naked eye. Microbes include bacteria and archaebacteria, protists, some fungi and even some very tiny animals that are too small to be seen without the aid of a microscope. Viruses and the recently discovered prions are also considered microbes. Visit the Microbe Zoo for more information.

Planet Pals

http://www.planetpals.com/

Learn all about ecology, including the great men and women of ecology, among then Henry David Thoreau. Thoreau earned his place in history on July 4, 1845, when he moved to Walden Pond, "to live deliberately." Over the past century and a half, millions have read his musings on his life there and been inspired. That day defined his life. His time at Walden, slightly over two years, demonstrated the natural harmony that was possible when a thinking man went to live simply, reading books, writing in his diary, cultivating his beans, and walking in the woods. The message that comes through most clearly from the pages of Walden is that this is, itself, a "Hero's journey." During his life, Thoreau was little known outside his small social and intellectual circle. Yet his reputation as a prophet for ecological thought and the value of wilderness, born at Walden, now grows with each passing year. He articulated the idea that humans are part of nature and that we function best, as individuals and societies, when we are concious of that fact. Visit the web site for more details on the Thoreau and, more importantly, the planet he strove to find harmony with.

The Secret Forest

http://www.afseee.org/sf/

Here you'll find links to cool researchers, scientists and rangers who live their lives studying and enjoying the great American woodlands. Why are these people so cool? They're scientists and teachers, and they get to spend most of their time in one of our 156 National Forests. Some hike, bike and climb cliffs to find evidence of endangered species, such as Peregrine falcons. Some work with kids like you to study the millions of little critters that live in the soil—and run the forest. Others work with community members to reintroduce important animals, such as beavers, into weakened streams. All of them LOVE to share their work with kids. These cool people can help you learn more about our National Forests—and they may even be able to help you answer a homework question about forest ecology. Don't be shy. These cool people are here to help you discover the mysteries—and the fun—of forest life. For example, consider Dave Mech who writes: "I have been studying wolves and deer in northeastern Minnesota since 1968, and wolves and caribou in Denali National Park, Alaska since 1986. I have also lived each summer since 1986 with a pack of wolves in the High Arctic to study their behavioral interactions and their predation on musk-oxen and arctic hares. This is probably the very coolest part of my job."

Neuroscience for Kids

http://faculty.washington.edu/chudler/neurok.html

Here are great neuroscience experiments and activities for kids. Make a model of the brain, a neuron or the retina. Fun for all. Check out the BRAIN recipes or take a peek at the Mammalian Brain Collection.

Can your eyes deceive you? How good is your memory? Do you like to play games or challenge your friends? Then check out the brain teasers, puzzles, games and jokes related to the nervous system. Also, get in on the neuroscience web search treasure hunt and compete for the "Golden Neuron Award". Next, check your reflexes. Quick! What was that? Jump, kick, and grab it before it hits the floor. How good are your reflexes? Quick and easy experiments are here for you to try. Then check your memory and learning skills. Would you be a good detective? Have you noticed what color eyes your best friend has? Can you remember what you had for dinner last night? Try techniques and activities to help you remember and understand how your brain "arranges" information. Finally, keep track of time with your internal clock. Our sleep patterns, body temperature, and our alertness are controlled by an internal clock. Would this internal clock still work if you were in the dark 24 hours a day? Do other animals have an internal clock? Find out.

Newton's Apple Television Program
http://ericir.syr.edu/Projects/Newton/

How do archeologists know where to dig? How do archeologists learn about people of the past? How can they turn bits and pieces of evidence into a big picture of the past? How did wild North American bison come back from near extinction? What role did bison play in North America's history? What factors contributed to their near extinction? What has been done to ensure their place in North America's future? What can we learn from our garbage? How much garbage do Americans throw away? What can we learn about individual life-styles from studying solid waste? What are some future solid waste disposal alternatives? How can windsurfers reach speeds faster than the wind that powers them? How does a windsurfing board use the wind to move? How does the windsurfer steer with the mast and sail? What are meteors and where do they come from? What is a meteor? When are you most likely to see meteors? Is there any way to predict them? What is permafrost? How can something be preserved for 30,000 years? How can humans adapt to permafrost? What can permafrost tell us about our past and future climate? Get the answers to all these questions and many more at the home page for the Newton's Apple television program.

Bill Nye, The Science Guy
http://nyelabs.kcts.org/

He's Mr. Wizard for the nineties! Bill Nye appears several times a week on Public Broadcasting, and appeals to kids of all ages, from 5 to 55. The Bill Nye site offers a fun way to learn about science. Simply go to the site and play! Activities—Activity 1: Do the Demo of the Day. Usually a simple experiment using everyday items to explain scientific phenomenon. Activity 2: Play a Quick time video that deals with a current science topic. Here you can also get details on Bill Nye's popular "Stop the Rock" CD. Using this entertaining CD, kids solve science riddles by experimenting with virtual equipment. Of course, "Bill Nye the Science Guy" is a series of 85 1/2 hour long programs designed to make science accessible and interesting to kids by relating science to their interests and everyday activities. Basic concepts are presented in a humorous and exciting format. The program's host, Bill Nye, conducts demonstrations and experiments in a variety of studio and field locations. Each program features a diverse cast of children, scientists and celebrity guests. Visit the web site for more information.

Optics for Kids
http://www.opticalres.com/kidoptx.html

What is light?

It's a kind of energy called "electromagnetic (EM) radiation" (but this kind of radiation is not harmful, except for an occasional sunburn). There are other kinds of EM radiation too (radio waves, microwaves, x-rays, etc.), but light is the part WE can see, the part that makes the rainbow. How does light travel?

FAST and STRAIGHT. How FAST? About 186,000 miles per second [300,000 kilometers per second], so light from the sun takes about 8 minutes to go 93 million miles [149 million kilometers] to earth. Does this seem SLOW? Well, if you could DRIVE to the sun at 60 mph [100 kph], it would take you 177 years to get there! In one second, light can go around the earth 7 times! How STRAIGHT? Perfectly straight, until something bends it. The straight paths of light are called LIGHT RAYS. What are lenses?

Lenses bend light in useful ways. Most devices that control light have one or more lenses in them (some use only mirrors, which can do most of the same things that lenses can do). Tune into "Optics for Kids" for other great questions and answers.

Science Made Simple
http://www.sciencemadesimple.com/

How do boats float? Why are leaves green? How do refrigerators work? Why do I get sick? What is plastic? How do light bulbs work? Why do I breathe? What is a rainbow? What makes the seasons? Why do the days get shorter? Why do people need eyeglasses? How do I hear sounds? How do batteries work? How do airplanes fly?

What's inside the Earth? Why is ice slippery? Why do dogs bark? How do trees grow? How do fish breathe underwater? Why is ocean water salty? Why is their water in a well? How do planes fly? How do birds fly? Why do elephants have tusks? Where does rain come from? Why are there no more dinosaurs? Why don't snakes have legs? Get easy answers for each question. Each answer has four sections: The main section gives a clear, detailed answer to the question. "I Can Read " pages are written in simple, clear language for young readers. "Learn More About It" pages are more difficult and cover additional information in more depth. Projects are included for each topic.

Spiders!

http://www.discovery.com/exp/spiders/spiders.html

Get the scoop on spiders from Kefyn M. Catley, Ph.D., Staff Scientist for Biodiversity, National Center for Science Literacy, Education and Technology and the Center for Biodiversity and Conservation at the American Museum of Natural History. Kefyn, a native Welshman, has a joint appointment at the museum. He splits his time between the Department of Entomology, where he studies spider systematics as a research fellow and the National Center for Science Literacy, Education and Technology, where he is the staff scientist for biodiversity. His current research involves a collaborative effort monographing the gnaphosoid ground spiders of Australasia. He has studied spider biodiversity in temperate South America, Australia, Europe and throughout North America. The author of many scientific papers and popular articles, Kefyn frequently gives presentations on various aspects of the natural world and teaches biodiversity classes for the museum. He is responsible for the scientific integrity of products relating to biodiversity emanating from the National Center, but also has a keen interest in biodiversity education, in particular integrating field studies into the curriculum. He leaves no question about spiders unanswered at this splendid web site dedicated to the whims, nature and lore of these multi-legged insects.

Reeko's Mad Scientist Lab
   http://www.spartechsoftware.com/reeko/

What can we say about Reeko? (In case you're wondering, Reeko is head mad scientist that runs this site). He's a big science fan. He spends most of his spare time watching the Discovery Channel and Beakman's World. Lives alone with his 3 cats. Oh yeah, and he's a computer nut too. Oh, you want to know about Reeko's Web site? OK, well, Reeko developed this Web site for three reasons: First, he has always been fascinated with science. It's still one of his favorite hobbies. Secondly, Reeko hopes he can instill his love of science into his two young kids. And lastly, Reeko is a professional programmer/analyst/Webmaster with too much free time on his hands. Reeko hopes the kids will find this page fun and hence foster a love for science. Reeko hopes parents will find this page interesting. Hopefully they'll sit down with their kids and attempt some of these experiments. Reeko believes they will have read the science facts so they understand the underlying principles behind these experiments. Then when the little one begins peppering them with questions, they'll explain the how and why of these experiments to their kids. Reeko believes you should always give your child the benefit of a doubt, no matter how difficult you think the topic may be—they may surprise you!

Water Science for Schools
   http://ga.water.usgs.gov/edu/

What makes water water? Water is a lot more than just wet—it has special properties that make it unique and valuable to all life on earth, including you. How much water is there on Earth? Where is it located? In what forms does it exist? Other water topics of interest are here as well. Find out if acid rain will turn your hair orange, look at how saline water is used, and examine water-quality issues. And there is more. Over the years, the U.S. Geological Survey has compiled a lot of data on how water is used in the United States. Here you'll find detailed water-use information by the category of use: public supply, domestic, commercial, industrial, irrigation, mining, electric power, hydroelectric power, livestock, and wastewater treatment. Is salt water used for anything in the U.S.? How can we have a 100-year flood two years in a row? What is an estuary? Why is the Hudson River more like a fjord than an actual river? Where does the city of Los Angeles get its water? Why are some water supplies innoculated with fluoride? Get the answers to all these questions and more at the web site Water Science for Schools.

The Why Files

http://whyfiles.news.wisc.edu/

The Why Files writers answer a host of engaging questions, such as: How do they remove ancient dinosaur fossils from the ground without wrecking them entirely? How do they mount fossils for public enjoyment—without wrecking them for science? Answer: The fundamental steps of fossil preparation have changed little since gung-ho dinosaur hunters roamed the range in the 1800s. First you unearth the fossils, then you extricate them from the matrix—the rock sticking to them. Finally, you mount the best specimens for study and stand back for the oohs and aahs. Consider Sue, the most complete T. rex ever found. Since the Field Museum paid more than $8-million for her, it stands to reason that she'd thrash some theories and substantiate others. One early casualty—based on holes in her jaw—was that she'd

been bitten by another dinosaur. The holes, however, don't match the tooth pattern of anything stupid enough to nibble a full-grown T. rex. Perhaps they were caused by infection, dinos being kinda weak in the flossing department. Did Sue neglect dental hygiene due to her acute sense of smell? Perhaps. Visit the site for these and other details.

WonderNet Experiments for Kids
http://www.acs.org/wondernet/activities/activities.html

Check out all sorts of interesting topics, such as simple matter. Matter is another word for the material that makes up all the stuff in the whole world. The matter we see around us every day is either a solid, a liquid, or a gas. These are called the three states of matter. One of the interesting things about the states of matter is that you can change a substance from one state to another. A good example is water. It can easily be changed from a solid (ice) to a liquid by warming it up. Also get the "skinny" on the science of color. Color is used all the time and in many different ways in chemistry. Color can help us figure out what a substance is, can help us tell when a substance has changed, and can even help tell us how strong or weak a substance is. Want more? How about all the ins and outs of chemical reactions? One of the most amazing things about chemicals is the way they can break apart and join together in new ways to form different chemicals. In fact, that's what a chemical reaction is: the process that changes one chemical into another.

Woodsy Owl
http://www.fs.fed.us/spf/woodsy/

In 1970, a fanciful creature named Woodsy Owl entered the lives of children all around the country. This outdoorsy new friend from the forest invited them to help him spread the word on protecting the environment, "Give a Hoot. Don't Pollute." As years passed, more children became Woodsy's allies by developing awareness of the local environment and a desire to use its resources in appropriate ways. Today, Woodsy has a new motto, "Lend a Hand—Care for the Land!" With this motto, this Forest Service symbol befriends another generation of children and motivates them to form healthy, lasting relationships with nature. Caring, friendly, outdoorsy, and wise, Woodsy is a good friend and partner. He is also a whimsical fellow and he's got his heart set on motivating kids to form healthy, lasting relationships with nature. As Woodsy flies across our land, he encourages youngsters to marvel at and explore the natural world, even in the city. He encourages everyone to make a positive difference in the world. Join the USDA Forest Service in introducing children to this fanciful creature. Woodsy is coming to you with simple, hands-on land stewardship activities—and there's so much more ahead.

15

MATHEMATICS

A Brief History of Algebra and Computing
http://www.museums.reading.ac.uk/vmoc/algebra/algebra.html

The first treatise on algebra was written by Diophantus of Alexandria in the 3rd century AD. The term derives from the Arabic al-jabr or literally "the reunion of broken parts." As well as its mathematical meaning, the word also means the surgical treatment of fractures. It gained widespread use through the title of a book ilm al-jabr wa'l-mukabala—the science of restoring what is missing and equating like with like—written by the mathematician Abu Ja'far Muhammad (active c.800-847), who subsequently has become know as al-

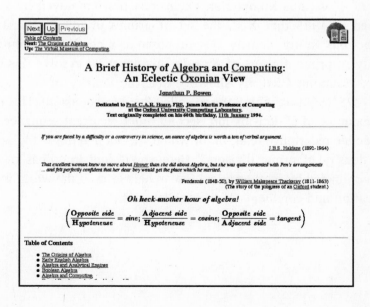

Khwarazmi, the man of Kwarazm (now Khiva in Uzbekistan). He introduced the writing down of calculations in place of using an abacus. Algorism (the Arabic or decimal system of writing numbers) and algorithm both derive from his name. Algebra was brought from ancient Babylon, Egypt and India to Europe via Italy by the Arabs. In the first half of the 16th century, Cuthbert Tonstall (1474-1559) and Robert Recorde (1510?-1558) were two of the foremost English mathematicians [2]. They were the first mathematicians at the University of Cambridge whose lives have been recorded in any detail and as such may be considered founders of one of the most important centres of mathematics in the world. Tune into this web site for more info.

Algebraic Number Theory Archives
http://www.math.uiuc.edu/Algebraic-Number-Theory/

Here is an example of the type of thing we have here, this item related to prime divisors of the Lagarias sequence. "For integer a let us consider the sequence $X_a=\{x_0,x_1,x_2,\dots\}$ defined by $x_0=a$, $x_1=1$ and, for $n>=1$, $x_{n+1}=x_n+x_{n-1}$. We say that a prime p divides X_a if p divides at least one term of the sequence. It is easy to see that every prime p divides X_1, the sequence of Fibonacci numbers. Lagarias, using a technique involving the computation of degrees of various Kummerian extensions first employed by Hasse, showed in 1985 that X_2, the set of primes dividing some Lucas number has natural density 2/3 and posed as a challenge finding the density of prime divisors of X_3. In this paper we resolve this challenge, assuming GRH, by showing that the density of X_3 equals 1573727S/1569610, with S the so called Stephens constant. This is the first example of a 'non-torsion' second order recurrent sequence with irreducible recurrence relation for which we can determine the associated density of prime divisors." Here you'll find hundreds of such items uploaded by mathematical researchers around the world for the edification and comments of their colleagues.

American Mathematical Society
http://www.ams.org/

The American Mathematical Society was founded in 1888 to further mathematical research and scholarship. The Society currently has approximately 30,000 members throughout the United States and around the world. It fulfills its mission through programs that promote mathematical research, increase the awareness of the value of mathematics to society, and foster excellence in mathematics education. The American Mathematical Society provides many professional services to the community and is a major publisher of mathematics, with offices in four locations. The headquarters office in Providence (with approxiately 150 employees) supports most publication and membership service activities. A warehouse and printing facility is located nearby in Pawtucket, Rhode Island. Mathematical Reviews, a major reviewing journal used by mathematicians around the world, is produced by the AMS office in Ann Arbor, Michigan, with a staff of approximately 75 people. The Society also has a Washington office that deals with matters of science policy and education, and serves as a resource to many agencies and organizations in the Washington area. Most recently, the AMS has been a leader in electronic publication. Since 1996, all journals of the Society have been available in electronic form over the web. Mathematical Reviews is available as MathSciNet, providing access to the mathematical literature from 1940 until the present.

Bell Labs Computing and Mathematical Sciences Research Division
http://www.bell-labs.com/org/112/

The Math Center consists of roughly four dozen members of technical staff, who conduct research primarily in the areas of statistics, mathematics of networks, performance analysis, mathematical foundations of computing, communication theory, and core mathematics. As they write: "We produce fundamental knowledge and experimental development and performance analysis tools in areas of interest to Lucent Technologies. We also consult for Lucent's business units and collaborate with them on joint projects. Additionally, we interact with other centers and laboratories across the Bell Labs research area." In an historic event, a sizable portion of the Math Center was 'spun off' in early 1996 to help start up an information sciences research organization in the new AT&T Labs. The Bell Laboratories Math Center retained its classical strengths in the mathematics of networks and networking, statistics, and communication theory. "We are actively rebuilding in network design and optimization, cryptography, foundations of computing, and various aspects of core mathematics. Current plans are to return to nearly our pre-spin-off size and breadth of coverage over several years. Some topics currently receiving research emphasis in the Center are broadband networking design tools and methods, ATM admission control, traffic characterization and modeling, simulation methods for networks and systems, statistics of large databases, fraud detection, statistical software, statistics of software development, experimental design, data mining and visualization, modeling/analysis/design principles for wireless communications systems, signal processing, coding, and information theory."

Calculus and Mathematica
http://www-cm.math.uiuc.edu/

Calculus&Mathematica is a revolutionary way of approaching teaching calculus. It presents a complete rethinking of: The mathematics of calculus, Calculus as a first course in scientific measurement, Mathematics as an empirical science, How to present calculus ideas visually, What students do in calculus, What motivates students to do calculus, How to motivate students to write about calculus, and How technology should be used in mathematics education. Traditional Mathematics courses emphasize the learning of mathematics through rote work, memorization, and mastery of hand methods of solving problems. Although this can result in creating a good human calculator, it is not conducive to in-depth and substantive understanding of mathematical concepts. Calculus and Mathematica does away with this traditional approach. Since students use Mathematica software to help them step through the boring routines of traditional mathematical learning, they are free to achieve a better conceptual understanding of the material while still gaining a good knowledge of

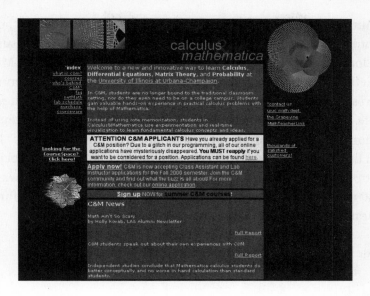

the methods of problem-solving. The end result is a student who really understands the material he or she is working on. Many prospective students are concerned that if they take C&M classes, they will not actually learn how to do any of the math, since "The computer does all the work for you." Fortunately, this is simply not true. Students must understand the problem well enough to be able to give Mathematica the right instructions to solve it.

Classification Society of North America
http://www.pitt.edu/~csna/

As the webmaster writes: "Welcome to the home page of the Classification Society of North America (CSNA). The CSNA is a nonprofit interdisciplinary organization whose purposes are to promote the scientific study of classification and clustering (including systematic methods of creating classifications from data), and to disseminate scientific and educational information related to its fields of interests. The CSNA is a member of the International Federation of Classification Societies (IFCS)" Founded in 1985, the IFCS is a federation of national, regional, and linguistically-based classification societies. It is a non-profit, non-political scientific organization, whose aims are to further classification research. Amongst other activities, the IFCS organises a biennial conference, publishes a newsletter, and supports the Journal of Classification. In addition to the participating Member Societies , the IFCS comprises a Group-at-Large, which serves the interests of individuals for whom there does not yet exist an appropriate classification society. (Find out more about the Internation Federation of Classification Socieities at its own web site: http://edfu.lis.uiuc.edu/~class/ifcs/) The site for the Classification Society of North America includes links to great downloadable software for clustering and multivariate analysis. Visit the two web sites for more information.

Guide to Available Mathematical Software
http://gams.nist.gov/

The Guide to Available Mathematical Software project of the National Institute of Standards and Technology (NIST) studies techniques to provide scientists and engineers with improved access to reusable computer software which is available to them for use in mathematical modeling and statistical analysis. One of the products of this work is an on-line cross-index of available mathematical software. This system also provides centralized access to such items as abstracts, documentation, and source code of software modules that it catalogs; however, rather than operate a physical repository of its own, this system provides transparent access to multiple repositories operated by others. Currently four software repositories are indexed: three maintained for use by NIST staff (but accessible to public), and netlib, a publically accessible software collection maintained by Oak Ridge National Laboratory and the University of Tennessee at Knoxville (netlib in Tennessee) and Bell Labs (netlib at Bell Labs). This represents some 10,000 problem-solving modules from more than 100 software packages. The vast majority of this software represents Fortran subprograms for mathematical problems which commonly occur in computational science and engineering, such as solution of systems of linear algebraic equations, computing matrix eigenvalues, solving nonlinear systems of differential equations, finding minima of nonlinear functions of several variables, evaluating the special functions of applied mathematics, and performing nonlinear regression.

Math.Com: The World of Math Online
http://www.math.com/

Mathematics has been vital to the development of civilization; from ancient to modern times it has been fundamental to advances in science, engineering, and philosophy. As a result, the history of mathematics has become an important study; hundreds of books, papers, and web pages have addressed the subject in a variety of different ways. The purpose of this site is to present a small portion of the history of mathematics through an investigation of some of the great problems that have inspired mathematicians throughout the ages. Included are problems that are suitable for middle school and high school math students, with links to solutions, as well as links to mathematicians' biographies and other math history sites. In the history of mathematical thought, several paradoxes have challenged the notion that mathematics is a self-consistent system of knowledge. Presented here are Zeno's Paradox and Cantor's Infinities. One of the most famous theorems in mathematics, the Pythagorean theorem has many proofs. Presented here is one that relies on Euclidean algebraic geometry and is thus beautifully simple. The site offers much more as well. Visit and discover a rich slice of mathematical information.

Mathematical Quotations Server
http://math.furman.edu/~mwoodard/mqs/mquot.shtml

Come here for a rich archive of mathematical utterances. For example: "Life is good for only two things, discovering mathematics and teaching mathematics"—Siméon Poisson. And can you guess the authors of the following? "The Mean Value Theorem is the midwife of calculus—not very important or glamorous by itself, but often helping to delivery other theorems that are of major significance." "The art of doing mathematics consists in finding that special case which contains all the germs of generality." "Medicine makes people ill, mathematics make them sad and theology makes them sinful." "Every new body of discovery is mathematical in form, because there is no other guidance we can have." "A scientist worthy of his name, above all a mathematician, experiences in his work the same impression as an artist; his pleasure is as great and of the same nature." "Mathematics is the cheapest science. Unlike physics or chemistry, it does not require any expensive equipment. All one needs for mathematics is a pencil and paper." "Mathematics is a language." "In my opinion, a mathematician, in so far as he is a mathematician, need not preoccupy himself with philosophy—an opinion, moreover, which has been expressed by many philosophers."

MuPAD Software

http://www.mupad.de/

MuPAD is a computer algebra system developed by the MuPAD Research Group under direction of Prof. B. Fuchssteiner at the University of Paderborn(Germany). In essence, it is a general purpose computer algebra system for symbolic and numerical computations. Users can view the library code, implement their own routines and data types easily and can also dynamically link C/C++ compiled modules for raw speed and flexibility. In addition to basic data types like numbers, polynomials, strings, lists, sets, and many more, domains are used to define new data types. Via the function domain, the user may create new domains. By domattr or using the :: operator the methods of a domain can be accessed. Many system functions can be overloaded by domain methods. For instance, defining a domain method _plus, the usual operator + can be used to add domain elements in a user-defined fashion. Domains allow the implementation of polymorphic algorithms. MuPAD offers various pre-defined domains, including Matrix (matrices over some commutative ring), SquareMatrix, GaloisField, AlgebraicExtension and more. These domains are provided by the MuPAD library Dom. Visit this web site for more details on the software and, of course, a free download.

Isaac Newton Institute for Mathematical Sciences
http://www.newton.cam.ac.uk/

The Isaac Newton Institute for Mathematical Sciences was opened in July 1992, after four years of careful preparation. For a number of years and a variety of reasons, a need had been felt for a UK national institute in theoretical physics and mathematics. The realisation of this idea became possible with the availability of "pump-priming" financial support from Cambridge Colleges, notably St John's College and Trinity College (through the Isaac Newton Trust). St John's offered to provide a purpose-built building on land it owned in West Cambridge, promising to subvent the rent by GBP150,000 for five years and Trinity offered GBP200,000pa towards running costs for the first five years. Further support and endorsement came from the London Mathematical Society (LMS) at its retreat in May 1989 at the Isle of Thorns. This was followed by negotiations with the Science and Engineering Research Council (SERC), since replaced by the Engineering and Physical Sciences Research Council (EPSRC), which invited proposals from universities wishing to develop a mathematics institute and, after consideration of proposals from Cambridge, Edinburgh (Edinburgh and Heriot-Watt Universities), London, Oxford and War-

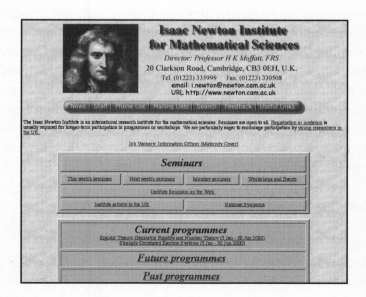

wick, recommended the funding of the Cambridge proposal and offered a 'rolling grant' of about £ 366,000pa for the first four years. This grant is reviewed every two years. Visit the web site for more details.

Emmy Noether

http://www.math.neu.edu/awm/NoetherBrochure/AboutNoether. html

In 1935, the year of Emmy Noether's death, Albert Einstein wrote in a letter to the New York Times, "In the judgement of the most competent living mathematicians, Fraulein Noether was the most significant creative mathematical genius thus far produced since the higher education of women began." Born in 1882 in Germany, Emmy Noether persisted in the face of tremendous obstacles to become one of the greatest algebraists of this century. Known primarily for her profound and beautiful theorems in ring theory, Emmy Noether's most significant achievement runs deeper: she changed the way mathematicians think about their subject. "She taught us to think in simple, and thus general, terms ... and not in complicated algebraic calculations," said her colleague P.S. Alexandroff during a memorial service after her death. In this way, she cleared a path toward the discovery of new algebraic patterns that had previously been obscured. Despite her intellectual achievements and the recognition of such mathematicians as David Hilbert and Hermann Weyl, Emmy Noether endured years of poor treatment by German universities, where for a time she could not even lecture under her own name. Weyl later wrote that, even when the Nazis prevented her from lecturing, "her courage, her frankness, her unconcern about her own fate, her conciliatory spirit, were, in the midst of all the hatred and meanness, despair and sorrow ... a moral solace." Visit the web page for more information on this remarkable woman.

Number Theory Web

http://www.math.uga.edu/~ntheory/web.html

The Number Theory Web uses the resources of the World Wide Web to collect and disseminate online information of interest to number theorists everywhere. As the webmaster writes: "Number theorists are encouraged to supply me with links to their homepages (which should contain an email address), to those of any group to which they belong, to descriptions of their (and other's) books—new and old (if these are not provided by publishers) together with errata, online lecture notes, links to regular seminar series (with abstracts or even better—the actual seminars), online problem collections, surveys, recent theses, conferences, number theory calculator programs, awards, addresses to meetings, videos, libraries with good collections in number theory and with online search facilities, death notices and to any other items of potential interest. I would also like to encourage enthusiastic workers in various branches of number theory to prepare pages depicting state-of-the-art accounts of their subjects, with lists of workers—past and present, outstanding problems, encyclopaedic references to papers and books. As examples I cite Michael Mossinghoff's pages on Lehmer's Conjecture, Chris Caldwell's Prime Page and Stéfane Fermigier's Elliptic Curves Page."

Random Numbers and Monte Carlo Methods
http://random.mat.sbg.ac.at/links/index.html

Numerical methods that are known as Monte Carlo methods can be loosely described as statistical simulation methods, where statistical simulation is defined in quite general terms to be any method that utilizes sequences of random numbers to perform the simulation. Monte Carlo methods have been used for centuries, but only in the past several decades has the technique gained the status of a full-fledged numerical method capable of addressing the most complex applications. The name "Monte Carlo" was coined by Metropolis during the Manhattan Project of World War II, because of the similarity of statistical simulation to games of chance, and because the capital of Monaco was a center for gambling and similar pursuits. Monte Carlo is now used routinely in many diverse fields, from the simulation of complex physical phenomena such as radiation transport in the earth's atmosphere and the simulation of the esoteric subnuclear processes in high energy physics experiments, to the mundane, such as the simulation of a Bingo game or the outcome of Monty Hall's

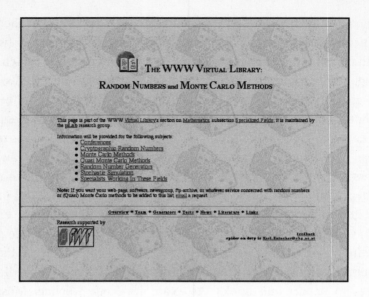

vexing offer to the contestant in "Let's Make a Deal." The analogy of Monte Carlo methods to games of chance is a good one, but the "game" is a physical system, and the outcome of the game is not a pot of money or stack of chips (unless simulated) but rather a solution to some problem. Let this web site tell (and show) you more.

Society for Industrial and Applied Mathematics
http://www.siam.org/

Inspired by the vision that applied mathematics should play an important role in advancing science and technology in industry, a small group of professionals from academe and industry met in Philadelphia in 1951 to start an organization whose members would meet periodically to exchange ideas about the use of mathematics in industry. This meeting led quickly to the organization of the Society for Industrial and Applied Mathematics (SIAM) in 1952. The goals of SIAM were to Advance the application of mathematics to science and industry; Promote mathematical research that could lead to effective new methods and techniques for science and industry; and Provide media for the exchange of information and ideas among mathematicians, engineers, and scientists. These goals haven't changed; they are more valid today than ever before. Applied mathematics, in partnership with computing, has become essential in solving many real-world problems. Its methodologies are needed, for example, in modeling physical, chemical, and biomedical phenomena; in designing engineered parts, structures, and systems to optimize performance; in planning and managing financial and marketing strategies; and in understanding and optimizing manufacturing processes. The SIAM web site is loaded with information about the group and its publications, meetings, conventions and educational programs.

StatLib from Carnegie-Mellon
http://lib.stat.cmu.edu/

As the webmaster writes: "Welcome to StatLib, a system for distributing statistical software, datasets, and information by electronic mail, FTP and WWW. StatLib started out as an e-mail service and some of the organization still reflects that heritage. We hope that this document will give you sufficient guidance to navigate through the archives." Be sure to check out the StatLib Mailing List WWW Gateway (LWGate). This service is intended to present information about a set of mailing lists, allow people to easily use mailing list commands, and provide a hypertext interface to list archives which exist on the StatLib server. The LWGate can support five major types of mailing list programs: LISTSERV(TM), ListProcessor 6, Majordomo, SmartList, and LetterRip. Depending on which program runs your mailing list, the form interface to your list may look different from others. Many functions of this interface are usable only to WWW clients which support forms. Also of interest: The great software archive wherein you will find: First Bayes (a teaching package for elementary Bayesian Statistics), plus a splendid collection of S functions (with interfaces to Fortran and C) that calculate properties of continuously monitored stopping boundaries for clinical trials.

Syngergetics on the Web
http://www.teleport.com/~pdx4d/synhome.html

This is one of several websites focusing in some way on an invented language, originally designed by R. Buckminster Fuller (b. July 12, 1895, d. July 1, 1983) to communicate his "explorations in the geometry of thinking" (the subtitle of the work). Fuller was a self-declared comprehensivist and often wrote about the cultural chasm identified by C.P. Snow, separating the humanities from the math-sciences. That's the chasm he set out to bridge. Synergetics is the result. Reading Synergetics is a challenge because it defies easy categorization. Readers looking for scientific content tend to be distracted by the "noise" of many-leveled metaphors. Like, is this a real computer, or some metaphoric "computer" we're reading about? Those trained in the humanities, on the other hand, may be turned off by its starkly geometric terminology, which perhaps strikes them as too cold and unfeeling. In other words, in attempting to cross Fuller's bridge, people on either side of C.P. Snow's chasm tend to confront their prejudices about the other side's style of communicating. A lot of would-be readers turn back, frustrated by an overwhelming sense that this work must be primarily intended for someone else. But stick with it, because it was intended for you.

Association for Women in Mathematics
http://www.awm-math.org/

In the mid-1980s, there was a flurry of work by a group of feminists theorists on gender and science. In commentary fairly critical of this work, Ann Hibner Koblitz succinctly summarized the main ideas behind the theory. "Put in its most general guise, the new 'gender theory' says that centuries of male domination of science have affected its content—what questions are asked and what answers are found—and that 'science' and 'objectivity' have become inextricably linked to concepts and ideologies of masculinity." She then lists eight criticisms of which I will mention only two, namely that gender theorists "seem unaware of the increasing numbers of women who have had satisfying lives as scientists" and "employ cartoon-character stereotypes of

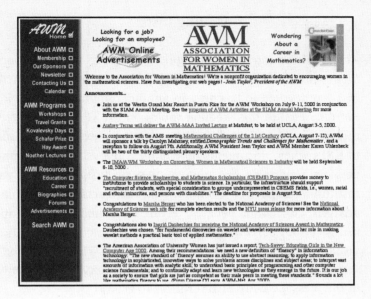

science, scientists, men, and women." The Association for Women in Mathematics is designed, in part, to correct these errors. As the webmaster writes: "The Association for Women in Mathematics (AWM) is a non-profit organization founded in 1971. Our continuing goal is to encourage women in the mathematical sciences. AWM currently has more than 4,100 members (women and men) representing a broad spectrum of the mathematical community—from the United States and around the world!"

Mailing Lists

CA-TEACH is an internet mailing list devoted to the discussion of the teaching of COMPLEX ANALYSIS. Though it is intended to be a list devoted to teaching in an undergraduate setting, it is not restricted to this. Regular topics on CA-TEACH could include: a discussion of Complex Analysis textbooks, broadcasts of URLs where documents on complex analysis can be found, personal reports on teaching complex analysis courses at your institution, impact of technology on the teaching of complex analysis, curriculum debates, lecture notes and examples of using various software packages to assist in complex analysis visualization, among others. To join the CA-TEACH mailing list, send a message to MAJORDOMO@abacus.oxy.edu with one line in the message body SUBSCRIBE CA-TEACH

MATHEDU is an open majordomo list for discussions about teaching and learning post-calculus mathematics, including graduate courses. To join the list, send an email message to majordomo@csv.warwick.ac.uk with the following command in the body of your email message: subscribe mathedu

NA-TEACH NA-TEACH is an internet mailing list devoted to the discussion of the teaching of NUMERICAL ANALYSIS. Though it is intended to be a list devoted to teaching in an undergraduate setting, it is not restricted to this. Regular topics on NA-TEACH could include: a discussion of new Numerical Analysis textbooks, broadcasts of URLs where documents on numerical analysis can be found, personal reports on teaching numerical courses at your institution, impact of technology on the teaching of numerical analysis, curriculum debates, reform of numerical analysis courses, etc etc. To join the NA-TEACH mailing list, send a message to MAJORDOMO@abacus.oxy.edu with one line in the message body SUBSCRIBE NA-TEACH

newsgroups

sci.math
sci.math.num-analysis
sci.math.research
sci.nonlinear
geometry.announcements
geometry.forum
geometry.research

16

METEOROLOGY

American Meteorological Society
http://www.ametsoc.org/AMS/

The American Meteorological Society was founded in 1919 by Charles Franklin Brooks of the Blue Hill Observatory in Milton, Massachusetts. Its initial membership came primarily from the U.S. Signal Corps and U.S. Weather Bureau and numbered just less than 600. Its initial publication, the Bulletin of the American Meteorological Society, was meant to serve as a supplement to the Monthly Weather Review, which, at the time, was published by the U.S. Weather Bureau. Many of the initial members were not practicing meteorologists, but after the dues were raised from $1 to $2 in 1922, the weather hobbyists began dropping their membership, and the Society moved toward a membership made up primarily of professionals in the field. The role of the Society as a scientific and professional organization serving the atmospheric and related sciences, which was established so well in the first few decades of the Society's history, has continued to the present. The AMS now publishes in print and online nine well-respected scientific journals and an abstract journal, in addition to the Bulletin, and sponsors and organizes over a dozen scientific conferences each year. It has published almost 50 monographs in its continuing series, as well as many other books and educational materials of all types.

Cooperative Institute for Meteorological Satellite Studies
http://cimss.ssec.wisc.edu/

CIMSS was established in 1980 to formalize and support cooperative research between the National Oceanic and Atmospheric Administration's (NOAA) National Environmental Satellite, Data, and Information Service (NESDIS) and the University of Wisconsin-Madison's Space Science and Engineering Center. Sponsorship and membership of the Institute was expanded to include the National Aeronautics and Space Administration (NASA) in 1989. CIMSS develops and successfully implements techniques and products for using geostationary weather satellite thermal radiation observations to improve forecasts of severe storms, including tornadoes and hurricanes. CIMSS plays a major role in the transfer of new technology into operational practice. CIMSS also plays a major role in instrument design and testing, and related software development, for improved space-based measurements of the earth's atmosphere. CIMSS is very active in national and international field programs, testing new instrumentation, data processing systems and assessing the geophysical utility of measurements. Current research focuses on the development and testing of computer-based analysis and forecast techniques that use observations from existing and planned spacecraft and ground-based weather observing systems as part of a national program to greatly improve weather forecast capabilities for

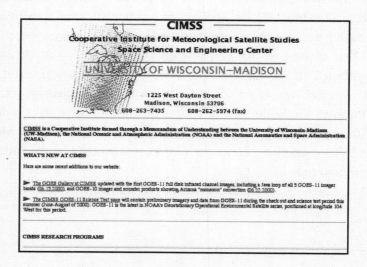

CIMSS

Cooperative Institute for Meteorological Satellite Studies
Space Science and Engineering Center

UNIVERSITY OF WISCONSIN–MADISON

1225 West Dayton Street
Madison, Wisconsin 53706
608-263-7435   608-262-5974 (fax)

CIMSS is a Cooperative Institute formed through a Memorandum of Understanding between the University of Wisconsin-Madison (UW-Madison), the National Oceanic and Atmospheric Administration (NOAA) and the National Aeronautics and Space Administration (NASA).

WHAT'S NEW AT CIMSS

Here are some recent additions to our website:

▶ The GOES Gallery at CIMSS updated with the first GOES-11 full disk infrared channel images, including a Java loop of all 5 GOES-11 imager bands (06.15.2000), and GOES-10 imager and sounder products showing Arizona "monsoon" convection (06.22.2000).

▶ The CIMSS GOES-11 Science Test page will contain preliminary imagery and data from GOES-11 during the check out and science test period this summer (June-August of 2000). GOES-11 is the latest in NOAA's Geostationary Operational Environmental Satellite series, positioned at longitude 104 West for this period.

CIMSS RESEARCH PROGRAMS

the next decade. The optimal use of satellite data in climate and global change studies has become another essential part of the CIMSS mission.

Fleet Numerical Meteorology and Oceanography Center
http://www.fnoc.navy.mil/

Come here for great NWP weather maps. What is NWP? NWP stands for "Numerical Weather Prediction," NWP is actually a bit of a misnomer as the computer models do not directly forecast the weather. Rather, meteorologists make "weather maps" from the output of the NWP model forecasts (e.g., winds and temperature) and/or diagnosistics (e.g., rainfall) and then infer the weather from the maps. These pages provide basic weather maps using data from the two leading NWP agencies in the United States: the Navy's Fleet Numerical Meteorology and Oceanography Center (FNMOC) and the National Centers for Environmental Prediction (NCEP). Two centers are used because model intercomparison is the key to model improvement and this web is arranged accordingly. This page currently contains the following global models: 1.the FNMOC Navy Operational Global Atmospheric Prediction System (NOGAPS or NGP in these pages). 2.the NCEP Medium Range Forecast (MRF) model—both the short range (0-72 h at 00, 06, 12 and 18 UTC) "Aviation" (AVN) run and the longer range (0-388 h at 00 UTC) MRF runs. These pages are best viewed with java-enabled browsers such as Netscape and Internet Explorer. Other browsers need not apply.

Integrated Science Assessment of Climate Change
http://frodo.atmos.uiuc.edu/isam/

Global climate change is perhaps the most significant environmental issue of our time. A comprehensive assessment of the scientific evidence by the Intergovernmental Panel on Climate Change (IPCC), co-sponsored by the United Nations Environment Program (UNEP) and the World Meteorological Organization (WMO) and made up of over 2000 scientific and technical experts from around the world, suggests that human activities are contributing to climate change and there has been a discernible human influence on global climate (Harvey et al., IPCC, 1996). The human activities, most importantly the burning of fossil fuels, as well as deforestation and various agricultural and industrial practices, have led to increased atmospheric concentrations of the number of greenhouse gases, including carbon dioxide, methane, nitrous oxide, chloroflurocarbons, and ozone in the lower part of the atmosphere. The basic heat-trapping property of these greenhouse gases is essentially undisputed. Although there is considerable scientific uncertainty about exactly how and when the earth's climate will respond to enhanced greenhouse gases in the future. The direct effects of climate change will be changes in temperature, precipitation, soil moisture and sea level. Such changes could have adverse effects on ecological systems, human health and socioeconomic sectors. Visit the web site for more details.

Global Change Master Directory
http://gcmd.gsfc.nasa.gov/

There is great need for an understanding of the relationships between human activities, potential changes to the Earth's climate, and the resulting ecological and economic impacts and other effects on human welfare from these changes requires an interdisciplinary perspective involving the physical, biological, social and political sciences. In response to this need, a new paradigm has emerged—one whose main purpose is not only the acquisition of scientific knowledge, but the assimilation and communication of scientific results. Here at this web site you have a splendid an interdisciplinary guide to general and technical information related to climate change resulting from human activities, particularly global warming by greenhouse gases and stratospheric ozone depletion. Much of the data here is comprised of literature citations accompanied by brief abstracts. The citations are broadly organized according to type of publication ("Professional Publications," "Reports," etc). Within those categories are subcategories based on content ("Climate Change Science," "Mitigation," etc). These documents are written for a diverse audience: policy makers, researchers, executives and administrators, librarians, students of various levels, and interested citizens. Entries of general appeal are designated, and the rest are grouped under specific topics so readers can quickly find the most interesting topics.

Hurricane Hunters
http://www.hurricanehunters.com/welcome.htm

Atlantic hurricanes making landfall create much more damage in La Niña years compaired to during El Niño years. La Niña refers to cooler-than-average sea surface temperatures across the eastern tropical Pacific Ocean. El Niño is an abnormal warming of the ocean temperatures across the eastern tropical Pacific Ocean. One major conclusion is that not only are there more storms in La Niña years, these storms are stronger, resulting in more damage from wind, storm surge, flooding caused by heavy rain. In terms of U.S. dollars, there is a 77 percent chance that more than $1 billion of damage will occur in a La Niña year and a 36 percent chance that more than $5 billion in damage will occur. These probabilities are much greater than the 32 percent and 14 percent chances, respectively, in El Niño years. These seasonal forecasts help resource and emergency managers prepare for the likelihood of more frequent and stronger hurricanes in La Niña years. However, El Niño

and neutral years do not mean no hurricanes will make landfall, and one hurricane can have large impacts. Hurricane Andrew is the most recent example of this phenomenon, a neutral-year storm that became one of the costliest natural disasters in U.S. history, with estimates of $30 billion in damage. Learn more at the Hurricane Hunters web page.

Institute of Global Environment and Society
http://grads.iges.org/home.html

The Institue of Global Environment and Society is dedicated to basic research in climate variability, climate predictability and climate change. It has been established to improve understanding and prediction of the variations of the earth's climate through scientific research, and to share both the fruits of this research and the tools necessary to carry out this research with society as a whole. The Institute consists of several centers of excellence, each dedicated to a particular scientific and societal goal. Currently there are two such centers, the Center for Ocean-Land-Atmosphere Studies (COLA) and the Center for Application of Research on the Environment (CARE). COLA is a group of uniquely qualified scientists dedicated to understanding the problem of seasonal to interannual and decadal climate fluctuations with special emphasis on the role of interactions between earth's oceans, atmosphere and land surface. The primary goal of COLA is to foster interdisciplinary research and to increase our understanding of the physical processes in the atmosphere, at the land surface, in the oceans, and the interactions among these components. Check the web site for more information on this excellent institution.

Integrated Earth Information Server at NSF
http://atm.geo.nsf.gov/

This server is a prototype Integrated Earth Information Server (IEIS, as in eyes on the globe). It is built on the infrastructure provided by the nation-wide Unidata Internet Data Distribution (IDD) network, in which participating universities have established information servers containing a range of earth-related data. Perhaps the best recent example of an IEIS product is the "Global Montage" which the

SSEC at the University of Wisconsin creates every six hours in graphic form and as an animation of the last week's images (2 MB). The information that appears on an IEIS arrives via the experimental nation-wide Unidata Internet Data Distribution (IDD) network, which automatically delivers real-time environmental observations from a variety of observing systems around the globe to servers at Unidata universities. At the heart of each server on each campus (and on this IEIS computer at NSF's Atmospheric Science Division) is a Unidata Local Data Manager (LDM), which captures the data and stores them as each site wishes. Sites may then use Unidata analysis and display programs to transform the data into easy-to-understand, familiar forms and to combine them with environmental data from other sources. As in the examples above, these form can then be made generally available on a university IEIS.

International Weather Satellite Images
http://www.people.fas.harvard.edu/~dbaron/sat/

As the webmaster writes: "This site is a listing of satellite images and movies taken by weather satellites around the globe. I have links to satellite pictures at other sites that are well known around the weather community and links to those that are practically unknown. Some of the pictures, especially those in visible light, offer stunning views of the Earth. Looking at weather satellite images gives you a chance to see weather events on a large scale. One can see the development of hurricanes, large frontal systems, the daily cycles of thunderstorms, and the repetitive weather patterns that cover many parts of the globe. Different images have different purposes, and some are easier to understand than others, but they all have important information about the world's weather." The International Weather Satellite Imagery Center is a comprehensive listing of weather satellite images from around the world and around the Internet. They are similar to and better than the ones seen on TV. It is intended both for professional meteorologists and for hobbyists. The purpose of this site is to list all of the weather satellite images on the Internet, possibly excluding redundant images.

MIT Weather Radio Lab

http://www-cmpo.mit.edu/Radar_Lab/Radar_Lab.html

What do all those colors mean on the TV radar images? Those colors are a way of plotting up the different values of reflectivity in a storm. The National Weather Service has established a set of five standard 'Levels' of reflectivity, to correspond to the types of rainfall usually associated with a given reflectivity—e.g., drizzle, light rain, heavy rain, etc. Most radars can actually see much more detailed distributions of reflectivity; the NWS 5-Level Scheme was constructed to simplify widespread distribution of radar data. NEXRAD (Next Generation Radar) is a generic term for the National Weather Service's program of implementing about 160 WSR-88D radars around the country. The current network of NWS weather radars is woefully outdated. After several years of contractual and technical difficulties, deployment of the WSR-88D's is finally underway in force. An integral part of the WSR-88D program is the development of a data processing and distribution network. In addition to the raw reflectivity and velocity data which the radars collect, the sites will generate a suite of analyzed products, including: Combined shear, severe weather analyses, echo top heights, weak echo regions, accumulated precipita-

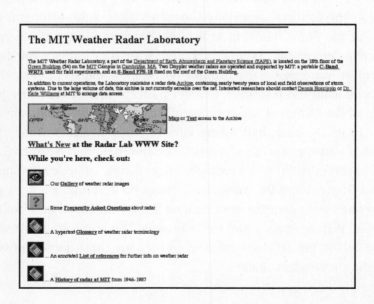

tion (1,3 hours, storm total), wind retrievals, vertically integrated liquid, storm tracking data, and more. Learn more at this web site.

National Climactic Data Center
http://www.ncdc.noaa.gov/ncdc.html

NCDC is the world's largest active archive of weather data. NCDC produces numerous climate publications and responds to data requests from all over the world. NCDC operates the World Data Center for Meteorology, Asheville which is collocated at NCDC. NCDC's web site has received a number of awards. NCDC supports a three tier national climate services support program—the partners include: NCDC, Regional Climate Centers, and State Climatologists. The NOAAServer, which will be replaced by the National Virtual Data System, offers search and access to NOAA data from all NOAA Data Centers. NCDC archives 99 percent of all NOAA data, including over 320 million paper records; 2.5 million microfiche records; over 500,000 tape cartridges/magnetic tapes, and has satellite weather images back to 1960. NCDC annually publishes over 1.2 million copies of climate publications that are sent to individual users and 33,000 subscribers. NCDC maintains over 500 digital data sets to respond to over 170,000 requests each year. Data are received from a wide variety of sources, including satellites, radar, remote sensing systems, NWS cooperative observers, aircraft, ships, radiosonde, wind profiler, rocketsonde, solar radiation networks, and NWS Forecast/Warnings/Analyses Products.

National Hurricane Center
http://www.nhc.noaa.gov/

The National Hurricane Center (NHC) maintains a continuous watch on tropical cyclones over the Atlantic, Caribbean, Gulf of Mexico, and the Eastern Pacific from 15 May through November 30. The Center prepares and distributes hurricane watches and warnings for the general public, and also prepares and distributes marine and military advisories for other users. During the "off-season" NHC provides training for U.S. emergency managers and representatives from many other countries that are affected by tropical cyclones. NHC also conducts applied research to evaluate and improve hurricane forecasting techniques, and is involved in public awareness programs. The Tropical Analysis and Forecast Branch (TAFB) provides year-round products involving marine forecasting, aviation forecasts and warnings (SIGMETs), and surface analyses. The unit also provides satellite interpretation and satellite rainfall estimates for the international community. In addition, TAFB provides support to NHC through manpower and tropical cyclone intensity estimates from the Dvorak technique. The Technical Support Branch (TSB) provides support for TPC computer and communications systems, including the McIDAS satellite data processing systems, the N-AWIPS workstations, and the WSR-88D computer systems. Visit the web site for more information.

National Weather Service
http://www.nws.noaa.gov/

The National Weather Service (NWS) provides weather, hydrologic, and climate forecasts and warnings for the United States, its territories, adjacent waters and ocean areas, for the protection of life and property and the enhancement of the national economy. NWS data and products form a national information database and infrastructure which can be used by other governmental agencies, the private sector, the public, and the global community. This is accomplished by providing warnings and forecast of hazardous weather, including thunderstorms, flooding, hurricanes, tornadoes, winter weather, tsunamis, and climate events. The NWS is the sole United States OFFICIAL voice for issuing warnings during life-threatening weather situations. As the webmaster writes: "The National Weather Service (NWS) is the U.S. federal agency charged with providing weather, water, and climate warnings and forecasts. We are a team of dedicated individuals who daily continue our tradition of service above self. Over the last several years, our collective focus has been on delivering necessary products and services while completing the myriad of activities associated with the NWS modernization and restructuring. Our new observing systems (space, radar, and ground); modern information technology assets; and training programs have combined to improve the quality of our products. By working with key partners, especially the emergency management community, we have been striving to ensure our products and services are responsive to the needs of the American public."

Scripps Climate Research Division
http://meteora.ucsd.edu/

Scripps Institution of Oceanography is playing a leading role in pioneering the interdisciplinary study of the earth as a unified system. In the Climate Research Division (CRD), scientists study a broad range of phenomena. These span time scales from a few weeks to several decades. Research themes include predicting the natural variability of climate and understanding the consequences of man<made increases in the greenhouse effect. Climate change caused by human actions is the paradigm that illustrates why traditional disciplinary barriers in the earth sciences are rapidly weakening. In the climate system, the atmosphere, the seas, the land surface, and the world of living things are tightly coupled. To understand these interactions, a variety of expertise must be brought to bear through a team approach to research.

Current research projects include the development of coupled global ocean and atmosphere models, assessing the role of cloud<radiation feedbacks in climate change, and modeling and predicting seasonal climate variability. CRD research combines the analysis of large observational data sets, the development of comprehensive numerical models of the climate system, and the exploitation of satellite remote sensing capabilities for monitoring the entire planet.

Texas Severe Storm Association
http://www.tessa.org/

The Texas Severe Storms Association (TESSA) is a 501(c)(3) national non-profit organization founded to bring together both amateur and professional severe weather scientists in an attempt to better understand dangerous storms through the collection and diffusion of knowledge. TESSA members can be found worldwide, from Texas to California to New York, Canada, Great Britain, Austria and Australia. Members include National Weather Service personnel, broadcast meteorologists, educators, researchers, emergency management personnel, storm chasers, school children and many others simply interested in severe weather. This web site includes a direct link to the National Weather Service's Storm Prediction Center (SPC). The SPC's mission is to provide timely and accurate forecasts and watches for severe thunderstorms and tornadoes over the contiguous United States. The SPC also monitors heavy rain, heavy snow, and fire weather events across the U.S. and issues specific products for those hazards. They use the most advanced technology and scientific methods available to achieve this goal. The SPC uses its suite of products to relay forecasts of organized severe weather as much as two days ahead of time, and continually refines the forecast up until the event is concluded. All products issued by the Storm Prediction Center are available on the Wide World Web.

Mailing Lists

Urban Climate Email List

The objective of this list is to exchange information about urban climate related events. This includes (but is not restricted to): conferences (regional, national and international); positions; funding opportunities; news; etc. If you have information likely to be of interest to others—please email me (see below) so that others can be informed. The list is open to anyone interested in urban climate or related topics. It is a moderated list. Email for distribution should be sent to Sue Grimmond (grimmon@indiana.edu). If you want to subscribe to this list email:grimmon@indiana.edu. In the body of your message put : subscribe urban_climate < your email address>

Newsgroups

SCI.GEO.METEOROLOGY

17

OCEANOGRAPHY

Acoustical Oceanography Research Group
   http://pulson.seos.uvic.ca/

As the webmaster writes: "Our goal is to advance our understanding of fundamental research problems in the upper ocean and coastal waters through innovative measurement and analytical approaches. The Acoustical Oceanography Research Group studies air-sea interaction and upper ocean processes, stratified flow over topography, high-frequency acoustical propagation and imaging, as well as applied topics in the long range detection of fish, wave impacts on offshore structures, sea-ice acoustics and marine mammal acoustics. Challenging environments demand innovative approaches and much of our work makes use of underwater sound, often requiring the development of specialized instruments. Acoustical techniques provide a window on the ocean that reveals phenomena inaccessible to traditional observational approaches. Students and visitors have the opportunity of participating in experiments, developing sophisticated instruments, analysing data and modeling ocean processes. The Acoustical Oceanography Research Group provides opportunities for graduate studies through the University of Victoria. Graduate students participate in the university graduate program just like other students, but their research arises through opportunities at the Institute of Ocean Sciences. (A few of our students also join us from the University of British Columbia, Dept of Earth & Ocean Sciences.) A wide range of projects are available to fulfill the requirements of a thesis at the MSc and the PhD levels."

AquaNet
http://www.aquanet.com/

The Aquatic Network provides information about living resources and technology relating to marine

and fresh-water environments. The Aquatic Network's mission is to: Promote sustainable use of aquatic resources; Serve as a clearing-house for information relating to aquatic environments; and Explore the use of the Internet and other new technologies to foster global communication and networking. The Aquatic Network includes a diverse collection of services, databases, news, editorials, art forms, advertisements, and products. The Aquatic Network welcomes a variety of information sources, including, but not limited to: articles, news releases, descriptions of products and services, literature and publication citations, employment and business opportunity information, non-profit resources descriptions, and business updates and meeting notices. Subject areas covered include aquaculture, conservation, fisheries, limnology, marine science and oceanography, maritime heritage, ocean engineering, and seafood. Be sure to check the link for the Southern Regional Aquaculture Center. The Southern Regional Aquaculture Center administered through the USDA provides a mechanism for assessing local aquaculture industry needs, establishing research and extension priorities, and implementing regional research and extension projects. Also check the great information on Tilapia. Tilapia is a fish that has been raised for centuries with little fanfare. In recent years with the worldwide emergence of aquaculture, increased attention is being focused on tilapia because of its superior culture possibilities.

Australian Institute of Marine Science
http://www.aims.gov.au/

Australia's ocean territory is the largest, most diverse and potentially most valuable, yet least understood, of all our natural assets. The Australian Institute of Marine Science (AIMS) was established the Commonwealth government in 1972 to generate the knowledge needed for the sustainable use and protection of the marine environ-

ment through innovative, world-class scientific and technological research. This web site has information about the Institute's research capabilities, laboratories, current projects and staff. In July 1995 the Institute moved from a general research program structure to a project-based organisation. This brought a renewed focus to the Institute's research activities. In March 1996 the Institute's support staff followed suit and took significant steps towards improving efficiency by documenting their objectives, all aimed at supporting their scientific 'clients'. AIMS researchers work primarily in the central Great Barrier Reef (GBR) region within the Great Barrier Marine Park. Frequent trips are also made to the northern and southern GBR, Western Australia and Papua New Guinea. The logistics of such an extensive operation are handled by the Field Operations Centre.

Center for Coastal Physical Oceanography
http://www.ccpo.odu.edu/

The State Council of Higher Education for Virginia (SCHEV) established the Commonwealth Center for Coastal Physical Oceanography (CCPO) at Old Dominion University in 1991 to promote research on the physical oceanography of the coastal ocean and related oceanographic processes. The coastal ocean is the focus of increasing research for reasons relating to both short-term anthropogenic impacts and longer-term global change. There is a variety of fundamental questions about coastal ocean physics that need to be answered if human impact and global change are to be assessed properly. Housed in Crittenton Hall, the Center is located six blocks east of campus on an attractive waterfront site curtained with stately live oaks. The 20,000 square-foot building contains all Center facilities: offices laboratories, classrooms, conference rooms, and display rooms, as well as two small apartments for overnight visitors. CCPO makes a significant impact on the economy of Hampton Roads. The Center is a high technology research center with a total operating budget of about $2,100,000. The center supports and facilitates innovative research on the physical oceanography of the coastal ocean and other coastal related processes through funding which allows faculty, visitors, students, consultants, and research associates to focus their efforts on specific research areas. The Center also participates in cost sharing activities with Federal and Commonwealth agencies on research of common interest and conducts outreach actiivities through the local public television station (WHRO), museums, and school systems.

Coral Reef Alliance
http://www.coral.org/

Coral reefs are a vital component of ocean ecosystems, providing shelter for nearly one quarter of all marine life. As one of the most spectacular and ancient forms of life in the world, coral reefs provide a home for over 4,000 species of fish, 700 species of coral, and thousands of other animals and plants. Coral reefs are also among the world's most fragile and endangered ecosystems. The loss of healthy coral reefs would mean the extinction of thousands of marine species, as well as the elimination of a primary source of food, income and employment for millions of people around the world. The Coral Reef Alliance is a nonprofit, member-supported organization that promotes coral reef conservation around the world. CORAL works with the dive industry, governments, local communities and other organizations to protect and manage coral reefs, establish marine parks,

fund conservation efforts, and raise public awareness with the mission to keep coral reefs alive. With the Conservation Program, CORAL helps create marine parks and other protected areas, and provides financial and technical support to conservation programs working in communities around the world. Through the Education and Public Awareness Program, CORAL provides information on the value of coral reefs, the threats they face, and what individuals can do to help protect the reefs.

Cousteau Society

http://www.cousteau.org/

The Cousteau Society is a membership-supported not-for-profit organization dedicated to the protection and improvement of the quality of life for present and future generations. Founded in 1973 by Captain Jacques-Yves Cousteau, the Society now has more than 150,000 members worldwide. The Society believes that only an informed and alerted public can make the decisions necessary to protect and manage the world's natural resources. Cousteau teams have explored the water system throughout the world for half a century. Their unique explorations and observations have been documented in more than forty books, eight sets of filmstrips, four feature films and 120 television films that have helped millions of people understand and appreciate the fragility of life on our Water Planet. Films to date have included studies of Haiti, Cuba, the Marquesas Islands and the Tuamotu Archipelago, New Zealand, Australia, Papua New Guinea, Thailand, the Andaman Islands, Borneo, Indonesia, Madagascar, South Africa, Lake Baikal and the Amazon, Mekong, Danube and Yellow rivers among others. Currently, Cousteau teams are carrying out an expedition to the St. Lawrence River of Canada.

JASON Project
http://www.jasonproject.org/

After discovering the wreck of the RMS Titanic, world-famous explorer and oceanographer Dr. Robert Ballard received thousands of letters from students around the world wanting to go with him on his next expedition. In order to bring the thrill of discovery to millions of students worldwide, Dr. Ballard founded the JASON Project, a year-round scientific expedition designed to excite and engage students in science and technology and to motivate and provide professional development for teachers. The JASON Project has been praised as the leader in distance learning programs, and continues to expand its reach by adding more components to the Project experience. The JASON Project components include: Scientific Exploration; Curriculum; Online Systems; Teacher Training; Live Broadcasts. Each year, JASON mounts a major scientific expedition that examines one or more of Earth's dynamic systems. Scientists and their work become the basis for developing a year-long, supplemental science and geography curriculum crafted for students in grades 4–9. Endorsed by the National Science Teachers' Association, the JASON Project curriculum enables teachers and their students to use the expedition as a framework for hands-on science learning throughout the school year. It is rich in opportunities for classes to do local experiments and data gathering that mirror the research being conducted at the site.

Monterey Bay Acquarium Research Institute
   http://www.mbari.org/

The Monterey Bay Aquarium Research Institute (MBARI) was founded in 1987 by David Packard, who wrote: "The mission of MBARI is to achieve and maintain a position as a world center for advanced research and education in ocean science and technology, and to do so through the development of better instruments, systems, and methods for scientific research in the deep waters of the ocean. MBARI emphasizes the peer relationship between engineers and scientists as a basic principle of its operation. All of the activities of MBARI must be characterized by excellence, innovation, and vision." To carry out its mission, the institute has defined six main goals: Identify important areas of marine science where research progress is limited by lack of appropriate technology. Develop sophisticated systems for investigating aspects of the marine environment and its inhabitants where high scientific potential exists. Meet the highest possible performance standards for the operation of its equipment and technological systems. Conduct high-quality, innovative research that maximizes effective management and use of all MBARI assets. Develop, in collaboration with the Monterey Bay Aquarium, creative programs that maximize the educational value of MBARI's research results. Transfer research results, technology, and operational techniques to the marine science community worldwide.

NOAA Coral Health and Monitoring Program
   http://coral.aoml.noaa.gov/

Scattered throughout the tropical oceans of the world, coral reefs provide an invaluable resource to global populations of marine and human life. Biologically, coral reefs are the second most productive systems in the world after tropical rainforests. They are home to a colorful array of over several thousand species of fish and other marine organisms. This intricate environment is essential to many marine and coastal species. To human populations, their value is inestimable. Their ecosystems and those they support are among the most diverse in the world. Unfortunately, they are also a living example of a severely threatened resource. Their degradation has spurred global concern for reef health as well as an effort to reverse current negative trends. The mission of the Coral Health and Monitoring Program is to provide services to help improve and sustain coral reef health throughout the world. Long term goals are: Establish an international network of coral reef researchers for the purpose of sharing knowledge and information on coral health and monitoring; Provide near real-time data products derived from satellite images and monitoring stations at coral reef areas; Provide a data repository for historical data collected from coral reef areas; and Add to the general fund of coral reef knowledge.

NOAA Fisheries Service
http://www.nmfs.noaa.gov/

Fish. The word evokes many thoughts and images—deep-fried shrimp, a tuna sandwich, cod fillets, oysters on the half shell. Or, a salmon tugging on the line, a leaping marlin, or maybe just a slap of the waves and the brisk sea air. But for the nation, fish have always been important, first for food and trade, often for recreation, and even as a key component of national security. So it should not be too surprising that the Nation's first Federal conservation agency, initiated in 1871, was devoted to the protection, study, management, and restoration of fish. This agency was the United States Commission of Fish and Fisheries, usually just called the "Fish Commission." Later it was renamed the Bureau of Fisheries, and still later it became the Bureau of Commercial Fisheries. Today its direct descendant is NOAA's National Marine Fisheries Service (NMFS) or just "NOAA Fisheries". The National Marine Fisheries Service (NMFS) or "NOAA Fisheries" is a part of the National Oceanic and Atmospheric Administration (NOAA). NMFS administers NOAA's programs which support the domestic and international conservation and management of living marine resources. NMFS provides services and products to support domestic and international fisheries management operations, fisheries development, trade and industry assistance activities, enforcement, protected species and habitat conservation operations, and the scientific and technical aspects of NOAA's marine fisheries program.

Ocean Studies Board of the National Research Council
http://www4.nas.edu/cger/osb.nsf

The Ocean Studies Board was established by the National Research Council to advise the federal government on issues of ocean science, engineering, and policy. In addition to exercising leadership within the ocean community, the Board undertakes studies at the request of federal agencies, Congress, or other sponsors, or upon its own initiative. The Board explores the science, policies, and infrastructure needed to understand and protect coastal and marine environments and resources. In recent years, the Board has conducted studies in the following areas: the status of marine and coastal environments, the ocean's role in the global climate system, technology and infrastructure needs, ocean-related aspects of national security, fisheries science, fisheries management and policy, living and nonliving marine resources, ocean education, reviews of specific agency programs, and the future of the discipline in the United States and abroad. The wide-ranging expertise of the Board members reflects this broad agenda.

The Board provides an open forum for those interested in ocean issues to bring technical and policy concerns for discussion and possible action. A primary responsibility of the Board is to initiate studies and ensure that they are carried out successfully.

Ocean Voice International
http://www.ovi.ca/

Destructive fishing methods such as the use of explosives to capture food fishes (above) and the spraying of sodium cyanide solution from plastic bottles (below) on coral heads to stun aquarium fishes to make them easy to capture, damage coral reefs. Ocean Voice and their partner the Haribon Foundation for Conservation of Natural Resources provides education on these issues. Ocean Voice International works for harmony between people, marine life and the envi-

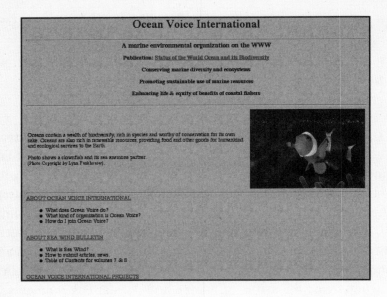

Ocean Voice International

A marine environmental organization on the WWW

Publication: Status of the World Ocean and its Biodiversity

Conserving marine diversity and ecosystems

Promoting sustainable use of marine resources

Enhancing life & equity of benefits of coastal fishers

Oceans contain a wealth of biodiversity, rich in species and worthy of conservation for its own sake. Oceans are also rich in renewable resources, providing food and other goods for humankind and ecological services to the Earth.

Photo shows a clownfish and its sea anemone partner.
(Photo Copyright by Lynn Funkhouser).

ABOUT OCEAN VOICE INTERNATIONAL

- What does Ocean Voice do?
- What kind of organization is Ocean Voice?
- How do I join Ocean Voice?

ABOUT SEA WIND BULLETIN

- What is Sea Wind?
- How to submit articles, news.
- Table of Contents for volumes 7 & 8

OCEAN VOICE INTERNATIONAL PROJECTS

ronment. It is environmental, humanitarian and global in its concerns. OCEAN VOICE works through education, training, research, appropriate technologies and partnerships. OCEAN VOICE's goals are: To conserve the diversity of marine life; To protect and restore marine ecosystems & ecological services; To enhance the quality of life and equity of benefits for coastal fisher peoples; and To promote the ecologically and socially sustainable harvest of marine resources. OCEAN VOICE achieves its goals: By partnerships to educate and train people to use environmentally sound marine resource harvesting methods; By engaging in and sharing results of marine life scientific research, indigenous and traditional knowledge; By fostering the participation of marine harvesters in environmental decision making, management and mutual co-operation; By writing, soliciting, publishing and communicating relevant articles, periodicals, manuals, books, videos, diskettes, and CD ROMs.

Oceanographer of the US Navy
http://oceanographer.navy.mil/

Today, under the direction of the Oceanographer of the Navy, Naval Oceanography embraces five major areas of responsibility: oceanography; meteorology; mapping, charting, and geodesy (known as MC&G); astrometry (the science of accurate astronomical measurements); and precise time-keeping. In serving the last of these, the Master Clock of the United States, from which all other national time standards are derived, is maintained at the Naval Observatory in Washington, which—incidentally—also hosts the Headquarters of the Oceanographer in his capacity as a member of the staff of the Chief of Naval Operations. The Naval Oceanography community today includes about 3,000 people, most of whom are civilians, at 65 locations around the world. In addition to the Naval Observatory, the most important of these are the Naval Oceanographic Office in Bay, St. Louis, MS, the Fleet Numerical Meterology and Oceanography Center in Monterey, CA, and four regional centers for direct support of the Fleet in Norfolk, VA, Pearl Harbor, HI, Guam, and Rota, Spain. Additionally, the oceanographic survey fleet consists of eight ships, assisted by three special purpose aircraft. On a day-to-day basis, ocean and weather observations are collected worldwide from civil and military sources, processed ashore, and used to make both oceanographic and meteorological forecasts in near-real-time to support the Fleet wherever it is operating.

Scripps Institute of Oceanography
http://www.sio.ucsd.edu/

Founded in 1903, Scripps Institution of Oceanography is one of the world's oldest, largest, and most important centers for global science research, graduate training , and public service. As part of the University of California, San Diego , Scripps Institution today is world renowned for its preeminence in scientific disciplines relating to biology, physics, chemistry, climatology, geosciences, and geophysics. Research at Scripps encompasses a wide range of scientific disciplines because understanding the oceans and their features requires a comprehensive knowledge of how the entire planet works. Most of the research efforts are interdisciplinary with a special focus of how the physical environment and life systems interact on a global basis. As the coming millennium approaches, we face daunting questions about the earth's future. What impact will global warming have on the planet's climate? Will overfishing and pollution destroy the sea's productivity, on which millions of people depend? Can the oceans provide new drugs to treat the diseases that continue to plague us? These are only some of the issues that scientists at Scripps Institution of Oceanography are now addressing.

Smithsonian's Ocean Planet

http://seawifs.gsfc.nasa.gov/ocean_planet.html

As the webmaster writes: "Ocean Planet, premiered at the Smithsonian Institution's National Museum of Natural History from April 1995 to April 1996, where it attracted nearly two million visitors. This electronic online companion exhibition contains all of the text and most of the panel designs and images found in the traveling exhibition. Learn more about the project by reading an overview of the exhibition, a message from the curator, or a copy of the final report which presents information about visitation, educational programming and materials, publicity, and the results of the visitor studies. Learn about the variety of educational materials associated with Ocean Planet, including a set of lessons and marine science activities which adapt several themes of the exhibition for use in the middle and high school classroom." Ocean Planet is the brainchild of Gene Carl Feldman. Gene has been an oceanographer at NASA / Goddard

Space Flight Center since 1985. He has been involved with the production, archival and distribution of the satellite-derived ocean color data sets, first as observed by the Nimbus-7 Coastal Zone Color Scanner and now, for the new ocean color mission called SeaWiFS which was successfully launched on August 1, 1997.

Woods Hole Oceanographic Institution
http://www.whoi.edu/

The Woods Hole Oceanographic Institution is a private, independent, not-for-profit corporation dedicated to research and higher education at the frontiers of ocean science. Its primary mission is to develop and effectively communicate a fundamental understanding of the processes and characteristics governing how the oceans function and how they interact with the Earth as a whole. To fulfill this mission, WHOI must successfully: Recruit, retain, and support the highest quality staff andstudents and provide an organization that nurtures creativity and innovation; Stress a flexible, multidisciplinary, and collaborative approach to the research and education activities of its staff within an equitable working environment; Promote the development and use of advanced instrumentation and systems (including ships,

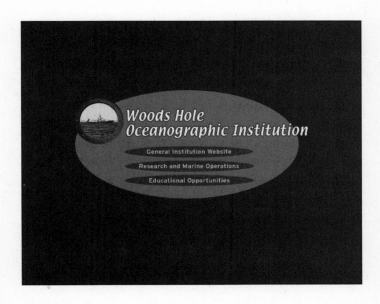

vehicles and platforms) to make the required observations at sea and in the laboratory; Make the results of its research known to the public and policymakers and foster its applications to new technology and products in ways consistent with the wise use of the oceans; Secure the essential resources to sustain these activities, a responsibility that the Trustees and Corporation Members must jointly share with management and staff. It is the goal of the Institution to be a world leader in advancing and communicating a basic understanding of the oceans and their decisive role in addressing global questions.

Mailing Lists

The Coral-List Listserver

The purpose of the Coral-List list-server is to provide a forum for Internet discussions and announcements among coral health researchers pertaining to coral reef health and monitoring throughout the world. The list is primarily for use by coral health researchers and scientists. Currently, about 1600 researchers are subscribed to the list. If you wish to subscribe to the coral-list, please send an e-mail message to majordomo@coral.aoml.noaa. gov, with the following message (only!) in the body of the text: subscribe coral-list

MARINE-L, The Marine Studies and Information List

This is an open Forum for the discussion and development of marine related topics. If you are interested in joining this list, you can subscribe by sending a message to LISTSERVER@cgc.ns.ca with the words SUBSCRIBE MARINE-L (first name, last name) in the body. Do not attach a signature and do not place anything in the SUBJECT line.

Newsgroups

bionet.biology.deepsea
sci.bio.fisheries
sci.engr.marine.hydrodynamics
sci.geo.eos
sci.geo.fluids
sci.geo.geology
sci.geo.hydrology
sci.geo.meteorology
sci.geo.oceanography
sci.mech.fluids
sci.physics.computational.fluid-dynamics

18

PALEONTOLOGY AND
PALEOANTHROPOLOGY

DinoDon.Com [note web site revised from what was on site map]
  http://www.dinodon.com

Here is the web site of"Dino" Don Lessem, a world-renowned dinosaur expert and writer. He has written on dinosaurs and other scientific subjects or numerous newspapers and magazines, including The Boston Globe, The New York Times, Smithsonian and Omni. He is a former Knight Science Journalism Fellow at M.I.T. and the author or co-author of many books on dinosaurs, including Bigger than T. rex, Dinosaurs Rediscovered, and with Dr. John R. Horner, The Complete T. rex and Digging Tyrannosaurus rex. He has been a host and writer of NOVA documentaries and is the creator and host of the largest and most successful traveling dinosaur exhibit in North America—The Dinosaurs of Jurassic Park/The Lost World. Don also produces the Giganotosaurus.com Web site, devoted to information and news about the largest carnivorous dinosaur ever found. Be sure to click on the link for Cryolophosaurus and learn about the "frozen crested reptile" which is a large early meateater with a singular bony crest that sweeps up its forehead like a pompadour. Geologist Dr. William Hammer of Augustana College in Illinois who excavated the dinosaur on a polar geological research trip, nicknamed it "Elvis" for the Presley-style sweep of the skull crest.

Dinosaur Trace Fossils

*http://www.emory.edu/COLLEGE/ENVS/research/ichnology/
dinotraces.html*

As the webmaster writes: "If all of the dinosaur bones in the world disappeared tomorrow, paleontologists still would have plenty of evidence for the existence of dinosaurs through dinosaur trace fossils. A trace fossil is indirect evidence of ancient life (exclusive of body parts) that reflects some sort of behavior by the organism. Examples of trace fossils are tracks, trails, burrows, borings, gnawings, eggs, nests, gizzard stones, and dung. In contrast, a body fossil is direct evidence of ancient life that involves some body part of the organism. Dinosaurs left trace fossils represented by tracks, tooth marks, eggs, nests, gastroliths, and coprolites. Body fossils of dinosaurs include bones and skin impressions. As an example of the distinction between dinosaur body fossils and trace fossils, skin impressions are not trace fossils unless they were made while the dinosaur was still alive, such as the skin impressions that might be associated with a footprint." The purpose of this web page is to give a brief summary of dinosaur trace fossils that will supplement paleontological information already given by dinosaur body fossils.

Dinosauria Online

http://www.dinosauria.com/

In the marketplace today there are many publications one can turn to for information about dinosaurs. However, the information in these publications tend to be about a single subject, overly scientific, badly out-of-date, or singular expositions of the author's thought. Dinosauria On-Line is intended to give the reader a broader exposure to dinosaur science. I've tried to bring together discussions about the topics that are hot among dinosaur enthusiasts today. This allows the reader not only to see a subject from many points of view, but allows him to see what others think about ideas and questions that the reader has wondered about but not been able to pose to knowledgeable people. Dinosauria On-Line is meant for the serious enthusiast and rank

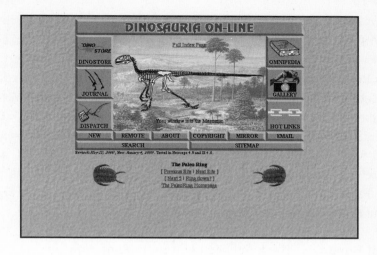

amateur alike. Discussions are both technical and at a level at which those without formal education in paleontology can understand and enjoy. Original articles written specifically for Dinosauria On-Line are intended to clear up certain issues, such as the meaning of the term "warm-blooded," for those just starting out in their hobby, and to clarify meaning for those already deeply enmeshed. Dictionaries, maps, and lists aid enthusiast, amateur, casual researcher and professional alike by defining important terms, listing known genera, and clarifying the technical information presented both here and in publications. Pictures are used where possible to clarify or emphasize important points.

Richard Dawkins Web Site
http://www.world-of-dawkins.com/

Richard Dawkins was educated at Oxford University and has taught zoology at the universities of California and Oxford. He is the Charles Simonyi Professor of the Public Understanding of Science at Oxford University. His books about evolution and science include The Selfish Gene, The Extended Phenotype, The Blind Watchmaker, River Out of Eden, Climbing Mount Improbable, and most recently, Unweaving the Rainbow . Richard Dawkins won both the Royal Society of Literature Award and the Los Angeles Times Literary Prize in 1987 for The Blind Watchmaker. The television film of the book, shown in the 'Horizon' series, won the Sci-Tech Prize for the Best Science Programme of 1987. He has also won the 1989 Silver Medal of the Zoological Society of London and the 1990 Royal Society Michael Faraday Award for the furtherance of the public understanding of science. In 1994 he won the Nakayama Prize for Human Science and in 1995 was awarded an Honorary D.Litt. by the University of St Andrews. Humanist of the Year Award 1996. Since 1996 has been Vice President of the British Humanist Association. Elected a Fellow of the Royal Society of Literature in 1997.

Fossil Hominids: The Evidence for Human Evolution
http://www.talkorigins.org/faqs/homs/

These web pages are intended to refute creationist claims that there is no evidence for human evolution. To do this, it is first necessary to summarize the current thinking about human evolution and the fossil evidence supporting it. If you are not interested in creationism, you can read only those pages. If you are only interested in creationism, you can skip to the pages on creationist arguments; they will contain links to the fossils under discussion when necessary. Why bother refuting creationist arguments about human evolution? Because creationism is dreadful science. In fact, it's not science so much as a campaign to evangelize fundamentalist religion. Creationists are running scared from the evidence for human evolution, as well they should be. They have no good explanation for the fossils, and human evolution is a topic on which the creationists are especially vulnerable because they can't afford any compromise. If humans evolved, then the whole rationale for creationism collapses. Why is creationism more of a threat than other equally silly pseudosciences such as astrology? The difference is that astrologers aren't engaged in a highly organised and well-funded campaign to have their pseudoscience taught in schools.

Leakey Ancestors

http://www.ants-inc.com/inhandmuseum/LeakeyAncestors.html

According to the webmaster, this web site features "a series of half-size skulls and fossil replicas aims to provide basic information about the various different species and the more significant fossils that play a part in the evolutionary history of modern humans. The series includes four extinct species, Australopithecus afarensis, Australopithecus boisei, Homo erectus, and Homo neanderthalensis, as well as three modern skulls for comparison; the sole surviving species in our own lineage, Homo sapiens, and two African apes, Gorilla gorilla (the lowland gorilla) and Pan troglodytes (the chimpanzee). Additional skulls and other fossils will be added to the series in the future. Each object is a scaled down but accurate replica. Information relating to the discovery, classification, time of existence, and significance is provided in an easy to read, attractively illustrated format. The web site offers detailed information on paleoanthropology in general, and early hominid finds in particular. The information is layered, but there will be a complete page for each species—right now H. ergaster and A. boisei and A. afarensis are fairly complete, but there are only a few paragraphs on each of the other species right now. This will be updated at frequent intervals until the baseline site is completed. Also, a number of new replicas will be available shortly, and details about each will be added here as they are released."

Monash University's Dinosaur Dreaming Site

http://www.earth.monash.edu.au/dinodream/

The PalaeoLab is housed in the Department of Earth Sciences at Monash University, and is run jointly by the Department of Earth Sciences and the Monash Science Centre. Established in 1986 to prepare the material excavated from the Dinosaur Cove site, it is a repository and research hub for material from all the expeditions and excavations run by the PalaeoLab staff and volunteers. As they write: "The PalaeoLab is part of the Monash University Department of Earth Sciences. We also work closely with the Monash Science Centre, an organisation committed to supporting science education in the community."

Become a Friend of Dinosaur Dreaming and support the excavation of the only working dinosaur site in Australia. Receive up-to-date information on the exciting research being carried out by palaeontologists on the 120 million year old fossils being recovered from the Dinosaur Dreaming site near Inverloch. All subscriptions directly assist the funding of the annual dig at Dinosaur Dreaming and support the ongoing research program. This research is vital to the study of what Australia, and Victoria in particular, was like over 100 million years ago.

Museum of Paleontology at UC Berkeley
http://www.ucmp.berkeley.edu/

UCMP's mission is the conservation of paleontological materials, collections development, and research and instructional support. The Museum's enormous collections are ranked 4th in America in size, and include protists, plants, invertebrates and vertebrates. The Museum of Paleontology was established at Berkeley in 1874 by the California State Legislature, when the collections of the California Natural History Survey and the Second (Whitney) Geological Survey were deposited in the University Museum. Other collections were added in the late 1800's and early 1900's. Miss Annie Alexander of Oakland provided an endowment to fund the Museum permanently. Later the University recognized the academic and scientific value of the Museum and provided additional, continued funding. Research, collections development, student support and special projects are currently funded from various donors, granting agencies, and contracts. The Museum of Paleontology's purpose is twofold. First, the Museum serves as a unique and invaluable storehouse for collections of fossil and modern organisms. Second, the Museum provides research oppurtunities to faculty and students. UCMP is widely known for advancing new technologies such as environmental scanning electron microscopy and molecular paleontology. These two separate avenues, collection and research, document the history and evolution of life.

Neanderthal Heaven
http://members.iinet.net.au/~chawkins/heaven.htm

Some people think that the Neanderthals were a separate species to modern humans i.e. Homo neanderthalensis compared with Homo sapiens. We can never know if this is true, as the only way to tell if two organisms belong to the same species is to see if they can breed together to produce fertile offspring. As fossil organisms can't interbreed, we can't test this hypothesis! If the Neanderthals were the same species (which the majority of paleontologists seem to say), then they would have been able to interbreed with modern humans. It seems they may have been a bit shy though. If the two groups of hominids were regularly interbreeding, then we wouldn't expect to find such distinct differences between them; interbreeding would "smooth out" the features. This does not seem to be the case. There are definite differences between the features of modern humans and the Neanderthals. Just recently, a discovery has been made that suggests that maybe there was some interbreeding going on. What stopped them partying? Paleontologists have suggested that maybe the Neanderthals and the modern humans waged a war of survival, ending in the extinction of the Neanderthals. Visit this great web site for more info.

Paleoanthropology: A Short Journey Through Time
http://www.uea.ac.uk/~x9706887/

The word Paleoanthropology is built up out of two separate words; "Anthropology" meaning: the study of man, his origins, physical characteristics, institutions, religious beliefs and social relationships and "Paleontology" which means: the study of fossils to determine the structure and evolution of extinct animals and plants and the age and conditions of deposition of the rock strata in which they are found. Together these two words form an exciting, rapidly changing field of research which is one of the most hotly debated sciences. As the webmaster writes: "On this page, I have attempted to summarise the main important discoveries made so far and place them in this evolutionary timeline. Many opinions may differ from mine, ranging from the place of many hominids in the timeline I have adapted for this page, to the place of origin of many of these species, to their ancestral roots. However, I have tried to give an objective view of the whole subject matter and I hope you find this science as interesting as I do." The site is loaded with great essays, images and FAQs, and thus comes highly recommended.

The Record of Human Evolution
http://www.natcenscied.org/delson.htm

What does it means to say that early mammals evolved into primates or that humans evolved from nonhuman primates? Evolution is the concept of biological change through time. Most scientists today understand it as a complex process involving genetic change from one generation to the next, under the control of natural selection. This term, devised by Charles Darwin in 1859, means that in a group of individuals of any one species, in a given environment some individuals will be better able than others to find food, escape from predators, protect their living space, find a mate, and care for their offspring. These more successful individuals are said to be better adapted to their environment, or more "fit" than their fellows of the same species. The best adapted individuals must also produce offspring who can carry the genetic heritage of their well-adapted fore-

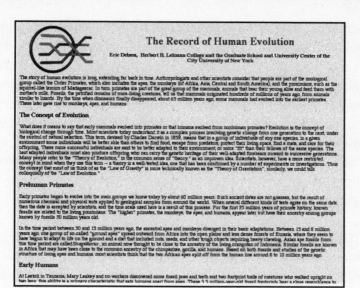

The Record of Human Evolution

Eric Delson, Herbert H. Lehman College and the Graduate School and University Center of the City University of New York

The story of human evolution is long, extending far back in time. Anthropologists and other scientists consider that people are part of the zoological group called the Order Primates, which also includes the apes, the monkeys (of Africa, Asia, Central and South America), and the prosimians, such as the squirrel-like lemurs of Madagascar. In turn, primates are part of the great group of the mammals, animals that bear their young alive and feed them with mother's milk. Fossils, the petrified remains of once-living creatures, tell us that mammals originated hundreds of millions of years ago, from animals similar to lizards. By the time when dinosaurs finally disappeared, about 65 million years ago, some mammals had evolved into the earliest primates. These later gave rise to monkeys, apes, and humans.

The Concept of Evolution

What does it mean to say that early mammals evolved into primates or that humans evolved from nonhuman primates? Evolution is the concept of biological change through time. Most scientists today understand it as a complex process involving genetic change from one generation to the next, under the control of natural selection. This term, devised by Charles Darwin in 1859, means that in a group of individuals of any one species, in a given environment some individuals will be better able than others to find food, escape from predators, protect their living space, find a mate, and care for their offspring. These more successful individuals are said to be better adapted to their environment, or more "fit" than their fellows of the same species. The best adapted individuals must also produce offspring who can carry the genetic heritage of their well-adapted forebears onward to successive generations. Many people refer to the "Theory of Evolution," in the common sense of "theory," as an unproven idea. Scientists, however, have a more restricted concept in mind when they use this term – a theory is a well-tested idea, one that has been confirmed by a number of experiments or investigations. Thus the concept that most of us think of as the "Law of Gravity" is more technically known as the "Theory of Gravitation"; similarly, we could talk colloquially of the "Law of Evolution."

Prehuman Primates

Early primates began to evolve into the main groups we know today by about 60 million years. Such ancient dates are not guesses, but the result of numerous chemical and physical tests applied to geological samples from around the world. When several different kinds of tests agree on the same date, then the date is accepted by scientists, and the time scale used here is a result of this process. For the first 35 million years of primate history, known fossils are related to the living prosimians. The "higher" primates, the monkeys, the apes, and humans, appear later but have their ancestry among groups known by fossils 30 million years old.

In the time period between 30 and 15 million years ago, the ancestral apes and monkeys diverged in their basic adaptations. Between 15 and 8 million years ago, one group of so-called "ground apes" spread outward from Africa into the open plains and less dense forests of Eurasia, where they seem to have begun to adapt to life on the ground and a diet that included nuts, seeds, and other tough objects requiring heavy chewing. Asian apes fossils from this time period are called Sivapithecus, an animal now thought to be close to the ancestry of the living orangutan of Indonesia. Similar fossils are known in Africa that may have been close to the common ancestry of the chimpanzee, gorilla, and humans. Based on both fossils and studies of the genetic structure of living apes and humans, most scientists think that the two African apes split off from the human line around 8 to 10 million years ago.

Early Humans

At Laetoli in Tanzania, Mary Leakey and co-workers discovered some fossil jaws and teeth and two footprint trails of creatures who walked upright on two legs; this ability is a primary characteristic that sets humans apart from apes. These 3.5 million-year-old fossil footprints bear a close resemblance to

bears onward to successive generations. Many people refer to the "Theory of Evolution," in the common sense of "theory," as an unproven idea. Scientists, however, have a more restricted concept in mind when they use this term—a theory is a well-tested idea, one that has been confirmed by a number of experiments or investigations. Visit this web site for more info.

Paul Serano's Dinosaur Web Site
http://dinosaur.uchicago.edu/

When not teaching or writing papers at the University of Chicago, Paul Sereno and his students are likely to be found searching museum collections or combing deserts to find fossil evidence that will impact on our understanding of large-scale evolution during the dinosaur era. Discoverer of dinosaurs on several continents, Paul Sereno fuses his mission of scientific research with his educational mission, engaging his students directly in the process of discovery. His field work began in 1988 in the foothills of the Andes in Argentina, where his team unearthed the first complete skeletons of the primitive dinosaur Herrerasaurus. Known previously only from bones of the hind limb, the new fossils allowed Sereno and several sculptors to reconstruct its skeleton and create a flesh model of this 12-foot-long dinosaur, now on display at the Field Museum of Natural History in Chicago. Returning to this area in 1991, Sereno's team discovered a small skeleton belonging to a new species they named Eoraptor ("dawn raptor). A primitive cousin of Herrerasaurus, Eoraptor measures only 3 feet from snout to tail tip. Ancient volcanic ash beds discovered near these early dinosaurs allowed Sereno's team to determine their age—228 million years old—and date the dawn of the dinosaur era. These discoveries shed light on the roots of the dinosaur family tree and on how and when dinosaurs came to dominate the land.

USA TODAY Paleontology articles
http://www.usatoday.com/life/science/paleo/lspindex.htm

Come here for all the latest dino news. For example: The oldest known fossil of a baby bird shows that it had a head and neck like a meat-eating velociraptor but was otherwise similar in its development to modern birds, researchers report Friday. The discovery further supports the link between birds and dinosaurs. The fossil represents a remarkable combination of ancient and modern physical features, says Luis Chiappe, American Museum of Natural History, New York. Another example: A 7-foot-long, fleet-footed meat-eating dinosaur, the most bird-like ever seen, has been found in Argentina, say paleontologists. The predator existed at the same time as birds but was a living relic, a member of the missing dinosaur line that led to birds, says paleontologist Fernando Novas of the Museo Argentino de Ciencias Naturales in Buenos Aires. And another: Researchers studying the 250-million-year-old fossil of a flying lizard say it had a wing structure unlike any other known in nature. The study, published in the journal Science, found the wings of Coelurosauravus jaekeli—the first known reptile to fly—consisted of a membrane stretched between hollow rods that grew out from the skin instead of attaching to a skeleton.

Wyoming Dinosaur Center
http://wyodino.org/

The Wyoming Dinosaur Center located in north-central Wyoming is known for some of the largest dinosaur fossil quarries in the world. Join Wyoming paleo-technicians in the field as they uncover large Jurassic dinosaurs such as Allosaurus, Apatosaurus, Camarasaurus and Diplodocus. Visit the center's spectacular online museum. See 19 full-size mounted skeletons, including 8 dinosaurs, such as: Allosaurus, Triceratops and Tyrannosaurus Rex. There are also displays on geology and prehistoric life on earth. Shop for fossils, gems, minerals, posters and great educational books, games and toys in the center's unique museum shop. Watch as technicians prepare dinosaur bones and fossils for exhibit.

See fossils and life-forms from earliest geologic time periods in displays that place them into a time-perspective. The central hall houses 19 full size mounted skeletons including 8 dinosaurs, with a stunning display of Tyrannosaurus Rex ("Stan") attacking Triceratops horridus. Also on display: premier collection of dinosaur eggs. And, as the webmaster adds: "Coming spring 2000:27-foot-long Cama-rasaur, first full skeleton to be mounted from our dig sites." There is much to learn here, and much to see and do, at the web page of the Wyoming Dinosaur Center.

Mailing Lists:

CBR-L
  Craniofacial Biology Research—send message "subscribe cbr-l" to
  majordomo@po.cwru.edu

HUMEVO-L {moderated}
  Human Evolutionary Research—send message "sub HUMEVO-L
  first-name last-name" to listserv@freya.cc.pdx.edu

Paleodiet
  Primitive diets and their relevance to modern life ("semi-private,
  semi-moderated")—Contact Dean Esmay at esmay@syndicomm.
  com

Newsgroups:

sci.bio.paleontology

19

PHYSICS

American Institute of Physics
http://www.aip.org/

The American Institute of Physics (AIP) was founded in 1931 in response to funding problems brought on by the Great Depression. At the urging of the Chemical Foundation, which provided initial funding, leaders of American physics formed a corporation for the "advancement and diffusion of knowledge of the science of physics and its application to human welfare," especially by achieving economies in the publishing of journals and the maintenance of membership lists. Broader concerns also argued for cooperation. With the advent of esoteric theory in quantum, nuclear, and relativity physics, the worlds of academic and industrial physics seemed to be drifting apart. Meanwhile the public found physics increasingly hard to comprehend, and some blamed science-based technology for the perils of modern warfare and economic collapse. Thus while the bulk of AIP's efforts would always be devoted to publishing and membership services, from the outset the Institute also worked to foster cooperation among different segments of the physics community and to improve public understanding of science. At the time of its formal incorporation in 1932, AIP comprised five societies with a total membership of some 4,000 individuals: The American Physical Society, the Optical Society of America, the Acoustical Society of America, The Society of Rheology, and the American Association of Physics Teachers. Visit the web site for more info on the Institute today.

Atomic Data for Astrophysicists
http://www.pa.uky.edu/%7Everner/atom.html

The Atomic Data for Astrophysics server provides links to basic atomic data required for calculation of the ionization state of astrophysical plasmas and for quantitative spectroscopy. Most of these data are utilized in the photoionization code Cloudy and other radiative-collisional, photoionization, and coronal plasma codes. The data are regularly updated. This server is maintained by Dima Verner at the Department of Physics and Astronomy, University of Kentucky, who writes: "Your comments, questions and suggestions are welcome. If you find this server helpful, and use the data retrieved through the server for your research, I would appreciate acknowledging it in your papers." Here you'll find atomic data related to Photoionization, Recombination, Collisional ionization and autoionization, Charge transfer, Auger processes, Energy levels, wavelengths, transition probabilities, Collision strengths, excitation rates, Stark broadening and Opacities. Here you will also find elegant Fortran subroutines for Photoionization cross sections and Radiative recombination rates. There is no resource quite like this anywhere else on the Internet. All astrophysicisits are bound to find this data absolutely indispensable, as well as easy to access. Dr. Verner is to be thanked for an absolutely splendid contribution to scientific information.

Bell's Theorem
*http://faraday.physics.utoronto.ca/GeneralInterest/Harrison/
BellsTheorem/BellsTheorem.html*

In the late nineteenth century the logician Hilbert used to say "Physics is too important to be left to the physicists." In retaliation, J.A. Wheeler has stated: "G"del is too important to be left to the mathematicians." Finally, although deductive logic is fairly well understood, nobody has succeeded in codifying iron-clad rules for inductive logic that work consistently. Mills tried very hard to do this, but the following story by Copi shows one problem: "A favorite example used by critics of the Method of Agreement is the case of the Scientific Drinker, who was extremely fond of liquor and got drunk every night

Bell's Theorem

Click here to go to the General Interest "Virtual Physics Bookshelf."

Click here to go to the JPU200Y home page.

AUTHOR

This document was written in February 1999 by David M. Harrison, Department of Physics, University of Toronto, mailto:harrison@physics.utoronto.ca. This is version 1.14 of the document, date (m/d/y) 04/07/00.

This document is Copyright © 1999, 2000 David M. Harrison.

INTRODUCTION

In 1975 Stapp called Bell's Theorem "the most profound discovery of science." Note that he says *science*, not *physics*. I agree with him.

In this document, we shall explore the theorem. We assume some familiarity with the concept of wave-particle duality; a document on this may be found here. We also assume considerable familiarity with the Stern-Gerlach experiment and the concept of a correlation experiment; a document on these may be found here.

The origins of this topic is a famous paper by Einstein, Rosen and Podolsky (EPR) in 1935; its title was *Can Quantum-Mechanical Description of Physical Reality be Considered Complete?* They considered what Einstein called the "spooky action-at-a-distance" that seems to be part of Quantum Mechanics, and concluded that the theory must be incomplete if not outright wrong. As you probably already know, Einstein never did accept Quantum Mechanics. One of his objections was that "God does not play at dice with the universe." Bohr responded: "Quit telling God what to do!"

In the early 1950's David Bohm (not "Bohr") was a young Physics professor at Princeton University. He was assigned to teach Quantum Mechanics and, as is common, decided to write a textbook on the topic; the book is still a classic. Einstein was at Princeton at this time, and as Bohm finished each chapter of the book Einstein would critique it. By the time Bohm had finished the book Einstein had convinced him that Quantum Mechanics was at least incomplete. Bohm then spent many years in search of *hidden variables*, unobserved factors inside, say, a radioactive atom that determines when it is going to decay. In a hidden variable theory, the time for the decay to occur is not random, although the variable controlling the process is hidden from us. We will discuss Bohm's work extensively later in this document.

In 1964 J.S. Bell published his theorem. It was cast in terms of a hidden variable theory. Since then, other proofs have appeared by d'Espagnat, Stapp, and others that are not in terms of hidden variables. Below we shall do a variation on d'Espagnat's proof that I devised.

PROVING BELL'S INEQUALITY

We shall be *slightly* mathematical. The details of the math are not important, but there are a couple of pieces of the proof that will be important. The result of the proof will be that for any collection of objects with three different parameters, A, B and C

---

of the week. He was ruining his health, and his few remaining friends pleaded with him to stop. Realizing himself that he could not go on, he resolved to conduct a careful experiment to discover the exact cause of his frequent inebriations. For five nights in a row he collected instances of a given phenomenon, the antecedent circumstances being respectively scotch and soda, bourbon and soda, brandy and soda, rum and soda, and gin and soda [ugh!]. Then using the Method of Agreement he swore a solemn oath never to touch soda again!" What of the validity of logic? Bell's Theorem tests the question.

Black Holes and Neutron Stars
http://antwrp.gsfc.nasa.gov/htmltest/rjn%5Fbht.html

It is impossible for a human to travel very near a high gravity star which has a mass like that of the Sun. If, somehow, a person could survive the extremely harmful radiation that would be emitted on or near these objects, the high gravity itself would likely pose insurmountable problems. The person could not stand casually on the surface of such a star because the high surface gravity would tend to flatten them. (Lying down wouldn't help.) Were a person to orbit the star in a spaceship, however, the immense gravitational field would be overcome by a large outward centrifugal acceleration. The problem in this case, however, is the extreme change in gravity between the head and toe of the person, the extreme tidal pull, would surely prove much more than annoying for any human. Nevertheless it is informative and interesting to wonder what it would look like to visit such a high gravity environment. Here, at this wonderful web page, the visual aspects of a journey to several different types of high gravity stars are discussed and described in some detail and presented along with computer generated illustrations highlighting the perceived visual distortions. The three types of stars discussed are a) a "normal" neutron star having relatively weak surface gravity, b) a black hole, and c) an "ultracompact" neutron star [13] having relatively strong surface gravity.

Cosmology FAQ
http://www.astro.ucla.edu/%7Ewright/cosmology%5Ffaq.html

Question: What is the evidence for the Big Bang? Answer: The evidence for the Big Bang comes from many pieces of observational data that are consistent with the Big Bang. None of these prove the Big Bang, since scientific theories are not proven. Many of these facts are consistent with the Big Bang and some other cosmological models, but taken together these observations show that the Big Bang is the best current model for the Universe. These observations include: The darkness of the night sky—Olbers' paradox; The Hubble Law—the linear distance vs redshift law; Homogeneity—fair data showing that our location in the Universe is not special; Isotropy—very strong data showing that the sky looks the same in all directions to 1 part in 100,000; and Time dilation in supernova light curves. Question: How can the Universe be infinite if it was all concentrated into a point at the Big Bang? Answer: The Universe was not concentrated into a point at the time of the Big Bang. But the observable Universe was concentrated into a point. The distinction between the whole Universe and the part of it that we can see is important. Tune into this web site for more insightful Q&A.

Frequently Asked Questions in Cosmology

Tutorial : Part 1 | Part 2 | Part 3 | Part 4 | Age | Distances | Bibliography | Relativity

- What is the evidence for the Big Bang?
- What is this "anti-gravity"? (The cosmological constant)
- Why do we think that the expansion of the Universe is accelerating?
- How old is the Universe?
- If the Universe is only 10 billion years old, why isn't the most distant object we can see 5 billion light years away?
- If the Universe is only 10 billion years old, how can we see objects that are now 30 billion light years away?
- How can the Universe be infinite if it was all concentrated into a point at the Big Bang?
- How can the oldest stars in the Universe be older than the Universe?
- Can objects move away from us faster than the speed of light?
- What is the redshift?
- Are quasars really at the large distances indicated by their redshifts?
- What about objects with discordant redshifts, like Stephan's Quintet?
- Has the time dilation of distant source light curves predicted by the Big Bang been observed?
- Are galaxies really moving away from us or is space just expanding?
- Why doesn't the Solar System expand if the whole Universe is expanding?
- Is the Universe expanding or is it just that our definitions of length and time are changing?
- Why haven't the CMBR photons outrun the galaxies in the Big Bang?
- Where was the center of the Big Bang?
- What is meant by a flat Universe?
- Is the Big Bang a Black Hole?
- What is the Universe expanding into?
- What came before the Big Bang?
- Doug Scott's Cosmic Microwave Background Radiation (CMBR) FAQ
- Can the CMBR be redshifted starlight?
- Why is the sky dark at night?
- Will the Universe expand forever or recollapse?
- What is the dark matter?
- What is the value of the Hubble constant?
- What can a layperson do in cosmology?
- Ask your own question!

What is the evidence for the Big Bang?

The evidence for the Big Bang comes from many pieces of observational data that are consistent with the Big Bang. None of these *prove* the Big Bang, since scientific theories are not proven. Many of these facts are consistent with the Big Bang and some other cosmological models, but taken together these observations show that the Big Bang is the best current model for the Universe. These observations include:

- The darkness of the night sky - Olbers' paradox.
- The Hubble Law - the linear distance vs redshift law. The data are now very good.
- Homogeneity - fair data showing that our location in the Universe is not special.
- Isotropy - very strong data showing that the sky looks the same in all directions to 1 part in 100,000.
- Time dilation in supernova light curves

Dark Matter
http://cfpa.berkeley.edu/darkmat/dm.html

There is perhaps no current problem of greater importance to astrophysics and cosmology than that of "dark matter". The controversy, as the name implies, is centered around the notion that there may exist an enormous amount of matter in the Universe which cannot be detected from the light which it emits. This is "stuff" which cannot be seen directly. So what makes us think that it exists at all? Its presence is inferred indirectly from the motions of astronomical objects, specifically stellar, galactic, and galaxy cluster/supercluster observations. The basic principle is that if we measure velocities in some region, then there has to be enough mass there for gravity to stop all the objects flying apart. When such velocity measurements are done on large scales, it turns out that the amount of inferred mass is much more than can be explained by the luminous stuff. Hence we infer that there is dark matter in the Universe. There are many different pieces of evidence on different scales. And on the very largest scales, there may be enough to "close" the Universe, so that it will ultimately re-collapse in a Big Crunch. This is the issue explored by the Dark Matter web site.

Fundamental Physical Constants
http://physics.nist.gov/cuu/Constants/index.html

As the webmasters write: "Welcome to the NIST Reference on Constants, Units, and Uncertainty, one of the technical activities of the Fundamental Constants Data Center of the NIST Physics Laboratory. The contents of this site have been prepared by Barry N. Taylor of the Data Center in close collaboration with Peter J. Mohr of the Physics Laboratory's Atomic Physics Division. This site was designed, edited and programmed by Michael Douma under the direction of Drs. Taylor and Mohr. All material has been authored or co-authored by Drs. Taylor and Mohr, with the exception of sections otherwise identified. The bibliographic database portion was designed and programmed by Michael Douma and Dr. Mohr in collaboration with Dr. Taylor, and is maintained by Drs. Mohr and Taylor. This web server is maintained by the Office of Electronic Commerce in Science and Engineering Data (ECSED) of the Physics Laboratory of the National Institute of Standards and Technology (NIST), an agency of the U.S. Department of Commerce." The site features Acrobat (pdf) files authored in TeX in a unix environment, and Adobe Pagemaker and Illustrator on a Power Macintosh. Wherever possible, the typefaces are set in Times Roman to minimize file sizes by avoiding subset font files. In TeX, this laborious process is accomplished using MathTime fonts available from Y&Y which allow TeX to use postscript fonts in place of its default bitmapped fonts.

Gravitational Wave Detection/TIGA
http://www.physics.umd.edu/rgroups/gen%5Frel%5Fexp/gwave. html

The TIGA project is a cooperative effort among three Universities (University of Maryland, Louisiana State University and the University of Rochester) to design and build a spherical, resonant-mass gravitational-wave detector. A gravitational wave detector is in essence a telescope that can see the universe in waves of space-time. There are two main approaches, laser interferometry and resonant mass. The TIGA project is a collaboration of American scientists working on the resonant mass approach. The detector is constructed from a large sphere of aluminum, or some metal, cooled to very near absolute zero to reduce thermal noise. This sphere is suspended from a vibration isolator, to keep out noise from the room that it is in. All this noise isolation is necessary because the oscillations created by the gravitational wave that the sphere is trying to detect can be less than the diameter of a proton. A spherical detector has many advantages that will make it a useful complement to the laser interferometer detectors already being built, such as LIGO and VIRGO . Becauce of its spherical symmettry, a TIGA detector is equally sensitive to gravitational radiation from any direction. The tensor character of the gravitational waves in Einstein's general relativity require that the energy will mainly go into the l=2 modes of the sphere.

Stephen Hawking's Official Web Pages
http://www.hawking.org.uk/

Dr. Stephen Hawking has spent his life trying to define the basic laws which govern the universe. With Roger Penrose he showed that Einstein's General Theory of Relativity implied space and time would have a beginning in the Big Bang and an end in black holes. These results indicated it was necessary to unify General Relativity with Quantum Theory, the other great Scientific development of the first half of the 20th Century. One consequence of such a unification that he discovered was that black holes should not be completely black, but should emit radiation and eventually evaporate and disappear. Another conjecture is that the universe has no edge or boundary in imaginary time. This would imply that the way the universe began was completely determined by the laws of science. Dr. Hawsking's many publications include The Large Scale Structure of Spacetime with G F R Ellis, General Relativity: An Einstein Centenary Survey, with W Israel, and 300 Years of Gravity, with W Israel. Stephen Hawking has two popular books published; his best seller A Brief History of Time, and his later book, Black Holes and Baby Universes and Other Essays.

The Light Cone

http://www.phy.syr.edu./courses/modules/LIGHTCONE/introduction.html

The Theory of Relativity is really a physical theory about time and space. In fact, it actually says that there is no such thing as time and there is no such thing as space. Instead, it is a theory of "a new thing called Spacetime". Spacetime is the history of an entire universe, that is, the set of all of the events that happened in that universe. "Our plan," writes the author of this web site, " is to follow a pseudo-historical development of how we came to understand 'Spacetime', the spacetime of General Relativity. We do so by considering a sequence of models for spacetime. Each model represents "how we understood space and time" at various stages in our human history. Specifically, we will consider: Aristotle's view, Galileo's view , and Einstein's view." The Light Cone is a mathematical model that very neatly encodes the causal structure of Einstein's Spacetime. Each event in Spacetime has a double-cone attached to it, where the vertex (i.e., the tip) corresponds to the event itself. By convention, "time" runs vertically in all of our diagrams. The upward-directed cone opens to enclose the directions pointing towards events to the future of this event. The downward-

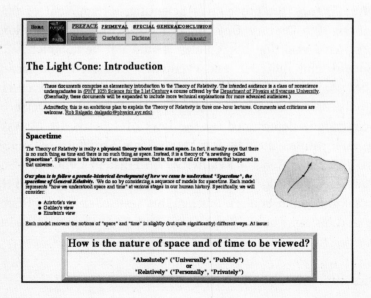

directed cone directions pointing towards events to the past of this event. Visit the web site for more information.

National Nuclear Data Center
http://www.nndc.bnl.gov

The National Nuclear Data Center (NNDC) is funded by the U.S. Department of Energy to provide services in the field of low and medium energy nuclear physics to users in the United States and Canada. In particular, the Center can provide information on neutron, charged-particle and photonuclear reactions, nuclear structure and decay data. Extensive bibliographic files, as well as experimental and evaluated data files, are available through the Center's On-line Data Service or by contacting the NNDC directly. Direct access to the NNDC's computer data bases is possible via electronic networks. Other requests are satisfied with computer retrievals which may be transmitted in the form of listings, plots, and/or files which can be formatted to satisfy most needs. More general needs can often be satisfied by one of the Center's many publications. The information available to the users of NNDC services is the product of the combined efforts of the NNDC and cooperating data centers and other interested groups, both in the United States and worldwide. The Center is responsible for the coordination of CSEWG, the Cross Section Evaluation Working Group, under a cooperative agreement of many laboratories within the U.S. and Canada to produce specific nuclear reaction data evaluations which contain the complete information needed for application studies.

Particle Data Group
http://pdg.lbl.gov/

As the webmaster writes: "The PDG is an international collaboration that reviews Particle Physics and related areas of Astrophysics, and compiles/analyzes data on particle properties. PDG products are distributed to 30,000 physicists, teachers, and other interested people. The Review of Particle Physics is the most cited publication in particle physics during the last decade. Plots of PDG statistics are available."

The Summary Tables give the Group's best values of measured properties—masses, lifetimes, widths, branching ratios, etc.—of the gauge
bosons, leptons, quarks, mesons, and baryons that we consider to be
well established. The Summary Tables also give search limits for
hypothetical particles such as Higgs bosons, massive neutrinos, and
supersymmetric particles. There is an extensive summary of tests of
conservation laws. The much larger Particle Listings list, evaluate,
average, and reference all the data we use to obtain the best values
and limits in the Summary Tables. These data come from both particle
physics and astrophysics. The Listings also contain many brief notes
(reviews) summarizing experimental or theoretical aspects of a given
particle or property, such as those on top quarks, Higgs bosons, neu-
trino oscillation experiments, B mixing and CP violation, rare K
decays, and supersymmetry.

Physics on the Web
http://www.alcyone.com/max/physics/

The Universe is big. The Universe has differing physical structure
over a range of distances that exceed 1040. This is a staggering number; by comparison, the total number of people on the Earth today is
considerably less than 1010; the total estimated number of stars in the
observable Universe is only something like 1022. From quarks to
atoms to bacteria to people to stars to galaxies to superclusters, all
these scales intermix and fade into one another. Erik Max Francis
ponders this and other questions—among them the question of
torque—in these splendidly rendered web pages. Of torque he writes:
"Essential to proving Kepler's second law (and further laws) is the
concept of torque. A torque is a tendency to change something's state
of rotation; it is the rotational analogue of force. For instance, if I
apply torque to a wheel, I'm providing a tendency to rotate that
wheel. Torque is in rotational mechanics what force is in linear
mechanics." Of Kepler, Francis writes: "It is interesting to note that,
should Kepler have been studying another planet, he would not have
noticed any discrepancy between its true and predicted (circular)
orbit."

Quantum Teleportation

http://www.almaden.ibm.com/st/disciplines/quantuminfo/

Two years ago an international group of six scientists, including IBM Fellow Charles H. Bennett, confirmed the intuitions of the majority of science fiction writers by showing that perfect teleportation is indeed possible in principle, but only if the original is destroyed. Meanwhile, other scientists are planning experiments to demonstrate teleportation in microscopic objects, such as single atoms or photons, in the next few years. But science fiction fans will be disappointed to learn that no one expects to be able to teleport people or other macroscopic objects in the foreseeable future, for a variety of engineering reasons, even though it would not violate any fundamental law to do so. Until recently, teleportation was not taken seriously by scientists, because it was thought to violate the uncertainty principle of quantum mechanics, which forbids any measuring or scanning process from extracting all the information in an atom or other object. According to the uncertainty principle, the more accurately an object is scanned, the more it is disturbed by the scanning process, until one reaches a point where the object's original state has been completely

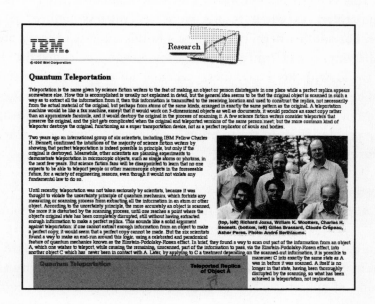

disrupted, still without having extracted enough information to make a perfect replica. Visit this web site for more details.

Rudiments of Quantum Theory
http://www.chembio.uoguelph.ca/educmat/chm386/rudiment/rudiment.htm

As mathematical physics reached a plateau one century ago, new vistas were being suggested as new experiments produced unexpected results. Spectroscopy and heat capacities, black body radiation and the photoelectric effect, all presented simple results that stood in stark contrast to accepted theories of nature.

With Planck's bold suggestion of the quantum nature of light and Einstein's equally impressive explanation of the photoelectric effect in quantum terms, Bohr, who was working with Rutherford on the nuclear scattering experiments, took another step and developed a mathematical framework to explain the spectroscopy of the hydrogen atom. He invoked the ideas of standing waves to justify the quantal stability of certain levels in the atom and this simple process provided such startlingly good results that the world was hooked on the quantum. This came to be known as the "Old Quantum Theory" since its comparatively excellent results were nevertheless limited in their scope. For another decade, extensions to this quantum theory proved unsatisfying. It was Prince Louis de Broglie who challenged the scientific world with his Ph.D. thesis wherein he suggested that if light could behave as particles, then matter could also behave as waves. He wrote down his famous de Broglie relation which was taken up by many people—often to try to prove that it was wrong. Visit this web site for the rest of the story.

Spacetime Wrinkles
http://www.ncsa.uiuc.edu/Cyberia/NumRel/NumRelHome.html

In 1916—eleven years after pronouncing the Theory of Relativity—Einstein challenged conventional wisdom by describing gravity as the warping of spacetime, not a force acting at a distance. Since then, Einstein's revolutionary insights have largely stood the test of time.

One by one, his predictions have been borne out by experiment and observation. But it wasn't until much later that scientists accepted one of the most dramatic ramifications of Einstein's theory of gravitation: the existence of black holes from whose extreme gravity nothing, not even light, can escape. Major advances in computation are only now enabling scientists to simulate how black holes form, evolve, and interact. They're betting on powerful instruments now under construction to confirm that these exotic objects actually exist. Now, after nearly a century of intense study by some of the world's most brilliant mathematicians and physicists—Hilbert, Dirac, Chandrasekhar, Einstein himself, and many others—full solutions to the complex equations of Einstein's theory of gravity are at last in sight. These solutions will not be analytical, but will instead generally take the form of numerical data generated on powerful computers, or dynamic representations of this data as animated scientific visualizations. Coupled with novel experimental approaches for detecting gravitational radiation, these numerical solutions will provide answers to many elusive and scientifically important questions.

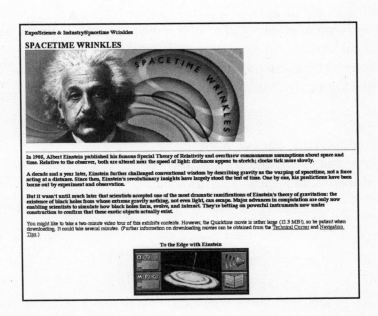

Mailing Lists:

These lists use the standard LISTSERV protocol.

phys-l
> Physics teacher discussion list
> server address: listserv@uwf.cc.uwf.edu
> list address: phys-l@uwf.cc.uwf.edu

physlrnr
> PHYSics LeaRNing Research list. Discussion of physics education
> specifically. server address: listserv@idbsu.idbsu.edu
> list address: physlrnr@idbsu.idbsu.edu

tap-l
> Technical Aspects of Physics List. Discussion of lab equipment,
> demonstrations, and so on.
> server address: listserv@lester.appstate.edu
> list address: tap-l@lester.appstate.edu

physhare
> Discussion of physics and physics teaching, primarily on the high
> school level.
> server address: listserv@psuvm.psu.edu
> list address: physhare@psuvm.psu.edu

phy-stu
> Physics student discussion list
> server address: listserv@uwf.cc.uwf.edu
> list address: phy-stu@uwf.cc.uwf.edu

newsgroups:

sci.physics is an unmoderated newsgroup dedicated to the discussion of physics, news from the physics community, and physics-related social issues.

sci.physics.research is a moderated newsgroup designed to offer an environment with less traffic and more opportunity for discussion of serious topics in physics among experts and beginners alike. There is an archive copy of the charter for this group and also a regular administrivia posting.

alt.sci.physics.new-theories is an open forum for discussion of any topics related to conventional or unconventional physics. In this context, "unconventional physics" includes any ideas on physical science, whether or not they are widely accepted by the mainstream physics community.

sci.physics.particle is an unmoderated newsgroup dedicated to the discussion of all aspects of particle physics by people with all levels of expertise.

sci.physics.accelerators is an unmoderated newsgroup for issues relating to particle accelerators and the physics of beams.

alt.sci.physics.acoustics is an unmoderated newsgroup for issues relating to sound and acoustics.

sci.physics.cond-matter is an unmoderated newsgroup dedicated to the discussion of the physics of condensed matter.

sci.physics.computational.fluid-dynamics is an unmoderated newsgroup for discussion of computational fluid dynamics.

sci.physics.electromag is an unmoderated newsgroup with its own FAQ dedicated to the discussion of topics pertaining to electromagnetics.

sci.physics.fusion is an unmoderated newsgroup with its own FAQ dedicated to the discussion of nuclear fusion.

sci.physics.plasma is a moderated newsgroup serving the plasma science and technologies community.

sci.physics.relativity is an unmoderated newsgroup for discussions about the theory of relativity.

20

PHYSIOLOGY AND MEDICINE

American Academy of Orthopaedic Surgeons
http://www.aaos.org/

The American Academy of Orthopaedic Surgeons provides education and practice management services for orthopaedic surgeons and allied health professionals. The Academy also serves as an advocate for improved patient care and informs the public about the science of orthopaedics. Founded at Northwestern University as a not-for-profit organization in 1933, the Academy has grown from a small organization serving less than 500 members to the world's largest medical association of musculoskeletal specialists. The Academy now serves about 24,000 members internationally. Members of the Academy, called fellows, are orthopaedists concerned with the diagnosis, care, and treatment of musculoskeletal disorders. The orthopaedist's scope of practice includes disorders of the body's bones, joints, ligaments, muscles, and tendons. Fellows have completed four years of medical school and at least five years of an approved "residency" in orthopaedics. In addition, they must pass a comprehensive oral and written examination, be certified by the American Board of Orthopaedic Surgery, and submit to stringent membership review processes prior to admittance to the Academy. Visit the web site for many more details on this very important medical academy.

American Hyperlexia Association
http://www.hyperlexia.org/

The American Hyperlexia Association is a non-profit organization comprised of parents and relatives of children with hyperlexia, speech and language professionals, education professionals, and other concerned individuals with the common goal of identifying hyperlexia, promoting and facilitating effective teaching techniques both at home and at school, and educating the general public as to the existence of the syndrome called hyperlexia. AHA is dedicated to the advancement of the education and general welfare of children with hyperlexia. Hyperlexia is a syndrome observed in children who have the following characteristics: A precocious ability to read words, far above what would be expected at their chronological age or an intense fascination with letters or numbers; Significant difficulty in understanding verbal language; and Abnormal social skills, difficulty in socializing and interacting appropriately with people. In addition, some children who are hyperlexic may exhibit the following characteristics: Learn expressive language in a peculiar way, echo ro memorize the sentence structure without understanding the meaning (echolalia), reverse pronouns; Rarely initiate conversations; Demonstrate an intense need to keep routines; Demonstrate Normal development until 18-24 months, then regression; and Difficulty answering "Wh—" questions, such as "what," "where," "who," and "why."

American Lung Association
http://www.lungusa.org/

The American Lung Association (ALA) is the oldest voluntary health organization in the United States, with a National Office and constituent and affiliate associations around the country. Founded in 1904 to fight tuberculosis, ALA today fights lung disease in all its forms, with special emphasis on asthma, tobacco control and environmental health. ALA is funded by contributions from the public, along with gifts and grants from corporations, foundations and government agencies. ALA achieves its many successes through the work of thousands of committed volunteers and staff. The American Lung Associ-

ation has many programs and strategies for fighting lung disease. Among these are Open Airways For Schools, the ALA's elementary-school education program for children with asthma. Open Airways teaches children with asthma to understand and manage their illness so they can lead more normal lives. A key part of the program is ALA's facilitation of asthma-care partnerships involving school nurses and educational staff as well as physicians, families and ALA volunteers. ALA also offers a variety of smoking control and prevention programs targeted to specific groups-some aimed at adults, others intended for school use, and still others designed to build bridges between the home and school and involve community leaders along with parents and educators.

American Medical Association

http://www.ama-assn.org/

The AMA is much more than a voluntary membership organization of physicians. It is the patient's advocate and the physician's voice. It sets standards for the profession of medicine. It is medical education, "The Principles of Medical Ethics," the Journal of the American Medical Association, the AMA House of Delegates, policy matters affecting the fabric of American medicine and patient care, and much more. More than anything else, the American Medical Association represents the best of each and every one of its members men and women who have chosen a caring profession, a profession whose everyday task is healing patients and saving lives. By choosing AMA membership, they have expressed their commitment to medicine and professionalism. As the webmaster writes: "Founded over 150 years ago, AMA's strategic agenda remains rooted in our historic commitment to standards, ethics, excellence in medical education and practice, and advocacy on behalf of the medical profession and the patients it serves. AMA's work includes the development and promotion of standards in medical practice, research, and education; strong advocacy agenda on behalf of patients and physicians; and the commitment to providing accurate, timely information and discourse on matters important to the health of America. The AMA strives to serve as the voice of the American medical profession. Being that voice is our mission."

Breast Cancer Answers
http://www.medsch.wisc.edu/bca/

Q: What are the symptoms of breast cancer? A: Early breast cancer usually does not cause pain. In fact, when breast cancer first develops, there may be no symptoms at all. As the cancer grows, the following changes may be noted: A lump or thickening in or near the breast or in the underarm area; A change in the size or shape of the breast; A discharge from the nipple; A change in the color or feel of the skin of the breast, areolas, or nipple (dimpled, puckered, or scaly). These changes do not always mean breast cancer, but are changes a women should have checked by her doctor. Q: How often should I get a mammogram? How accurate are they? A: The National Cancer Institute recommends that women in their forties or older get screening mammograms on a regular basis, every 1 to 2 years. Women who are at increased risk for breast cancer should seek medical advice about when to begin having mammograms and how often to be screened (for example, a doctor may recommend that a women at increased risk begin screening before age 40, or change her screening intervals to every year). The American Cancer Society recommends women age

40-49, have a routine screening mammogram every 1-2 years, and those over the age of 50 have an annual screening mammogram. Visit the web site for more vital Q&A.

Cancer Research Foundation of America
http://www.preventcancer.org/

The Cancer Research Foundation of America is a national non-profit health organization whose mission is the prevention of cancer through scientific research and education. Founded in 1985, the organization's commitment is fueled by the fact that certain cancers are preventable through lifestyle changes, yet more than 550,000 Americans die from the diseases annually. Since its inception, the Foundation has supported research, education and early detection programs in excess of $36 million. "When I lost my father to cancer in 1984, I was determined to do everything I could to help others fight cancer. So, in 1985, I opened the doors of CRFA to prevent cancer through scientific research and education programs. We believe the best way to defeat the disease is to attack it at the front end," said CRFA President and Founder Carolyn Aldige. Since its inception, the Foundation has provided funding to more than 200 scientists at more than 100 leading academic institutions across the country. Through the Foundation's public education programs, thousands of men, women and children have received life-saving information about cancer, including early detection and prevention. When the Foundation first began its efforts 13 years ago, cancer prevention was not on many people's radar screens, but today prevention research is booming, and enormous gains are being made. The Cancer Research Foundation of America has played a crucial role in instigating these critical changes.

The Gross Physiology of the Cardiovascular System
http://cardiovascular.cx/

The cardiovascular system has ten unique characteristics that make it an unusually complicated hydraulic system. Understanding how the cardiovascular system functions requires insight into a larger set of variables than that which governs the function of most pump, pipe, and fluid systems found in the world of man-made machines. A few of the characteristics peculiar to the cardiovascular system are: The system is a closed circle rather than being open-ended and linear. The system is elastic rather than rigid. The system is filled with liquid at a positive mean pressure ("mean cardiovascular pressure"), which exists independent of the pumping action of the heart. The right and left ventricles, which pump into the same system that they pump out of, are in series with two interposed vascular beds (systemic and pulmonary). The heart fills passively, rather than by actively sucking. As a consequence of the heart's passive filling, the circulation rate is normally regulated by peripheral-vascular factors, rather than by cardiac variables. The flow from the heart is intermittent, while the flow to it is continuous. Normally, there is an excess expenditure of energy by the heart needed for the circulation rate imposed by peripheral vascular regulators ("pump energy excess"). Check these web pages for more info.

Journal of Applied Physiology
http://jap.physiology.org/

The Journal of Applied Physiology publishes original papers that deal with diverse areas of research in applied physiology, especially those emphasizing adaptive and integrative mechanisms. Adaptive physiology includes 1) inherent adaptations such as those related to development, aging, and pathophysiological conditions; and 2) adaptations to the external environment such as those occurring with exercise, microgravity, hypoxia, hypo- and hyperbaria, and hypo- and hyperthermic conditions. Integrative physiology includes 1) horizontal integration across organ systems and 2) vertical integration from molecule to cell to organ. In all areas of applied physiology, the use of cutting-edge techniques, including genetics and molecular and cellular biology are especially welcome. The list of research interests of the Journal is not intended to be exhaustive. However, the boundaries of physiology have clearly been enlarged because demarcations between concepts and techniques in the physiological, pharmacological, and biochemical sciences are becoming increasingly blurred. The interdependence of physiology on other fundamental sciences is increasing, and disturbances in physiological function often shed light on normal physiological function. Moreover, the focus is not confined to experimental studies, since theoretical articles dealing with research at any level of biological organization, ranging from molecules to humans, fall within the broad range of interest of the Journal. It should be underscored that the wide scientific span of the Journal rests on physiology as its keystone.

National Library of Medicine
http://www.nlm.nih.gov/

The National Library of Medicine (NLM), on the campus of the National Institutes of Health in Bethesda, Maryland, is the world's largest medical library. The Library collects materials in all areas of biomedicine and health care, as well as works on biomedical aspects of technology, the humanities, and the physical, life, and social sciences. The collections stand at 5.8 million items—books, journals, technical reports, manuscripts, microfilms, photographs and images. Housed within the Library is one of the world's finest medical history collections of old and rare medical works. The Library's collection may be consulted in the reading room or requested on interlibrary

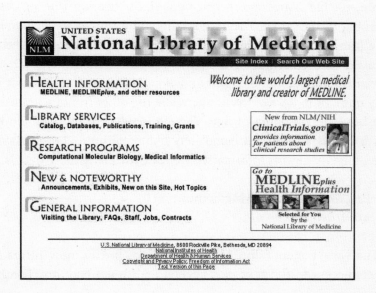

loan. NLM is a national resource for all U.S. health science libraries through a National Network of Libraries of Medicine®. For more than 100 years, the Library has published the Index Medicus®, a monthly subject/author guide to articles in 3400 journals. This information, and much more, is today available in the database MEDLINE® via the World Wide Web. MEDLINE has more than 10 million journal article references and abstracts going back to the early sixties. Other databases provide information on monographs (books), audiovisual materials, and on such specialized subjects as toxicology, environmental health, and molecular biology.

Neuroanatomy and Physiology
http://www.bethisraelny.org/inn/anatomy/anatomy.html

The nervous system is divided into two parts, the central nervous system and the peripheral nervous system. The central nervous system consists of the brain and the spinal cord. The peripheral nervous system is made up of 12 pairs of cranial nerves and all the remaining nerves of the body. The skull is formed by the bones of calvaria and the skull base. The calvaria is comparatively large to accommodate the brain. In the newborn, it is about 25% of its adult size. It reaches about 75% of its adult size by the end of the first year. The newborn skull is made up of thin, pliable bones due to incomplete ossification (the process of hardening of the bone). They are separated by fibrous or membranous tissue (the sutures). The membranous gaps are called fontanelles and are larger at the corners of the parietal bones. The centerally located anterior frontanelle is the largest and diamond-shaped. It does not fully ossify until 18 to 24 months of age while the other frontanelles usually close by 2 to 3 months of age. The sutures where most of the bone growth occurs also do not completely obliterate until approximately 8 years of age. Visit this informative web site for many more details.

New England Journal of Medicine
http://www.nejm.org/

The New England Journal of Medicine On-line now offers subscribers access to full text plus several additional features. The Journal On-line continues to offer to all users many selections from the Journal, including abstracts of all scientific articles. The current issue becomes available on the Web Wednesday at 5 PM. The abstracts of Original Articles (reports of original clinical research) and Special Articles (reports of research on health policy) are available on-line, along with the names and institutional affiliations of the authors. If you wish to read an entire article, you can have it sent to you by mail or fax. In addition, the full text of the following features is available on-line: Images in Clinical Medicine, Editorials, Sounding Board articles (opinion pieces), Correspondence, and Book Reviews. For Review Articles, Brief Reports, and Case Records of the Massachusetts General Hospital, which have no abstracts, only the titles and authors' names and affiliations are available on-line. You may have these articles sent to you as well. Articles of interest can be saved to a personal archive. The results of searches can also be saved. The full text of the Journal is available beginning with the first issue of 1993. In addition, the database for searches includes the citations for all articles published since 1990.

Online Journal of Physiology
   http://www.cpb.uokhsc.edu/ojvr/ojp.htm

The Online Journal of Physiology (OJP) is a reviewed journal with six Doctoral-Professorial editorial members. The journal specializes in system and molecular physiology including functional genetics/genomics. The OJP provides physiological scientists with a medium to present interactive methods and results in the form of programs, applets or movies. The site consists of updated and archived full-text articles and abstracts and provides physiological scientists with an opportunity to rapidly submit and disseminate peer-reviewed work globally. All submissions are peer reviewed by three (3) persons qualified in the field chosen from the editorial board or commissioned from another institution. Articles posted on OJP should be able to be read by persons not specialized in the field and data can be presented in graphs and photographs. Articles are usually published within 14 days of acceptance. Presently, full text articles may be viewed without fees. It is the Editorial Board's policy to remain at "Arms Length" of any institution. All articles are permanently available, archived and updated when relevant information is received. Accepted articles are immediately posted throughout all the major web-search engines and OJP posts the relevant key words of articles on the World Wide Web.

American Pain Society
http://www.ampainsoc.org

The American Pain Society (APS) had its beginnings on March 6, 1977 at a now historic meeting in Chicago of the Ad Hoc Advisory Committee on the Formation of a National Pain Organization. Important events preparing the way for the Chicago meeting were significant increases in public awareness of pain management and research; the need for a national organization of pain professionals; the existence of two regional pain societies, the Eastern and Western USA Chapters of the International Association for the Study of Pain (IASP); and the growth of the IASP. It was realized that the new IASP in its early years would have to rely heavily on financial and membership support from the US Consequently, there was some urgency for the creation of a US national pain organization to work with and become an integral part (i.e., chapter) of the IASP, as well as represent the interests of the various local and/or regional pain groups within the US. Preliminary discussions between representatives of the eastern and western chapter leaders resulted in the decision to hold a joint face-to-face conference. Drs. John J. Bonica and B. Berthold Wolff were asked to invite interested pain professionals from across the US, covering a wide disciplinary range, to the Chicago meeting. Visit these web pages for more details.

Physiology Online
http://www.physoc.org/

This is the online home of The Physiological Society. Physiology is a key life science and is essential to the progress of medicine and biomedical sciences. With increasing research specialisation, especially in the fields of cellular and molecular biology, physiology today plays a crucial role in relating molecules and cells to the function of tissues and organs, and ultimately to the whole body. Physiology is therefore integral to the advancement of health and medicine. The Physiological Society was founded in 1876 and throughout its history the Society's primary objectives have remained the same: To promote the advancement of physiology; To facilitate communication between physiologists and with other scientists; And to provide an interface between research, education, government and the general public. It has done this largely through frequent meetings of the Society, support for physiologists, publication of scientific journals and books, and representation on various councils and committees. During the last few years the society has expanded rapidly not only in the number of Members—now over 1800—but also in the activities which it supports worldwide. These span from encouraging science in schools to preserving scientific history and promoting physiology in the media. Groups of Society Members (sub-committees) initiate and organise such activities.

World Health Organization
http://www.who.int/

The objective of WHO is the attainment by all peoples of the highest possible level of health. Health, as defined in the WHO Constitution, is a state of complete physical, mental and social well-being and not merely the absence of disease or infirmity. In support of its main objective, the Organization has a wide range of functions, including the following: To act as the directing and co-ordinating authority on international health work; To promote technical co-operation; To assist Governments, upon request, in strengthening health services; To furnish appropriate technical assistance and, in emergencies, necessary aid, upon the request or acceptance of Governments; To stimulate and advance work on the prevention and control of epidemic, endemic and other diseases; To promote, in co-operation with other specialized agencies where necessary, the improvement of nutrition, housing, sanitation, recreation, economic or working conditions and other aspects of environmental hygiene; To promote and co-ordinate biomedical and health services research; To promote improved standards of teaching and training in the health, medical and related professions; To establish and stimulate the establishment of international standards for biological, pharmaceutical and similar products, and to standardize diagnostic procedures; To foster activities in the field of mental health, especially those activities affecting the harmony of human relations.

Mailing Lists

med-ed

Mailing list request address: majordomo@aamcinfo.aamc.org
The AAMC has launched an electronic mail discussion group, or listserv, for developers and users of medical education software in undergraduate, graduate, and continuing medical education. This forum will allow a broad-based and swift exchange of ideas on courseware, authoring tools, and evaluation criteria and methods, along with other infrastructure and technical issues.
The listserv is not intended for advertising commercial courseware or authoring products, but rather, encourages discussions about integrating both commercial and faculty-authored materials into the medical school curriculum.

Medical Physics Internet Server List

A Canadian-based conference mailing list in which the subscribers have a particular interest in Medical Physics. The listserv was established by Trevor Cradduck at the University of Western Ontario.
To subscribe send an e-mail message to: cradduck@uwo.ca. Subject can be anything (it's ignored).
Single line of TEXT: "subscribe canada-l" (that is an ell for List, not a one).

Newsgroups

sci.med.diseases.cancer

alt.support.cancer

sci.med.prostate.cancer

misc.health.alternative

alt.support.arthritis

alt.support.crohns-colitis

alt.support.headaches.migraine

sci.med.cardiology

sci.med.immunology

alt.support.scleroderma

alt.support.skin-diseases

alt.med.cfs (chronic fatigue syndrome)

alt.med.fibromyalgia

21

PSYCHOLOGY

American Psychological Association
http://www.apa.org/

Based in Washington, DC, the American Psychological Association (APA) is the largest scientific and professional organization respresenting psychology in the United States. With more than 159,000 members, APA is also the largest association of psychologists worldwide. Like the federal government, APA's governance has a complex system of checks and balances that help make the system operate fairly and democratically. Because of its complexity, many members are not aware of how the parts of the structure operate together and exercise control over each other. As the webmaster writes: "First of all, APA is a corporation chartered in the District of Columbia. Our certificate of incorporation determines and limits the kind of organization we can be and what we can do. Fortunately, the limits are broad, but the charter takes precedence over all of our internal documents, even our bylaws. Because of the nature of our organization, we are given favorable tax treatment by the federal government and by the District. But that, too, limits our activities. If we should deviate too far from our primary role of promoting psychology in the public interest, we could lose our favorable tax status and that would make it far more expensive, if not impossible, to operate at our current level of services and activities." Visit the web site for more details.

Classics in the History of Psychology
http://www.yorku.ca/dept/psych/classics/

Classics in the History of Psychology is an effort to make the full texts of a large number of historically significant public domain documents from the scholarly literature of psychology and allied disciplines available on the World Wide Web. There are now over 20 books and over 100 articles and chapters on-line. The site also contains links to over 170 relevant works posted at other sites. The target audience is researchers, teachers, and students of the history of psychology, both for use in their courses on the history of psychology, and for the purposes of primary academic research. To assist undergraduate teaching, in particular, orignal introductory articles and commentaries, written by some of the leading historians of psychology in North America, have been attached to a number of the most importatn works. The initial set of documents was chosen by the Editor of the project, Christopher D. Green of York University, in consultation with a number of other professional historians of psychology. Many of the subsequent documents were selected in response to the requests of the site's users.

Sigmund Freud and the Freud Archives
http://plaza.interport.net/nypsan/freudarc.html

In 1880 and 1881 Dr. Josef Breuer of Vienna, a well-known physician and experimental physiologist, was occupied in the treatment of a girl who had fallen ill of a severe hysteria while she was nursing her sick father. The clinical picture was made up of motor paralyses, inhibitions, and disturbances of consciousness. Following a hint given him by the patient herself, he put her into a state of hypnosis and contrived that, by describing to him the moods and thoughts that were uppermost in her mind, she returned on each particular occasion to a normal mental condition. By consistently repeating the same laborious process, he succeeded in freeing her of all her inhibitions and paralyses. Nevertheless, Breuer refrained from following up his discovery or from publishing anything about the case until some ten years later, when Sigmund Freud prevailed on him to take up the subject afresh and embark on a joint study of it. These two, Breuer and

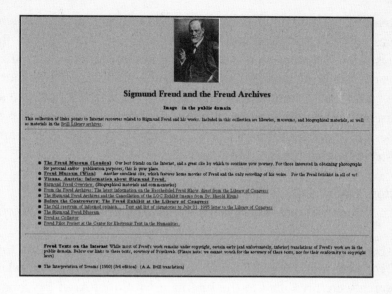

Freud, published a preliminary paper On the Psychical Mechanism of Hysterical Phenomena in 1893, and in 1895 a volume entitled Studies on Hysteria (which reached ist fourth edition in 1922), in which they described their therapeutic procedure as cathartic. There is much more info to be had at the web pages for the Sigmund Freud Archives.

Freud Museum (London)

http://www.freud.org.uk/Index.html

The Freud Museum, at 20 Maresfield Gardens in Hampstead, was the home of Sigmund Freud and his family when they escaped Nazi annexation of Austria in 1938. It remained the family home until Anna Freud, the youngest daughter, died in 1982. The centrepiece of the museum is Freud's library and study, preserved just as it was during his lifetime. It contains Freud's remarkable collection of antiquities: Egyptian; Greek; Roman and Oriental. Almost two thousand items fill cabinets and are ranged on every surface. There are rows of ancient figures on the desk where Freud wrote until the early hours of the morning. The walls are lined with shelves containing Freud's large libraryof reference books. The house is also filled with memories of his daughter, Anna, who lived there for 44 years and continued to develop her pioneering psychoanalytic work, especially with children. It was her wish that the house become a museum to honour her illustrious father. The museum is now being developed as a cultural and research center of outstanding value to the professional community. The Freud's were fortunate to be able to bring all their furniture and household effects to London: there were splendid Biedermeier chests, tables and cupboards, and a fine collection of 18th and 19th-century Austrian painted country furniture.

History of Psychology Calendar
http://www.cwu.edu/~warren/calendar/datepick.html

Let's pick a date at random, say April 28. On April 28. 1905: Alfred Binet and Theodore Simon's first intelligence test and related research were presented to the International Congress of Psychology in Rome. Their paper, read by Henri-Étienne Beaunis, was titled "New Methods for Diagnosing Idiocy, Imbecility, and Moron Status." 1905: George A. Kelly was born. Kelly developed the personal construct theory of personality and psychotherapy, emphasizing individual interpretations of a setting as the determinants of individual differences in behavior. Kelly's Role Repertoire Test was the basis of many studies of personality. 1933: Wolfgang K"hler wrote, for the newspaper Deutsche Allgemeine Zeitung, the last anti-Nazi article to be published openly in Germany before World War II. The article defended Jewish professors recently dismissed from their university posts and pointed to the many contributions Jews had made to German culture. How about June 24? 1795: Ernst Weber was born. Weber is best known for his work on the sense of touch, leading to the discovery of the just-noticeable difference in sensation and Weber's law of psychophysics. 1933: The Society for Research in Child Development was organized. 1959: The first All-Union Congress of the Russian Soviet Federal Socialist Republic Psychological Society began in Moscow and continued until July 4, 1959. A. A. Smirnov was elected chairman. Click on any date of the calendar year for similar info.

Internet Mental Health
http://www.mentalhealth.com/

Internet Mental Health is a free encyclopedia of mental health information. It was designed by a Canadian psychiatrist, Dr. Phillip Long, and programmed by his colleague, Brian Chow. The idea of creating Internet Mental Health resulted from a Canada-Japan Mental Health Exchange in 1994 arranged by Mr. Mikio Kuraki. During that exchange, Robert Winram and Dr. Phillip Long visited Japanese psychiatric hospitals and lived for one week with psychiatric patients as guests in their homes. The Canadian delegation was amazed to find that, in Japan, the average length of stay in psychiatric hospital for a patient with schizophrenia was four years. In Canada, the same patients would be hospitalized for only four weeks, then followed as outpatients. As the webmasters write: "The most outstanding need in Japan, our hosts told us, was for more information concerning our mental health sytem in Canada. Thus the concept of Internet Mental Health was born. By using Internet, our hope was that we could freely share whatever information we have on mental health with the world." The site includes have online diagnostic programs that can be used to diagnose: Anxiety Disorders, Attention-Deficit Hyperactity

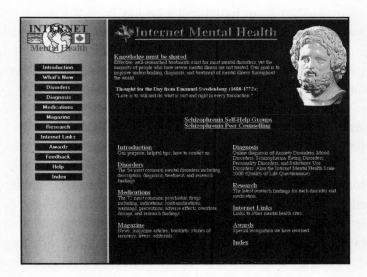

Disorder, Eating Disorders, Mood Disorders (Depression, Bipolar Disorder), Personality Disorders, Schizophrenia and Substance-Related Disorders.

Jung Institute
http://members.aol.com/~cgjungbos1/

C. G. Jung was convinced that the psychological problem of today is a spiritual problem, and that focus on the material has deprived humanity of a sense of meaning in the world. Jung described personal myths as a way of finding meaning in modern life. Jung also said that "civilized man in his dreams reveals his spiritual need." ANd Jung believed that the Catholic sacrament of confession, general confessing and confession in analysis all share their roots in the same archetypal structure or pattern. All three function to facilitate some type of rapprochement or "right relationship." The C.G. Jung Institute—Boston is chartered by the New England Society of Jungian Analysts (NESJA) and is dedicated to the healing discipline of Analytical Psychology. As the webmaster writes: "Our vision is to nourish the human endeavor for psychological transformation and wholeness. Our mission and task is to understand the human psyche through the psychological theories and therapeutic methods pioneered by Carl Gustav Jung." The Jung Institute is empowered to designate Jungian Analyst status. A Jungian Analyst is an individual who has been granted a diploma by a training institute accredited by the International Association of Analytical Psychology. The diplomate, as a member of the International Association, may then use the designation, "IAAP" after his or her name.

National Electronic Library for Mental Health (UK)
http://cebmh.warne.ox.ac.uk/cebmh/nelmh/

From 1992 to 1997, the Health of the Nation (HOTN) strategy was the central plank of health policy in England and formed the context for the planning of services provided by the NHS. It represented the first explicit attempt by government to provide a strategic approach to improving the overall health of the population. In July 1999, the goverment published a White Paper entitled: The Saving lives : Our Healthier Nation (OHN). It is a comprehensive Government wide public health strategy for England which specifically addresses mental health . The National electronic Library for Health (NeLH) is a new initiative, announced in the Government's Information for Health strategy. The NeLH aims to: provideeasy access to best current knowledge improve health and healthcare, clinical practice and patient choice. The main principle determining the inclusion of knowledge which the NeLH feels must be made available to every NHS worker, and patients, is that there should be access to sources of knowledge which are quality assured and improved. The mission of the NeLH is to provide easy access to best current knowledge. The NeLH will give priority to sources of knowledge that are regularly updated, thus relieving the end user from the worry that the knowledge they are looking at might have been superseded by newer information.

The Psychoanalytic Connection
http://www.psychoanalysis.net/

As the webmaster writes: "The Psychoanalytic Connection began way back in the dark ages of electronic communications (the dark ages meaning way back before the Web became first a fad then a trend then currently an increasingly central feature of mainstream cultural and economic life). Our originating idea was to give clinicians and scholars in private offices and disparate locations access to the same kinds of shared communications tools as those used by people who all work in the same location. As we've grown and participated in the "digital revolution" we've added significantly to the tools we make available for individuals (as well as adding an entirely new set of services for organizations). We continue to provide a growing array of services both to individuals and organizations. Our newest service makes it easy for members to share information with the wider public using our WEB-DIRECT service. With WEB-DIRECT members can easily and directly present information about professional training opportunities, mental health services offered, and information about meetings and conferences of interest to psychoanalytic professionals, as well as hear directly from journal editors who are Connec-

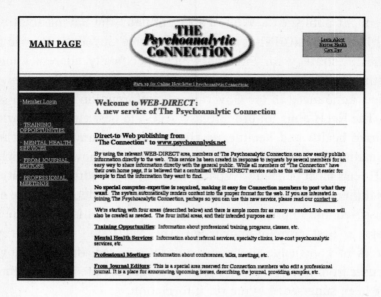

tion members. If you are an individual who is part of the international psychoanalytic community we hope you will apply for your own personal membership."

Psych Central

http://www.psychcentral.com

Looking for an online support group? A Website? A resource in psychology, mental health, psychiatry, or social work? This resource directory, compiled online since 1991, is one of the oldest in existence today. It sports resources for both consumers and professionals in the field. Got a question relating to the symptoms or treatments associated with a specific mental disorder? Find the answer here. Take an automated, brief quiz on depression, mania, or adult ADD. Participate in free, live interactive chats every week, on the Web where the site's proprietor answers your general mental health, relationship and psychological questions. Who is the proprietor? John M. Grohol, Psy.D. is a Boston author, online expert, and researcher. He built drkoop.com's mental health center and was the co-founder and director for nearly 4 years of Mental Health Net, one of the top 10 most-trafficked mental health Websites online (according to PC Data). As the youngest chief operating officer in the behavioral healthcare industry today, he oversees the continuing development of HelpHorizons.com, an e-therapy services provider. Trained and educated as a clinical psychologist at Nova Southeastern University, he now acts as a patient advocate, mental health educator, and online services innovator. While he has been involved in online services as early as 1981, he began on the Internet in 1991 as a regular contributor to the Internet's discussion forums, Usenet newsgroups. He has founded and moderated a number of newsgroups since then.

Psychology Info Online
http://www.psychologyinfo.com/

As the webmaster writes: "Psychology Information Online was created to provide a central place on the Internet for information about the practice of psychology. Psychology Information Online provides information about psychological diagnosis, disorders and problems, psychotherapy and counseling (including family therapy, couple counseling and group therapy), behavior therapy (stress management and relaxation skills training, assertiveness training, desensitization for phobias, parenting skills, etc.), psychological evaluations and testing, and other treatment services, and also provides information about Forensic psychology and psychological consultations for legal matters. This information can be helpful to consumers, psychologists, undergraduate and graduate students of psychology, and anyone interested in accurate information about the practice of psychology. When you need to talk to a psychologist, you should look for an experienced and licensed psychologist close to your home. To help you find one, Psychology Information Online hosts the National Directory of Psychologists. The Directory contains a listing for every State Psychological Association and State Psychology Licensing Board in the United States, as well as listings for licensed practicing psychologists in individual state directories. The Directory also contains links to the individual web sites of practicing psychologists who have provided us with their Internet address. Psychology Information Online does not charge for these listings, and does not recommend any specific psychologists because they are listed. This is an information service to assist you in finding information about psychologists on the Internet."

Psych Net
http://www.psychnet-uk.com/

"As Psychologists," the webmaster wites, " we have all become frustrated trying to locate different sources of information over the Internet. With this in mind, PsychNet-UK was designed and conceived to address this very problem, enabling the most current and up to date Web Sites to be accessed from one single access point." PsychNet-UK was born after recognizing a need to search and collate published information which may be often sought, on a regular basis, by persons engaged in the mental heath professions. It is also meant to provide a meeting point for the dissemination of information and ideas. PsychNet-UK is a privately owned and run Web Site developed and therefore does not owe its allegiance to any academic body, institute or organisation it therefore exists through the contributions of sponsors, advertisers and other interested parties. But be sure to check out the joke section. How many Narcissistic P.D. does to take to change a lightbulb? Just one. To hold the lightbulb but he has to wait for the whole world to revolve around him. How many Borderline P.D. does to take to change a lightbulb? Just one. To threaten suicide if you don't change it for him/her. How many Obsessive-Compulsive P.D. does to take to change a lightbulb? Just one. But he has to check it 100 times, one for each watt.

Psych Web
http://www.psychwww.com/

Effective, well-researched treatments exist for most mental disorders, yet the majority of people who have severe mental illness are not treated. The goal of this web site is to improve understanding, diagnosis, and treatment of mental illness throughout the world. This site aspires to be the premier World Wide Web gathering place for mental health professionals and applied behavioral scientists—a place where professionals of every discipline can feel at home. This web site currently includes over 200 discussion lists, 50 web sites, 17 ftp sites, and 15 gopher sites of particular interest to psych faculty and students. You will also find psychology-oriented newsgroups, email addresses for APA and APS personnel and other professional and student organizations, and a list of programs you can download from America OnLine. There are also about 100 support group and other non-professional discussion lists. The site also gives you a searchable index of almost 30,000 journal articles, books, and book reviews in psychoanalysis going back to 1920 . . . links to home pages of over 1,000 psychology and social sciences journals, with notations of which feature abstracts, tables of contents, and full text articles . . . and several searchable databases that provide references to research literature on sociological, psychological, and medical aspects of substance abuse.

Sleep Medicine
http://www.users.cloud9.net/~thorpy/

About 120 million Americans suffer from sleep disorders including narcolepsy, sleep apnea, restless legs syndrome, the insomnias and simple sleep deprivation. Most are unaware. Sleep is vital to our

health and well being. Yet millions of us are cutting ourselves short on the amount of sleep that we get or suffer from other sleep problems. For example, surveys conducted by the National Sleep Foundation reveal that 60 percent of adults report having sleep problems a few nights a week or more. In addition, more than 40 percent of adults experience daytime sleepiness severe enough to interfere with their daily activities at least a few days each month—with 20 percent reporting problem sleepiness a few days a week or more. At least 40 million Americans suffer from sleep disorders, yet more than 60 percent of adults have never been asked about the quality of their sleep by a physician and fewer than 20 percent ever initiated a discussion. Poor sleep has a price. Millions of individuals struggle to stay alert at home, in school, on the job—and on the road. Tragically, fatigue contributes to more than 100,000 highway crashes, causing 71,000 injuries and 1,500 deaths each year in the United States alone. Visit the Sleep Medicine web site for more information.

Listservs and Subscription Services:

BIOMED-L@mcgill1: Association of Biomedical Communication

BIOMED-L@ndsuvm1: Biomedical ethics

BRAIN-L@mcgill1: Mind-brain discussion

CADUCEUS@utmbeach: History of medicine

DRUGABUS@umab: Drug abuse education information and research

MEDCONS@finhutc: Medical consulting and case description

Psyche-l@nki: Psyche-L: Consciousness and the brain

Psycoloquy@pucc: Psycoloquy: Psychology, neuroscience, behavioral biology

QUALRS@uga: Qualitative research in health sciences

STOPRAPE@sbrownvm: Sexual assault activist list

22

SOCIOLOGY

Pierre Bourdieu

http://www.massey.ac.nz/~NZSRDA/bourdieu/home.htm

"Sociology of education is not a secondary discipline. It is the core of any sociology."

Pierre is a substantial French social scientist, which has studied various power structures in teaching. He describes, "school actually reproduces the cultural division of society in many visible and invisible ways despite its apparent neutrality." So writes contemporary French social scientist Pierre Bourdieu. What is social action and it's structure? Bourdieu's theory is that social action is its structure, which is interchangeable. Negotiations within a culture for example are out of the consciousness mind of habitus. He speaks of strategies arising form the habitus and this change ascribes the "primitive mind" in Bourdieu's mind. According to Bourdieu, "on the individual level, habitus means the system of attitudes and dispositions which are relatively permanent and transferred from one object to another, which simultaneously both integrates all the previous experiences of an individual's ways to see and value things and act" He also describes his meaning of science: "the concern to control his discourse, that is the reception of his discourse, imposes on the sociologist a scientific rhetoric which is not necessarily a rhetoric of scientificity: he needs to inculcate a scientific reading, rather belief in the scientificity of what is being read—except in so far as the latter is one of the tacit conditions of a scientific reading."

457

Emile Durkheim

http://granny.lang.uiuc.edu/durkheim/

In 1898, Durkheim founded the Année sociologique, the first social science hournal in France. In fact, Durkheim's intellectual virtuosity up to 1900 had implicitly contradicted one of his central arguments, namely that in modern societies, work (including intellectual work) should become more specialized, though remaining part of an organic whole. In 1896, therefore, putting aside his work on the history of socialism, Durkheim devoted himself to establishing a massive program of journalistic collaboration based upon a complex division of intellectual labor. Supported by a brilliant group of young scholars (mostly philosophers), the Année was to provide an annual survey of the strictly sociological literature, to provide additional information on studies in other specialized fields, and to publish original monographs in sociology. His "science of morality" offended philosophers, his "science of religion" offended Catholics, and his appointment to the offended those on the political Right. The appointment also gave Durkheim enormous power. His lecture courses were the only required courses at the Sorbonne, obligatory for all students seeking degrees in philosophy, history, literature, and languages; in addition, he was responsible for the education of successive generations of French school teachers, in whom he instilled all the ferbour of his secular, rationalist morality.

Electronic Journal of Sociology

http://www.sociology.org/

As the webmaster writes: "Recognising that the current scholarly communication system is in financial crises caused by the predatorial practices of a handful of commercial publishers, and recognising that there is considerable potentials inherent in information technology to reduce the cost of distributing scholarly information, it is the mission of the EJS and ICAAP to demonstrate that high quality, low cost, and non commercial alternatives to the commercial system are possible. The EJS is thus offered free of charge to individuals, libraries, academic and commercial organizations. It is part of, and a model for, a

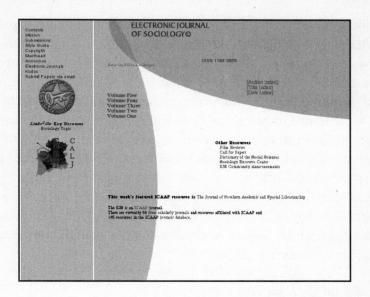

new publishing paradigm whereby the scholars themselves retain control over all aspects of the scholarly communication process. The EJS receives free production assistance and expertise from the International Consortium for Alternative Academic Publication (ICAAP)." Recent articles address: Timeless Moral Imperatives in Causal Analysis of Social Functioning, Power and Powerlessness in the Global Village, The Veil of Piacular Subjectivity, Emergent Clusters of Denotative Meaning, Unacknowledged Roots and Blatant Imitation, Social Psychological Dimensions of Electronic Communication, A Content Analysis of Internet-Accessible Written Pornographic Depictions, and related topics.

Norbert Elias and Process Sociology
http://www.usyd.edu.au/su/social/elias.html

As the webmaster writes: "The kind of imagination best suited to life in the twenty-first century will be one which recognizes that we are also moving from one millennium to another. It will be enormously useful to draw on the work of thinkers whose perspectives are broader than a single decade or even a whole century, who ask questions emerging from a truly historical conception of social life. What does it actually mean to be a 'modern', 'civilized' person? How are we to understand the ways in which an understanding of our history can contribute to a more effective response to current human problems? Can we explain the contemporary world in terms of its genealogy, and where is it headed in the future? What is the significance of differing social configurations in producing particular kind of human beings, who relate to each other, themselves and their social world in specific, often self-destructive ways? How is our concern with individual autonomy and independence related to the very real patterns of inter-dependence which characterize all human social life? These are the kinds of questions which Norbert Elias addressed for over half a century between the 1930s and the 1980s, developing a unique approach to sociology which is now beginning to take root in contemporary sociological research and theory."

CyberSociology Web Zine
  http://www.socio.demon.co.uk/magazine/magazine.html

Cybersociology is a non-profit multi-disciplinary webzine dedicated to the critical discussion of the internet, cyberspace, cyberculture and life online. According to the editors: "Cybersociology Magazine is a forum for the discussion of the social scientific study of cyberspace. Every few months, this e-zine will strive to publish at least three original articles dealing with cyberspace, the Internet, and online communities. Each issue will also contain book and site reviews. Although it is hoped that most contributions will come from post-graduate students and professional researchers, undergraduates are also welcome to send articles for consideration." Issue topics include: "Cyber-Romance, Cybersex, and Cyber-Eroticism," "Online (Virtual?) Communities," "Digital Third Worlds and Questions of Net Access," "Grassroots Political Activism Online," "Research Methodology Online," and "Religion Online and Techo-Spiritualism." Forthcoming issues will explore techniques for getting grants for ongoing web discussion of topics related to the sociology of the digital village. Recent articles include: "Cyberpunks: A Sociological Analysis With Special Interest In The Description Of Their Online Activities," "Net Ideologies: From Cyber-liberalism to Cyber-realism," "There Are No Last Words Online," "Bringing The Net To The Masses: Cybercafes In Latin Amer-

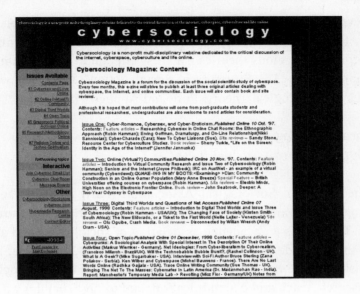

ica," "Cyberpower and the Meaning of Online Activism," and "Men and Women's Gender Display in Text-based Communication."

The Dead Sociologists Society
http://abacus.bates.edu/~jfrizzel/lrid/DSS/DEADSOC.HTML

We are talking about such dead sociologists as Talcott Parsons (1902-1979). He was a US sociologist who attempted to integrate all the social sciences into a science of human action. He was converted to functionalism under the influence of the anthropologist Bronislaw Malinowski.

In "The Social System" 1951, Parsons argued that the crucial feature of societies, as of biological organisms, is homeostasis (maintaining a stable state), and that their parts can be understood only in terms of the whole. Parsons began his career as a biologist and later became interested in economics and sociology. He studied in Heidelberg, Germany. He taught sociology at Harvard from 1931 until his death, and set up the Department of Social Relations there. He published more than 150 books and articles.

Like the German sociologist Max Weber, whose work he translated, Parsons wanted to describe convincingly logical types of social relation applicable to all groups, however small or large. His great achievement was to construct a system or general theory of social action to include all its aspects, drawing on several disciplines and reinterpreting previous theories. His first attempt at this systematization appeared in "The Structure of Social Action" 1937, followed by "Essays in Sociological Theory, Pure and Applied" 1942.

European Sociological Assocation
http://www.valt.helsinki.fi/esa/

The European Sociological Association (ESA) aims to facilitate sociological research, teaching and communication on European issues. The ESA is an academic association of sociologists and a non-profit Europe-wide association made up of over 700 members. It was established in the early 1990s in order of facilitate European sociological research, teach and communication, and to give sociology a voice in European affairs. Europe is in the midst of massive changes, including the transformations in east and central Europe and the increasing integration of the European Union. Sociology has much to contribute at a European level to debates on these and other developments. The ESA has an important role to play in organizing the debate and setting the agenda. The First European Conference of Sociology in Vienna in August 1992 attracted 631 sociologists from East, West, North and South Europe, and from a total of 33 countries. The conference was organised by both international and local programme committees with the cooperation of 38 panel organisers from 19 different European countries. It was at this conference that a meeting of representatives from the national sociological associations of Europe and other interested parties endorsed the desire to form a European Sociological Association and charged a Steering Committee with the task of building this.

George Herbert Mead
http://paradigm.soci.brocku.ca/~lward/

As a writer, Mead had a curious style—he rarely presented his ideas as original contributions. Instead, he portrayed them as minor modifications to the work of others. While admirably modest at the time, at the end of the twentieth century, this creates more than one problem for any n"ive reader. A lot can happen in a century, especially in emerging fields like social psychology. Two barriers stand in the way of easily understanding of Mead's work. First, over half a century has elapsed since Mead last published. Simply locating the documents that Mead commented on or included in his syntheses can be difficult. The second problem, is a bit more difficult. Neither Mead's ideas nor those he drew upon existed in a vacuum. There is a broader context, assumed by the work but only occasionally directly referenced. These are the ideas that fill out the intellectual landscape of the time. What was the intellectual background against which Mead is proposing his ideas? What did the rest of psychology, philosophy, sociology look like when Mead wrote? These questions are harder to answer. The net has to be cast wider, drawing in sources that are only indirectly related to the central goal of Mead Project. Documents that provide this type of background will also appear here. As the webmaster writes: "Deciding which documents to include requires more than a little editorial license, so bear with us. If you have suggestions, drop us a line—or better yet—send the file."

George Simmel
   http://socio.ch/sim/index_sim.htm

Georg Simmel was born on March 1, 1858, in the very heart of Berlin, the corner of Leipzigerstrasse and Friedrichstrasse. This was a curious birthplace—it would correspond to Times Square in New York—but it seems symbolically fitting for a man who throughout his life lived in the intersection of many movements, intensely affected by the cross-currents of intellectual traffic and by a multiplicity of moral directions. Simmel was a modern urban man, without roots in traditional folk culture. Upon reading Simmel's first book, F. Toennies wrote to a friend: "The book is shrewd but it has the flavor of the metropolis." Like "the stranger" he described in his brilliant essay of the same name, he was near and far at the same time, a "potential wanderer; although he [had] not moved on, he [had] not quite overcome the freedom of coming and going." One of the major theorists to emerge in German philosophy and social science around the turn of the century, he remains atypical, a perturbing and fascinating figure to his more organically rooted contemporaries. Visit the web site for more details on this most fascinating 19th century social scientist.

Society for Applied Sociology
http://www.appliedsoc.org/

The Society for Applied Sociology, founded in 1978, is an international organization for professionals involved in applying sociological knowledge in a wide variety of settings. As they write: "We believe that, in the practice of sociology, it is the responsibility of members, above all else, to knowingly do no harm to those they serve or their research subjects. This responsibility includes all individuals and social groups regardless of the member's assessment of the legitimacy or role in society of that person or group. Human subjects will not be coerced to participate in research. Study designs should assume voluntary cooperation on the part of the research subjects if their participation is required; informed consent of subjects is encouraged whenever possible. All identifying information associated with participants in a study is to remain confidential, unless prior permission to release the information has been granted by the subjects or their

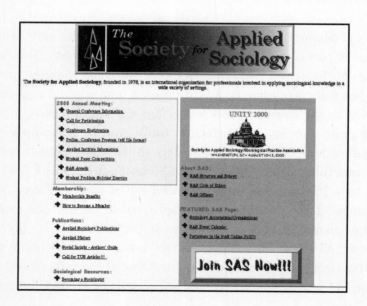

legally designated representatives. In addition to their subjects, we believe members have equally important responsibilities to those they serve; students, employers and clients. Members will provide those they serve with a realistic representation of their qualifications and limitations as they relate to the professional activity in question. Members conducting research for clients should also clarify specific details of a project with their clients, either verbally or (preferably) in writing, prior to the beginning of a study."

SocioWeb

http://www.socioweb.com/~markbl/socioweb/

The SocioWeb is an independent guide to the Sociological resources available on the Internet and is founded in the belief that the Internet can help to unite the sociological community in ways never before possible. Originally launched in October, 1995, The SocioWeb has grown at a steady pace along with the growth of the Internet. Unfortunately, the original architecture of The SocioWeb was exceptionally difficult to maintain in light of the increasing amount of new listings and address changes. In July, 1997 the current version of The SocioWeb was launched with a new interface and an an architecture which will be much easier to maintain. As the webmaster writes: "My apologies to all who have experienced out-of-date links or a lack of email response in the past. As The SocioWeb has no funding and is essentially a one-man effort, the outdated architecture made the ongoing maintenance difficult to conduct on a regular basis. Thank you very much for your patience during this period. I invite you to explore The SocioWeb and to let me know what you think about the new design, and what you might be interested in seeing in the future. Your suggestions are critical to the future growth of The SocioWeb."

Sociological Tour Through Cyberspace

http://www.trinity.edu/~mkearl/index.html

Within the topic-based pages at this site you will find considerable use of the General Social Surveys of the National Opinion

Over twenty years ago columnist Lewis Lapham made the following observation:

There no longer exists a theater of ideas in which artists or philosophers can perform the acts of the intellectual or moral imagination. In nineteenth-century England Charles Darwin could expect *On The Origin of Species* to be read by Charles Dickens as well as by Disraeli and the vicar in the shires who collected flies and water beetles. Dickens and Disraeli and the vicar could assume that Mr. Darwin might chance to read their own observation. But in the United States in 1979 what novelist can expect his work to be read by a biochemist, a Presidential candidate, or a director of corporations, what physicist can expect his work to be noticed, much less understood, in the New York literary salons? ("A Juggernaut of Words," *Harper's Magazine*, June 1979, pp. 12-13)

Conditions have hardly improved in 2000. Now in the supposed "Information Age" six out of ten American households do not purchase a single book, and one-half of American adults do not read one. In 1965 when the Gallup Organization asked young people if they read a daily newspaper, 67 percent said yes. Three decades later, less than 30 percent answer affirmatively. And yet "they" say we are saturated with informational overload!

I am most interested in the potential of this cyberspace medium to inform and to generate discourse, to truly be a "theater of ideas." This site features commentary, data analyses (hey, we've become a "factoid" culture), occasional essays, as well as the requisite links, put together for courses taught by myself and my colleagues. Additions and updates are made daily. If you do give feedback on one of the message pads scattered across these pages and wish a reply, please include your e-mail address.

And now for some sites to stimulate the *sociological imagination*
(or, at a minimum, prepare one for *Sociology Jeopardy*):

➤ General sociological resources
➤ Sociological theory
➤ Data resources and some useful web tools
➤ Methods and statistics
➤ Guide to writing a research paper

Research Center (NORC). These face-to-face surveys of random samplings of English-speaking Americans 18 years of age and older, conducted nearly annually from 1972 through 1996 (and bi-annually for the near future), are some of the best information available to social scientists. Details about them can be obtained with just one click on a hyperlink that will take you to the University of Michigan's General Social Survey Data and Information Retrieval System. One can, in fact, even perform one's own crosstabulations using Berkeley's CSA tools, all downloadable from this site. One can also click and go to Queens College to either download an electronic searchable version of NORC's Annotated Bibliography of Papers Using the General Social Surveys or use their own online search engine. Another resource used at this site comes from the International Social Survey Programme. Conducted annually, each year features a different subject module, such as social inequality (1987,1992), women, work and family (1988,1994), religion (1991,1998), national identity (1995), and environment (1993,2000). Be sure to check out all these wonderful online resources.

Sociological Research Online
http://www.socresonline.org.uk/

Sociological Research Online was launched in March 1996 in time for the Research Assessment Exercise in the UK. Unlike most journals, this is an electronic journal distributed over the World Wide Web and, also innovatively, it is free for anyone to access provided they have the freely available software to do this. Sociological Research Online is the result of a consortium chaired by Professor Nigel Gilbert at the University of Surrey, and includes the Universities of Surrey and Stirling, the British Sociological Association and SAGE Publications Ltd. The journal is edited by Dr. Liz Stanley (University of Manchester) who is supported by an editorial board reflecting a wide range of sociological interests and representing a number of prestigious departments. The journal is truly global in nature, being available to readers around the world, provided that they have Internet access. To reflect the interests of such a range of academics, the Editorial Board is aided by a team of International Correspondents. Initially, Sociological Research Online is being funded by the Electronic Libraries Programme. This programme was set up as a direct result of the Follett Report, chaired by Sir Brian Follett (Vice-Chancellor of the University of Warwick), which studied the continuing revolution in electronic information.

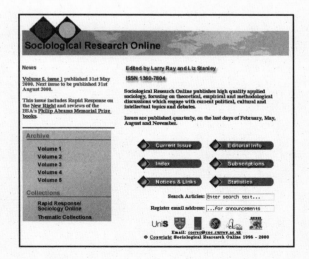

Timeline of Sociology

http://www.ac.wwu.edu/~stephan/timeline.html

The term "the history of sociology" is most frequently used to refer to the chronicle of the discipline's general theories and theorists. But other issues investigated in this scholarship include: methodological advances; the politics of the profession; the discovery and introduction of the forgotten theorists; biographies of significant contributors to the discipline's subfields; accounts of departments and of their influence at particular historic moments; the work of applied sociologists; the administration and staffing of the association; chronicles of the annual and regional meetings; and the gender, race, and class politics that have influenced the professionalization of the discipline (and the construction of and challenges to the canon of "sociology's founding texts"). On the one hand, the History of Sociology is an established and influential area of research and teaching in the discipline. On the other hand, as we approach the end of the twentieth century and recognize more than a century and a half of sociological work, there is still no organizational home for this subdiscipline, no section in the American Sociological Association devoted to bringing together this body of scholarship. This web-based timeline will therefore prove a useful tool.

Sociology Mailing Lists:

The Journal of World-Systems Research: send a message to list-proc@csf.colorado.edu: "subscribe wsn <your e-mail address>".

The Progressive Sociologists Network: send a message to list-proc@colorado.edu "subscribe psn <your_name>".

The Communication Research and Theory Network: send a message to listserv@psuvm.psu.edu: "subscribe CRTnet <your_name>".

SOCBB—information for sociologists in the UK: send e-mail to socbb-request@soc.surrey.ac.uk.

Social Theory: send a message to mailbase@mailbase.ac.uk: "join social-theory <your_name>".

Rural Sociology: send a message to listserv@ukcc.uky.edu: "subscribe rursoc-l <your_name>".

SOS-DATA: NewsNet: bit.listserv.sos-data or send a message to listserv@unc.edu: "subscribe sos-data <your_name>".

Public Opinion Research (POR): send a message to listserv@unc.edu: "subscribe por <your_name>".

Socgrads: send a message to listserv@ucsd.edu "sub <your e-mail address> socgrad".

Newsletter of the European Sociological Association: send a message to mailbase@mailbase.ac.uk "join european-sociologist <first_name> <last_name>".

OIC—the Organizational Issues Clearinghouse: send a message to listproc@ursus.jun.alaska.edu "subscribe oic <your_name>".

ASQ, Administrative Science Quarterly listserver: send a message to ASQ@umich.edu , first line: <your e-mail address>, second line: <your name and affiliation>.

Econsoc: send a messages to majordomo@uclink4.Berkeley.EDU "subscribe economic-sociology".

Symbolic Interaction: send a message to listproc@sun.soci.niu.edu "subscribe interact <your name>".

TeachSoc: send a message to listproc@irss.unc.edu "subscribe teachsoc <your name>".

SOCNET: send a message to listserv@nervm.nerdc.ufl.edu "subscribe SOCNET <your name>".

The Australian Sociological Association Email List: send a message to mailserv@cc.newcastle.edu.au with a blank subject line and the message "subscribe tasa" on the first line and "end" on the second line.

Social-Class: send a message to listserv@listserv.uic.edu with the message "SUB SOCIAL-CLASS <firstname> <surname>, <school>".

SOC, the Sociology Omnibus Cafe: To subscribe send a message to mailserv@uaa.alaska.edu with the message: subscribe SOC <your firstname> <your lastname>.

Bourdieu Forum: To subscribe send a message to majordomo@lists.village.virginia.edu with the message: subscribe bourdieu.

ABSLST-L, the listserv of the Association of Black Sociologists: to subscribe send the message "SUB ABSLST-L <your real name>" to LISTSERV@CMUVM.CSV.CMICH.EDU.

For more sites visit
www.sciam.com